*PART OF* **KENT**

*Ashurst* Grombridg
*Lamb-hurst*
*Scrotney*

*Waldehurst*
*Flymwell*
*Tychurst*
*P.yhley*
*Borsill*
*Harmer*
*Erid*
*Whitll*
*San.thurst*

**Anderida**
now
Newenden
*Rother R.*

*Fairfield*
*Breckland*

*Oxney Island*

*Kent Ditch*

*Rother Alu.*
*Brucksmall*
*Franchis*
*Burwash*
*Etchingham*
*Sale hurst*
*Bodyham*
*Tustens*
*Northam*
*Beckley*
*Peasmersh*

**PEVENSEY RAPE**
*Mayfield*
*Crowborow hill*

*Hartley Beacon*
*Hawk wood*
*Bughill*
*Rotherbridg Abby*
*Ewhurst*
*Staplehurst*
*Gate*

*Iden*
**Rye**

*Guilford*

*Burwash Beacon*
*Secknoys*
*Rotherbrig*
*Stapley Beacon*

*Hyndall*
*Buckstell*
*Pownsley*
*Dallington forest*
*Brigling*
*Mundsidl*
*Selcomb*
**HASTINGS**
**RAPE**
*Udimore*

*Plaxden*
*Marsh*

*Wittersham*
*Camberhall*
*Camber ey*
*Camber Falls*

*D* *A*

*Catbret*
*Dallington*
*Breed*
*Wigfield*
*Winchelsey*

**VINDELES**
*Bromshill church decayed*
*Old Winchelsey Drowned*

*Heathfield*
*Earwood*
*Darum wood*
*Penhurst*
**Battel**
*Bromeham*
*Maxfield*
*Pamelbridg*
*Pett*
*Gestling*
*Stonslinch*

*Framfield*
*Blackhefe*
*Waldern*
*Crooksted*
*Searlets*
*Crawl*
*Ashburnham*
*Nunfield*
*Standard hill*
*Fairleigh*
*Crawhurst*
*Cure*
*Peplsham*

*Little Horsted*
*Wylie*
*E. Hoadly*
*Chickman*
*Buckslepe*
*Hellingley*
*More Hall*
*Cattesfield*
*Cros*
*Hellinst*
**Hastings**

*Northyam*
*Park*
*Vert wood*
*Hoo*
*Buckhole*
*Silley*
*Weryham*

*The Breke*
*Bentley*
*Chittinsley*
*Hollingly*
*Boreham Street*
*Hurst monceaux*

*Swartling*
*Beekes hill*
*Bexill*
*The Pell*

*Laughton*
*Ripe*
*Dyke*
*Havisham*
*Michelham*
**Pevensey Marsh**
*Nords Chap*

*Hastings haven intended*

*Chauton*
*Claverham*
*Bulverhyth*

*Stensham*
*Marling*
*Glyne*
*Fyrle*
*Ludley*
*Glynley*
*Westham*
*Priest hawes*
*Pevensey*
*Cromlepond*
*Langle*

*Cliffs*
*Southram*
*Bedingh*
*Selmeston*
*Berwyke*
*Wotton*
*Willington*
*Fowington*

*Alciston*
*Middleton*
*Winton*
*Willington*
*Ratton*
*East Born*

*Terring*
*Norton*
*Frogsull*
*Alfriston*

*Hayton*
*Denton*
*Bletchington*
*Sutton*
*West Deans*
*Jevington*
*Fryton*
*South*
*The Beach*

*Pillinghe*
*Bishops*
*Seaford*
*Excete*
*East Deane*

*New Haven*
*Cuckmere Haven*
*Pevensey Haven*

*ENGLISH CHANEL*

Sold by Abel Swale Awnsham and John Churchill.

KIM LESLIE

# SUSSEX

## Tales of the Unexpected

### Five Centuries of County Life

west
sussex
county
council

First published in the United Kingdom in 2008 by
West Sussex County Council
County Hall
Chichester
West Sussex
PO19 1RQ

Kim Leslie
West Sussex Record Office
County Hall
Chichester
West Sussex
PO19 1RN

Telephone: 01243 753602
Fax: 01243 533959
E-mail: kim.leslie@westsussex.gov.uk

British Library Cataloguing in Publication Data
A catalogue record for this book is available from the
British Library

ISBN: 978-0-86260-577-3

Design and production: Mike Blacker
Blacker Design
Hillcroft Barn
Coombe Hill Road
East Grinstead
West Sussex
RH19 4LY
info@blackerdesign.co.uk

Printed and bound in China by 1010 Printing
International Ltd on behalf of Compass Press

*Front endpapers: Sussex by Robert Morden, 1695*
*Back endpapers: Sussex by W. Schmollinger, 1836*

*Dedicated*
*with love and thanks*
*to*
*Jenni, Victoria and Justin*
*who made the book*
*a family affair*

# 1749

*. . . be so kind as never to go into Sussex . . .*
*the whole county has a Saxon air, and the*
*inhabitants are savage . . . Sussex is a great*
*damper of curiosity.*

Horace Walpole in a letter to George Montagu,
26 August 1749, quoted in Charles G. Harper,
*The Brighton Road: Old Times and New on a Classic Highway*
(Chatto & Windus, 1892)

# 1912

*Paradise . . . this Eden which is Sussex still.*

Hilaire Belloc, *The Four Men* (Nelson, [1912])

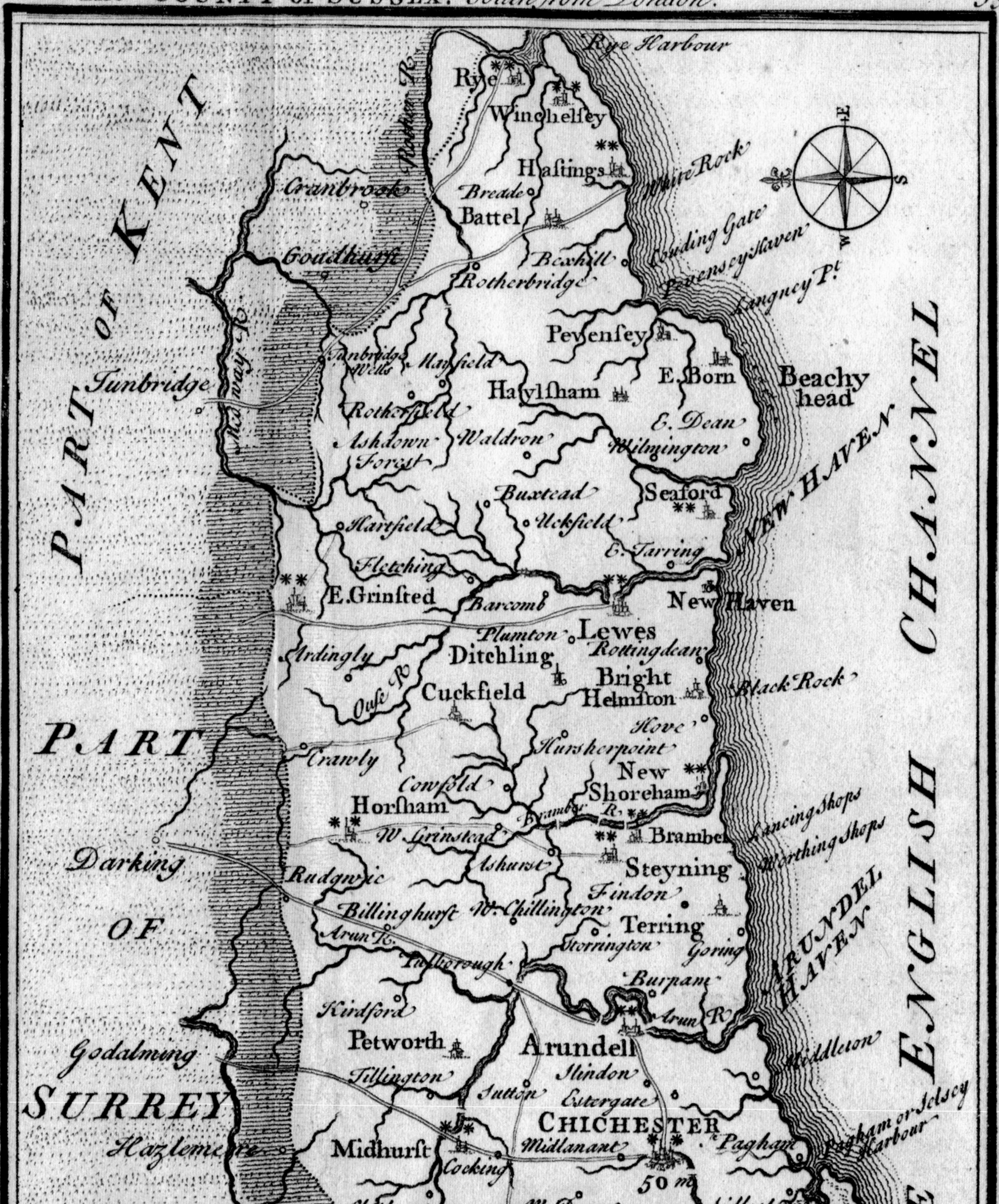

PART OF KENT

Tunbridge

Rother R.

Rye Harbour

Rye
Winchelsey
Hastings
Breade
Battel
Bexhill
Rotherbridge
White Rock
Louding Gate
Pevensey Haven
Langney Pt.

Cranbrook
Goudhurst

Tanbridge Wells
Mayfield
Rotherfield
Ashdown Forest
Waldron
Hartfield
Fletching
E. Grinsted

Haylsham
E. Born
E. Dean
Wilmington
Buxstead
Ucksfield
E. Tarring

Beachy head

NEW HAVEN

Pevensey

Seaford

Barcomb
Plumton
Lewes
Rottingdean
Ditchling
Ardingly
Ouse R.
Cuckfield
Bright Helmston
Hove
Black Rock

New Haven

PART

Crawly

Hursherpoint
New Shoreham

OF

Cowfold
Horsham
W. Grinstead
Ashurst
Bramber R.
Bramber
Steyning
Lancing Shops
Worthing Shops

Darking

Rudgwic
Billinghurst
W. Chillington
Findon
Terring
Goring

ARUNDEL HAVEN

SURREY

Arun R.
Pulborough
Kirdford
Petworth
Tillington
Sutton
Slindon
Estergate
Arundell

Storrington
Burpam
Arun R.
Middleton

THE ENGLISH CHANNEL

Godalming

Hazlemere
Midhurst
Cocking
Chithurst
Rogate
Harting
Marden

Midlanant
W. Dean
Funtington
Wt. Bourne

CHICHESTER
Pagham
Pagham or Selsey Harbour

50 m
Sidlesham

Wittering

CHICHESTER HAVEN

Petersfield

A Scale of Miles

5     10     15

Publish'd by the Proprietor H. Toms Sept. 29. 1742.

H. Toms Sculpt.

# Contents

*Opposite:* The County of Sussex *by Thomas Badeslade, 1742*

CONTENTS

# Preface

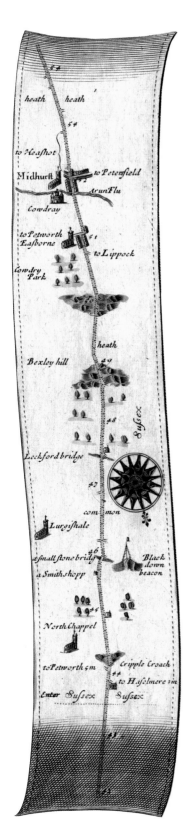

*Detail from* The Road from London to Chichester *by John Ogilby,* 1675

THIS BOOK IS BASED ON a series of weekly articles first published in the *West Sussex Gazette* in 2003 to commemorate the newspaper's one hundred and fiftieth anniversary. They were the idea of the then editor, Dorothy Blundell, happily in charge of that very special birthday year.

'The West Sussex', as it is affectionately known, has long been one of the bedrocks of the county's identity. More than just a local newspaper, this much-loved weekly has featured an enormous diversity of subjects, from farming to wildlife, from Sussex dialect to life in the countryside and copious amounts of local history. Over its many years it has always been a goldmine of information about the county's past and present, and more lately renowned for its superb colour photography of the local scene. Its bound copies, year after year since 1853, are preserved in West Sussex Record Office. This book is in some small tribute to the *WSG* for its generosity in making them available for local history research in this way and in recognition of the fact that without its initiative this series of articles would never have seen the light of day.

From the original weekly articles published throughout 2003, some thirty-nine have been chosen for this book, and to these has been added one that originally appeared in the magazine *West Sussex History*.

In putting this book together for publication, the opportunity has been taken to make corrections and amendments to the original articles, to add considerably to the number of illustrations first used, and to rearrange the order in which they were first published so that they can now be presented in much more of a chronological sequence. One major addition is a section on the sources used in the research that wouldn't have been appropriate in the newspaper.

My first thanks must inevitably go to Dorothy Blundell, past editor of the *West Sussex Gazette*, who gave me the opportunity to write the articles in the first place, and to the present editor, John Hammond, for his permission to reprint them here. Then special thanks must go to colleagues at West Sussex Record Office: first and foremost to Richard Childs, the County Archivist, for his constant support and encouragement; to Clare Snoad for scanning the documents and pictures; to David Milnes for photography in the Record Office and in Chichester District Museum; to archivists Caroline Adams, Bill Gage, Sue Millard and Alan Readman for all their many kindnesses; to Sarah Head for her ever-ready help on the administrative side. Mike Blacker and Cindy Edler of Blacker Design in East Grinstead brilliantly transformed ideas into reality in the design and preparation of the book for publication. The many days spent working with them, with support from Elwyn and Simon Blacker, have all been most pleasurable, marked with their own very special brand of sound advice, abundant hospitality and generosity.

A great debt of gratitude is owed to so many others who have kindly given help and guidance, both with the sharing of information and easing my path at many different locations across the county. To Winifred Abbott (on coastal erosion at Middleton); Ali Beckett and Nicky Horter, both of Chichester Harbour Conservancy, and Gillian Edom, of West Sussex Record Office (all giving information on wadeways); Christine Colthurst (access to the John White memorials at Broadwater);

Sarah Corn and Sheila Fennings of East Grinstead Museum (access to turnpike tickets); the Dean and Chapter of Chichester Cathedral (for their kind permission to photograph memorials by Eric Gill); David Drummond (on Pullinger mouse traps); Roderick Gordon (on the Gordon family of Harting); Frances and Marjorie Guthrie (about the Pear Tree Press); Tim Harding and Jeremy Woods (locating the photograph of the Slinfold road accident); Anne Harvey (much about Eleanor Farjeon); Oliver Hawkins and Chloe Fisher (for their guided tour around Humphrey's Homestead and Shed Hall at Greatham); Ron Iden (loan of the very scarce dustwrapper on his copy of *The Fortnight in September* and for other Bognor illustrations used in the Sherriff article); Peter Jerrome and Miles Costello (on the site of Petworth Prison and locating the little-known bricks scratched with prisoners' names and dates); David Johnston (loan of the Petworth Prison button); Simon Kitchin of Chichester District Museum (organising photography in the museum); Rosemary and Tony Laker and Clifford Pinhey (about the site of Ladyholt) and Christopher North (for his permission to walk the site); Jenni Leslie of the Library of the University of Chichester (acquiring copies of learned journals); Wendy Lines (identifying Gillmans Cottage near Billingshurst); Monica Maloney (loan of Dean Burgon's amusing sketch sent to her aunt); Sara Rodger, Assistant Librarian to His Grace the Duke of Norfolk (about 'the Collector Earl' as well as the American Eagle Owls of Arundel Castle); the Reverend Keith Smith (access to the Becket banner at Pagham); Nick Stride and Derek Bowerman of Stride & Son, Chichester (access to Dangstein when it was put up for sale by the National Trust).

Parts of this book would have been the poorer without the use of illustrations and text protected by copyright. Agencies, trustees and 'permissions' staff have all been most helpful in their guidance and, indeed in some cases, with overwhelming generosity regarding fees. All these copyright holders are acknowledged towards the end of the book.

The articles were originally researched and written against a weekly timetable that had to be fitted into other responsibilities around the county and in the Record Office. Coping with unforgiving deadlines meant that so much of the work necessarily spilt over into so many evenings and most weekends. That I could do it at all owed much to a most understanding family who lost me for the best part of a year. My wife Jenni, and Victoria and Justin, played their own crucial part both at the time of the original articles in 2003 and more lately with the preparations for the book, commenting, proofing, coming to my rescue with the computer at home so that it ran like clockwork, getting out and about with me to take photographs, following up clues in the field, holding back the barbed wire and – importantly – carrying the sandwiches. They were there and that made all the difference. That's why this book is a family affair and is dedicated to them.

THE DEAN THINKING ABOUT DODO.

Kim Leslie                                                                                July 2008
West Sussex Record Office
Chichester

# Preamble

*The past is a foreign country. They do things differently there.*

L.P. Hartley, *The Go-Between* (1953)

AND JUST HOW DIFFERENTLY and far away from our own times things were in the past comes out so vividly from all these stories spanning some five centuries of Sussex life.

Some of the things described here are so starkly different from what we are used to today, when day-to-day life could be nasty, brutal and short. They tell of scrofulous women in search of a cure stroking the hand of a dead robber waiting to be gibbeted on a windswept heath near Midhurst in 1799. When hard labour in Petworth Prison meant 'grinding the wind' – ten long hours of useless labour a day on the dreaded treadmill in the mid-nineteenth century. When an eighty-two year old woman could be transported to Australia for perjury in the 1780s. When to be poor was to be criminalised, pauper wives taken from their pauper

husbands under the poor law rule of separation. And when sixteenth-century Chichester, 'very mierie, full of water and dirty places both loathsome and noysome', ran like a sewer and it was nothing out of the ordinary for a housewife to be charged 'for throwing owte of her fylthy watter and for other of her fylthey doungs'. Centuries on and one Sussex soldier-poet, mired in his own horrific nightmare 'of a blood-stained field' in the Great War, could but dream of better times and a better place back home – his one comfort the 'dream that comes to men in hell'.

These are just a few of the stories told here – of times cruel and hard, of lives and experiences straight out of hell.

And yet here also is at least some redemption from all these horrors by way of sharp provoking contrasts, some light as well as shade.

From his hell in a trench on the Western Front our Sussex soldier could but dream of home, of 'A sun-kissed cottage nestling in a vale of peace', a vision of the stillness and beauty of home 'Where all to God and Mother Nature yield' – his wistful glimpse of heaven on earth, so close and yet so far.

Other stories tell of this heaven-at-home, of a Sussex that seemed such a perfect paradise. There was Lady Dorothy Nevill whose 'exotic groves' of rare plants, silkworms and aviaries at Dangstein attracted some of the most famous botanists, scientists and explorers of the nineteenth century. There was nothing quite like it outside Kew. Loving the strange and exotic, pigeon whistles were sent specially from China for her avian orchestra. Clipped to pigeons' tails, the little whistles winged their way across the lawns, delighting guests with their heavenly music in this sanctuary of beautiful sights and sounds, a place of wonder in full gaze of the Downs as its constant backdrop, so much the reassuring symbol of Sussex and all that it represents.

Of such perfection that it was marked out by heaven – that was how Hilaire Belloc rated his adopted county in his pugnaciously philosophic panegyric *The Four Men*, describing their walk through 'this Eden which is Sussex':

> *... there are only two things in Sussex which Sussex deigns to give its name to, and the first is the spaniel, and the second is the sheep. Note you, many kingdoms and counties and lands are prodigal of their names, because their names are of little account and in no way sacred, so that one will give its name to a cheese and another to a horse, and another to some kind of ironwork or other, and another to clotted cream or to butter, and another to something ridiculous, as to a cat with no tail. But it is not so with Sussex, for our name is not a name to be used like a label and tied on to common things, seeing that we were the first place to be created when the world was made, and we shall certainly be the last to remain, regal and at ease when all the rest is very miserably perishing on the Day of Judgment by a horrible great rain of fire from Heaven. Which will fall, if I am not mistaken, upon the whole earth, and strike all round the edges of the county, consuming Tonbridge, and Appledore (but not Rye), and Horley, and Ockley, and Hazelmere, and very certainly Petersfield and Havant, and there shall be an especial woe for Hayling Island; but not one hair of the head of Sussex shall be singed, it has been so ordained from the beginning ....*

Wills's Cigarettes

Hilaire Belloc

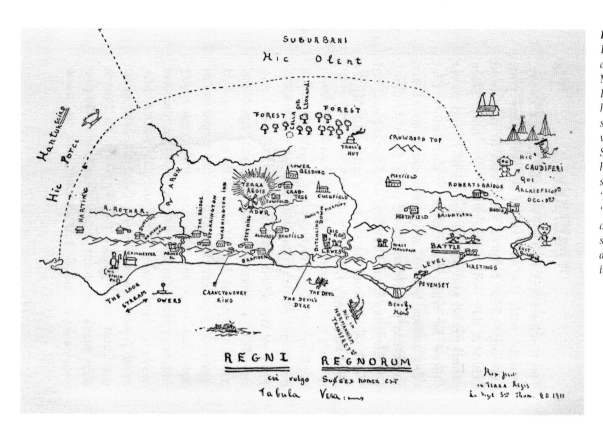

*Belloc's Sussex*
*Belloc's hand-drawn map accompanying* The Four Men *is centred on 'Terra Regis' – or 'King's Land' – his home in its radiant setting at Shipley, at the very heart of the county. Sussex, his ' holy place', his 'Paradise', was surrounded by alien 'shapeless things' and 'waste': by Hampshire full of hogs, Surrey with its suburban inferior things and Kentish men, insolent imps with devil's tails.*

Belloc, that arch-protagonist of all things good about the county, loved Sussex with a passion.

Then there was writer Eleanor Farjeon who made Sussex her own very special arcadia in the 1920s and '30s. The part most particularly sweet to her was the Arun valley from Billingshurst down through the Wildbrooks to the top of the Downs – 'Eleanor Farjeon Country' – her books and verse a magic carpet into this mysterious and exquisitely beautiful land 'that it might be Eden grown tiny', she wrote. Of her beloved Downs enfolding her little thatched cottage down Mucky Lane, near Amberley, she confessed 'They've healed me more, and given me more strength and certainty and peace, than any other living thing'.

There was Eric Gill, one of the greatest artist-craftsmen of the twentieth century, sculptor, engraver and designer of beautiful letters whose typefaces transformed print and design, his *Gill Sans* letters, simple and dignified, still making the BBC's logo to this day. In the 1890s the youthful Gill succumbed to the spell of Chichester and its neat and tidy street plan, small in scale, planned and well-ordered: 'the human city, the city of God, the place where life and work and things were all in one and all in harmony ... something as human as home and as lovely as heaven'.

The intensity with which Sussex has been both loved and praised is caught in these pages, but so also is Belloc's warning cry in his prophetic questioning on whether it could all last. 'Can Sussex endure?' he asked in 1936, fearing for the future of his much-loved county. And for the answer? Look around and judge for yourself, some seventy years later.

Between these two opposite extremes of hellish lives and heavenly landscapes are sandwiched many more real-life stories, some extraordinarily unusual, like Lord Egremont's revolutionary early nineteenth-century piggery at Petworth, one of the earliest-known farm battery units in the country – live pigs in at the front, smoked bacon out at the back. Another is of the hubbub that came to Birdham in 1824 with the all-England – and quite illegal – prize-fighting championship, seventy-seven punishing rounds, the vanquished John Langan knocked insensible with a 'blow on the smeller' and a 'left-handed nobber', the victor Tom Spring rewarded with an incredible £500 – more like a quarter of a million in today's money – and the field of victory down by the canal renamed in his honour, Spring Field as it is to this day. Yet another story tells of two pioneer schemes that would have built Britain's first motorway from London to Brighton, one planned way back in 1906, the other in 1928 because of 'dangerous congestion' and the mounting number of cars on the roads each year even then – two of the might-have-beens of history that came to nothing. Surrey and Sussex thus lost the chance of introducing this revolutionary type of road to the country and it then took thirty more years of planning after the second scheme failed before Britain's first motorway was opened in Lancashire.

Then there are tales of just ordinary everyday life, about eighteenth-century road travel along the clay-clogging highways of the Weald, when one wag of a visitor told of his journey to Shermanbury, penetrating 'a land desolate and muddy … the oxen, the swine, the women, and all other animals … so long-legged' maybe 'from the difficulty of pulling the feet out of so much mud'.

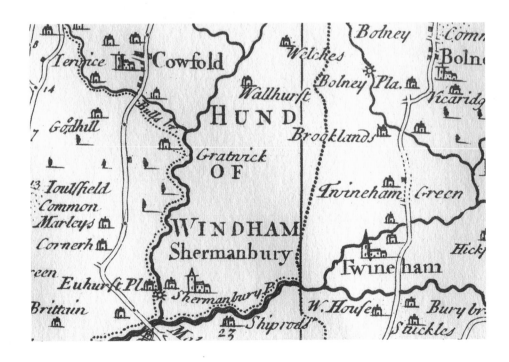

There is daily life in a remote downland penny-a-week Victorian school, driven by 'Tickets and Rewards', when Saturdays were the only weekly holiday and church attendance compulsory. When the Victorian Sunday, hedged about with puritanical prohibitions, shut up everywhere but the church, tidying away children's amusements except for the Noah's Ark, a device for religious instruction, not a toy just for mere play. Two centuries before the Victorians, the fanaticism of the Puritans had turned the world upside down, banning the celebration of Christmas and even the eating of plum pudding – wicked excuses for 'carnal and sensual delight' – and stopping all worldly traffic on Sundays, when even the urgency of the harvest and getting to market ran up against the church. A world where Robert Wadlington carried some wood at Burpham and Richard Hall used his windmill at Felpham on this holy day – both therefore sinners on Sunday – both to be charged and punished by the courts as 'sabbath-breakers' in the 1620s. The legacy of intolerance ran deep.

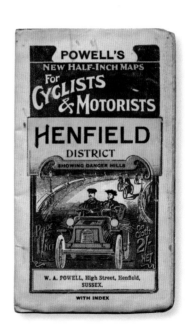

In other times we look at West Sussex through tours across an early eighteenth-century map and later hand-in-hand with guidebooks to the county. One, of 1894, was written by a consummate snob repelled by Haywards Heath as a 'colony of cockney villas' and bemused at seeing Petworth House crowded with herds of casual visitors, 'uninterested and uneducated', carrying away nothing more than a confused jumble of impressions. Another guidebook, of 1904, rich in anecdote and penned by an inveterate searcher of nostalgia, tells of a lady at Harting sick with the mulygrubes and of Lord Thurlow who laid an egg in Arundel Castle. Its author searched out thinly-populated places, peaceful and silent, in one place finding, 'clinging to the hill side, an almost Alpine hamlet', in another 'an unpopulated country ... by way of one of the pleasantest and

*'At Pulborough.'*

narrowest lanes that I know', in another place stumbling on 'one of the most remote of Sussex villages'. The book may have been written a hundred years ago, but its off-the-beaten-track discoveries still point to countryside little changed since then. Away from the coastal belt and roar of the main roads, through lanes and footpaths, the feeling of lost lands and other times can still be uncovered even today if you know where to look. Guided by old maps, documents and books there is still much to be discovered out and about in Sussex. Hopefully these pages will point the way.

# 1 'Loathsome and Noysome': Tudor Chichester

CHICHESTER'S EARLIEST STREET PLAN, dated 1595, captures the very essence of the city as a place of order and regularity, its four main streets centred on the Cross imposing their own unifying symmetry. Each street terminates at one of the four ancient gateways opening to the four quarters of the world, each dividing the city into near-equal quadrants, neatly enclosed within its encircling walls.

On paper – as a map – Chichester all looks very appealing in its harmony and balance. Compact and on a human scale. The queen herself, Elizabeth I, had come here a few years earlier in 1591. A good place to visit.

But dig under the surface a little. In the real world of Tudor Chichester the evidence points to neglect and decay, to dirt and smells, its social life disturbed by poverty and crime. Its citizens faced enormous problems in their daily lives.

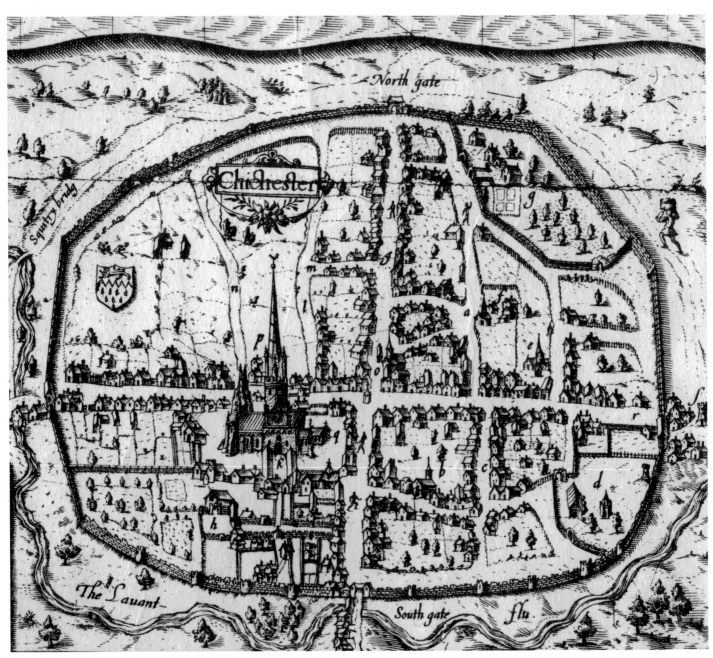

*Chichester's earliest street plan, by John Norden, 1595*

2

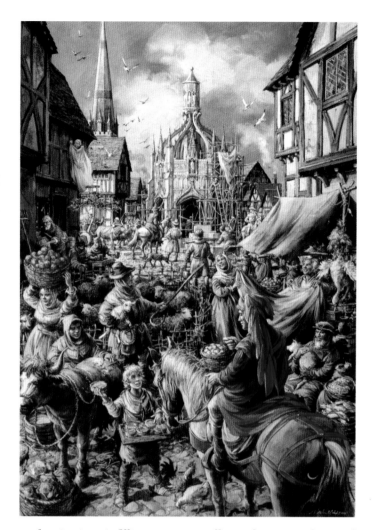

This is the dismal picture to be drawn from records of sixteenth-century Chichester. Much earlier in the century, in 1534, the mayor and citizens petitioned Henry VIII touching 'the ruin and decay' of their city, and in 1540 there was an act of parliament for the 're-edifying of decayed houses in sundry towns and places of the realm' that included Chichester. And then in 1596, just a year after the street plan was made, there was a most damning indictment of the state of the city in yet another petition appealing for financial relief as 'the citty ... doth so fast decay and run to ruine ... the cittysens doo not meinteine the citty as thei ought...'. The poor were being driven to beggary, threatening to drive out 'the better sorte' of residents, whilst thieves were running amok because of the ease by which they could come and go as the city gates and walls were falling apart. Maybe it's a thief running away across South Street? Chichester's defences were down, not quite the picture of a well-ordered city suggested by the plan.

This went for the streets as well, described as 'very mierie, full of water and dirty places both loathsome and noysome'. Regular cattle markets were held between the houses in East Street. Butchers with their slaughterhouses – known as shambles – congregated around the St Martin's area. The 'Crooked S' passageway between North Street and St Martin's was once called Shambles Alley.

Commercial premises throughout the city were intermingled with the houses, in so many cases poorly-built timber frames needing constant repair. Sixteenth-century building accounts reveal that workmen were constantly underpinning, infilling gaps in walls, replacing timber and tiles all the time. The overall impression suggests that these houses were cold, damp and draughty.

The city's court books indicate the many health hazards facing the population. In 1574 the following orders and charges were made:

- *Mr Hargrave to carry away his dounge in Savery Lane* [the early name for Little London]
- *John Lowe layeth his shaveings of his shop in Savery Lane in the Queene's hye waye*
- *Hence's wife for throwing owte of her fylthy watter and for other of her fylthey doungs in West Street*
- *John Benet the butcher is anoyed by a gutter that cometh from Mr Mayor's backsyde*

Was life any better in the cloistered calm of the cathedral? It doesn't seem so. There are strong suggestions of neglect equally scandalous. Disturbances to worship from visitors were frequent and in going up the tower to admire the view they were even damaging the bells and stealing lead from the roof. The vicars choral were all too frequently cited for drunken brawling in the cloisters. In 1594 one verger was told to find a deputy because he was 'aged, impotent, and unable to execute his office as he ought'. In the following year the choirmaster was admonished for not applying himself diligently to teaching the choristers and, soon after, two of the sextons had to be warned to attend services on the sabbath; another, John Grygorye, a lay vicar, often absented himself from divine service because he went bowling. Devotional discipline seems to have been at an all-time low.

The Chichester plan forms an inset to a map of Sussex by the cartographer John Norden (1548–1625). It is the earliest street plan for any Sussex town. Many of the features shown and the overall street plan are still familiar today.

The most noted surviving Tudor addition to the street scene was the Market Cross, built in 1501. To the north of the Cross, Norden shows another building in the middle of the road. It stood close to St Olave's church – now a Christian bookshop. This was Chichester's Market Hall,

*For Tudor Chichester's 'poore peple': the Cross at the centre of the city is one of the chief glories of Tudor Chichester. Built as a covered market for 'the poore peple to sell theire Chafer' (their wares), it was a gift from the Bishop of Chichester, Edward Storey, made in 1501.*

*Tudor Chichester might have been in ruin and decay, but the city's civic dignity was enhanced in 1570 by a grant of arms to the mayor, aldermen and citizens: a shield sprinkled with fourteen droplets of blood under the heraldic lion of England. The significance of these devices is unknown. Curiously its representation on Norden's city street plan of 1595 – the earliest known copy in print – features two errors, changing the straight dividing line under the lion into a zigzag and reducing the droplets of blood to eight.*

incorporating an open covered space at street level for the sale of produce, and a small 'Cage' – a lock-up cell for prisoners – with a council chamber above. (It would have been similar to Titchfield Market Hall at the Open Air Museum at Singleton.) It was demolished in 1731, replaced by the imposing arcaded Council House further up North Street.

'The Lavant flu' – 'flu' the abbreviated Latin form of 'flumen' or river – then washed the city's walls on three of its sides. Unlike today it once turned northwards by West Gate, then flowed along the side of Squitry Lane (now Orchard Street) and under Squitry bridge before its southwards journey towards Apuldram and the harbour.

The north-west quadrant was the one comparatively empty quarter of the city. It was an open area, mainly pasture, some smallholdings and gardens, much of it today dominated by County Hall. Its two principal streets were then known as West Lane (now Tower Street) and East Lane (now Chapel Street). Our present Crane Street was known as Crane Lane.

There were small suburbs outside three of the gates, the biggest of which was St Pancras, famed for its needle-making industry, whilst beyond North Gate there were fields and open countryside leading on to the little hills of the Broyle overlooking the city on its north side.

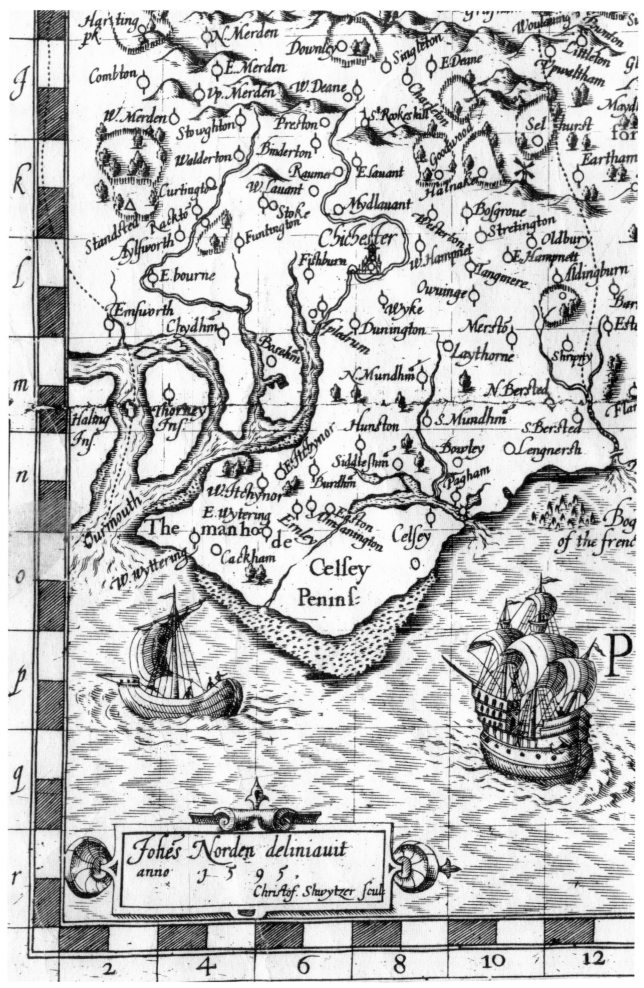

*Coast and countryside around Chichester in 1595, by John Norden*

# 2 Bohemia to Arundel: Wenceslaus Hollar

THE DISTINCTIVE SHAPE and skyline of this seventeenth-century scene echoes a townscape still familiar today. Even without its give-away title there could be few locals who could not identify this jewel in the crown of Sussex towns from this old print. Wedged between downland and riverside, watched over by its massively-fortified castle and hilltop parish church, here is a view still as popular as ever with artists, calendar makers and postcard merchants.

This particular print of Arundel, dated 1644, represents a milestone in the making of Sussex views. It is the earliest dated landscape print in West Sussex Record Office, one of just a handful of Sussex views made by Wenceslaus Hollar (1607–77) from Prague in Bohemia. He is said to have been the most distinguished topographical draughtsman working in England in the seventeenth century. Importantly he was one of the first to work in this field, leaving a remarkable visual record of immense historical value. He played a key role in popularising print-making and the appreciation of engravings and etchings.

Hollar's work was ground-breaking. Consider some types of Sussex 'views' we have from before his time. The eleventh-century Bayeux Tapestry

*Hollar's portrait shows a table full of the tools of his trade, in the background a glimpse of Prague, his native city, and in his hands he holds a Raphael portrait of Saint Catherine from the Arundel collection*

*Arundel in 1644 by Wenceslaus Hollar of Prague*

A Prospect of
ARRVNDELL CA=
=stle & Towne, on y.e West =
=side.

*Hollar's patron, Thomas Howard, Earl of Arundel – 'the Collector Earl' with his wife, by Anthony Van Dyck. His insatiable extravagance in collecting works of art and antiques took him to the verge of bankruptcy and planning to take his vast collection to Madagascar, to which he points on the globe. He abandoned his plans on discovering that the island was infested with fleas.*
                                                                                                                                                                  Arundel Castle

with its glimpses of Bosham and Hastings; the Saxon cathedral by the shore at Selsey, painted in the 1530s and displayed in Chichester Cathedral; maps like that of Steyning in 1639, preserved in the Record Office, its main street lined with little timber-framed houses. All these buildings are either shown as conventional artistic impressions or as small detail within a wider overall theme. What they are not are landscapes conveying the idea of recognisable localities.

It was Hollar who led the way in transforming the style in which buildings and the land were represented. And by producing multiple copies he made sure that his views were seen by a wide audience.

Hollar was born in the Bohemian city of Prague where, as a boy, he took great delight in drawing maps. He took up sketching and drawing his favourite places, and, as a way of making his hobby profitable, started engraving and then

moved on to the fairly new craft of etching. As an etcher he became an outstanding European figure.

He moved around a lot, plying his craft in Frankfurt, Stuttgart and Strasbourg and then Cologne where his fine etchings attracted the close attention of 'the Collector Earl', Thomas Howard, Earl of Arundel (1585–1646), then leading a diplomatic mission for Charles I at the imperial court. It was the Howard link that was to change Hollar's life for good. He joined the earl's entourage, eventually returning with him to London. In this way the art of topographical recording in this country owes as much to Thomas Howard as it does to Wenceslaus Hollar.

Howard is regarded as the greatest of the English collectors and patron of the arts of his time. Art and antiques were his passion, his house more like a museum and art gallery; wherever he travelled he sought out treasures to take home. His collections were vast, including forty-four Holbeins, thirty-three Titians, fifty-five Van Dycks, woodcuts by Dürer and drawings by Leonardo. Today many of his prints and drawings are in the Royal Library at Windsor. There were several hundred busts and statues known as the Arundel Marbles, many badly damaged in the Civil War. Remnants of his collection of marbles are now in the Ashmolean Museum at Oxford.

As well as seeking out artistic treasures, Howard used his wealth to support a remarkable 'Academie' of scholars, heralds, genealogists, painters, sculptors and print-makers. Of him, Dr Eustace, the historian of Arundel, has written that 'there was scarce an artist of ability, or a scholar of eminence, either here or on the Continent, who had not some reason to be grateful for his liberality'.

It was this liberality that supported Van Dyck in his earliest days in England as well as the architect Inigo Jones. So impressed was Howard with Hollar's etchings that he brought him back to make a pictorial record of his collections in his London home, Arundel House in the Strand. It was through this link that Hollar eventually came to produce his 1640s print of Arundel.

But sadly art gave way to politics and war. Both patron and artist became embroiled in the Civil War. The royalist Howard fled to the Continent where he died in exile in Padua in 1646. His heart and entrails were left there under a slab of black marble, his body buried in Arundel's Fitzalan Chapel, but his wish for a monument amongst his ancestors was never carried out. [However, a fitting tribute to 'the Collector Earl' was opened by Prince Charles in the grounds of Arundel Castle in 2008: the re-creation of what his Jacobean garden may have been like in London, featuring fountains, gateways and pavilions.]

The war took its toll on Hollar as well. He is said to have entered the royalist ranks as a soldier in the regiment of the Marquis of Winchester, another patron of the arts. This got him ensnared in one of the most critical episodes of the war in southern England – the long-drawn-out siege of Basing House in Hampshire. Putting every opportunity to his advantage, Hollar produced a noted wartime print of the siege showing the attacker's hastily-built breastworks used to freeze-out the garrison. From here Hollar escaped to the safety of Antwerp where he was documented as a 'platsneyder' – a plate-cutter or engraver.

Returning to England in 1652, it was now to a life

without his great patron, the earl. Fortunately he had made good connections before the war when he taught drawing to the young Prince Charles. When Charles became king at the Restoration in 1660, Hollar was appointed 'His Majesty's Scenographer', for whom he made one of his chief works, 'The Coronation of Charles II at Westminster'.

Hollar's overall output was phenomenal, his prints covering an enormously wide range of subject matter: biblical scenes, maps, portraits, views of towns and cities, animals, flower and fruit pieces. He is credited with producing nearly three thousand prints.

Perhaps his most notable English prints were his views of London. As his recent biographer, Gillian Tindall, has remarked: 'Whenever an illustrated history refers to seventeenth-century London, or some scene-setting

*Gillian Tindall's biography emphasises Hollar's important work in recording the buildings of seventeenth-century London*

material is needed for an exhibition of Van Dyck, say, or the Restoration, or the Plague and Fire of London, or Sir Christopher Wren, it is the work of Wenceslaus Hollar that is called upon'. And today it is his version of the Tower of London that is printed on the plastic bags carried away by the tourists. A Hollar view was chosen by the Royal Mail for one of its postage stamps to celebrate seven hundred years of Parliament in 1965. As long as there is a call for London's visual history, Hollar's work will live on.

*The Royal Mail celebrated the history of Parliament in 1965 with this commemorative stamp showing Hollar's seventeenth-century Thames-side view of London*

All his London views are highly important records of the capital – there are no others like this – and they are drawn and printed in exquisite detail with the most ambitious proportions, such as his 'Long View of London from Bankside' which was finished in exile in Antwerp in 1647. Seven-and-a-half feet long (2.3 metres), this magnificent bird's-eye panorama shows both sides of the Thames ranging from Whitehall to the Tower and beyond. So accurate were Hollar's drawings that his detail was used as crucial evidence in the reconstruction of Shakespeare's Globe Theatre in the 1990s. His map of the Covent Garden–Holborn area of about 1660 combines a bird's-eye perspective with all the qualities of a conventional map and is seen by one authority as 'the finest example of a map-view in existence'.

After the Great Fire of London, Hollar, by royal appointment, was authorised to make an exact plan of the city as a basis for rebuilding, and on which land claims could be made after so many landmarks and points of reference had been obliterated. His map distinguishes between the unburnt portion of the city and its outskirts in bird's-eye view, while the burnt centre is in two-dimensional street-plan style. No wonder that Tindall's book on Hollar is entitled *The Man Who Drew London*. Certainly no study of the seventeenth-century London he surveyed is possible without reference to his work. Hollar's London views are his most enduring monument.

From the sixteenth century onwards there was a growing enthusiasm for historical studies, particularly amongst antiquarians who travelled the length and breadth of the country searching for the past, looking at ruins and seeking out old documents. The first county histories and county maps began to appear and it is from this time that the study of local history in this country can first be dated. It is within this context that Hollar's work in the next century should be seen, as part of a much wider movement to document and record. His own contribution to county history is in the plates to William Dugdale's *The Antiquities of Warwickshire Illustrated* (1656) and Robert Thoroton's *Antiquities of Nottinghamshire* (1677).

Considering his links with the Earl of Arundel, it is perhaps surprising that Hollar produced so few Sussex prints until it is realized that his patron's main home was Arundel House in London's Strand, and his country retreat was not Arundel at all but Albury Park in Surrey.

In the case of Hollar's etchings of the castles at Bramber and Pevensey and of Wiston Place, the original drawings on which they are based are attributed to John Dunstall senior, a military surveyor turned Chichester stationer. Of Hollar's other Sussex prints: a prospect from the Downs behind Old

Shoreham, Chichester Cathedral and this view of Arundel, the original artists are unknown, although the overall feel of the Arundel print and the little buildings suggest similarities with his own drawings of London.

By the time Hollar produced the Arundel etching in 1644, the Civil War had wrought its destruction. Guns had been set up on the church tower and all around the town to pound the royalist-held castle into submission during a seventeen-day siege right at the end of 1643 and into the new year. The castle and its defences were severely damaged, houses were burnt, some deliberately pulled down. The Hollar view is definitely not of a town sacked by war, so clearly it was drawn before 1644. Eustace suggests 1642, but cites no evidence. We do know that Hollar's habit was to hoard stocks of his drawings away for much later use. He might have done so in this case and etched the plate once he was in the safety of Antwerp in 1644.

What we see is the medieval castle topped by its Norman keep and fourteenth-century Great Hall, distinguished by its embattled gable ends and roof lantern. Down at the bottom end of the town are the riverside quays with trading vessels, one under sail and a moored three-decker galleon. In Hollar's time, Arundel was a major trading port for Wealden timber on its way to the naval dockyards and European ports. At this period ships were built along the banks of the Arun.

A little wooden bridge crosses the river, making Arundel the lowest bridging point along its course. Hollar's bridge

looks as though it is complete, but in reality it was falling down in the early 1640s and it was not until 1646 that a new wooden structure was in place.

Other detail – or more correctly the lack of it – suggests that the print is perhaps just a little misleading: a large fifteenth-century mansion that was once at the east end of Tarrant Street called Nineveh is not recognisable at all. As he was known for his exactness of detail – 'The exact nature of place was his passion' says Tindall – this may just be a clue that perhaps it was not his original drawing at all. But whatever the case this is an outstanding print – one of the earliest Sussex townscapes – from this most remarkable man from Bohemia.

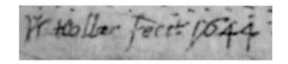

Richard Budgen's map of Sussex is a landmark in local map-making. Published in 1724, it is the first large-scale printed map of the county – at three-quarters of an inch to one mile.

Significantly it reflects the increasing application of scientific principles used in the eighteenth century to advance cartographic accuracy: it is the first map of the county to be orientated to true north, the first to indicate magnetic variation, the first to have parallels and meridians and the first to have a scale bar in statute miles. Whilst we might take these features for granted on maps today, in the eighteenth century they were an enormous leap forward. To show how far he had come in his mathematical techniques, just take a look at another Sussex map produced in 1695 by Robert Morden that actually shows three different measures for the mile, a good suggestion of the confusion that Budgen was trying to avoid in his more painstaking and careful work.

The configuration of the coastline makes this yet another first: the first to accurately show its proper length and shape. Budgen even goes so far as adding some nautical data, showing the depth of the sea around the treacherous sandy shoals and rocks around Selsey Bill and in Chichester Harbour.

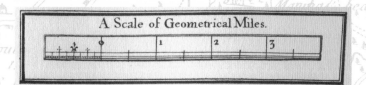

*Richard Budgen's Sussex map of 1724 was the first map of the county to use the standardised or statute mile*

*Choose the length of your mile! Robert Morden's Sussex map of 1695 offers three scales varying between the long, middle and short mile – these were 'local' or 'vulgar' measures and varied throughout the country*

## A MAP FOR TRAVELLERS

Budgen's prospectus advertising his map of Sussex proposed that it would include:

*… not only … the Post Roads that cross the County, but likewise all the principal Roads that are of Note or Use to Travellers, inserting the Names of all Commons, Downs, Forests, Greens, Cross-ways, Villages, Streets, &c. that shall lye in or near the Roads. Describing all Lanes and By-ways, that shall turn out of the Roads, to what places they lead. To delineate and lay down the Roads thus survey'd exactly, according to their several Angles, Turnings, Bearings and Situations, noting the Miles between Town and Town, whereby the Distance, not only of the Towns, but also of other interjacent Places will appear by Inspection.*

# ... Tours with Richard Budgen in 1724

The key to the symbols – in what he calls his 'EXPLANATION' – is appropriately enclosed within a sumptuous border of marine life redolent of Sussex-by-the-Sea – dolphins, shells, lobsters, fish, nets and Neptune's tridents. Here Budgen shows signs pointing to a wealth of detail never before attempted on a Sussex map, including stone quarries, iron furnaces and forges, watermills, churches 'Drawn According to their Several Forms' – that is whether they have towers or spires – little rowing boats that 'Shews how far ye Rivers are Navig[able], 'Gentlemen's Seats' and by the use of 'prick'd Parellels' even that a road is 'open' – that is without a boundary fence or hedge, an important consideration when roads were so bad, meaning that travellers could then walk or ride alongside neighbouring land instead of on a muddy, rutted highway. Mileages on major routes are indicated by numbers and dots. Budgen's map was a really practical map and such an advance on its smaller-scale, more decorative predecessors.

So with Budgen as our guide we will travel across Sussex in nine little tours, looking at the county – at least the western part of it – with 1724 as our starting point. In nine sections of the map we will go from east to west across the Weald and then return from west to east along the Downs and coastal plain. Where practical each section of the map has been reproduced to overlap adjacent sections. The scales have been enlarged and reduced from the original.

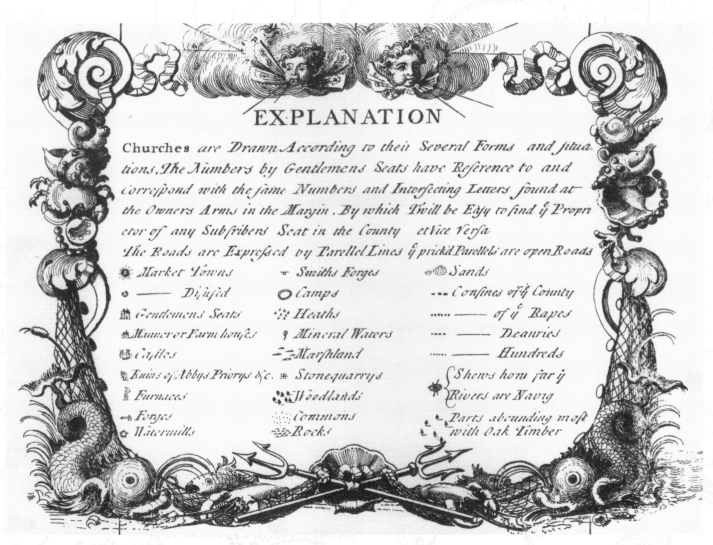

# 3 Tour One: 'The Appian Way for the high nobility'

THIS FIRST TOUR focuses on mid-Sussex. The area shown was once part of East Sussex long before local government reorganisation in 1974 moved the West Sussex boundary eastwards. But in Budgen's time the two halves of the county were not known as East and West Sussex at all. There was just one county and because of its abnormal length of nearly eighty miles it was divided into two 'Divisions'. One side was called the Eastern Division and the other the Western Division until Victorian legislation created the two quite separate counties. Administratively we may be two counties today, but geographically we are still one county (including the separate city of Brighton and Hove which – just administratively – is now independent and in neither).

In 1724 there were just two towns within the area of the map – East Grinstead and Cuckfield – both noted for their markets. Budgen's symbol of the radiant sun indicates a market town.

The sites of Burgess Hill and Haywards Heath are shown here as just heath and common land, as 'Heyworths heath' and 'St Johns Comon'. Names familiar in both towns today can be discovered such as Muster Green, 'Scarce bridg' (Scrase Bridge) and 'Vales bridge' (Valebridge). Scattered in and around St John's Common in the early eighteenth century – and not revealed on the map – were brick and tile works that eventually became the initial stimulus for the growth of Burgess Hill. Haywards Heath was far more of a railway-stimulated new development after the Brighton line opened in 1841.

This is the first county map to detail the road network.

The Comet *coach through Cuckfield plied the shortest and most fashionable route between London and Brighton, in an engraving after a painting by James Pollard, 1822*

Tour One: mid-Sussex in 1724 when East Grinstead and Cuckfield were market towns – indicated by the radiant suns. Crawley was then a tiny village and the sites of the future towns of Haywards Heath and Burgess Hill were covered by heathland and commons.

Before the main London to Brighton road was made a turnpike through Bolney in the early nineteenth century – now the A23 – there were two rival coach routes heading southwards, one through Cuckfield, the other through Lindfield. Eventually, even when there was the choice of the three ways to Brighton, the Cuckfield road was a cut above the rest, popularised by the Prince Regent. One commentator of the time remarked that it was 'the Appian Way for the high nobility of England'. He described the other routes as 'vulgar'.

Several small cogwheel symbols on rivers and streams indicate watermills. Two windmills are shown, both in elevation, one on Chailey Common, the other at East Grinstead. Also shown in elevation are large houses and churches, whilst built-up areas, the centres of towns and villages, are shown by block plans.

Look for the place name Horsted Keynes, by Budgen spelt 'Horsted kayns', emphasising the old Sussex way to pronounce its name. It is not to rhyme with the new city of Milton Keynes – as we say in Sussex, you can always tell a furriner!

## EAST GRINSTEAD TURNPIKE

Because the road from London was 'very ruinous' and at times 'almost impassable', powers were granted to erect turnpike gates between the city and East Grinstead in 1717. Tolls were charged at each gate to pay for road improvements:

> For every Horse, Mule, or Ass, laden or unladen, and for every Chaise, Cart, Dray, or Carriage drawn by One Horse only, the Sum of One Peny.
>
> For every Coach, Chariot, or Calash drawn by Two or more Horses, before they shall be permitted to pass through the same, the Sum of Six Pence.
>
> For every Waggon not laden with Hay or Straw, the Sum of Six Pence.
>
> For every Waggon laden with Hay or Straw, the Sum of Three Pence.
>
> For every Cart, Dray, or Carriage laden with Hay or Straw, or other Goods, the Sum of Two pence.
>
> For every Drove of Oxen or Neat Cattle, the Sum of Eight Pence per Score, and so in proportion for every greater or lesser Number.
>
> For every Drove of Calves, Hogs, Sheep, or Lambs, the Sum of Four Pence per Score, and so in proportion for every greater or lesser Number, as well with respect to the Tolls and Duties imposed by this or the former Acts, or any of them, over and besides the Tolls and Duties already imposed or granted by the said former Acts.

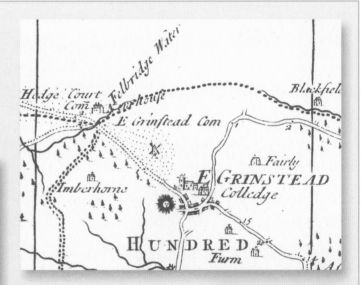

*Left: Tolls to be paid for animals and wheeled traffic using the turnpike road through East Grinstead, authorised by Act of Parliament, 1730–1*

*Right: Milepost in East Grinstead marking 30 miles from London, the bow and bells decoration a punning device representing Bow Bells, signifying London. A series of these milestones was erected in the eighteenth century along the London – Uckfield – Lewes and Uckfield – Hailsham roads.*

*Left: East Grinstead turnpike tickets*
East Grinstead Museum

# 4 Tour Two: 'Desolate and Muddy'

THIS SECTION OF BUDGEN'S MAP continues our westward journey across the northern part of the county, centred on Horsham, St Leonard's Forest and the upper Adur valley.

The road pattern is deeply revealing. Most roads run from north to south, notably those crossing the sticky Wealden clays on the lower land south of the forest. Far fewer are from east to west, reflecting the much more difficult conditions created by the underlying geology. Even today, nearly three hundred years later, road journeys crossing these parts can be lengthy. Try the east-west route between Twineham and Shermanbury measured against the crow's flight. By road it's twice the direct distance. The footprint of the past still strongly persists in these rural parts.

*Sir Charles Merrik Burrell (1774–1862) by whose influence much of the Cuckfield-Billingshurst road was built in the early 19th century – giving easier access to his home and estate at Shipley. It transformed east-west communications across the Weald. It is now the A272.*

For the most part today's route of the A272, the main east-west artery across central Sussex, was completely absent in 1724. It wasn't until a hundred years later that parliamentary powers were given to build the road across this part of the county. The new road became a turnpike or toll road, meaning that all horse-drawn traffic and droves of animals had to be charged for every journey. Shipley's historian, M.M. Hickman, said that it was Sir Charles Merrik Burrell of Knepp Castle – 'Nep' on the map – who first decided that a road should run from east to west. Besides the convenience of passing his own front door, this would then connect with the numerous roads running from north to south. She said that Burrell himself pegged out the course the road was to take.

### Knepp Castle – the old
*All that remains of the 12th- century castle, a fragment of the keep on top of its defensive mound, built by William de Braose. He was a powerful supporter of William the Conqueror.*

### Knepp Castle – the new
*The castellated gothic mansion built by Sir Charles Merrik Burrell in 1809, designed by John Nash. Destroyed by fire in 1904, it was rebuilt in its original flamboyant style.*

Tour Two: the Weald of Sussex in 1724 when roads were notoriously bad

Many of the older roads that were upgraded to turnpike status continued to follow their ancient routes as they meandered across the countryside. But those turnpikes built as completely new roads were generally made as straight as possible, hence some of the arrow-like stretches on either side of Shipley today, tell-tale signs of a nineteenth-century highway construction.

**The West Grinstead Paved Way**
*Sandstone slabs pave the way across the fields on either side of the Adur footbridge south of the parish church, one answer to the notorious mud in these low-lying parts*

**Roads as straight as an arrow – a Burrell legacy**
*On either side of the Burrell estate at Shipley – between Coneyhurst and Bolney – the modern A272 is noted for several straight alignments, a characteristic of completely* new *roads built in the 18th and 19th centuries*

The idea of paying for the distance travelled on the roads was quite revolutionary. In Sussex this meant that travellers met a tollgate on average every four miles of their journey.

At the time the map was published there was just one short stretch of road in this area operated on the toll system, the Sussex section of the Reigate to Crawley road, gated by an act of 1697. This was only the fourth road to be turnpiked in the whole of the country. The very first English road to be turnpiked was on the Great North Road in 1663, between Wadesmill in Hertfordshire and Stilton in Huntingdonshire.

In Sussex most north-south main roads were turnpiked between 1750 and 1800, the east-west routes between 1800 and the 1840s. Once the railways arrived there were no new turnpikes, although the last tolls were still being taken on some Sussex roads well into the 1880s.

Wealden roads were notoriously bad. When Dr John Burton journeyed from Oxford to Shermanbury in 1751 he wrote as if he were entering hostile territory as soon as he came into Sussex:

> *I fell immediately upon all that was most bad, upon a land desolate and muddy, whether inhabited by men or beasts a stranger could not easily distinguish, and upon roads which were, to explain concisely what is most abominable, Sussexian.*

> *Why is it that the oxen, the swine, the women, and all other animals, are so long-legged in Sussex? May it be from the difficulty of pulling the feet out of so much mud by the strength of the ankle, that the muscles get stretched, as it were, and the bones lengthened?*

So much mud meant that one of the best forms of transport in the Weald, particularly in the winter, was by water. The rivers then came into their own. Budgen emphasises their

*Mock Bridge today* *where the bank of the river was levelled to make a wharf for trade up and down the river*

importance for communication by indicating the highest points of navigation. His sign is a little boat, shown in plan view. There is one here by the Adur at 'Mokes bridge' (Mock Bridge today), just north of Henfield. To the riverside landing here, deep in the country, came coal, chalk and flints from Shoreham and the Downs. Logs and timber from the forest country to the north were hauled here for the river journey down to the coast, especially for shipbuilding.

Forest land dominates the northern part of the map. St Leonard's Forest is said to derive its name from a now-lost medieval chapel dedicated to this sixth-century French hermit. His cult was popularised in the eleventh century, but is still strong in Germany where he is the patron saint of farm animals. In the early-middle ages St Leonard's Forest was noted for its wild animals, notably deer and horses.

On the edge of the forest, near Mannings Heath, Budgen marks a fair: 'St Leonards Fair'. This took place annually on the saint's feast day of 6 November and can be traced back to at least 1438. It was probably a horse fair, trading in the wild horses of the forest. Horsham, at the very gates of the forest, was once pronounced and frequently spelt 'Horsam', and is said to have been a settlement or enclosure for horses.

Hilaire Belloc, always ready to defend the ancient ways of Sussex, had this to say of the place-name in his anonymously-written book *Sussex* in 1906:

> *Two generations ago everybody called the town Hors-ham. It became a considerable railway station. Many were led to read the name who had never heard of the little county town until the railway was built. Its own inhabitants did not defend the traditional pronunciation with sufficient vigour, and Horsh-'m it has now fallen to be in spite of the most vigorous efforts of those who love their county to restore its original and significant name, and in spite of the fact that a horse even in Horsham is not yet a Horsh.*

# 5 Tour Three: An 'Engine to Raise Water'

TRAVELLERS VENTURED into these parts at their peril. Twenty years or so before Richard Budgen produced this map, King Charles of Spain journeyed to Petworth House for Christmas. An aide recorded his painful progress:

> ...we set out at that time (six o'clock in the morning) by torchlight and did not get out of the coaches, save only when we were overturned or stuck fast in the mud, till we arrived at our journey's end. 'Twas hard service for the Prince to sit fourteen hours in the coach that day, without eating anything, and passing through the worst ways that I ever saw in my life ... the nearer we approached the Duke's house, the more unaccessible it seemed to be. The last nine miles of the way cost us six hours time to conquer them.

Atrocious highways led to isolated communities, no more so than in the northern reaches of the county towards the Surrey border. To ease worshippers from difficult journeys along rough and muddy roads to their parish churches, chapels-of-ease were built in scattered hamlets. These were at Loxwood for Wisborough Green ('Green' on the map), at Plaistow for Kirdford and at North Chapel – hence the village name (but today spelt as one word) – for Petworth. But the roads were so bad around Plaistow that the Archbishop of Canterbury even gave Kirdford's parson special dispensation from holding weekly services there in the 1760s. For this reason he need only go to Plaistow once in a month or even six weeks 'as he should think necessary, or convenient'.

### Hunger Lane, between Tillington and Rotherbridge
*This narrow gorge through the sandstone rocks near Rotherbridge funnelled the ancient road between Petworth and Chichester. The perils of using this road were heightened by tales of supernatural terrors, smuggling and violence against travellers.*

*Dispensation granted to reduce the frequency of chapel services at Plaistow because of 'the badness of the Roads', recorded in the Kirdford parish register, 1768*

The best length of road on this section of the map was the old Roman military Stane Street on its journey from Chichester to London. Over the centuries much of the engineered road surface had been destroyed by local farmers, but the length through Billingshurst and Pulborough was still remarkably well preserved with its firm and unbroken Roman surface, according to Dr John Burton in 1751. He said that it was only when he left 'this stone causeway' that things got difficult.

Scattered across the Sussex map are many references to 'Hundreds'. The Hundred of Rotherbridge is marked near Petworth.

These hundreds were ancient subdivisions of most English counties, dating from Anglo-Saxon times. The significance of the term is obscure. Originally it might have meant a hundred hides of land. A hide was equal to anything between sixty acres (24 hectares) and nearly two hundred acres (80 hectares), depending on local custom, or it might have referred to a district which supplied a hundred warriors for battle, but there is no certainty at all as to its meaning.

Awfold

Parsonage Rudg

Durn gate · Anfold barn · Shire hedg · Christmas Com · Wanford Gr · Wats Corn

Upper Rundhurst · Fishes Street · Shillingly Park · Wild Carkfield · Plaston Chap · Loxwood Pla · Loxwood Chap · Ickfale · Kinglate · Collins Gr

Lower Rund hurst · Frith furnas · Loxwood bridg · Drenfwick br

Blackdown house · Eastlands · North Chap · Rumbald · Crouchlands · Beggers bush · Trenchmore · Bounder Street Common · Haver

Earthen br. · Monvant hill · Weaphurst · Holmbushes · Buckmans

Lurgafale · Dial Oak · Fnickes · Ebernold Common · Hills Green · Brockland · Dunhurst · Pucket · 5 Oaks

Addingsold · Bells br · Lodge · Colthook Common · Bellchambers · Barkfold · Bexhall brook · Prats · Summers

LIBERTY of LODSWORTH · Burls Cops gate · Hoxds Common · Lladeland · Kirdford · Linfold · Green · Ivals · HUND

Limfo · Linfold bridg · Billinghurst

HUNDRED OF ROTHERBRIDGE · Idehurst · Parbrook

Upperton Com · River · Upperton Street · Moore · Battlehurst · Andrens hill · OF

Lodsworth · Dane · Hampkhurst Com · Palingham · Lordings · Hadfoldhern · Pococks

Netherland · Tillington · Parsonage · Blunsbury · Broadford bridg

Critnum · Lodg bridg · Hutlands · Petworth · New Grove · Bynorth street · Wharfe · Banqueting house · West North Heath · Hunger

Crosland · Cross · Hallgate · Common · Green · Lee Farm · EASWRITH · Redlai

Kilnsham · Rother brid · Egdean · Stopham Parsona · Great Comblands · WChilington

Horsebar bridg · Conder hall Mills · Stopham bridg · Old Place · New Place · Pulborough · Leebrook

Burton · Coates · Heshworth str · Stopham br · Finhouse · Wickfield bridg · Southlands

Burton Park · Engine to Raise Water · Horncroft · Fittleworth · Fittleworth br · Larm br · Hardham brook · Wiggonholt bridg · Heath Mill

Wollavington · Fulling mill · Duncton · Horncroft Common · Coldwaltham · Causway · Hardham · Parson age · Munkmead Common · Thakcham

Barlavington · Parsonage · Bignor Park · Gritham br · Herringham · Wiggonholt · Hurstor · Champion Thakcham · Won

sutton · HUND · Watersfield Street · Hurston Mill · Round about · Greenhurst Common

Upwaltham Donn · Bignor · OF BURY · Gritham · Fryon · Heath Common

Nomans Land · Gumworth · Trottron · W Burton · Bury · Wildbrook · Racomb Common · Parham · EAST

Parsonage · Amberly · Cross gate · Ruins of Racomb Chap · Storrington · Chantry · Rowdell

Amberly Castle · Racomb · Sullington

DLANRIL · loughton

***Rotherbridge near Petworth***
*Meeting place for the Hundred of Rotherbridge, one of the largest Sussex hundreds extending from the Surrey border near Haslemere to the edge of Slindon on the Downs, from where judicial, military and administrative duties were dispensed by the hundred court. The riverside site commanded a strategic crossing of the Rother on what was the main route between Petworth and Chichester. Wide enough for cattle and wheeled traffic, the medieval stone bridge was demolished around 1800 when the turnpike road was diverted via Coultershaw, since when it has been replaced by several different types of footbridge, including one that floated on barrels. The present iron structure dates from 1961.*

What we do know is that each hundred was a collection of parishes originally united for local government matters at a meeting called the hundred court. Traditionally these courts were held in the open-air at some central spot quite away from any settlement. Sometimes they were held by a well-known landmark, invariably in a fairly neutral place by a parish boundary – so the spot became known as 'No Man's Land' as a distinct place-name. One is marked south of Upwaltham Down.

The court for the Hundred of Rotherbridge, covering twelve ancient parishes north and south of the Rother, met close to the Petworth/Tillington parish boundaries by the river at Rotherbridge. Budgen marks this significant place on his map, lying astride the old Petworth – Chichester highway. This ancient route is now a green lane, as around 1800 it was diverted by a new river crossing a little to the east at Coultershaw – today the A285.

At Coultershaw – note Budgen's spelling – the little cogwheel symbol signifies the site of the watermill, erroneously marked here as 'Mills' in the plural. It was one of the oldest watermills in West Sussex. Various mill buildings occupied this site until the last was burnt down in the 1970s.

What is still here today, and in working order, is the restored water-driven beam pump installed in the 1780s. It was used for pumping river water to Petworth House and town, an extraordinary mechanical survival of an early

public utility. A mile or so further south from here is Burton Park. By the watermill symbol the legend says 'Engine to Raise Water', another and even earlier installation than at Coultershaw and used to pump water for the big house at Burton. (A similar engine was installed at nearby Harting

23

to pump water up the hill to Uppark. The little engine house still survives at Engine Farm, by the roadside at the foot of Harting Hill.) Then a little way to the south again is Duncton where the mill site is shown as a 'Fulling mill'. The process of fulling involves the cleansing of cloth for the woollen industry, once important in this area of downland sheep pasture.

Yet another use of waterpower was in the iron industry, both for pumping the huge bellows used in the furnaces and for driving the big hammers at the forges. The Weald was once the most important iron-producing area in the country during the sixteenth and seventeenth centuries. There were fast-flowing streams for power, the local raw material itself in the form of iron-bearing sandstone, and plenty of woodland for the charcoal used in the furnaces. All the essential ingredients for this forest-based heavy industry were to be found around here.

But by Budgen's time the industry was in decline. In these parts the single clue to its survival in 1724 is 'Frith furnace' on the north-west of the map. Originally an Elizabethan furnace, the works was mainly for the production of bar iron until its closure in 1776. It was then one of the last of the West Sussex iron-making sites.

In the commentary for the first tour around the map, reference was made to Budgen's spelling of place-names and the light it can throw on local – and traditional – pronunciation. Today's Greatham, by the Arun just south of Pulborough, is here shown as Gritham, another illustration of the value of maps in discovering and understanding the historic roots of the local and vernacular.

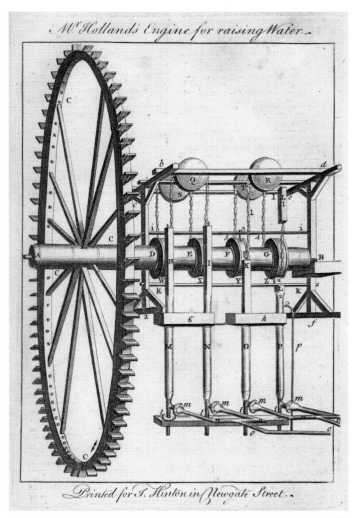

*Maybe similar to the water pump at Burton Park, 'Mr Holland's Engine for raising Water' was built for a country estate in 1755. The water- wheel rotated about five times a minute to pump sixty gallons of water each hour.*

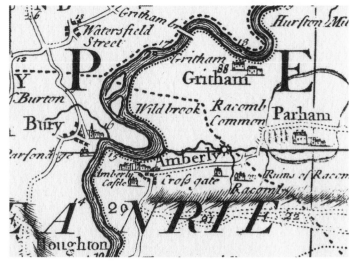

# 6 Tour Four: 'Peculiar' Jurisdictions

CAN YOU FIND Hampshire in Sussex? It is one of two places on this part of Budgen's Sussex map that, whilst geographically firmly within the county, yet was once quite outside the county's jurisdiction and authority.

Hampshire had an 'island' of territory well within West Sussex – it lay east/north-east of Midhurst – and by its side the bishops of London exercised their own rule beyond the reaches of local and even national officers of the law. The reasons for these peculiarities are rooted deep in medieval history.

One quite distinctive feature of medieval jurisdiction was the way in which territorial control, either by counties, parishes or the church, was fragmented, so that portions of land were detached as satellites from the main body.

In the church, the archbishops of Canterbury held parishes that were outside the authority of the diocese by which they were surrounded. They were known as 'peculiars'. Pagham, Slindon, South Bersted and Tangmere were among several Sussex 'peculiar' parishes subject to the archbishop rather than the bishop of Chichester (see map, page 44).

The early Saxon colonists in Sussex created their main settlements – the mother parishes – and then in many places went on to develop outlying settlements several miles away. In the Sussex Weald this was often for seasonal pig pastures in the autumn and winter. Thus people from Upper Beeding went on to settle Lower Beeding, with Upper and Lower used in the sense of main and subsidiary rather than in physical height, for Upper is lower than Lower. Thus some parishes had detached portions elsewhere.

In this way the early settlers of Steep in Hampshire colonised a narrow finger of land some eight miles from north to south and half-a-mile or less in width, a dozen miles or more by road and track from the main parent parish. This sinuous strip of Hampshire in Sussex with its ancient boundaries is clearly shown by Budgen.

It incorporated the twin settlements of North and South Ambersham, although only the southern hamlet is spelt out on the map. Ambersham people were forced to travel to their parish church at Steep for all their baptisms, marriages and burials. When this little bit of Hampshire was finally surrendered to Sussex in 1844 it was only in respect of civil county matters. Steep and the Diocese of Winchester continued to exercise their authority over the Ambershams until as late as 1890. It was an extraordinary medieval survival into the late Victorian period.

The 'Liberty of Lodsworth' on the map refers to the freedoms enjoyed by the bishops of London who had owned the manor here since the early twelfth century. The bishops held their own courts at the Manor House, with power to imprison and execute. Capital offenders were hanged at Gallows Hill, on the parish boundary with Graffham. The original charter granting these rights confirmed that the bishop's jurisdiction was exempt from any authority of the Sheriff of Sussex, the Chamberlain of the King's Household and the Earl Marshal of England. Those who lived within the bounds of the Liberty were exempt

*Manor House, Lodsworth, originally built in the 13th century. With its courtroom and dungeon it was once the administrative headquarters of the Liberty of Lodsworth.*

Tour Four: Midhurst's countryside in 1724, with its two 'peculiars' belonging to Hampshire and the bishops of London (added in colour for emphasis)

*Budgen's map is an exceptionally fine specimen of early eighteenth-century cartography. But errors can be found. Can you spot the error in the spelling of a place-name that had been noticed and then rather clumsily corrected by the engraver? (And this is not the only example of this type of error on the map – another can be found south of Cowfold, see map, page 18.)*

from paying tolls for selling their produce in any market or fair throughout England or Wales.

The manor of Lodsworth eventually passed from the church to the Cowdray Estate in the 1540s, and so came into the ownership of the Montague family. Just under the symbol for Easebourne church there is a tiny coronet indicating the residence of the then current owner in 1724, the sixth Viscount Montague. Close to the coronet is a small figure '11'. Numbers like this next to the big houses and

estates refer to the display of numbered coats of arms of the respective owners printed around the edge of the map.

The Montague's Cowdray Park, an ancient deer park, is shown surrounded by a continuous paling fence. See how cleverly the illusion of perspective has been created by some very fine line work. The original map shows that detail such as this has been exquisitely executed.

The map was printed from an engraved metal plate. A close look across the whole of the map reveals so much very careful attention to detail in the quality of the engraver's craftsmanship. Each tree has its own little shadow.

The way in which the steep north face of the Downs is shown is another good example of what has been achieved. All the earlier map-makers faced one of their greatest challenges in trying to depict the changing levels of landscape on a flat sheet of paper. From the Tudor period onwards hills were generally shown pictorially by little hillocks, but they give no indication of the overall shape and feel of the land.

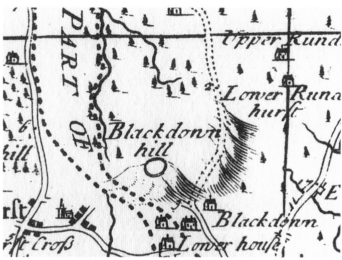

Budgen shows the lie of the land much more effectively, suggesting the curve of the downward slopes with little lines – called hachures – drawn from the top of the hills. The feel of the steep escarpment is beautifully conveyed as the downland ridge sweeps across the map. Blackdown – the highest point in Sussex at 919 feet (280 metres) – is shown in a similar way, crowned with a circle to represent the comparatively flat summit.

As on other areas of the map we have noticed many watermills, shown by the use of a little waterwheel sign. One of the two Midhurst mills – the South Mill – is marked as a 'Fulling Mill'. As at Duncton this is where cloth was cleansed for the local woollen industry, hereabouts so important with all the downland sheep pasture. Midhurst was an important centre of the trade. Indeed the foundation of Midhurst Grammar School in 1672 was based on an endowment made by Gilbert Hannam whose wealth was derived from making coverlets, or quilts.

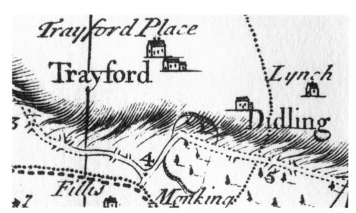

The other important mill site was Pophole on the county boundary north of Lynchmere village. Just to the left side of the mill's name is a small symbol of a hammer indicating a hammer pond used for the production of iron. The ironworks dates from the sixteenth century when the Weald was the major iron-producing area in the country. By Budgen's time the industry was in decline, with Pophole being one of the last surviving sites.

## WATER POWER FOR THE IRON INDUSTRY

The Pophole site on the river Wey straddles the county boundary where West Sussex meets with Hampshire and Surrey. The area is known as Hammer today and several other 'Hammer' place-names perpetuate the link with this former industry: Hammer Coppice, Hammer Hill, Hammer Lane, Hammer Moor, Hammer Vale.

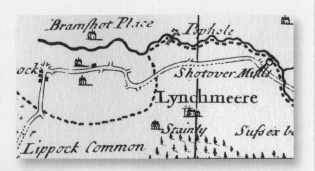

*Sluices breaching the bay of the former Pophole hammer pond, built to operate a water-powered hammer*

*The working of a water-powered hammer: this drawing shows how the water wheel turned the drum with projecting knobs (F) that forced the hammer (A) against the elastic spring of wood (C) forcing it down onto the anvil (G). The hammer could strike the anvil as much as 150 times a minute.*

*Tell-tale signs of ironstone at Pophole – the waterlogged ground is saturated with a rust-coloured iron deposit*

# 7 Tour Five: On the County Boundary

OUR JOURNEY WESTWARDS has finally brought us to the county boundary with Hampshire. In Anglo-Saxon days Hampshire was then part of Wessex, the kingdom of the West Saxons.

Sussex was another, and at times rival, Saxon kingdom, the home of the South Saxons.

So a long time ago this extreme western part of Sussex was border country between two ancient kingdoms, their joint frontier a significant political divide. Over the centuries the kingdom boundary between warring tribes became a more peaceable county boundary, and – with just a few minor changes along its course – has lasted into the twenty-first century much as it has been for well over a thousand years. The persistence of this ancient alignment today as a county border is a typical, but nonetheless remarkable, survival from the local government of early medieval England.

Budgen's eighteenth-century map marks the division quite emphatically. He indicates a fairly straight boundary line marching across country between Ditcham and Ladyholt. Between these two points there is an ideal demonstration of how an ancient boundary was demarcated on the ground.

Boundaries – whatever their status, either national, county or parish – are marked out by either natural or man-made features. Both types can be seen in this isolated stretch of countryside, best viewed on the ground with the aid of the Ordnance Survey's Explorer map to the area.

*Downley Bottom where topography influences the line of the Sussex-Hampshire boundary along the bottom of the valley. Looking north, Hampshire is on the left side of the valley.*

From the crest of the downs high above Old Ditcham, the county boundary sweeps southwards into the bottom of a dry valley, a perfect example of how landscape has been exploited for separating and defining territorial jurisdiction.

Then south of Downley Bottom the boundary sharply abandons the natural grain of the land, striking across what is now a thickly pine-forested downland slope. Without any natural depression or ridge to follow, the boundary here was man-made as a linear earthwork, raised as an embankment, ditched on either side. Throughout their whole territory, Saxon settlers dug thousands of miles of these earthwork boundaries to mark their territories, a colossal undertaking in manpower.

In some places boundary stones were also set up as prominent marker points. At one point a rough-hewn tapered block of sandstone four feet (1.2 metres) high marks the West Sussex side of the embankment. This is on private land south-east of Ditcham close to where the Sussex Border Path crosses the boundary between land called The Harris (in Hampshire) and The Harrows and Harehurst Wood (in West Sussex). All three local

*Victoria Leslie discovers one of the ancient county boundary stones east of Ditcham Park, marking the division between Harting, West Sussex and Buriton, Hampshire*

*The county boundary east of Ditcham Park, partly defined on this 6-inch Ordnance Survey map of 1914 by 'B.S' signs to indicate boundary stones (shown at reduced scale)*

Tour Five: where Sussex meets Hampshire: the Sussex borderland in 1724

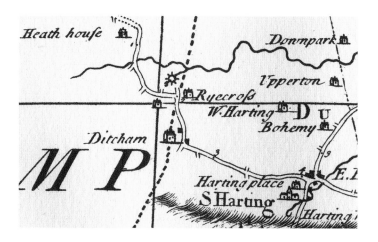

put across old administrative boundaries considerable legal confusion can result. In one Sussex case a dispute arose between two local authorities about the maintenance of a pauper. The boundary cut right through where he lived, his bed being in two different parishes. Counsel decreed that the pauper must be supported by the parish in which his head usually lay at night.

This border landscape is a scatter of small villages and farmsteads, the main population, as today, being concentrated along the Rother valley and at the foot of the Downs, notably at Harting.

In Budgen's time the most thinly-populated area was the extensive heath or common land to the north of Rogate. Here were just a handful of manorial tenants whose lives depended on ancient commoners' rights: the right to gather wood, to dig turf for fuel and graze their animals. To them this wild land was an economic necessity.

Others saw heathland as sinister and inhospitable. Roads crossing heathland were notoriously haunted by footpads. William Cobbett, travelling around the country in the 1820s, described these bleak wastelands as 'villainous' and 'rascally'.

place-names are possibly derived from the Old English word 'har' meaning a boundary. In this way maps, old documents and the landscape itself, taken together, are steeped in clues that unlock the past.

The boundary on Budgen's map is shown going straight through a building marked as 'Ditcham'. This single building represents the farming settlement of Old Ditcham, marked on the modern OS map. Where buildings have been

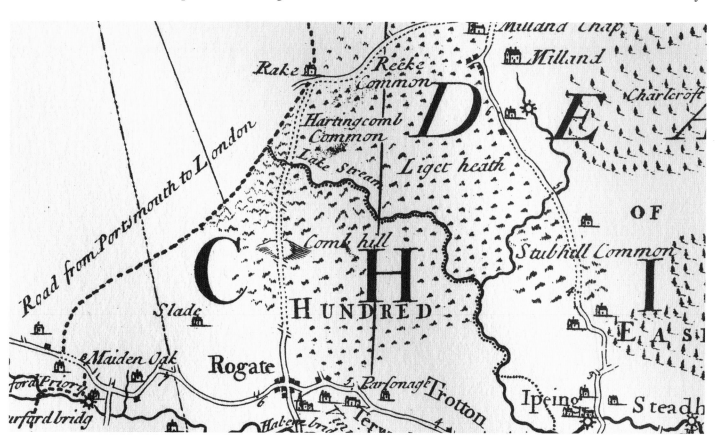

# LADYHOLT – A LOST MANSION IN ITS PARK

*The front elevation facing north-east, the only known illustration, made as a rough sketch about 1760 when the addition of the wings shown at either end of the house was planned*

British Library

### The site today
*What was once a paradise of trees, gardens and sumptuous living and creativity, is now but a ploughed field where a scattering of broken bricks and tiles forever marks the site. The mansion stood between the tree on the left and the cottages in the distance. These two cottages mark the site of domestic outbuildings including the deep well, still in water.*

*The Caryll family, as Lords of Ladyholt, are still remembered here today by this 'millennium' coat of arms erected in 2000*

*One of the Ladyholt cottages marks the site of the former stables*

On the south-western extremity of the map there is a much more different story to tell. Two country estates are shown, each denoted by the symbol of a house (one with a coronet by its side), with avenues of trees ringed by fences, finely shown in perspective.

Ladyholt and Uppark brought wealth, fame and a cosmopolitan lifestyle into an otherwise little disturbed countryside. When Budgen made his map in the early 1720s both were fairly new.

So much is known and has been written about Uppark, built in the late 1680s, almost destroyed by fire in 1989, and since, wonderfully reborn.

But what of the lost mansion and estate of Ladyholt, just two miles away?

The big house has long since vanished. It stood for just a few years short of a century, hidden deep in downland south-west of Uppark. But the plough still turns up fragments of building rubble. Two cottages, marking the site of its domestic outbuildings, ensure that this remote spot is still inhabited: one marks the site of the old stables and maybe a coach house, the other, possibly the former laundry, dairy and brewhouse. The well – at two hundred and forty feet (72 metres) one of the deepest in these parts (and once worked by a donkey wheel, long since broken up) – still survives.

Ladyholt was the home of the wealthy and influential Caryll family who held extensive lands in West Sussex, mainly at West Grinstead, Shipley and Harting. The mansion was built sometime in the 1670s by John Caryll (1625–1711), a leading Catholic, classicist, playwright and diplomat. It had been completed by the beginning of 1680.

It was his nephew, another John Caryll (1666–1736), known as the Squire of Ladyholt, that made the place sparkle with new life, finishing and improving the house and surrounding estate. We find him leading and glazing, bringing in furnishings from the royal bedchamber at Windsor, erecting outbuildings, deepening the great well, making ponds, creating orchards and new cultivations. Into the park he brought three hundred red deer and did much tree planting: belts of trees as windbreaks, trees as ornamental specimens, and a great avenue from the house over Harting Down almost to the edge of Harting, a good two miles in length. Budgen shows the avenue striding across the Downs, giving vistas that integrated the gardens with the surrounding landscape.

Ladyholt's most noted and frequent visitor was the poet Alexander Pope (1688–1744) who confessed that he 'long had a partiality' for the place. Squire Caryll was his oldest and best friend. It was he who suggested the story that turned into one of Pope's most well known verses 'The Rape of the Lock' in which he immortalised his friend with the line 'This Verse to *Caryll*, Muse! is due'. Pope loved to come to Ladyholt for its peace and serenity, his perfect rural idyll. 'A Type of Paradise, the Rural Scene!' – the crescendo to his 'Lines on Solitude and Retirement' – might well have been written for Caryll's little bit of heaven tucked into the Sussex Downs. Its lifestyle and surroundings doubtless inspired many of his poetic works – he worked on his translation of Homer's *Iliad* here – and certainly it was the inspiration behind Pope's less well-known interest in landscaping and garden design.

One of Pope's letters to Caryll suggests that cheap smuggled drink found its way into this remote spot. 'When a hogshead of good French wine falls into Ladyholt Park, whether out of the skies or whatever element that pays no customs, you will favour me with about twelve dozen of it at the price you give.'

The Carylls spent lavishly and well. In debt, the Squire's grandson, yet another John, was finally forced to sell Ladyholt. It ended up in the ownership of Sir Matthew Fetherstonhaugh of Uppark. By 1770 Ladyholt had been razed to the ground.

Viewing the site today it seems incredible that this secluded downland place witnessed such transformations three hundred years ago, now all but vanished but for a few clues on the ground and a name on the map.

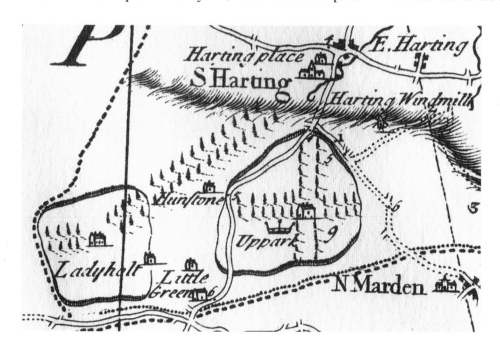

# 8 Tour Six: A Watery Landscape

FROM THE WEALD AND DOWNS we now come down to the flat lands of the coastal plain, dominated by Chichester, its cathedral, markets and harbour. The Manhood Peninsula thrusts the county southwards into the Channel. Selsey Bill – at its tip the most southerly latitude of Sussex – can't be traced as a place-name far back into history. In fact Richard Budgen's 1724 map is the very first county map to name this somewhat blunt-shaped promontory in this way. Portland Bill in Dorset is similarly named. They possibly both mean a projection of land resembling a beak.

A watery necklace bounds this landscape of rifes and rithes, marsh and mud, for the most part not much higher than sea level. Finger-like creeks and channels eat into the land offering easy access to safe havens at Emsworth, Itchenor, Bosham and Dell Quay. But when storms lashed and tides ran high great swathes of this fragile coastline were completely cut off from the mainland. Both islands – Hayling (on the extreme western edge of Budgen's map, unnamed and only partly shown) and Thorney – as well as the Selsey Peninsula (once an island) were then unreachable. Otherwise all three places were linked across the water by either the choice of a ferry boat or a 'wadeway', a causeway through the water, only safe to be used when weather and low tides permitted. Carts, carriages, horses and livestock had little choice but to follow a wadeway. (Budgen doesn't mark any of these wadeways.)

The Thorney Wadeway snaked for nearly a mile across the mud and deep-water channels by a treacherous route that claimed lives in the eighteenth century. Thorney's burial register records:

*1743  Hannah Fuller accidentally drown'd in ye wade-way*
*1752  Richd Smith drowned in the Wade-Way*
*1796  John Harfield drowned in the Wadeway*

To his memorial in Thorney church, Harfield's widow, Sarah, added this timely warning:

*Time swept by his fast-flowing tide*
*My faithful partner from my side,*
*And you of yours deprived may be,*
*As unexpectedly as me.*

Just how much the wadeway must have affected the daily rhythm of life is shown in the previous century. In 1625, farmer John Hargood had to watch the tides when harvesting on Thorney. He was charged by the church for

*Bosham from over the water at Cutmill Creek*

*'Causeway for Carriages at low Water': Thorney Island Wadeway, 1778*

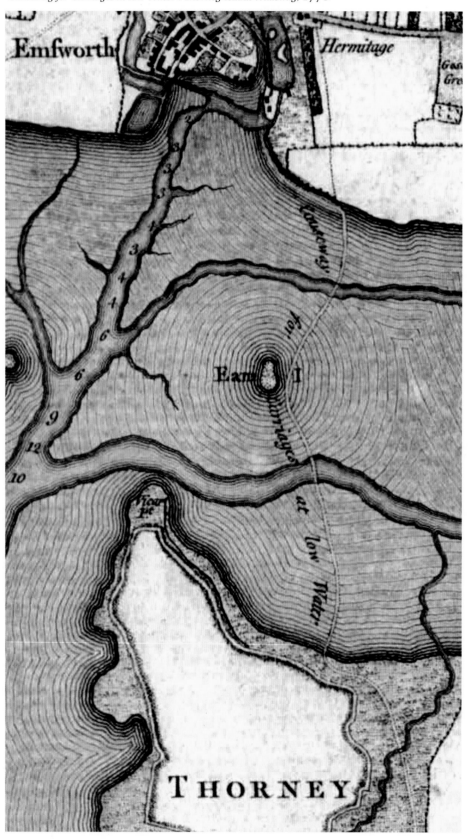

working on a Sunday: for 'bringing his cart and horses over the water upon a Sabbath day ... being constrayned thereunto by necessity, the tide falling out so that he could not possibly passe over uppon the Saturday by reason of fowle weather'.

The Thorney Wadeway across Little Deep and Great Deep has long been abandoned and lost, but just a mile or so westwards into Hampshire – but still technically in Chichester Harbour at almost its furthest reach – the Hayling Wadeway for the most part still survives today. Once linking Hayling Island to the mainland at Langstone, it was cut in two by the deepening of the channel for the Portsmouth and Arundel Canal in the 1820s. Even so the wadeway here is an outstanding example of this type of tidal causeway, of great archaeological significance and listed by Hampshire County Council as a countryside heritage site. When wind and tidal conditions are favourable it can still be walked on safely for a maximum of three hours on either side of low tide.

Yet more evidence of the constant struggle against water in these coastal flatlands is found in the pattern of drainage, so much of it man-made by the drainers, those doughty diggers who were the real heroes of these parts they won from sea and flood. As 'plumbers of the land' they have dug, scoured and repaired these ancient watercourses, sluices, banks, bridges and sea walls over the centuries. Without their constant vigilance this land would be under water.

The main streams here are called rifes, such as Bremere Rife and Pagham Rife draining into Pagham

*Hayling Island Wadeway at Langstone*

*Top right: Bremere Rife, east of Sidlesham*

*Right: 'winding through the mud and ooze', Pagham Harbour*

Harbour. And then into these rifes fall an intricate web of man-made ditches and drains (in times past called 'gutters'); they criss-cross the landscape as its essential arteries, the life-blood of these marshlands, making fields grow rather than drown (and best appreciated today from the Ordnance Survey's local Explorer Map). Then at low tide in Chichester Harbour are exposed the rithes – main channels like little rivers and streams winding through the mud and ooze, at times just a trickle of water, as at Mengham Rithe at Hayling, Fowley Rithe between Emsworth and Thorney and School Rithe at Bosham. In Pagham Harbour they are called 'channels' – Ferry Channel and Mill Channel.

Some decisive historical events have been played out on these shores. The Romans penetrated to Fishbourne and Chichester. The first invading Saxons made their landfall at a spot on the former shoreline now under the waves off Selsey. Saint Wilfrid came this way to spread Christianity, building his monastic cathedral at what later became known as Church Norton, the predecessor of Chichester Cathedral. The Venerable Bede tells Wilfrid's story at Selsey in one of the nation's earliest history books, in his *History of the English Church and People*, finished in 731. And nearby is Bosham that played its vital part in the countdown to the Norman Conquest, its church famously pictured on the Bayeux Tapestry under the headline 'Ad Bosham Ecclesia'. These are hallowed shores.

And more lately the Manhood's 'forward' position was exploited during the Second World War. There were two RAF Advanced Landing Grounds in fields at Apuldram and Church Norton. The D-Day invasion of Normandy was practised at Bracklesham Bay, whilst the sea between Selsey and Bognor was a Mulberry Harbour construction site, from where prefabricated sections were towed to Arromanches for the troop landings in 1944.

The dramatic events that have taken place on these few miles of coastline over the centuries have been of such magnitude that they represent much more than just local history. They are the very stuff of national history, played out locally.

Just when Budgen was preparing his map of Sussex, a very famous author came touring through these parts in the early 1720s. This was Daniel Defoe (1660–1731) whose *Robinson Crusoe* (1719) created one of the most enduring and famous adventures in English literature. As well as a novelist he was a man of many parts: businessman, pamphleteer and government agent, gathering information and testing the political climate to relate back to the politicians. For this he travelled widely, publishing his *Tour Through the Whole Island of Great Britain* in three volumes between 1724 and 1726, so his observations were contemporary with Budgen's map. Here are some extracts from what he wrote about Chichester at the time:

> *I cannot say much for the city of Chichester, in which, if six or seven good families were removed, there would not be much conversation, except what is to be found among the canons, and dignitaries of the cathedral . . .*
>
> *They have a story in this city, that when ever a bishop of that diocess is to dye, a heron comes and sits upon the pinnacle of the spire of the cathedral. This accordingly happen'd . . . when Dr John Williams was bishop. A butcher standing at his shop-door . . . saw it, and ran in for his gun . . . and shot the heron . . . at which his mother was very angry with him, and said he had kill'd the bishop, and the next day news came . . . that Dr Williams . . . was dead . . .*

After his anecdotes about Chichester life – Defoe the novelist

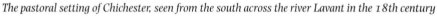

*The pastoral setting of Chichester, seen from the south across the river Lavant in the 18th century*

Tour Six: a watery landscape of tidal creeks, rifelands and marsh in 1724

*Fishbourne Mill, c.1900, one of many mills once dotted around the harbourside. Watercolour by Dr Arthur Evershed of Fishbourne (1836–1919).*

loved picking up good gossip and stories like this – he went on to describe the local grain trade. With his own background in trade, he was always keen to note matters of business and commerce. For Chichester, Defoe tells how grain merchants from around the harbour had built large granaries 'near the Crook, where the vessels come up', by which he meant Dell Quay. '. . . here they buy and lay up all the corn which the country . . . can spare; and having good mills in the neighbourhood, they grind and dress the corn, and send it to London . . . by Long Sea, as they call it' rather than, as previously, sending it by road to Farnham, in Surrey 'the greatest corn-market in England, London excepted'.

Transport by road being so slow and difficult, there was nothing unusual in preferring sea travel for internal communication in the eighteenth century. When Jane Austen's Dashwood family in *Sense and Sensibility* moved their home from Sussex to Devonshire, all the heaviest goods went by boat.

Dell Quay – 'Dellkey' on Budgen's map – was Chichester Harbour's chief wharf since at least 1275. By the eighteenth century it had built up a considerable coastal trade with other English ports with a wide range of cargoes from farm produce, fish and oysters to timber, stone and coal.

The success of the local grain trade through the Dell Quay granaries was closely linked to the numerous corn mills dotted around the harbourside. Reflecting the rich cornlands of the coastal plain, these mills were a sign of considerable prosperity, pointing to a golden age in farming during much of the eighteenth and nineteenth centuries.

A few were windmills, but most were water-powered. The most unusual of the watermills were the tidemills, the Chichester area having one of the largest concentrations of these anywhere in the country. By the nineteenth century there were seven tidemills working here, six in Chichester Harbour, one in Pagham Harbour.

The incoming water operated the mill wheel as it rose to its full height, the sea water being impounded until released on the falling tide. So these mills were as reliable as the daily tides, unlike ordinary watermills that might stand idle for lack of water in a dry summer, or be totally useless in a district where streams were seasonally intermittent. The Lavant is a good case in point. Dry in the summer and autumn, it once powered at least four watermills: at Lavant, Westhampnett (the only one marked by Budgen), Chichester and Apuldram.

In Budgen's time the tidemills were at Nutbourne, Fishbourne (called the 'Saltwater Mill' on the map), and at Sidlesham, which was massive, the largest of them all with three wheels driving eight pairs of stones. It was described as one of the largest mills in the country, with phenomenal production.

Sidlesham's mill might have been geographically in Pagham Harbour, but it was nevertheless legally within the Port of Chichester, the Port defined as a customs' jurisdiction. In 1680 its bounds were set between Hermitage Bridge on the county boundary by Emsworth and extending to the most easterly part of the parish of Felpham. So all the Selsey and Bognor coastline fell within the Port's control.

In distant days Selsey was once all at sea, literally an island – the Isle of Seals. By Budgen's time the area was known as Selsey Peninsula – 'nearly an island'. The sea was on all three of its sides, cut off from Sidlesham and Chichester by what was a much more extensive Pagham Harbour than today, plunging south-westwards, almost reaching the sea. When flooded, the low-lying marshland at Medmerry and Thorney would sever Selsey from the mainland. Even a fairly recent guide to Selsey insists that it is still technically an island because the Broad Rife, linking the head of Pagham Harbour to the sea at Bracklesham, completes the water boundary around the parish.

From earliest times Selsey's connection with the mainland across Pagham Harbour was by two low-tide tracks, one the Wadeway, suitably suggestive of the watery journey facing travellers, the other the deeper Horseway. Then, close-by, a ferry operated, later replaced by a causeway and road bridge taking the main road over the water. The little settlement here is still called the Ferry, one of its properties keeping the name 'Lower Wadeway'. It's been said that even today many Selsey residents have developed a distinct 'island mentality' so that when they cross the Ferry they think of themselves as back home.

What is shown as the headland of Selsey Bill in 1724 is certainly not the present coast-line. Erosion has been relentless over the centuries. The farm-house marked by Budgen at 'Medmery' was in ruins by 1905, cut by the shoreline, its site now completely underwater.

If Selsey's beaches are ever dramatically breached – maybe permanently by the effects of global warming in the future – then it is highly likely that Budgen's map suggests the route of any incursion that might make Selsey an island once more.

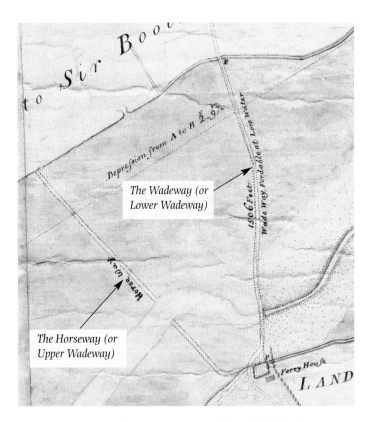

*The Wadeway (or Lower Wadeway)*

*The Horseway (or Upper Wadeway)*

*Selsey Wadeway and Horseway, 1774. Although both have long since been obliterated, the site of the old Ferry House by the sharp bend in the road is still a feature on the road to Chichester.*

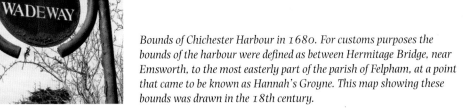

*Bounds of Chichester Harbour in 1680. For customs purposes the bounds of the harbour were defined as between Hermitage Bridge, near Emsworth, to the most easterly part of the parish of Felpham, at a point that came to be known as Hannah's Groyne. This map showing these bounds was drawn in the 18th century.*

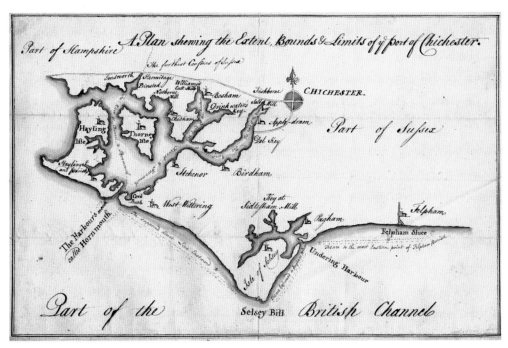

# 9 Tour Seven: Lost Lands

THIS EARLY-EIGHTEENTH CENTURY coastline between Pagham and Littlehampton harbours was bleak and desolate, few people living right on the shoreline as they do today. The invading sea was swallowing up acres of farmland year by year. Each storm brought fresh dangers.

Significantly Budgen makes the point: 'The South Wall of Middleton Church stands about 60 feet from ye Full' (i.e. 18 metres above the full, or high, tide mark). The situation was becoming desperate.

Here, a century before, in 1606, the old village of Middleton had been mapped in great detail: every field shown, a few cottages lining the lane leading to the manorial hall, rectory and church, but even so the place was being described in the 1630s as 'much decayed, wasted and consumed with the sea whereof divers houses and landes are eaten away'. Budgen's map shows both church and manor perilously close to the edge. A century later, in 1837, the church was finally abandoned to the waves.

The last burial in this sea-girt churchyard was in June of that year, for a little three-day-old boy. Surely a double tragedy for the grieving family, with the grave about to go

## MIDDLETON – LOST TO THE WAVES

*The original village in 1606, all since lost to the sea. The church stands to the south of the 'Hall'.*

*Budgen's note on his map in 1724 suggests impending trouble*

**The Gentleman's Magazine *records the unhappy plight in 1796:*** *'the sea . . . gains on the land in a rapid manner: it has devoured the churchyard, with great part of the chancel, and threatens the whole fabrick, which, from the ruinous and desolate situation it is in, appears to be irreparably hastening to its total dissolution . . .'*

under the water. Middleton could then have no more burials until the new Victorian church was opened on a safer, more inland, site in 1849. In its churchyard a solitary tombstone salvaged from the old graveyard can still be seen (at the foot of the steps by the west door) – to Henry Sparkes, dated 1775.

The site of the old church is just off the beach at the seaward end of the second groyne westwards from the end of Sea Lane, according to local historian Winifred Abbott. Traces of five of the old village wells were last sighted on the beach here in 1996.

Without adequate sea defences, the erosion of the coastline was unstoppable. Groynes were erected by one eighteenth-century vicar of Felpham – named as 'Grynes' by Budgen – but they were never as effective as the more modern concrete seawall or the nearby rock islands off Elmer. The remains of some of the early groyning can still be discovered at low tide along Felpham's beach, smoothed down almost to the level of the sand. Today's narrow greensward along the edge of the beach by the Summerley Estate at Felpham was wide enough for a game of cricket, and this was within living memory.

There have been other lost villages along this battered coastline, but long gone by Budgen's time. Sea Lane, Pagham, and Barrack Lane, Aldwick, once met on dry land at a place called Charlton. Now about half-a-mile from the foreshore, its lands were mostly under the waves by the mid-seventeenth century. And between Middleton and Littlehampton there was a village called Cudlow that disappeared in the late sixteenth century. This whole stretch of coastline is a graveyard of lost souls.

Budgen's map is some seventy years before Sir Richard

### Charlotte Smith's Landscape of Melancholy

*Charlotte Smith's sonnet, first published in 1789 and reprinted in The Gentleman's Magazine in 1797, was illustrated by this engraving of the church with her note that 'the sea . . . approaches within a few feet . . . . The wall, which once surrounded the church-yard, is entirely swept away, many of the graves broken up, and the remains of bodies interred washed into the sea; whence human bones are found among the sand and shingles on the shore'.*

Gent.Mag. Sept.1797. Pl.I. p.729.

*Middleton Church, Sussex. N.E.*

### Written in the Churchyard at Middleton in Sussex

Press'd by the Moon, mute arbitress of tides,
While the loud equinox its power combines,
The sea no more its swelling surge confines,
But o'er the shrinking land sublimely rides.
The wild blast, rising from the Western cave,
Drives the huge billows from their heaving bed;
Tears from their grassy tombs the village dead,
And breaks the silent Sabbath of the grave!
With shells and sea-weed mingled, on the shore
Lo! their bones whiten in the frequent wave;
But vain to them the winds and waters rave;
They hear the warring elements no more:
While I am doom'd – by life's long storm opprest,
To gaze with envy, on their gloomy rest.
*Charlotte Smith (1749-1806)*

### The lone tombstone from Middleton's watery past

In Memory
of
HENRY SPARKES
who died July 28th 1775
With sweat and toil I long
hath till'd the ground
But until now no fitting
place be found

*Tour Seven: the Sussex coast in 1724. Along this bleak and desolate coastline the invading sea was swallowing up acres of farmland year by year. The boundary (coloured for emphasis) defines the Hundred of Aldwick and its 'peculiar' parishes under the jurisdiction of the archbishops of Canterbury. A narrow finger of land connects Slindon to the other 'Canterbury' parishes.*

RED

High ditch Woods

Warren Lodg

W Dean

RAP

Upwaltham

R

OF

BURY

P

Barlavington

HUND

Bignor Park

Bignor

Watersfield Street

Gritham br.

Gritham

M. Burton

Wildbrook

Bury

Amberly

Cross gate

Upwaltham Down

DEANRI

Selhurst Park

Lodg

Nomans Land

Gumworth

Trottron

Houghton

Houghton bridge

Goodwood Park

Slindon Windmill

Part of Aldwick Hundred

Madhurst

N Stoke

S Stoke

Halnecker Wind.

Eartham

Wareheed

Slindonplace

Slindon Park

Hebedon

Arundel Park

Offham

E Lavant

Halnecker Park

HUNDRE

OF

Halnecker Street

Boxgrove

Streetington

Cocker hill

W Hamptnet

Peastree

Filkinses hole

ARUNDEL

Arundel Castle

Aldingbourne

Aldingbourne P.

Walberton

Tortington Priory

Badworth

Wormin street

Hamptnet Pla

Tangmeer

Knightam 101

Estergate

A

Tortington

Limister

AND

Oveing

HUNDRED

HUNDRED

Binstead

Marsh Farm

Holticor Sluce

Black Dike

Poleing

Riimbaldweek

OF

Yapton

Ford

Courtweek

OF

TOCKBRIDGE

Leethorn

DEAN

Yapton Place

Merston

OF RIE

Poole

Shripney Street

Climping

Vicareds

North Ways

N Mundham

Boars bridg

Barnham Wind.

Barnham

Climping Windmill

Little Hampton

X

Hunsto

North Berstead

Lagnersh

Shripney Wind.

Lidsey

A VISFORD

Atherington

Sefter

ALDWEEK

S Berstead

Flansham

Bailiess Court

Bowley

Bennets

PAGHAM

Bognor

Felpham

Middleton

Tolsham

Newtimber Green

Aldweek

Grynes

Middleton point

Elmor

ARUNDEL H.

Grove

Fishing houses

*The South Wall of Middleton church stands about 60 feet from y Full*

Pagham

Felpham Sluces

Barn Rocks

Bognor. Rocks

A) Gravel dry y first ¼ Ebb

3½

3½

3

B) Gravel dry at ¼ Ebb

Pagham Siddlesham or Selsey Harbour

4

4

4½

3

2½

3½

4

4½

5

2

4½

5½

6

2½

4½

5

The Park Good Anchoring Ground

6½

7

Ph 6

Baker John Esq at Mayfield.

Qc 10

Blackmore Raymund Esq of Bailey.

Qd 7

Ash St James

Barton Tho. Gent.

Mb 11

Board John Esq.

Hotham started to develop Bognor as a genteel watering place, the beginning of a new age in fashionable seaside history. In the 1720s Bognor was merely a tiny hamlet of fishing huts and farm buildings. The map marks 'Fishing houses' along the shoreline. These were possibly net houses of the type that survive at Hastings.

Throughout the whole map there is a hierarchy of place-names. The size of the lettering suggests the relative status of each place. Significantly the crescent-shaped reef called Bognor Rocks in the sea is much larger as a place-name

than Bognor on the land. That's the reason why Gerard Young, Bognor's historian, commented that 'It was a place that had seldom appeared on a map and was usually called Bognor Rocks – not for itself but because of the character of its coast'. Clearly Bognor hardly existed then.

The coastline hereabouts, backed by the marshy rifelands immediately to the north, would have seemed isolated and cut-off, particularly as there was then no through road across the Arun at Littlehampton. The river acted as a most effective barrier to communications. One vicar of Climping remarked that many of his labourers never visited the town at all, despite its proximity, although there was a rowing boat to take foot passengers across.

So all other traffic, horse-ridden or horse-drawn, had to be funnelled through Arundel as the lowest-bridging point over the river until 1825, when a chain-ferry, or floating bridge, came into operation at Littlehampton. But it wasn't until as late as 1908 that an iron swing-bridge finally transformed Littlehampton's connection with the west side of the Arun.

In the Bognor area one of the oldest roads featured by Budgen was the link between Pagham and Slindon. At least medieval in origin, parts of the route today still follow much of its ancient alignment along Chalcraft Lane, across to North Bersted Street and thence on to Shripney. Many medieval archbishops of Canterbury and their stately retinues travelled this way ever since Saint Wilfrid, the Saxon bishop, gave both parishes to the archbishopric. Hence Pagham and Slindon were known as archbishops' 'peculiars', being under the jurisdiction of Canterbury rather than subject to the diocese of Chichester. This is why Pagham's parish church was dedicated to St Thomas à Becket, and even today the archbishop is still patron of the living.

*The Becket Banner*
*Thomas à Becket is shown holding Pagham church on his lap, traditional symbolism of the special care a church receives from its patron saint. The banner is worked on a background of blue watered silk, recalling the sea and its ever present influence on Pagham's life and history.*

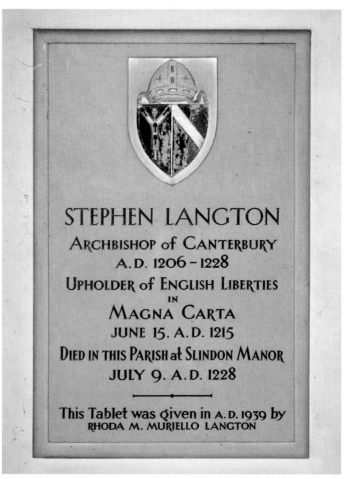

STEPHEN LANGTON
ARCHBISHOP of CANTERBURY
A.D. 1206 - 1228
UPHOLDER of ENGLISH LIBERTIES
IN
MAGNA CARTA
JUNE 15. A.D. 1215
DIED IN THIS PARISH at SLINDON MANOR
JULY 9. A.D. 1228

This Tablet was given in A.D. 1939 by
RHODA M. MURIELLO LANGTON

*At Slindon the archbishops owned a country house and estate – on the site of what is now Slindon College. A single castellated tower is a remnant of the former palace. They frequently stayed at the palace when visiting their Sussex properties, as did Stephen Langton who died here in 1228. His memorial is in the parish church.*

What also united Pagham and Slindon – as well as Tangmere and South Bersted – was that they were all parishes within the Hundred of Aldwick. They were also linked with a detached portion of the archbishops' peculiar within the walls of Chichester, the parish of All Saints in the Pallant. (These hundreds, the ancient subdivisions of most English counties in the past, are briefly explained in Tour Three.)

The hundred court met at a site in Aldwick and so, as its headquarters or 'capital', gave its name to the whole hundred. Aldwick Parish Council recently commemorated this ancient centre of local government by a blue plaque outside number 28 Barrack Lane.

Budgen marks the hundred's boundary by a well-defined line from Pagham Harbour around Tangmere and Slindon and back to the coast between South Bersted and Felpham. Slindon is connected to the rest of the hundred by the narrowest of fingers of land dividing Eastergate and Aldingbourne, the whole roughly in the shape of an '8'. In this way the lands of the archbishops were united.

By status the borough of Arundel, with its mayor and corporation, was by far the most important place on the map. In 1730 the Reverend Thomas Cox, in his *Magna Britannia*, said that its situation on the Arun 'where ships of 100 Tuns may ride, render the Trade so considerable, that there are several Ships built there'. There were two weekly markets and four annual fairs, and the place was 'famous for Mullets, both for the Plenty, Largeness, and Goodness of them'.

On this site,
from about the mid-14th Century,
stood the

**HUNDRED HOUSE OF ALDWICK**

Courthouse and Centre for local government for tithings in the area from Aldwick to Pallant (Chichester) and across to Slindon in the east.

It was evidently rebuilt after 1617 and probably fell into disuse following the reform of local government in 1894. It was demolished about 1930.

See History of Pagham by Lindsay Fleming

This plaque was installed in 2002 by
Aldwick Parish Council

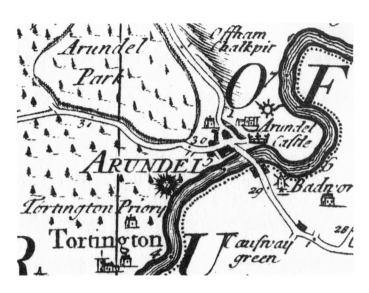

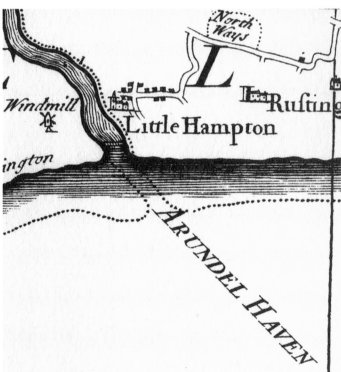

Such was the dominance of Arundel that the harbour mouth at Littlehampton was called Arundel Haven. Littlehampton didn't become the major port on the Arun until well into the nineteenth century after engineering work to the piers and deepening the river made possible the building of ocean-going vessels. Then, for a short time, passenger-carrying steamboats operated between here and France and the Channel Isles.

In the bottom right-hand corner of this section of the map there are five coats of arms. Across the whole map there are a hundred and forty-eight of these altogether, with twelve blanks. These were the arms of all the subscribers whose financial support made publication of the map possible. Presumably twelve didn't pay up. By the side of most of these there are upper and lower case letters followed by a number, making it possible to find the geographical location of the seat of each subscriber. The map is ruled by a reference grid with upper case letters at top and bottom and lower case to the left and right. The number by each shield is the number printed next to a house symbol on the map. Thus Yapton Place has '46' beside it, and looking at the map – beneath the town of Shoreham in this case and not shown in this section – we find that these are the arms of Laurence Elliot who lived there. Its symbol at Yapton shows that, according to Budgen's key, the property was a 'Gentleman's Seat', just the type of person to whom Budgen made his appeal for funding the map.

Arundel mullets, prized as a local fish dish, have long been celebrated as one of the 'Seven Good Things of Sussex' (the others being Selsey cockles, Chichester lobsters, Amberley trout, Pulborough eels, Rye herrings and Eastbourne wheatears). This fish became so interwoven with the good fortunes of Arundel that anyone born within its bounds has been called a mullet, the native aristocracy of the town.

# 10 Tour Eight: Of Fleas and Smugglers

Dr Richard Russell, by Benjamin Wilson
Brighton Museum and Art Gallery

THE SEASIDE and its attractions had hardly been 'invented' by 1724. The transformation of this stretch of coastline was still many years away. Yet the first signs were soon to emerge, hinting at what lay ahead to change this coastal landscape forever.

It was the lure of sea-water that did it, but using the sea not for recreational bathing and pleasure, but more as a hospital.

Dr Richard Russell of Lewes (1687–1759) popularised the fashion with his seminal book, *A Dissertation on the Use of Sea-Water in the Diseases of the Glands*, first published in Latin in 1750. It advocated the sea as a health cure: for drinking as a medicine and for immersion rather than swimming.

This was the sea for serious business, certainly not for fun.

Russell moved his practice to the little fishing village called Brighthelmston, whereupon the sickly-rich soon arrived to 'take the waters'. Brighton as a medical cure – 'Doctor Brighton' – was born. Worthing and scores of other coastal resorts followed the same pattern, owing much to the pioneer work of this Sussex doctor. Bottled sea-water from Sussex was even on sale in London for those unable to visit themselves.

The motto for this new fad can be discovered in Russell's memorial in South Malling church, Lewes. From the Greek it reads: 'The sea cures all the diseases of mankind'.

> **'The sea cures all the diseases of mankind'**
>
> *Dr Richard Russell of Lewes popularised bathing and the drinking of sea-water as a medical cure in his book first published in Latin in Oxford as* De Tabe Glandulari *in 1750. His views received wider circulation when the book was republished in English – without his permission – in an unauthorised pirated edition in Dublin in 1753. His work popularised the seaside for health and soon places like Brighton and Worthing transformed the Sussex coastline.*

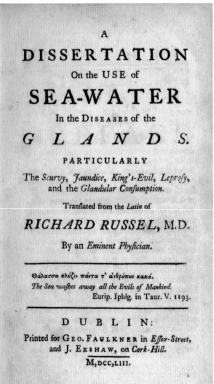

*Tour Eight: the empty coastline that smugglers turned to their advantage. The unnamed hamlet of Worthing, marked here in 1724 by four black squares south of Broadwater, was soon to be transformed into a fashionable seaside resort by a new fashion – 'taking the waters'. 'Worthing Shops' possibly refers to fishermen's huts.*

The whole notion of the sea and seaside development underwent a dramatic change in the eighteenth century. For in Budgen's time, in the 1720s, the coast was far from being the magnet it was later to become. Except for fishermen, and maybe farmers who harvested the seaweed for fertilizer, people didn't care to live right by the sea. It was seen as bleak, desolate and wind-blown, even hostile, in the front line of raids in time of war, the haunt of smugglers and at the full mercy of the waves. If anything it induced gloom and melancholia, as with Charlotte Smith at Middleton (page 43).

Significantly, when John Taylor – well-known as the somewhat eccentric but respectable 'water-poet' – rowed along the Sussex coast and landed at Goring in 1623, he and his fellow boatmen were promptly arrested as pirates, their oars stolen and hidden in a barleyfield, his indignities compounded by having to sleep in a bed 'all beleaguer'd with an host of Fleas'. The whole tenor of this versifying visitor was that this place was inhospitable and unwelcoming – somewhere to be avoided.

We have already seen the shoreline being eaten away in great chunks around Selsey, Pagham and Middleton, whole villages disappearing under the waters. Between Littlehampton and Worthing it was exactly the same story. Yet another Sussex church was lost to the waves, this time in the early seventeenth century. In 1626 the churchwardens reported that their chapel-of-ease at Kingston, was about to go under:

> *Our chappell is much decayed and out of repayre by reason of the sea, and now hath wrought away the land . . . so that it is not repayrable . . . suddenly the chappell will be ruinated by the sea.*

And indeed it was, for in 1641 they reported that 'Our chappell is utterly ruinated and demolished by the sea, and wee doe constantly resort to Ferring to service, being the mother church'.

Maybe the original village site around the chapel was indicated in 1981 when the base of an ancient well was found on the beach about five hundred feet (about 150 metres) from the present shoreline. East Preston's local historian, Richard Standing, has made the point that ancient footpaths through the fields in Kingston all run in the direction of this well site and the presumed lost village.

A study of large-scale maps in West Sussex Record Office suggests that the rate of coastal erosion between Rustington and Worthing during the eighteenth and nineteenth centuries has been anything up to nine hundred feet (275 metres), with the greatest losses in the region of central Worthing and decreasing westwards. This may have been due to the fact that whereas the land in front of Worthing was low, flat and open, further west it became thickly wooded as the remains of submerged fossilised tree trunks still indicate. In 1845 an old man of ninety-five said that as a boy he spoke with a man of eighty who remembered a park of large elm tress called Rushton Park in Rustington. Their felling in about 1700 encouraged more coastal erosion. The loss of lands and homes must have been a depressing sight.

So this rather unwelcoming coastline attracted few people to live here. The small villages lay a short distance inland, as if shunning the sea as in the case of 'old' Rustington and Ferring.

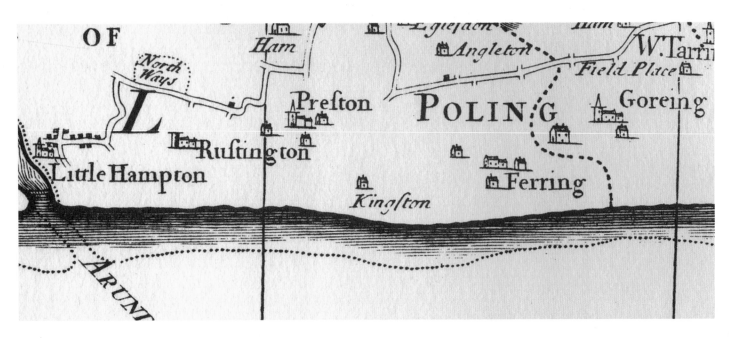

# THE BARBARITY OF SMUGGLING

The people who turned this isolated, empty coastline to their advantage were the smugglers. Sussex and Kent were notorious for this line of illicit trade. Indeed by the late eighteenth century there were more illegal imports coming through these two counties than anywhere else in the country. West Sussex was particularly favoured, being free of dangerous, rocky headlands and cliffs, with gently shelving beaches for easy unloading.

*A dispute over smuggled tea: the Hawkhurst Gang whip Richard Hawkins to death at Slindon in 1748*

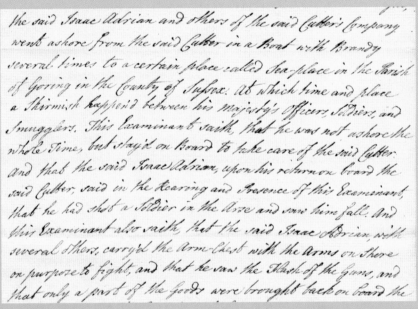

*Brandy smuggling at Sea Place, Goring, with a soldier 'shot . . . in the Arse', 1743*

*The dreadful warning, the grisly end: gibbeted smugglers on the seashore – two members of the Hawkhurst Gang suffered this fate at Selsey Bill in 1749*

After 1720 there was a huge expansion of this illegal trade, encouraged by the very high level of import duties imposed by the government. Tea and spirits were the main cargoes, with the best returns coming from smuggled tea from Holland. Around 1740 the cheapest grades cost six old pennies (2½p) for a pound weight of tea (half a kilogram), that could be sold for a six or eight-fold profit and yet still undercut legally-imported tea. There were big profits to be made, a welcome addition to a lowly-paid workman's wages.

But this 'free-trade' was far from being the romantic affair often portrayed. Ruthless gangs pursued their unlawful activities with violence and intimidation. Gangs of twenty, fifty, even a hundred, armed with guns, bludgeons and clubs, terrorised the county. The Hawkhurst Gang, with good support from West Sussex smugglers, was infamous for cruelty and murder as they worked the countryside between Kent and Dorset.

Some of their number were implicated in the fatal shooting of one of the dragoons drafted in to reinforce the local riding officer during a landing at Sea Place, Goring in 1744. Shots were fired at Ferring in 1720 when upwards of sixty armed men engaged with the preventive forces. Smugglers Walk and Smugglers Cottage are reminders today of the part played by this high-risk occupation in Ferring village in the past. At Rustington the name 'Broadmark' used in three road names today, derives from the broad mark, or broad arrow, signifying government property (and as once popularly known as the mark traditionally put on prison uniforms). The government property in this case being the local preventive officers' watch house. These were the armed coastguards of the day.

The first most dramatic change on this stretch of Sussex coast took place at Worthing. In the space of just two or three decades, from the late eighteenth century, this little fishing and farming community was transformed into a most fashionable and handsome watering place.

But in Budgen's time it was merely an obscure appendage to its mother parish. Worthing didn't even exist in its own right in local government terms. It was just a hamlet *within* the parish of Broadwater.

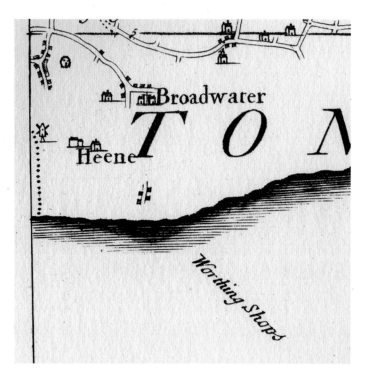

*44 High Street, Worthing: a fragment of the original hamlet of old Worthing*

Worthing was made up of a scattering of houses and cottages along its one main street – known as Worthing Street – representing the core of the place shown in simplified form by Budgen. It was so insignificant that it's not even named on the map.

Around the street, that became known as High Street about 1775 – and by which it is still known – were the ancient medieval common fields for crops and pasture lands for grazing. It was as much a farming community as it was for fishing. Its fishing side may possibly be suggested by Budgen's enigmatic 'Worthing Shops' printed on the map, well away from the main street. This might refer to the fishermen's net-drying and tackle sheds ranged along the beach.

Today's High Street marks the original heart of old Worthing. Sadly an orgy of modern town planning has left little of this once delightful street of old flint walls and cottages, now turned into an inner ring road, massive car parking and a supermarket. It's now all gone except for a fragment of the old village: numbers 44 and 46 on the east side of the road are precious survivals. Number 44 is finely built from smooth-shaped beach pebbles set in regular courses, a local building style occasionally glimpsed elsewhere along the Sussex coast. Research has suggested that emigrants from Sussex took the style to America in the early nineteenth century where they built similar houses around the Lake Ontario Plain of western New York State. There these homes are much admired and are appropriately known as cobblestone buildings.

# 11 Tour Nine: Bridges and 'Rotten Boroughs'

OUR EIGHTEENTH-CENTURY TRAVELLER moved slowly across the map. Journeys weren't undertaken lightly. When it's realised that the root of the word 'travel' is similar to 'travail', linked with the French *travail*, meaning painful effort or labour, then we are much nearer to understanding what early travellers faced in moving around the country. They needed patience, stamina and a very good reason for starting out.

Whatever our problems in travelling today, they are nothing to those suffered by our Georgian ancestors. They peppered their letters and diaries with horrendous descriptions of their roads, much as we discuss and write about the weather.

And indeed no one came into Sussex unless they really had to. That's the reason why the Sussex Spring Assizes in March were held at either East Grinstead or Horsham on the northern boundary of the county, preventing the itinerant circuit judges from having to face the bad roads further south. The Summer Assizes were held at Lewes, deep into the county, when the roads were so much better. One suffering barrister wrote to his wife after the Spring Assizes: 'I have come off without hurt ... through the Sussex ways which are bad and ruinous beyond imagination'.

Likewise the earliest turnpike roads from London into Sussex all stopped close to the county boundary, so that by 1717 these 'improved' roads only reached Tunbridge Wells, East Grinstead and Crawley. The need to go any further south towards the coast meant you went at your own peril.

In Budgen's day there was no through route hugging the coast as the A259 does today. It was a crumbling coastline broken by rifes, dykes and salt-water marshland. Even when the coastal road was eventually built between Worthing and Lancing in 1808 there was endless trouble, with the road being constantly washed away. At one time six hundred feet disappeared (just under 200 metres) and The Gap, as it was called, became a prominent feature of the landscape for fourteen years until the road was opened again in the late nineteenth century. Then by the end of the century the newly-established West Sussex County Council eventually got involved, whereupon it was suggested – Alice in Wonderland style – that there was no liability as the road had ceased to exist!

The main road held to the high ground through Arundel and the edge of Broadwater to Lancing, much the same overall route as the A27 today, but near the river Adur it came to an abrupt stop. Travellers either could add several miles to their journey by crossing at the lowest bridging point at Bramber, or, alternatively, make the crossing to Old Shoreham by one of two ways. They either forded on horseback, or used the ancient ferry. As several diarists tell us, both were risky ways across. In 1772 John Baker of Horsham wrote that his party 'rode over up to horses' bellies'. And the ferry was used with some trepidation. It was almost certainly a wide wooden raft that was poled across. Rafts like these were known as pads, possibly the origin of the name of the nearby old coaching inn, the Sussex Pad. Budgen marks this location as 'Pads'.

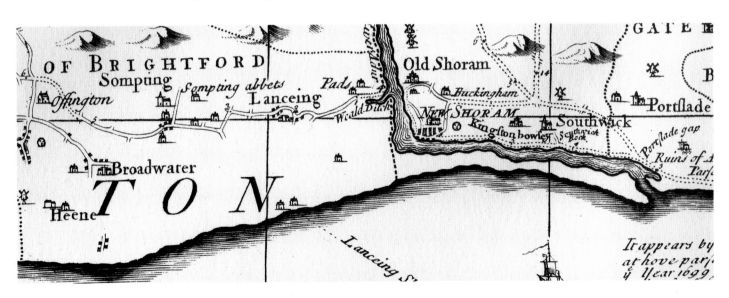

Partridg Green
Euhurst Pla
Shermanbury E
Twineham
Goather green
St Johns
Common
Wivelsfield
Brittain
Bines bridge
Mokes bridge
Shiproad
W. House
Bury br
Stuckles
Sawyers Common
Cabs mill
OF
Oathall
Bines Green
Chestlains bridge
14
Hamonds Pla
TEAD
Blakes
Ashurst
Etons
Hendfield
Wontly
Blackston
High Cross bridge
Uplies
Hurstperpoint
Woorke bridg
Barronhill
Blackston
Fstreet
Woodmancote
Alboune
W. Town
Wickham
Byneham bridg
Nut knowl
HUND. OF TIPNOAKE
Dany
Ditchling
HUND OF
Newhall
Stretham
Woods Mill
Newtimber Place
Wolsonbury hil
Clayton
Westmiston
Broadbourne Stream
BURBEECH
Newtimber
HUND.
Piecombe
Ditchling Cast.
STENNING
New br
Beeding
Horton
Todington
Truly
Edberton
Folking
Poynings
Pang dean
Standean
Part of Ring
Bramber Ca
Beeding Windmill
Folking
Sadlescomb
Poormans Wall
OF
Hundred in Deanries S. M.
Stammer
BRAMBER
New house
POYNINGS
Buttolphs
Coombs
Applesham
Erlingha Chalkpits
Erlingham
LEWE
White Lot
HUND. OF FISHERS GATE
Hangleton
HUND OF DEANE
Stammer Cross
Patcham
Patcham Windmill
Hollinsbury
HU
Old Shoram
Blatchington
Whiteing
Mousecomb
Hadshurfe
Lanceing
Pads
Buckingham
Portslade
HUND OF PRESTON
Preston
Preston place
Weald Ditch
NEW SHORAM
Kingston bowsey
Southwick
Southurst Rock
Portslade gap
Ruins of Aldrington th Parsonage
Hove
HUND OF WHALESB ONE
YOUU
N
Brighthelmston
Lanceing Shops
It appears by an Inscription at hove parsonage that since ye year 1699 ye Sea has gained on that coast 6 Perches.
Black Rock

# CROSSING THE ADUR – THE NEW BRIDGE OF 1782

To improve safe passage over the river, the Old Shoreham Toll Bridge was opened in 1782. For its period it was a remarkable achievement, and up to then was the most ambitious bridge yet to be constructed in the county.

*The new bridge, shown in this engraving of about 1800, was the most significant addition to Old Shoreham since the medieval church was built by the Normans*

The principal Sussex rivers had their lowest bridging points at strategic downland-gaps, at Arundel, Bramber and Lewes. At these points crossings could be reasonably short and on relatively firm foundations.

But in contrast – and this was its distinction – the new bridge at Shoreham was the first to be built in Sussex on the coastal plain below the downland-gap position, resulting in the need for both a considerable span and an artificial causeway over the mudflats on the Lancing side. The causeway, built on a foundation of wooden faggots, was across ground so bad that the superintending surveyor said that 'with his hand only he had driven a hop pole up to its head in the mire'.

The completed structure was the longest bridge that had ever been put up in the county. By this singular piece of engineering the one major obstacle to east-west communications along the coast had been solved.

Closed to vehicular traffic today, the bridge retains its original eighteenth-century design, curiously medieval in form with its pack-horse style passing places. It's strange to think that the bridge carried the A27 trunk road until 1970, creating enormous traffic jams as tolls were still being demanded. It was the last public road bridge in Sussex to be controlled by a toll.

*The new bridge and lengthy causeway over the Adur marshes is shown here for the first time on a Sussex map – by Yeakell, Gardner and Gream, 1795. (The map has been dissected, or cut into sections for ease of folding, hence the vertical dividing line.) For centuries the lowest bridging point of the river had been at Bramber. Its opening transformed local travel, according to the Sussex Weekly Advertiser (25 March 1782), promising 'the greatest advantages to the county of Sussex in particular, and the kingdom in general, by opening a communication, much wanted, between Portsmouth and Dover'.*

*The wooden bridge is curiously archaic for the late-eighteenth century, even medieval looking with its pack-horse style passing places – from an early 20th-century watercolour by W.H. Borrow*

Before the main road to Brighton was built through mid-Sussex (eventually becoming the A23), the little fishing town of Brighthelmston was approached from the London direction by a variety of meandering routes.

One of these bridged the Adur at Bramber before the steep climb over Beeding Hill and then crossed open downland towards the coast. Budgen marks it as unfenced (by using dotted points instead of continuous lines) and

with numbers for milestones, zeroed from Brighton. New Erringham – just south of milestone seven – served as a coaching inn. It continued to be the main road until superseded by the new turnpike in 1807, following the east side of the Adur valley with the express purpose of avoiding Beeding Hill. The old road across the Downs can still be followed today.

This road from London and Horsham, down through

*Road travel over the Downs to Brighton in 1780 – a view of the Henfield-Brighton turnpike at Poynings by S.H. Grimm. The town's eighteenth-century growth as a fashionable seaside resort depended on improved road communications by the introduction of turnpikes in the 1770s feeding in from three directions, from Lewes, Cuckfield and Henfield. Note the grass verge, useful for detours when the road was deeply rutted after winter storms. The chalk bank on the left suggests that the level of the road had been lowered to ease the gradient up the hill.*

British Library

Steyning and Bramber and thence on to New Shoreham, was of considerable antiquity. The linking of these Sussex places along this highway was of some significance, for they were all ancient borough towns, each with the right to send members to parliament, a privilege going back to the late thirteenth century. Then their political status reflected their economic and military importance in the medieval period. But by the eighteenth century many of these boroughs were but shadows of their former selves. The position seemed lunatic.

One Suffolk borough, Dunwich, continued to send two MPs to parliament, although the town had been washed away by the sea. Old Sarum in Wiltshire, merely a green mound with a ruined castle, similarly had two MPs. By contrast the rising industrial centres of the north, places like Manchester and Rochdale, with all their social problems, had no parliamentary representation at all. No wonder that places that had outlived their political usefulness were known as 'rotten boroughs'.

Daniel Defoe – of *Robinson Crusoe* fame – could thus write with some contempt of Bramber in the 1720s, for its two MPs represented just fifteen or sixteen families 'and of them not many above asking you an alms as you ride by'. In similar vein Steyning was described by another traveller as 'A mean contemptible Place, in which ... there is hardly an House fit to put an Horse in, yet this poor Place hath the Privilege of sending Burgesses to Parliament'. Rotten boroughs were unfair and unjust.

New Shoreham was the most prosperous and lively town in these parts with its considerable shipbuilding industry. Around 1700 it was famed for its men-of-war. Up to fifteen merchant ships were on the stocks at one time in the 1730s. But politically the place was corrupt, voters clubbing together to sell their votes to candidates offering money and the promise of lucrative shipbuilding contracts. Such places were the rotten boroughs of Sussex.

**The 'Rotten Borough' of Bramber**
*By the 18th century Bramber's glory lay in the past as an ancient castle-stronghold. But the tiny village around its walls still scandalously hung on to its former trappings of power with its two MPs representing just fifteen or sixteen families, according to Daniel Defoe.*

Bad roads, a crumbling coastline, the haunt of smugglers, corrupt politics. Budgen's Sussex certainly doesn't give the appearance that all was well down here in the eighteenth century. Maybe Lord Chancellor William Cowper's comment that the county was nothing better than 'a heap of dirt' had a ring of truth about it.

# 12 Bound for Botany Bay: Transportation to Australia

THE DATELINE WAS January 1788, the place Botany Bay, destination of eleven British boats that had been at sea for eight long months with its cargo of human misery, the rejects of English and Welsh society. Seven hundred and seventy-eight criminals had been loaded, banished by a judicial system to 'beyond the seas'. Their arrival signalled the beginning of Australia as a convict colony.

It was from this epic-making 'Noah's Ark of small-time criminality' that three convicts from Sussex stepped ashore, men tried and sentenced by Assize courts at Horsham and East Grinstead. Thus, in some small way, Sussex contributed to this momentous venture played out on the other side of the world.

The roots of transportation go back to 1597 when Elizabethan legislation to control rogues, vagabonds and beggars enacted the punishment of banishment 'out of this Realm'. Some thousands of convicts were exiled to the new colonies and plantations along the eastern seaboard of North America. All went well as long as the American colonies remained British, but with the door effectively closed by the declaration of American Independence in 1776, the government faced crisis point as prisons overflowed. Where to send them? It took ten years to decide on an alternative – Botany Bay.

*Leaving Portsmouth in chains: Australian stamp issued in 1988 to commemorate the bicentenary of the First Fleet*

*Below: Convicts embarking for Botany Bay, by Thomas Rowlandson*
National Library of Australia

Once the decision was reached there were months of feverish activity: boats to charter and refit as floating prisons, equipment, food and clothes to procure. Stores ranged from nails, hinges, hooks, axes and spades to wheelbarrows and carts, bricks and window glass, a printing press and even a piano. There were tents, a portable canvas house for the new governor, bedding, live cows, sheep, turkeys and chickens as well as dogs and cats as hunters and pets. Tons of food were supplemented by seeds, trees and plants. Then at last came the convicts themselves: pale, ragged and lousy, thin as sticks from their jail diet. Herded on board, the prisoners were at first to be kept below deck until the flotilla was out of sight of land.

After endless – and what to the convicts must have been agonising – delays, the little fleet – officially known as the First Fleet – weighed anchor on the Mother Bank between Portsmouth and Ryde in the early hours of 13 May 1787, setting sail on the first leg of its eight-month long haul to Australia.

*The First Fleet leaves England for Botany Bay, passing the Needles and the Isle of Wight, May 1787, by William Bradley, First Lieutenant on HMS* Sirius. *He kept a detailed journal illustrated by his watercolours.*
Mitchell Library, State Library of New South Wales

Most of the transportees were sentenced for crimes against property, the great majority just small-time criminals: pickpockets, burglars and poachers. Private property was sacrosanct, its violation punishable by laws of draconian severity. The value of the booty was quite immaterial. Thomas Hawell stole two hens, James Walbourne a linen handkerchief. Each got seven years' transportation. This rag-bag of humanity included both young and old. John Hudson was the youngest of them all, a chimney sweep boy only nine years old – seven years for stealing clothes and a pistol. The oldest was an incredible eighty-two, Dorothy Handland – 'an old clothes woman' – seven years for perjury.

What of the three convicts from Sussex? All three were put on board the *Alexander*, the largest in the First Fleet, but even so she was only a hundred and fourteen feet in length (35 metres) with a beam of thirty-one feet (just under 10 metres). Besides officers, crew and marines, there was the cargo itself: one hundred and ninety-

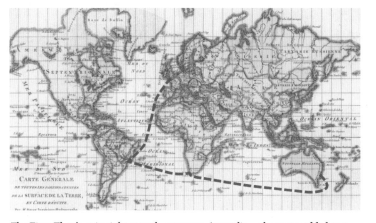

*The First Fleet's epic eight-month voyage to Australia – the route added to a map dated 1780*

five male convicts packed together below like sardines, horrifyingly ideal conditions for incubating and spreading disease. Even before sailing, the *Alexander* lost sixteen of her prisoners from infection, and on the voyage faced more troubles than any of the other transports, with more attempts at mutiny by both convicts and seamen than on any of the other ships. But the Sussex three survived the rigours of the journey and can all be traced – though fleetingly – on Australian soil.

First to be tried was Edward Varndell. By the time they sailed he had been in custody for more than three years, having been sentenced at the Sussex Lent Assizes at East Grinstead in March 1784. Court papers describe him as a twenty-five year old labourer from Lewes, charged with stealing two horses valued at £5 each. He was sentenced to hang, but reprieved with a sentence of seven years' transportation. By 1791 he had obviously made good as he was granted thirty acres (12 hectares) of land, a sure sign that he had won his freedom and wanted to stay on to make a new life in Australia. He was one of a new breed of ex-convict yeoman farmers, encouraged to become independent and show, by example, that transportation could reform.

The second Sussex man to be sentenced was Joseph Harbine, a shadowy figure for whom few records seem to exist. He was tried at Horsham in January 1786, but little so far has been traced, no age, occupation, not even the charge. Just a little more is known about him in Australia where he was in trouble again. In 1789 Harbine was accused of making a noise at an improper hour for which he was punished with a hundred lashes. In the next year he received thirty lashes for neglecting his work and going fishing without permission. Unlike Varndell who stayed, Harbine left the colony as soon as his sentence expired, leaving for Canton in 1793.

Three months after Harbine stood trial, James Richards, a twenty-two year old labourer, appeared before the Sussex Lent Assizes at East Grinstead in March 1786. The court calendar gives the charges as breaking and entering the Customs House at Shoreham and stealing fourteen casks of foreign spirits and one cask of foreign gin which had been seized, no doubt from smugglers. At another date he was accused of stealing, 'with force of arms', sixty-one gallons of brandy, two gallons of gin and fifteen wooden casks worth £31 7 shillings and 6 pence (£31.37½p), as well as taking a horse. Condemned to death, he was then reprieved. Transported for seven years, he only served a little less than three as he was reported drowned in Sydney Harbour in 1790.

The drowning incident occurred when Richards was out on a fishing trip with a small party of fellow convicts. As it happened the boat they were in belonged to the chief medical officer of the new colony – he had been chief surgeon on the First Fleet – Surgeon-General John White who, later in life, came to give Sussex its most prestigious link with the First Fleet. For White eventually retired to Sussex.

White's medical command of the voyage as its chief surgeon and doctor was outstanding. His insistence on the highest medical standards and the adequate provision of medical supplies and foodstuffs – supplied in the face of penny-pinching bureaucracy – did much to achieve a comparatively low death rate on the voyage. Forty-eight died on the First Fleet, just over six per cent, whereas on the Second Fleet two years later a quarter of the prisoners perished at sea.

*Final anchorage: the First Fleet and its cargo of convicts sails into Botany Bay, January 1788, by William Bradley*

Mitchell Library, State Library of New South Wales

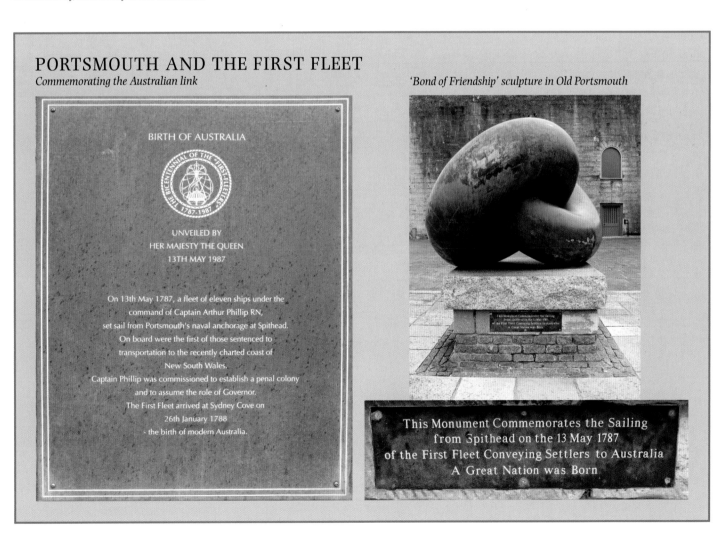

## PORTSMOUTH AND THE FIRST FLEET
*Commemorating the Australian link*

*'Bond of Friendship' sculpture in Old Portsmouth*

BIRTH OF AUSTRALIA

UNVEILED BY
HER MAJESTY THE QUEEN
13TH MAY 1987

On 13th May 1787, a fleet of eleven ships under the
command of Captain Arthur Phillip RN,
set sail from Portsmouth's naval anchorage at Spithead.
On board were the first of those sentenced to
transportation to the recently charted coast of
New South Wales.
Captain Phillip was commissioned to establish a penal colony
and to assume the role of Governor.
The First Fleet arrived at Sydney Cove on
26th January 1788
- the birth of modern Australia.

This Monument Commemorates the Sailing
from Spithead on the 13 May 1787
of the First Fleet Conveying Settlers to Australia
A Great Nation was Born

Even before the fleet sailed White seemed to be performing miracles. Fever struck the *Alexander*. To the complacent there was little that could be done, that it must run its course. To White the common-sense solution was to give the convicts a chance for exercise and fresh air, to give them fresh meat, vegetables and wine. His arguments won the day and even the order that they be totally incarcerated below deck until out of sight of land was relaxed so that each prisoner, under guard, was allowed an hour a day out on deck.

The *Alexander* itself needed scrubbing with creosote (used as a disinfectant and pesticide) and then swabbing with quicklime. White was very much in charge and was able to prevent what would otherwise have been a far worse outbreak of fever. His stringent measures during the voyage and his frequent inspection of the convicts went a long way in controlling scurvy, dysentery and all the other ills and diseases that constantly threatened. Once in the new country he laboured to set up the colony's medical care, including building Australia's first hospital.

Yet White still found time and energy to keep a detailed and perceptive journal that stands as one of the finest records to document the whole venture. There were other diarists who recorded their own stories – about a dozen in all – but White's *Journal of a Voyage to New South Wales*, published in 1790, is amongst the best. The publisher's prospectus gives the clue to its great interest to Europeans curious to see all this new exotica for the first time with its engravings of 'Non-descript Animals, Birds, Serpents, Lizards, curious Cones of Trees ... and other Natural Productions ...'. His interest in the natural sciences and in making contact with the native aboriginal tribesmen make his journal of enormous importance in appreciating Australia at the very beginning of colonisation.

*John White*
*Chief Surgeon to the First Fleet*

But White never fully settled in the new country. After all his good work he still saw the colony as 'a place so forbidding and so hateful as only to merit execration and curses'. He returned home in 1794, never to go back, resuming his naval career as a surgeon, working in Chatham and Sheerness dockyards until taking retirement in 1820. He came down to the Sussex coast where he lived in Brighton, then later in Worthing and was buried in the parish church of St Mary at Broadwater in 1832.

Here he is commemorated by a small diamond-shaped marble tablet set in the floor of the central aisle near the west end of the chancel.

A slightly more informative plaque was fixed to the south-east pillar of the tower in 1984 by the Fellowship of First Fleeters, an Australian-run association of those proudly proving descent from those who sailed with the First Fleet. One of their objectives is to mark the burial places of those who went on the original voyage with similar plaques. John White's at Broadwater was the first to be put up in England – for Sussex just one small and unassuming trace of this great pioneering venture to transport European civilisation half-way across the world.

*Engraving based on a drawing by John White. Many of the First Fleet diarists were keen naturalists and delighted in recording the strange and exotic.*

THE KANGOOROO.

# 13 'The bones that had laughed and had cried': Midhurst Highwaymen

HANGINGS WERE PUBLIC OCCASIONS with their own macabre souvenirs. The gallows spawned their own distinctive street literature, the penny broadsheets, allegedly representing the last words of the condemned before they were launched into eternity.

The broadsheets were called 'Last Dying Speeches' and sold in vast quantities. Almost two-and-a-half million sheets were printed for country-wide sale when husband and wife Maria and Frederick Manning were executed in London in 1849. It was big business. The centre of this grim trade was the Seven Dials area of London, its most noted publicist James Catnach who dominated this sub-world of literary culture with all types of penny and farthing chap books, ballads and broadsheets.

A stock woodcut commonly used for 'Last Dying Speeches'

West Sussex Record Office holds just two specimens of this rare type of street literature.

These 'Last Dying Speeches' usually give a summary of the crime followed by a few appropriate words supposedly uttered by the criminal. Most criminals facing the drop would hardly have had the composure to say much, especially in verse, however dreadful. One of these penny sheets ended:

*Farewell to all – the bell does toll,*

*Have mercy, God, on my sinful soul.*

Hack versifiers found much gainful employment from this type of ghost-writing. One of their fraternity freely admitted that 'I gets a shilling for the verses written by the wretched culprit the night previous to the execution'.

The essential point about these executions was the publicity. 'Sir', said Dr Johnson, 'executions are intended to draw spectators. If they do not draw spectators they don't answer their purpose.'

A good day's hanging had all the trappings of a carnival: special stands were erected to ensure the best view, tele-scopes were on hire, gingerbread, oranges and ginger pop for sale. Otherwise the spectacle was free. They even advertised excursion trains to one public hanging in Liverpool.

When John Lawrence was executed outside Horsham Gaol in 1844 the day was specially chosen, a Saturday when the annual sheep fair was held to attract the maximum gathering. Some three thousand turned up for the morbid proceedings. Costermongers came up from

'Last Dying Speeches' were hawked about the streets by peddlers. Here Thomas Rowlandson celebrates one of the Cries of London in this print of 1799 entitled 'Last dying speech and Confession'. The woman bawls the words so loudly that she must muffle her ears against her own howls and those of the dog.

Brighton with their wares and one beer-shop owner did such a roaring trade that he was heard to say that he wished a man was hanged every day of the week. A hack had been busy on Lawrence's behalf:

*My time is come, my glass is run,*

*I now behold my setting sun.*

The Record Office's 'Last Dying Speech' reproduced here is about the case of two Midhurst highwaymen, Robert and William Drewett – spelt Drewets by the printer – convicted of robbing the postboy carrying the Arundel to London mail at North Heath on 5 December 1798. (North Heath is the open heathland between Easebourne and Henley alongside the A286.) The Drewetts were eventually caught after arousing suspicion when trying to cash one of the stolen items, a bank draft, at the Chichester Bank. Following their trial at East Grinstead Assizes, they were sentenced to be hanged at Horsham on 13 April 1799. The *Sussex Weekly Advertiser* reported the execution and its grisly aftermath:

*Last Saturday the unfortunate brothers, William and Robert Drewett, were executed on Horsham Common, pursuant to their sentence, at our last Assizes, for robbing the Arundel Mail. A report having prevailed that they were to be rescued on their way to the gallows, a strong military guard was placed at the outer gate of the Jail, about seven in the morning, soon after which the malefactors were brought out, and having attended the cart, were escorted by the military to the fatal tree, where Robert appeared much agitated, and said nothing. William conducted himself with a becoming fortitude, and persisting in his innocence, said he hoped the sacrifice that was about to be made of him, would warn Jurors in the future, from convicting innocent men ... after about 40 minutes spent in prayer, they were launched into eternity.*

*William died without a struggle, but the convulsive twitches of Robert, exhibited life for some space of time after he was turned off. Their bodies, after hanging the usual time, were cut down, and ironed, and then conveyed in a cart to North-Heath,*

*Literature of the gallows: a rare specimen of a 'Last Dying Speech' broadsheet (the last figure in the date has been partly obliterated; it should read '1799')*

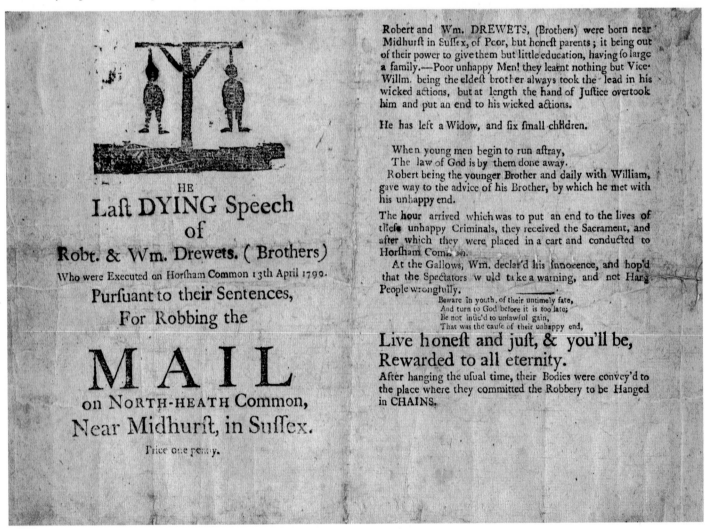

64

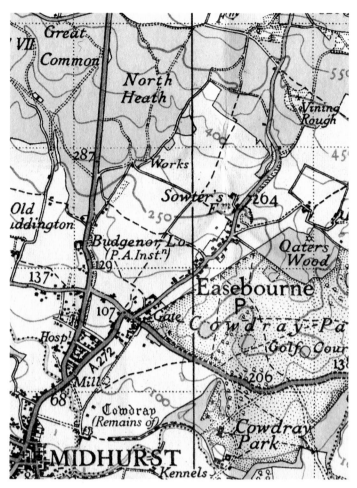

*North Heath, north of Midhurst, the wild and lonely landscape for the Drewett's highway robbery in 1798 and their ignominious end on a roadside gibbet*
Ordnance Survey, one inch to one mile, 1945 (shown enlarged)

*A grisly relic: body irons or 'skeleton dress' for securing a criminal's corpse on a gibbet. Most of the weathered skull survives. These irons held the rotting remains of John Breads, a butcher hung for murder in Rye in 1743. For fifty years his disintegrating skeleton hung by the riverside before it was finally removed. As his bones fell to the ground they were gathered up as a cure for rheumatism.*

Rye Town Hall

*and there hung on a gibbet 32 feet high, amidst at least two thousand spectators, for the accommodation of whom booths were erected as at a horse-race or a cricket-match. The persons employed at the gibbet were such novices at their business, that they were upwards of two hours in getting William, who was first suspended, to his exalted position.*

*In going through Petworth the crowd was so pressing to get a sight of the bodies, that the attendants were obliged to lock them up in a chaise house, whilst they baited their horses.*

Gibbeting, or hanging in chains at the spot where the crime took place, invariably followed execution as a warning to all who passed by. The bodies were often smothered in tar to make them last longer, then encased in made-to-measure body irons, or 'skeleton dress'. Rotting bodies swinging on high were a common sight on hilltops and crossroads in these brutal days. Chains and gibbet – symbols of horror and desolation – add their terrifying imagery to the opening scenes of Dickens' *Great Expectations*.

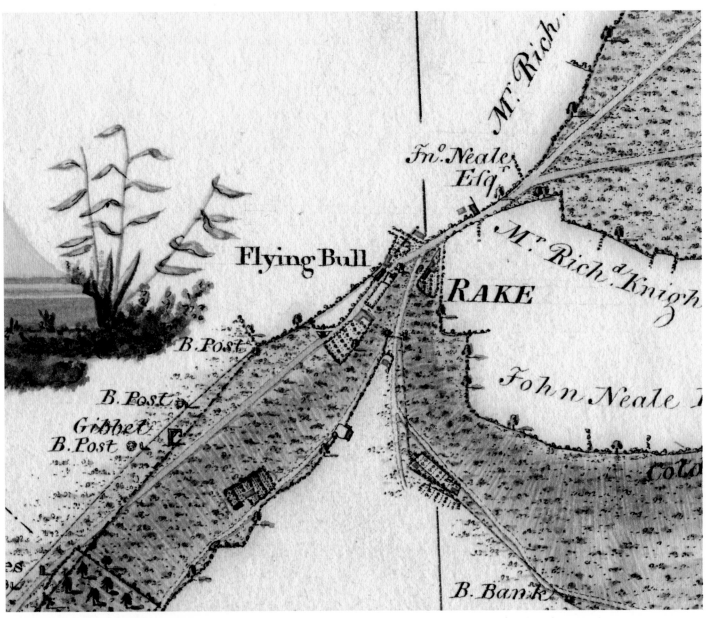

*The gibbet on the London – Portsmouth road near Rake, 1803. (The Sussex-Hampshire boundary is marked by three boundary posts.)*

As for the Drewetts it was later reported that when the bodies had arrived at the gibbet, 'two young women, of genteel appearance, labouring under scrofulous complaints, presented themselves to have their necks stroked with the hand of one of the dead men . . .'. To be touched by the hand of a dead felon was said to be an infallible cure for many other diseases and for barrenness. There was also the lucky hand – cut from a gibbeted corpse, dried and then a wick tied to each finger and the whole dipped in fat. This was 'The Hand of Glory' or 'Dead Man's Candle'. Once the human candles were set alight the new owner of the hand was reputed to possess occult powers.

Gibbeting stories reached the depths of pathos and human tragedy. After a similar case at Shoreham in 1793 a mother's love for her robber son turned into a gruesome

duty. One by one his bones dropped to the ground. At dead of night, in all weathers throughout the seasons, she gradually gathered together his mortal remains. Refused burial in the churchyard at Old Shoreham, she dug them in close to the outside of the wall. This story of love and tragedy is the basis for Tennyson's poem 'Rizpah'. Nightly he tells of how she came to grope for his scattered bones:

> *My baby, the bones that had suck'd me,*
> *The bones that had laughed and had cried...*

It is said that the Drewetts were the last to be gibbeted in Sussex, a practice abolished by law in 1834.

An apparent printing error on the Drewett broadsheet is more than likely a clever typographical device. Can you spot it?

*Making a 'Hand of Glory' from the hand of an executed criminal is explained in this old song taken from Harrison Ainsworth's novel about the highwayman Dick Turpin –* Rookwood *(1834). (The mansion called Rookwood Place is modelled on Cuckfield Place.)*

*'a wick tied to each finger and the whole dipped in fat'*

# The Hand of Glory

*From the cor[p]se that hangs on the roadside tree*
*(A murderer's cor[p]se it needs must be),*
*Sever the right hand carefully:*
*Sever the hand that the deed hath done,*
*Ere the flesh that clings to the bones be gone,*
*In its dry veins must blood be none.*
*Those ghastly fingers white and cold,*
*Within a winding-sheet enfold;*
*Count the mystic count of seven;*
*Name the Governors of Heaven.*
*Then in earthen vessel place them,*
*And with dragon-wort encase them,*
*Bleach them in the noonday sun,*
*Till the marrow melt and run,*
*Till the flesh is pale and wan,*
*As a moon-ensilvered cloud,*
*As an unpolluted shroud.*
*Next within their chill embrace*
*The dead man's Awful Candle place:*
*Of murderer's fat must that candle be*
*(You may scoop it beneath the roadside tree),*
*Of wax, and of Lapland sisame.*
*Its wick must be twisted of hair of the dead,*
*By the crow and her brood on the wild waste shed.*
*Wherever that terrible light shall burn*
*Vainly the sleeper may toss and turn;*
*His leaden lids shall he ne'er unclose*
*So long as that magical taper glows.*
*Life and treasure shall he command*
*Who knoweth the charm of the Glorious Hand!*
*But of black cat's gall let him aye have care,*
*And of screech-owl's venomous blood beware!*

# 14 A Rough Horse: Petworth Prosecuting Society

THIS WANTED NOTICE, issued by the Petworth Prosecuting Society in 1800, advertises two rewards for the arrest of James Page, allegedly a horse thief at Horsham Fair. Considering the horse's condition ('blind of the near Eye ... several Saddle Marks, and Hoofs a little broke'), and at a time when a Sussex farm worker earned an average of nine shillings a week (45p), it might seem surprising that such a substantial reward of fifteen guineas, or £15 and 15 shillings (£15.75), was being offered. This is equivalent to at least £14,000 for someone earning £400 a week today .

Yet was the horse really the temptation? Perhaps Page was after the 'very good Saddle' and all the riding tackle? Maybe it was a bit like stealing an old car just for its good radio and sound system. No local records have been found to indicate that Page was caught, so perhaps the broken down old horse made for a good escape out of the county. And he appears to have got away despite not only the reward but also the very graphic description of what he looked like. The 'dirty round Frock' he was wearing was an everyday working overall. It was like a smock, but without all the elaborate embroidery. On top he wore 'a small Hat slouched', that is, one with a droopy brim just like Paddington Bear.

Whatever the motive, the two-part reward was enormous, but this was typical of the times. Rewards – and punishments – might seem out of all proportion to the value of the property involved. But this would be a judgement from today's standpoint. Then, the value of the goods was not the point. What was at issue was the violation of private property.

This explains why three thieves who, according to Quarter Session records, 'burglariously' entered Jolesfield windmill at West Grinstead to steal a pair of leather shoes worth just one shilling (5p), were

each sentenced to transportation to Australia for seven years in 1801. The lesson to be demonstrated, for the sake of example, was that private property was sacrosanct.

When this incident happened there was no county police force. In most places law and order was in the hands of untrained parish constables, annually appointed, doing duty for a year as their turn came around in each parish. The origin of the local constable can be traced back hundreds of years to medieval roots. What is certain is that

# FIFTEEN GUINEAS
## REWARD.

WHEREAS on the 27th of NOVEMBER laft, JAMES PAGE fraudulently obtained from Mr. HENRY FORD, of *Midhurft*, Suffex, Malfter, at Horfham Fair, a handfome GREY GELDING, about 15 Hands high, 8 or 9 Years old, blind of the near Eye, Tail nicked, Head and Legs newly trimmed, but not the Tail; had feveral Saddle Marks, and Hoofs a little broke;---had on a very good Saddle, the Letter R engraved on the two fore Buttons, an old double Girth, and a double reined Bridle, with double Bits and Curb Chain, all plated.

The faid Mr. HENRY FORD, hereby offers a Reward of TEN GUINEAS, and the *Petworth Profecuting Society* FIVE GUINEAS more, to the Perfon or Perfons who fhall apprehend the faid JAMES PAGE; to be paid on his Conviction.

The faid JAMES PAGE is 5 Feet 7 or 8 Inches high, rather ftoutly made, about 29 or 30 Years old, of rather ruddy Complexion, light ftraight Hair, rather rough Voice, with partly a Weft Country Dialect, Walks upright, and has been a Soldier; had on a dark coloured dirty round Frock, with Silk Handkerchief round his Neck, dark coloured Worfted Stockings, Shoes tied with Leather Thongs, and a fmall Hat flouched. By order of faid *Henry Ford* and the faid Society.

M. J. DAINTREY, *Clerk to the faid Society.*

*Petworth, Suffex,* Dec. 2, 1800.

they operated a system quite inadequate for the needs of late Georgian England. The increasing poverty and crime wave of the late eighteenth and early nineteenth centuries – seen against the threat that what had happened in revolutionary France might well happen here – encouraged mutual self-help amongst property owners. Individuals banded together to form themselves into prosecuting societies. Lack of effective policing so easily leads to forms of self-help vigilantism. The objectives of these societies were to encourage detection, effect arrest and so increase the chances of conviction. Membership was by annual subscription, and with the funds, the societies were able to offer rewards to anyone giving information leading to successful prosecution.

Throughout West Sussex a number of prosecuting societies similar to the one at Petworth were established from the late 1780s. There was the Southwater Prosecuting Club, the Steyning Society for the Protection of Property and Prosecuting Thieves, and the Warnham Society for the Detection and Apprehension of Felons. Some others in the county were at Arundel, Chichester, Cowfold, Henfield, Horsham, Lancing, Lurgashall, Northchapel, Slinfold, West Tarring and Wisborough Green. The areas covered by each varied a great deal. Chichester's extended to the whole of the Rape of Chichester – an area about one-third of West Sussex – Warnham's to just the parish itself. Several societies covered members and their properties to a distance up to ten to fifteen miles away.

With the creation of proper police forces, many of these private societies ceased to be active in their original sense, although many continued as social institutions with an annual dinner. There can't be many that still keep going today. We have one in West Sussex. The Arundel Society for Prosecuting Felons and Thieves meets once a year for dinner at the Norfolk Arms. Conviviality, not prosecution, is now high on the menu. Go for a drink in the Lounge Bar and you'll find an original society poster of 1849 advertising their rewards for each category of crime.

*Perhaps the dubious-sounding horse fraudulently taken at Horsham Fair in 1800 met with a similar fate. In this early 19th-century engraving another rather sad and broken-down old nag has its merits talked-up by the shady looking dealer trying to sell it to the gullible looking fop. The dealer's accomplice smiles with satisfaction at the victim's innocence.*

# 15 Petworth Porkers: Lord Egremont's Piggery

PIGS WERE TREATED DIFFERENTLY at Petworth. In fact they were given model premises, their diets were carefully considered, they were watched and weighed, and even top people taken to see them. These very important pigs lived right next door to his lordship himself.

The date was around 1800, his lordship was the Earl of Egremont, his piggery – next to Petworth House – of pioneering design, one of the earliest-known examples of battery-meat production in the country. As a model piggery it anticipated modern factory-farming by well over a century.

The Petworth piggery could be taken as the Sussex symbol of the Agricultural Revolution – roughly the period 1750 to 1850 – when farming practices underwent massive advances to cope with the rapidly expanding population and the demands of an industrialising nation. Up to then, farming was stuck in the past: seeds sown by hand in almost biblical style; crops grown in open fields by antiquated rotations as they had been since medieval days; animals reared on common and waste land without restraint or control in their feeding and breeding. Methods were old-fashioned and out of date.

The new farming of Georgian England came from a small band of innovative farmers unlocking the secrets of the soil and the early science of stock-breeding. These were the men famous in farming who led the Agricultural Revolution, men such as Jethro Tull of Berkshire with his seed drill, Robert Bakewell of Leicestershire and Thomas Coke of Norfolk with their cattle- and sheep-breeding. The new ideas spread from farms such as theirs, but they spread slowly, Coke said at just one mile each year, such was the conservatism of the farming fraternity in following their old out-dated ways.

One key figure who came down to Sussex many times was Arthur Young, Secretary of the Board of Agriculture – 'the soul and inspiration of the progressive movement' – whose writings did so much to advertise and promote the new improvements taking hold across the country. King George III, known as 'Farmer George', who had his own model farm at Windsor, said: 'Mr Young, I am more obliged to you than to any man in my Dominions'.

Young toured the country extensively in searching out the new farming methods for his official reports to the Board. In Sussex he was in touch with about twenty leading farmers, the most significant being just three of these. In

East Sussex there was John Ellman of Glynde, famous for his South Down sheep, and Lord Sheffield with his model farm at Sheffield Park. In West Sussex, Lord Egremont at Petworth dominated the scene. Their pioneering work, communicated widely to the farming world by the Board of Agriculture, represented the county's major contribution to the country's Agricultural Revolution.

These plans of the Petworth piggery were engraved for a report drawn up for the Board of Agriculture by the Reverend Arthur Young, son of the Board's Secretary, with the title *General View of the Agriculture of the County of Sussex*, published in 1808. It was in such demand that it was reprinted in 1813.

The essence of the piggery's design was that it confined the pigs to a cycle of three distinct stages, following a flow-system that worked from the front to the back of the complex – pigs in at the front, bacon out at the back.

On the front side was a line of open-air sties, each with a feeding trough leading into the 'lodging' area under a roofed cover, presumably for sleeping and for weather protection. After this stage the pigs were eventually transferred to the little window-ventilated compartments known as 'fatting hutches' where they were closely-confined. Once here they weren't let out again; indeed the sign of a good fat pig was that it couldn't walk far anyway. They were finally removed to the rear of the building, the butchery quarters, where they were slaughtered, cut up, boiled and smoked – note the smoking chimney. Out through the back door went pork in all its many cuts: griskins, blades, thighs, spare-ribs, chines, belly-pieces, cheeks and flitches for bacon.

The total layout was all very neatly mechanistic, ensuring efficiency and control, the essential principles behind the factory-farming of a much later age.

Far in advance of its time, the building was revolutionary in its concepts, typical of its enlightened owner, Lord Egremont. What his system replaced was the old free-range method of pig-keeping where they foraged and rooted semi-wild in scenes more reminiscent of medieval times.

What was perhaps surprising was the piggery's location so close to the northern end of Petworth House and right by the side of one of the arboreal walks into the parkland. After all the pigs could have been on Egremont's model

# THE PETWORTH PIGGERY
*one of the earliest known animal batteries in the country*

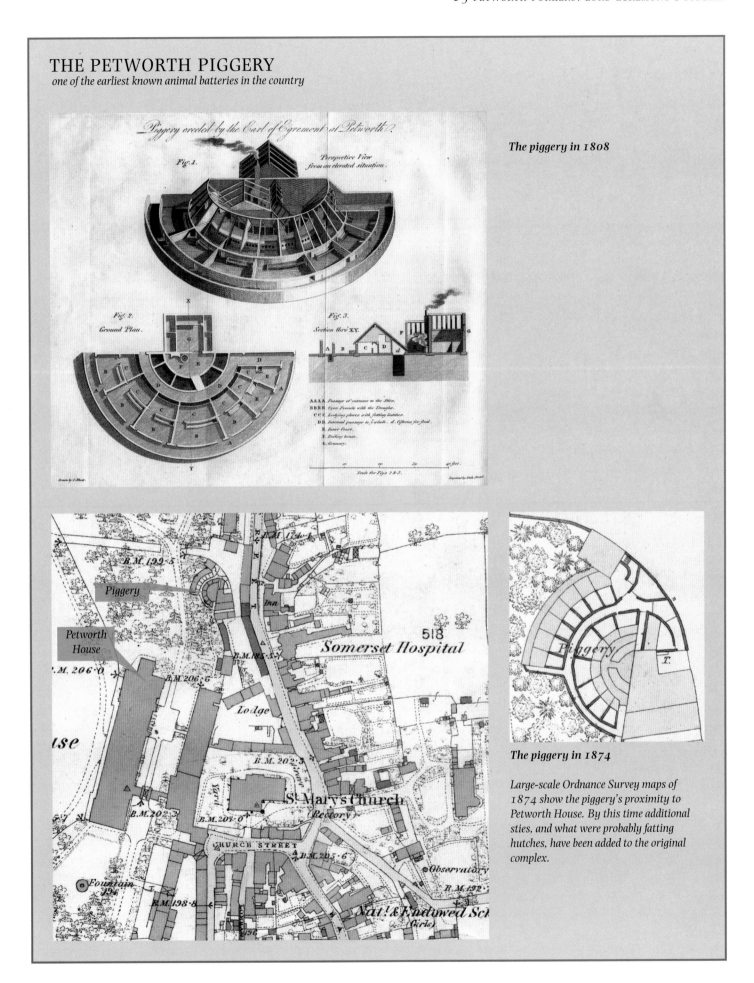

**The piggery in 1808**

**The piggery in 1874**

Large-scale Ordnance Survey maps of 1874 show the piggery's proximity to Petworth House. By this time additional sties, and what were probably fatting hutches, have been added to the original complex.

farm less than three miles away at Stag Park, a much better location for beasts commonly regarded at the time as quite beyond polite society.

Henry Fielding's Parson Trulliber (in his novel *Joseph Andrews* of 1742) was a farmer six-days a week, a parson on Sundays, but lost all his dignity with his pigsty 'but two steps from his Parlour Window'. Some things were just not done, a view that would have been exemplified by John Mills writing in the 1770s who expressed the attitude well: 'Of all the quadrupeds ... the Hog appears to be the foulest, the most brutish ... all its ways are gross, all its inclinations are filthy, and all its sensations concentrate in a furious lust, and so eager a gluttony ...'.

So, like Parson Trulliber, Egremont kept his pigs indecorously near to home, but like him, Egremont would not have bothered about fashionable thinking on the matter. He was his own man. He wanted his pigs close enough for regular visits to keep an eye on how his improvements were going on, close enough to show his new state-of-the-art piggery to his many visitors. The fact that the piggery was eventually demolished sometime between 1875 and 1895 no doubt reflects the swing of opinion against pigs in proximity to fine living. (In banishing the beasts from the edge of his house the then master of Petworth, Lord Leconfield, introduced his own bit of exotica to the estate, a Paxton-style glasshouse for banana production.)

Some of Lord Egremont's pig experiments were outlined in the Sussex report to the Board of Agriculture. In trials to determine the best feed for the most profitable return, he

*This remarkable early 19th-century pig was typical of livestock breeding of the time – bred for size and weight rather than quality of meat. Pigs were fed to immense and ungainly proportions so that their huge mounds of flesh made it difficult to even walk or stand. They frequently suffocated whilst asleep and so to help with their breathing were given wooden pillows to support their snouts.*
Lawes Agricultural Trust, Rothamstead Research

kept some out of doors in the traditional way, free-ranging on grassland in Petworth Park. Others, confined to cages and fed on barley, gave the best profit. In another experiment, seven pigs were fattened on as much barley as they could eat and compared with one fed on a mixture of one part barley to four parts boiled potatoes. The beast was caged 'so as to fit exactly the size of the hog, with small holes at the bottom for the water to drain from him, and a door behind to remove the soil. The cage stood upon four feet, about one foot from the ground, and was made to confine the hog so closely, that he could only stand up to feed, and lie down upon his belly'.

The caged pig, when slaughtered, weighed a stone or more (7 kilograms) than the other seven pigs, a result, concluded the report, 'extremely curious, and deserves to be farther examined in a variety of trials'. These were the sort of results that encouraged and justified the building of the new piggery and its principle of fattening in close confinement.

The champion and advocate of these new pig-rearing methods, the third Earl of Egremont (1751–1837), was a most remarkable man. His title derived from the town of Egremont in Cumberland. With some hundred and ten thousand acres (44,000 hectares), thirty thousand (12,000 hectares) of them here in West Sussex, he was one of the wealthiest landowners in the kingdom. This was a wealth he put to so many good and varied uses, supporting all sorts of new enterprises, such as improving communications through turnpike roads and new waterways, giving Petworth a pumped and piped water-supply, and taking an active interest in not only the arts – and notably by his patronage of Turner – but also in the new sciences and new technologies.

It was in this spirit that he built and equipped a scientific laboratory at Petworth House, buying electrical machinery and some of the latest books on experimental electricity. And in Petworth he set up a medical surgery and dispensary where vaccine supplied by Edward Jenner, the pioneer in vaccination against smallpox, was made available to local people. In these ways Egremont brought cutting-edge science to these rural parts. Through his many and varied interests, Petworth was far from being a rural backwater.

With the same eagerness to embrace new ideas and new thinking, Lord Egremont built his model farm at Stag Park where so many new farming practices were tried and tested: methods of land improvement, crop raising and stock breeding. His orchards, said to produce the best cider in Sussex, produced that deliciously nutty dessert apple that still bears his name, the Egremont Russet.

The *General View of the Agriculture of the County of Sussex* is a lengthy catalogue of Egremont's contribution to farming, with more references to his work than to any

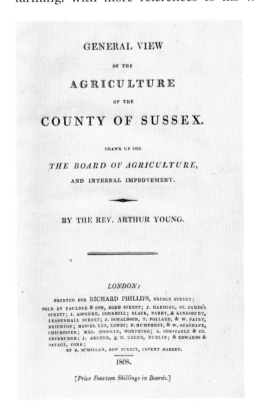

GENERAL VIEW

OF THE

AGRICULTURE

OF THE

COUNTY OF SUSSEX.

DRAWN UP FOR

THE BOARD OF AGRICULTURE,

AND INTERNAL IMPROVEMENT.

BY THE REV. ARTHUR YOUNG.

LONDON:

PRINTED FOR RICHARD PHILLIPS, BRIDGE STREET;
SOLD BY FAULDER & SON, BOND STREET; J. HARDING, ST. JAMES'S
STREET; J. ASPERNE, CORNHILL; BLACK, PARRY, & KINGSBURY,
LEADENHALL STREET; J. DONALDSON, T. POLLARD, & W. PAINE,
BRIGHTON; MESSRS. LEE, LEWES; P. HUMPHREY, & W. SEAGRAVE,
CHICHESTER; MRS. SPOONER, WORTHING; A. CONSTABLE & CO.
EDINBURGH; J. ARCHER, & M. KEENE, DUBLIN; & EDWARDS &
SAVAGE, CORK;
BY R. M'MILLAN, BOW STREET, COVENT GARDEN.

1808.

[Price Fourteen Shillings in Boards.]

*George O'Brien Wyndham, 3rd Earl of Egremont (1751–1837), by Thomas Phillips. Egremont's agricultural improvements included intensive methods of pig breeding.*
National Trust, Petworth House

other Sussex farmer. Its author made the comment that 'all the great improvements in our agriculture have been patronized, propagated, and encouraged by gentlemen of large landed property and scientific exertions. In this class, it is impossible ... not to mention the Earl of Egremont. To do justice to the exertions of this distinguished nobleman, is far above the reach of my humble capacity. Suffice it to say, that his Lordship's estates are conducted upon a great scale, in the highest style of improvement.'

That is why the Petworth piggery was so important, particularly as most stock-breeders at the time neglected the pig in favour of sheep and cattle. That Egremont was in advance of his time in his estimation of the worth of the pig says as much about him as his piggery does for his lead-position in the history of agricultural change in Sussex.

# 16 Smells, Filth and Flies: Chichester's Beast Market

*Beast Market, East Street, Chichester, by Joseph Francis Gilbert – an engraving after the original oil painting, c. 1813*

So IT MUST BE WEDNESDAY. Chichester's beast market was up and running again, clogging the city centre just as it had always been doing for centuries past.

East Street bustles with life: sheep in their pens, sheep being herded, farmers gathering, shoppers shopping, little boys up to no good, the city crier about his business. As to when it was all happening we know it was a Wednesday – market day as today – and we know it was winter, as in the summer months the sheep were moved to the shadier south side of the street; from the shadows it is still morning.

This engraving – the finest nineteenth-century Chichester street scene we have – was based on an oil painting dated about 1813 by Joseph Francis Gilbert (1791–1855). A Royal Academician, he specialised in landscapes, mainly

of Sussex scenery. His father ran a watch and clock-making business in East Street, and he himself was a Chichester drawing master. The painting was so well received that it was turned into a print in 1814, dedicated to the fourth Duke of Richmond. In the nineteenth century these prints were to be seen hanging on the walls of many a farmhouse around Chichester.

Gilbert's view of East Street on market day teems with life. The picture looks west from its junction with North Pallant and St Martin's Lane. Pens of sheep crowd the north side of the street. A few cattle stand loose whilst some sheep are driven away. Two are about to escape down North Pallant. Several farmers mill around chatting. Shepherds in their round frocks (or smocks) keep a keen eye on the sheep.

On the left the city crier rings his handbell announcing the day's news. How important to everyday life he was before the mass consumption of newspapers. One nineteenth-century catch-phrase sums up his position perfectly: 'The common people are to be caught by the ears as one catches a pot by the handle'. With the city gaoler, the crier was responsible for collecting the market dues and fixing up the wooden pens each market day.

The portly gentleman, centre foreground, was apparently a well-known personality, but his name isn't known. Is he about to be taunted or pick-pocketed by the two naughty boys? Reminiscences taken down in the 1870s about the old market talk of 'the terror of the street boys' earlier in the century.

By the St Martin's turn on the right side stands a bow-legged figure probably suffering from rickets, that curse of malnutrition then so common. Brush in hand, he was another well-known character, but in this case we do know his name, Billy Borem, the local chimney sweep.

East Street was a busy commercial centre, lined on both sides with little bow-windowed shops. There were grocers and tea dealers, a confectioner and fishmonger mixed in with fashionable establishments such as hatters, milliners, glove and dress shops. Elegant pedestrians and shoppers stroll along the pavements.

On the right middle distance under the hanging sign is the Swan, one of Chichester's principal coaching inns from where *The Union* coach went to and from Portsmouth every day. Perhaps this is where the Portsmouth butchers, who regularly came to market, regaled themselves. Today the Swan's site is occupied by the NatWest bank.

The street has all the grace and harmony imposed by its Georgian proportions. Houses and shops were either built like this as new, or much older timber-framed structures were cased in brick. East Street around 1813 shows this architectural fashion to perfection.

The Georgian city fathers had also started to modernise by introducing oil-lit street lighting – there are lamps on brackets above the shops – and by building pavements along the main streets. It all looks remarkably civilised. Indeed from Gilbert's picture it all looks remarkably clean and sanitised.

So much so that it doesn't tell the real story. And East Street wasn't the only thoroughfare affected as the market spilled into Little London, East Walls, up St John's Street and into New Town, and spread right up North Street. By the 1860s, to the consternation of the cathedral authorities, it had even strayed into West Street.

*Opposite: another view of the East Street market, photographed from Eastgate Square c.1870, not long before it closed and the new purpose-built cattle market outside the city walls opened in 1871*

The beast market brought smells and its own filth to this entire area. There was no proper drainage down the streets. In this respect Chichester was more a hangover from medieval days, not a city in the progressive nineteenth century.

Carcasses hang in the open-fronted butchers's shop, so close to the live animals in their pens. The problem was that no one then properly understood about infection through the carrying of airborne germs and the danger from flies. One cathedral dignitary, Canon Swainson, complained of

all the problems the market brought to city life in the 1860s. But he saw the market issue as part of a much wider problem. In a stirring pamphlet published in 1866: *A Few Words to those who have the welfare of Chichester at heart*, he pens a grim picture of a city in decay: 'a feeling of discontent is growing over the place: a feeling that there is a screw loose somewhere'. He tried to shame the city out of its lethargy. 'Will the Working Bees of Chichester listen to one of the unhappy?' he asked.

Chichester was in peril through its cavalier attitude to public health. All the water came from wells. For safety it all had to be boiled; there was no adequate drainage to carry away slops and sewage, with cesspools contaminating the

ground and courtyards with floods and trails of indescribable 'mud'. Raw sewage fouled the wells. Thus fever and sickness were rife, cholera and typhus a constant threat. The mind-set was the biggest problem. Improvement would cost money. Indeed one councillor summed up his policy to city electors: 'No Drainage of Town! No Drainage of Pocket!'

One anonymous wag – and it might even have been Swainson himself – took the drainage issue to Shakespearian heights:

*TO DRAIN or not to Drain, that is the question:–*
*Whether 'tis better in this town to suffer*
*The Smells and Odours of the City Cess-pools;*
*Or to take arms against the grim non-drainers,*
*And by opposing end them. To purge, – to drain,*
*No more, And by these drains to say we end*
*The fever and the thousand foul diseases*
*That cess-pools breed. 'Tis a consummation*
*Devoutly to be wish'd. To purge – to drain;*
*To drain! Perchance we shall, ay, there's the rub;*
*For when the City's drained, such good will come,*
*When we have rooted out this present system,*
*Must give us thanks. Health's the reward*
*That crowns the efforts of the Drainage Party.*
*Why should we bear these foul existing cess-pools,*
*The fever's scourge, disparaging statistics,*
*The want of proper drains, the long delay,*
*The ignorance of some folks, the contempt*
*That drained cities, healthier, hold us in,*
*When we ourselves might renovate the City*
*With proper Drainage?*

The market animals added their contribution to the mess by fouling the drainless streets. It was a constant and regular reminder of Chichester's backwardness. Swainson gave his hard-hitting comments on the situation:

*Even to drive into the chief stables in East street from the country, you subject your horses to the danger of being gored by some cattle in their market-day perplexities.... the Chichester shops are inaccessible. Indeed one cannot drive up to the shop doors on the previous afternoon, because of the pens.... And if beast-market-day is a wet day, as it very often is, the next two days are almost as bad.*

*The cattle and sheep and pigs stand in their own filth for so many hours that, when at last they are moved and driven off, they leave their marks behind on the pavement, and there they may be often seen until the Sunday morning; for it is of the essence of our local non-governors neither to clean the pavement themselves, nor to require the householders to do so. Indeed the latter would be unjust. And thus it is a fact that the better-dressed people avoid Chichester, not only on the market-day, but on two or three days after.*

He went on:

> The occupants of these houses . . . are beset with the sheep and pigs and their pens: they can neither give entertainments, nor, with any comfort, accept invitations on the fatal Tuesday. . . . Moreover, the houses are disturbed in the early morn by the arrival of the animals for sale, and by the talk that follows in the streets: invalids cannot live in them: the smell is described at times as suffocating.

Swainson's answer to all these problems was simple:

> If Chichester is to flourish . . . that market must be removed out of the streets. . . . The Market then must go.

Certainly he wasn't the only voice crying in a wilderness of tight-fisted officialdom. The *West Sussex Gazette* reported that even the national papers were aiming 'severe diatribes . . . against . . . the barbarism of the good people of Chichester for allowing a cattle market in the public thoroughfares'. And there was deep anger throughout the city. Eventually a petition pleaded for the removal of the beast market as being 'injurious to the health of the inhabitants'. The city council was goaded into action.

Finally, to great rejoicing, a church service and then a dinner, the new cattle market was opened on Wednesday 10 May 1871, significantly outside the Eastgate city walls in its own purpose-built accommodation. According to the *West Sussex Gazette*'s long and fulsome report the following day, the market was paved and drained with brick gutters. No one had to tread raw sewage any more. And animals were never sold in the Chichester streets again.

This new cattle market continued to sell livestock until 24 October 1990, bringing to an end many centuries of animal trading in the city.

## REMEMBERING THE OLD STREET MARKET

*The market was formerly held in the streets of the city, wooden wattles made into pens were placed from the curb to the middle of the street. In the East Street they reached from the Cross to Little London, on the north side of the street in the winter, on the south side in the summer – all for sheep. Beyond Little London to the Walls, iron posts were let into the pavement and chains ran along, and horses were tethered to them, heads to the pavement – the other side of the street from [the] Police Station to St John's Street had posts and chains along, and small droves of cattle stood there loose.*

*In the North Street the wattles reached from the Cross to the Walls. At the Cross were several pens of calves and after these sheep, till they met the pigs, which extended to and finished at North Gate. In the summer when the extra supply of sheep are sent to market, I have seen pigs on the south side of West Street down as far as the Prebendal School.*

Thomas Gordon Willis (written in the 1920s)

*From East Street the market spilled its stench and filth into North Street, photographed in 1870*

# REGULATIONS

FOR THE

# Conduct of the Watchmen,

APPOINTED BY THE

### Guardians of the Poor of the City of Chichester,

SEPTEMBER 28th, 1821.

## CHIEF WATCHMAN.

THE WATCHMEN are required to be at the Watch-house, at a quarter before Ten o'clock in the evening, at which time the Superintendent or Chief Watchman, shall there call over the names of the persons under his Superintendence. He shall also keep a book, in which, he shall insert the names of any Watchmen absent when the names are called over, and any other neglect of duty on the part of the Watchmen during the night, which book shall be laid before the Court of Guardians on the first Monday in every month, or if necessary, at any intermediate Court. He shall take charge of the Staves, Rattles, and Lanterns, with which the Watchmen are to be provided, and deliver to every man one of each of the above articles every evening at the beginning of the Watch, and receive them back at the time appointed for going off the rounds. The Guardians having resolved that any person dealing in Smuggled Liquors, or keeping a disorderly house, shall be ineligible to hold the situation of chief or subordinate Watchman; any one who shall be found so offending, or engaged in Poaching, or assisting in such practices, shall be dismissed.

Each man to start from the watch-house, and proceed to his respective box so as to cry the hour there, when the Cross Clock strikes Ten; to start from his box again at half-past Ten, and so continue to go every half hour while on the watch, crying the hour at about every 40 yards during his round. Each Watchman shall be required according to the provision of the Act of Parliament, to apprehend *all malefactors, disturbers of the King's Peace, and all suspicious persons, night walkers, and persons misbehaving themselves,* and secure them in the watch-house, to be taken by the Superintendent as soon as conveniently may be, before some Justice of the Peace for the City or County, to be examined and dealt with according to Law.

Every Watchman to continue on his round until Four o'Clock in the morning during the months of May, June, July, and August; until Five o'Clock in the morning during the months of March, April, September, and October, and until Six o'Clock in the morning during the months of November, December, January, and February—to cry the hour as he leaves his box, and proceed to the watch-house to deposit the various articles of equipment furnished at the beginning of the watch.

### No. 1—JOHN GALE,

From a box in the South Street, into Canon Lane, the Close, St. Richard's Lane, to Mr. Garland's, without Southgate, Theatre Lane, South and West Pallant, to his box.

### No. 2—HENRY DAY,

From the East Pallant, George St. Bafflin's Lane, Cross Street, Saint John's Street, East Street to the Cross, down South Street, to the White Horse, and return through East Street and the North Pallant, to his box.

### No. 3—HENRY LEE,

From the corner of St. John's Street, up the Hornet, to Mr. Hayllar's, St. Pancrass, to the Ship and Lighter, East Wall, East Row, up Little London, East Street, to his box.

### No. 4—THOMAS GOBLE,

From St. Martin's Square, to the Corner of St. Martin's Lane East Street, Shamble Alley, Friary Lane, out of North Gate, to Mrs. Philpot's Buildings, up North Street, Guildhall Street, to the Pound, at the East Wall, back to the corner of East Row, and return to his box.

### No. 5—JOHN FARNDELL,

From the Cross down North Street, Council House Lane, and return to North Gate, to Mr. Dendy's Store and back, round the North Wall, West Lane, Crane Street, return up West Lane, West Street, to the corner of Tower St. and back to his box.

### No. 6.—JOHN GARDNER,

From the watch-box West Street, down Tower Street, North Wall, out at West Gate, to the Tan Yard, Orchard Street, and to his box.

### No. 7—EDMUND COLLINS—*Summers Town,*

From a box at the Poor House, High Street, to Mrs. Forbes's, down the lane leading to West Gate, and back to Mr. Wills's Stable, back again to George Street, Cross Street, to his box.

*The routes of the watchmen's rounds – within the walls – can be followed on this 1820 street plan of the city. Most of them also had to patrol beyond the walls, whilst Edmond Collins was confined entirely to Summers Town, a suburb to the north-west of North Gate.*

Plan of the CITY of CHICHESTER, taken in the Year 1820. By Edward Fuller, Surveyor, CHICHESTER.

THE WATCHMEN OF ENGLAND have deep roots in history going back many centuries. Known as 'charlies', their ancient office was swept aside in the nineteenth century by the new police forces, by the 'bobbies' on the beat. The story goes that the charlies were nicknamed after King Charles II who considerably expanded London's force of watchmen in 1663. The bobbies (or 'peelers') on the other hand take their names from Sir Robert Peel who, as Home Secretary, created London's Metropolitan Police Force in 1829.

Chichester's charlies date from comparatively modern times and even then they were only short-lived. Set up in 1821 they were put out of their job by the city's police force, established in 1836. These watchmen were always *night* watchmen, in line with a centuries'-old tradition in law enforcement. Henry III ordered a nightly patrol of the London streets in 1253 because of street crime, or in the words of Elizabethan historian John Stow, the 'enormities in the night'. In the reign of Mary Tudor, bellmen did duty as a night-time force, armed with pike, lantern and bell. In eighteenth-century Nottingham the watchmen took an annual oath to 'well and truly keep this town till to-morrow at the sun-rising'.

That Chichester's band of watchmen fell under the jurisdiction of the local guardians of the poor might seem a little curious. The connection was that the essence of the poor law they administered was all about the control and regulation of paupers. Allow these poor people unfettered freedom and they would menace society as robbers, thieves and disturbers of the peace, threatening both life and property. So the Chichester poor were sent to the workhouse – situated in what had been the former Cawley Almshouses just outside the North Gate – whilst vagabonds and vagrants from outside the city were sent back to where they belonged. The poor law was much more about law and order than social welfare and philanthropy.

This is also why the Chichester guardians were empowered to provide the city

with street lighting – by oil – as much a measure of security as convenience. And so in 1753, by act of parliament, they were given authority not only to establish the poorhouse but also for 'enlightening in the Night-time the Streets, Lanes, Alleys and other public Places'. And hence would follow the guardians' responsibility to appoint watchmen to guard these same city streets during the hours of darkness.

In Chichester seven watchmen were taken on at a weekly wage of fourteen shillings (70p) for the long winter nights, reduced to ten shillings and six pence (52½p) when the days grew longer. There was also a superintendent or chief watchmen who was paid sixteen shillings (80p) a week irrespective of the seasons. Other costs involved the building of the watch-house to serve as a headquarters and as a small overnight lock-up. We don't know where this was positioned. But the notice gives good clues for the approximate sites of the seven watchmen's boxes put up around the city's streets.

Every watchman was given a warm greatcoat, a stave (otherwise called a staff) to act as a truncheon, as well as a rattle and a lantern. They each had to provide their own boots and hats.

*Watchmen armed with staves, rattles and lanterns crawl home after their long night vigil – a lithograph of 1829*

## 'NIGHT IS APPOINTED FOR DARKNESS'

*Soon after gas lighting was seen in Sussex for the first time in a private installation around the grounds of the Royal Pavilion in 1818 – and with the strong likelihood that it would be extended as a public scheme around the neighbouring streets of Brighton (as soon happened in 1824) – these objections were published in the* Sussex Weekly Advertiser *(10 May 1819):*

# THE BAD CONSEQUENCES OF LIGHTING THE STREETS

## ALL LIGHTING OF THE STREETS IS OBJECTIONABLE

**1 FOR THEOLOGICAL REASONS.** Because it seems to be a violation of the order established by Providence. According to this order, night is appointed for darkness, which is interrupted at stated times only, by the light of the moon. We have no right to interfere, to pretend to correct the plan of the universe, and turn night into day.

**2 FOR LEGAL REASONS.** Because the expenses of this illumination must be raised by an indirect tax. Why should you or I pay for a thing which is indifferent to us, or which perhaps even interrupts us in many avocations?

**3 FOR MEDICAL REASONS.** The exhalations proceeding from the oil and gas are injurious to delicate and nervous persons, the ground of many diseases is also laid, by making it more easy and pleasant to loiter in the streets, and this exposure to the night air brings on colds, coughs and consumptions.

**4 FOR PHILOSOPHICAL MORAL REASONS.** The morals of the people are injured by lighting the streets. The artificial light eradicates from the mind that horror of darkness which deters the weak minded from many sins. This light makes the drunkard confident, and induces him to remain at the alehouse till late in the night.

**5 FOR REASONS OF POLICE.** It makes horses shy, and thieves bold.

**6 FOR ECONOMIC REASONS.** Large sums annually go from us for oil or for coals, which is so much taken from our personal wealth.

**7 FOR PATRIOTIC REASONS.** The object of public festivals is to awake and cherish a sentiment of national pride; illuminations are peculiarly adapted to this purpose. But the impression is greatly weakened by nightly quasi-illuminations. Hence we may observe, that the peasant gazes with much more astonishment at the blaze of light than the citizen whose eyes are satiated with it.

## LET US THEN BE CAREFUL TO PRESERVE THE EMPIRE OF DARKNESS

*Gas lamp, Royal Pavilion gardens, dating from the reign of William IV*

When a similar force was set up in Lewes in 1793 – much earlier than in Chichester – they were given a felt hat as well, but again no boots, and the rattles were called ratchets. There they tried to fund just three men by asking for public subscriptions. This failed and so they had to resort to using the rates to pay them seven shillings (35p) each a week. As only two of the three watchmen were to be on duty at any one time there was an opportunity to save money by making them share their greatcoats and hats. Brighton was much more generous to its watchmen, paying them more than double the Lewes rate at fifteen shillings (75p) a week, and giving each man a smart uniform, a cut-away black tailcoat, white trousers and a black top hat, no doubt much more in keeping with Brighton's fashionable image.

In Chichester the cost of the watchmen was paid from a new rate payable by all city property owners – the watch rate – which was set at three pence (just over one new penny) in the pound.

But just how effective were these watchmen in fighting crime? The poster openly advertises information about their timings and precise routes so that everyone knew their movements from hour to hour during the night. Their approach would have been given away by their lanterns as well as by their shouting out the time as they trudged the streets. Someone said they were like clocks walking in the silent darkness. In some places they also cried out the state

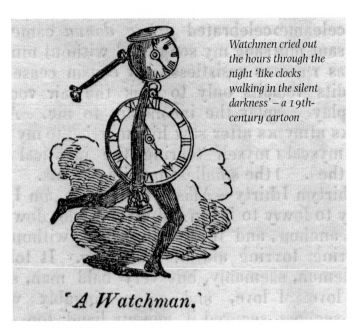

*Watchmen cried out the hours through the night 'like clocks walking in the silent darkness' – a 19th-century cartoon*

'A Watchman.'

of the weather as well. And in Brighton the white-trousered watchmen would have greatly increased their chances of being much more visible on their night-time rounds. There was little room for surprising the nocturnal evil-doer.

One big problem was that so many watchmen were just not up to the job. They were elderly and out of work, the poor law guardians of Chichester always of course having a ready supply of these types. So employing them as watchmen was one way of keeping them from being a burden on the rates, but as a nineteenth-century commentator observed, those they employed 'degenerated' so that 'in later times poor worn-out fellows filled the position of night watchmen'.

*The watchman sleeps! – a popular 19th-century view of the worn-out charlies*

These old men were frequently treated as figures of fun, giving much enjoyment to the high-spirited who tormented them. If they were caught asleep the box might be overturned or the door turned towards the wall. Teasing a charlie was a popular sport, a great wheeze for young bloods after a night out.

Chichester might have been rather late in setting up its force of watchmen compared with other cities and towns throughout the kingdom, but nevertheless was very early in modernising its street lamps.

The first city street lamps were lit by oil, but this was changed over to gas in September 1823. This made Chichester the first place in western Sussex to adopt gas for street lighting, even before the developing seaside resorts of Worthing (1834) and Bognor (1851). In fact the city was one of the first places in the country to be gas-illuminated, and even – just – pre-dating Brighton's public scheme (1824). Ancient Chichester must have seemed a most progressive place.

But no doubt the new hundred and twenty gas lamps around the city were as much a deterrent value as the seven watchmen. For within a month of the new gas lamps being turned on, the guardians reduced their number to just four men, and even then deliberated long and hard about cutting this number down to two.

These watchmen were certainly not greatly valued, and in any case were soon to pass away into the shadows of a vanished Chichester.

# 18 Evils of Tea Drinking: William Cobbett's *Cottage Economy*

HIS ENEMIES CALLED HIM a dangerous radical. To his friends he was a hero, the champion of the poor and oppressed, fighting the money-grubbing corruption of modern society: the loathsome politicians, evil tax gatherers and parasitic stock jobbers bleeding the nation and destroying the values of an older England.

From the troubled nineteenth century he saw the years of his early life in the eighteenth century as arcadian. He denounced the eating up of England by factories and industrial towns – the sprawling towns he called 'wens', spreading their tentacles across the countryside. He attacked the economic system that made paupers of countrymen living amongst fields of plenty. 'I knew that my country presented a scene of wretchedness and disgrace, compared with the scene it had presented at the time that I was born.'

G.K. Chesterton singled him out as 'the noblest example of the noble calling of the agitator'. For his beliefs he was lampooned, attacked – physically at times – bankrupted, even imprisoned.

He called himself Peter Porcupine, bristling with indignation, barbed in defence of his principles. His real name was William Cobbett and he lived between 1763 and 1835, years of such massive change and upheaval that he saw the country going to the dogs. As writer, campaigner – eventually as an MP – he made it his lifetime's mission to work for social justice through a return to another, better, way of life. And in Cobbett's creed it was the countryman's life, close to the land, that was best of all.

Born in Surrey, Cobbett farmed in Hampshire, yet he certainly knew Sussex well. He rode through here on many occasions, vividly recording his travels in the 1820s in *Rural Rides*. Reprinted many times, there is no better way of discovering the countryside he knew so well, sharpened by his constant stream of invective on all he found disagreeable. There was plenty of that. He was never dull. In Brighton he found the town's 'shifty ugly-looking swarm' – he meant the trying-to-get-noticed and trying-to-get-on types, otherwise known as 'expectants'. The Royal Pavilion he called 'the Kremlin', giving instructions on how to make a copy with turnips and garden bulbs on top of a box.

His other book, *Cottage Economy*, was published in 1822. One of the earliest books on self-sufficiency, this is a landmark work of its type, a manual of good housekeeping based on living off the land. Its claim to be a Sussex book is that it was written in a Sussex farmhouse, grounded in a

COTTAGE ECONOMY:

CONTAINING

Information relative to the brewing of BEER, making of BREAD, keeping of COWS, PIGS, BEES, EWES, GOATS, POULTRY and RABBITS, and relative to other matters deemed useful in the conducting of the Affairs of a Labourer's Family; to which are added, Instructions relative to the selecting, the cutting and the bleaching of the Plants of ENGLISH GRASS and GRAIN, for the purpose of making HATS and BONNETS.

BY WILLIAM COBBETT.

A NEW EDITION.

LONDON:
PRINTED FOR THE AUTHOR;
AND
PUBLISHED BY CHARLES CLEMENT, 183, FLEET STREET,

1824.

*Right: 'Peter Porcupine' – the bristling radical, otherwise William Cobbett (1763–1835), possibly by George Cooke*
National Portrait Gallery

*Left: The original classic on self-sufficiency first published in 1822 and still in print*

great deal of information and advice garnered from a Sussex farmer's wife.

From his earliest years around Farnham where he was born, Cobbett's roots went deep into the countryside. From as young as he could recall he laboured in the fields: 'I do not remember the time when I did not earn my living. My first occupation was driving the small birds from the turnip seed, and the rooks from the peas'. This was the practical education he prized so much in later life: 'I am perfectly satisfied that if I had not received such an education ... if I had been brought up a milksop ... I should have been at this day as great a fool, as inefficient a mortal, as any of those frivolous idiots that are turned out from Winchester or Westminster School or from any of those dens of dunces called Colleges and Universities.' This was Cobbett the down-to-earth no-nonsense man.

So when he bought property it was with land to cultivate. A five-hundred-acre (200 hectare) holding at Botley in Hampshire was his first farm, in 1805. Nearly twenty years on, in the rural outskirts of London, he took several acres at Kensington: 'We kept five fine cows. We had a pigeon-house to hold a hundred pair ... Pigs in stye, and a most abundant and fruitful garden.'

As Cobbett said towards the close of his life 'I was born and bred a farmer, or a sort of labourer; and I have never desired to have any rank, station, or name, or calling, more and other than that of a farmer'.

But his interests and skills were far wider than farming. He wrote dozens of books: on English grammar, another on how to spell, on gardening, history, emigration, hints to the poor and on politics. He served in the army – in Canada – ran a bookshop – in Philadelphia – started a daily newspaper, *Porcupine's Gazette*, and his weekly *Political Register*, reporting parliamentary debates. From Cobbett's foundations grew *Hansard*. From his pen gushed a vast output of books, pamphlets and periodicals on all the burning issues of the day. *A Bone to Gnaw for the Democrats*, *A Kick for a Bite* and *Tuppenny Trash* brought an enormous readership.

Cobbett mercilessly exposed corruption and maladministration in high places and the damage done to the country by tinkering with the economy in printing vast sums of paper money – 'rag money' – to replace 'real money' of gold and silver. There were even seven-shilling (35p) notes being pumped out by the banks in Kent. This depreciation, with

A GRAMMAR

OF THE

ENGLISH LANGUAGE,

In a Series of Letters;

INTENDED FOR THE USE OF SCHOOLS AND OF YOUNG PERSONS IN GENERAL, BUT MORE ESPECIALLY FOR THE USE OF SOLDIERS, SAILORS, APPRENTICES, AND PLOUGH-BOYS.

BY

WILLIAM COBBETT.

TO WHICH ARE ADDED

SIX LESSONS, INTENDED TO PREVENT STATESMEN FROM USING FALSE GRAMMAR, AND FROM WRITING IN AN AWKWARD MANNER.

*Cobbett's didactic books gushed from his pen*

ADVICE TO YOUNG MEN,

AND (INCIDENTALLY) TO

YOUNG WOMEN,

IN THE

MIDDLE AND HIGHER RANKS OF LIFE:

IN A SERIES OF LETTERS ADDRESSED TO

A YOUTH, A BACHELOR, A LOVER, A HUSBAND, A FATHER, A CITIZEN, OR A SUBJECT.

BY

WILLIAM COBBETT.

the piling up of the National Debt 'were all the causes of the ruin, the misery, the anguish, the despair' of the times. Their consequences, grinding taxation, poverty and unrest, were all fair game from his fearless pen.

Cobbett was equally scathing about another modern tendency. For now 'Scarcely anyone thought of providing for his own wants out of his own land and out of his own domestic means'. Markets and fairs had kept prices down in the old days, but were now replaced by shops run by 'locusts, called middle-men', the shop-keepers who creamed off all the profits made out of the labouring poor.

The practical alternative was to do-it-yourself: self-sufficiency in the home based on a little plot of land.

Hence his book called *Cottage Economy*.

It was written at Lodge Farm in the parish of Worth where he often stayed with his farming friends. 'Mrs Brazier, the farmer's wife, helped me a great deal; for she, though then nearly eighty years of age, had brought up forty children and grand-children, and had it said of her, that she had done more work herself than any woman in Sussex; and that there was not a working-man or woman in the parish who had not, first or last, either resided or been fed under her roof; and though she could neither write

nor read, understood well the making of bread, the brewing of beer, the keeping of cows, the rearing of pigs, and was able to teach me practically all that I myself did not know touching the subjects upon which I was writing. To her, who is now dead, I thus record my acknowledgements, and I would gladly, if I possessed the means, raise a monument to her memory in the churchyard at Worth.'

According to the Worth parish register, Elizabeth Brazier had died in January 1833, aged eighty-eight, just eleven months before Cobbett wrote these lines.

As she was such a noteworthy figure in Cobbett's life it seemed the right thing to try and find her grave. So we had a family hunt amongst hundreds of graves, some buried in bushes, lichen-covered and eroded, many quite impossible to read. After an hour of searching, Victoria found it by the hedge on the south side of the churchyard. At least we could read this one. Then confusion, for if the parish register is correct – as shown here – the stone-mason cut the wrong date and wrong age – 'February 8th 1832 aged 90 years'. And that the stone-mason, or whoever was responsible, could make mistakes is again suggested by the inscription below that of Elizabeth, to her husband Samuel – for his July date started off as February.

*Map showing Lodge Farm, Worth where* Cottage Economy *was born and where Cobbett stayed with his mentor, Elizabeth Brazier, on his frequent visits to Sussex. From the Worth Tithe Map of 1839-40. Today village and farm, half-a-mile apart, are sundered by the M23.*

*Victoria Leslie discovers the grave of Elizabeth Brazier at Worth. Elizabeth was the fount of much of the self-sufficiency advice in Cobbett's* Cottage Economy.

*Burial entry in Worth parish register for 1833*

Their book, *Cottage Economy* – of Elizabeth Brazier's practices wrapped in Cobbett's writings – advises on brewing beer, making bread, keeping all sorts of animals, even on how to make a simple ice-house for food preservation. Typically Cobbett couldn't resist attacking what he saw as modern fads coming into fashion.

In his section on how to make home-brewed beer, he swipes out at tea drinking:

## EVILS OF TEA DRINKING

THE DRINK which has come to supply the place of beer has, in general, been tea. It is notorious that tea has no useful strength in it; that it contains nothing nutritious; that it, besides being good for nothing, has badness in it, because it is well known to produce want of sleep in many cases, and in all cases, to shake and weaken the nerves. It is, in fact, a weaker kind of laudanum, which enlivens for the moment and deadens afterwards. At any rate it communicates no strength to the body; it does not in any degree assist in affording what labour demands. It is, then, of no use. And now, as to its cost, compared with that of beer. I shall make my comparison applicable to a year, or three hundred and sixty-five days. I shall suppose the tea to be only five shillings the pound, the sugar only sevenpence, the milk only twopence a quart. The prices are at the very lowest. I shall suppose a tea-pot to cost a shilling, six cups and saucers two shillings and sixpence, and six pewter spoons eighteen-pence. How to estimate the firing I hardly know, but certainly there must be in the course of the year two hundred fires made that would not be made, were it not for tea drinking.

Then comes the great article of all, the time employed in this tea-making affair. It is impossible to make a fire, boil water, make the tea, drink it, wash up the things, sweep up the fire-place, and put all to rights again in a less space of time, upon an average, than two hours. However, let us allow one hour; and here we have a woman occupied no less than three hundred and sixty-five hours in the year; or thirty whole days at twelve hours in the day; that is to say, one month out of the twelve in the year, besides the waste of the man's time in hanging about waiting for the tea! Needs there any thing more to make us cease to wonder at seeing labourers' children with dirty linen and holes in the heels of their stockings? Observe, too, that the time thus spent is, one half of it, the best time of the day. It is the top of the morning, which, in every calling of life, contains an hour worth two or three hours of the afternoon. By the time that the clattering tea-tackle is out of the way, the morning is spoiled, its prime is gone, and any work that is to be done afterwards lags heavily along. If the mother has to go out to work, the tea affair must all first be over. She comes into the field, in summer time, when the sun has gone a third part of his course. She has the heat of the day to encounter, instead of having her work done and being ready to return home at an early hour. Yet early she must go too; for there is the fire again to be made, the clattering tea-tackle again to come forward; and even in the longest day she must have candle light, which never ought to be seen in a cottage (except in case of illness) from March to September.

Now, then, let us take the bare cost of the use of tea. I suppose a pound of tea to last twenty days, which is not nearly half an ounce every morning and evening. I allow for each mess half a pint of milk. And I allow three pounds of the red dirty sugar to each pound of tea. The account of expenditure would then stand very high; but to these must be added the amount of the tea-tackle, one set of which will, upon an average, be demolished every year. To these outgoings must be added the cost of beer at the public-house; for some the man will have, after all, and the woman too, unless they be upon the point of actual starvation. Two pots a week is as little as will serve in this way; and here is a dead loss of ninepence a week, seeing that two pots of beer, full as strong, and a great deal better, can be brewed at home for threepence. The account of the year's tea drinking will then stand thus:

|  | £ | s. | d. | £ | p |
|---|---|---|---|---|---|
| 18lb. of tea | 4 | 10 | 0 | 4 | 50 |
| 54lb. of sugar | 1 | 11 | 6 | 1 | 57½ |
| 365 pints of milk | 1 | 10 | 0 | 1 | 50 |
| Tea-tackle | 0 | 5 | 0 |  | 25 |
| 200 fires | 0 | 16 | 8 |  | 83½ |
| 30 days' work | 0 | 15 | 0 |  | 75 |
| Loss by going to public-house | 1 | 19 | 0 | 1 | 95 |
|  | 11 | 7 | 2 | 11 | 36 |

. . . But I look upon the thing in a still more serious light. I view the tea drinking as a destroyer of health, an enfeebler of the frame, an engenderer of effeminacy and laziness, a debaucher of youth and a maker of misery for old age.

# 19 A 'blow on the smeller': A Great Fight near Chichester

*When Sussex – at Crawley Down – was a mecca for bare-knuckle prize-fighting: the Jack Randall-Jack Martin fight in 1819*

*Reader, have you ever seen a fight? If not you have a pleasure to come, at least if it is a fight like that between the Gas-man and Bill Neat. The crowd was very great when we arrived on the spot; open carriages were coming up, with streamers flying and music playing, and the country people were pouring in over hedge and ditch in all directions. . . .*

ESSAYIST WILLIAM HAZLITT gave his classic description of a momentous occasion in the annals of pugilism, setting the scene as thousands flocked to watch Bill Neat hammer Tom Hickman – 'the Gas-man' – into the ground in 1821. The fun and excitement of a carnival, with a bloody contest thrown in for good measure, was just the same sort of scene on the road down towards Birdham, just south of Chichester. There, 'thousands poured into an out-of-the-way Sussex field to watch a scrap of no-mean proportions three years later in 1824.

Modern boxing with padded gloves bears little resemblance to the classic days of prize-fighting in the eighteenth and nineteenth centuries. Then bare-fisted contests could last for more than seventy punishing rounds, rules of fairplay were a mockery, brutal injury, even death, not uncommon. Amazingly many lived to fight another day. As a sport the prize-fight was illegal so that contests had to take place in remote country areas with little advance publicity about the venue.

Sussex has been the setting for many great fights. One of the earliest international matches was fought at Hailsham in October 1805 between the all-England champion, Tom Cribb, and Bill Richmond from Staten Island, New York. And at least a dozen fights were staged at Crawley Down between 1800 and 1823, immortalised in literature by Sir Arthur Conan Doyle's *Rodney Stone* (1896).

By far the most important fight staged in the western

# A GREAT Fight,

Which took place this day between Spring and Langan, for the Championship, & 500l. aside, near Chichester.

Cribb, and Gully, passe[d] thro' Guildford, on Sunday, on their way to Chichester, to be present at the Great Battle Langan on Sunday, passed by Virginia Water, to the place of Action, and Spring on the same day, left Reigate, both men were in excellent condition

THIS morning June the 8th, at an early hour, the road was covered with vehicles of every description, and the numerous barouches and four, were filled with Swells, of the first quality, to witness Spring again exhibit his Pugilistic powers.

The toddlers were scanty indeed But in addition to the great Folks on the road anxious to participate in the sports of the Prize ring, the hero of the Castle, took the shine out them all, the fight was a good turn for this road the lively groupes all in rapid motion, the blunt dropt like waste paper, and no questions asked made all parties pleasant and happy,

The delicate fair ones were seen peeping from behind their window curtains the tradesmen leaving their counters to have a " York " at their doors; the country girls grinning, the Joskins starring, the Old Folks hobbling out astonished the Propriety, people stealing a look, with all their notion of respectability and decorum. Indeed it might be asked how could they help it, who does not love to see a bit of life, if they can't enjoy it. A peep cost nothing, the fun met with on the road, going to a " Mill " Is a prime treat and more good characters are to be witnessed than at a Masquerade, view the Swell handle his ribbands and push his tits along with as much style and ease, as if he wou'd ride with a Ladies neck

*Pitts, Printer, 6 Great st. Andrew street 7 dial*

lace. the bit of blood from his fleetness think ing it no fin to hurl the dirt up in people's eyes such is fancy of going to a mill, till the fancy get on the ground. It was two to one, all round the ring, before the Combatants made their appearance and at One o' Clock. almost at the same time. Spring and Langan threw their hats into the ring attended by their Seconds.

First round, considerable caution was observed on both sides, both of them dodged each other, a little while, made offers to hit and got away Spring endeavoured to plant a blow. but it fell short, from the retreating system adopted by Langan Spring again endeavoured to make a hit which alighted on Langan's right arm. the latter by way of derision patted it and laughed Spring at length went to work, and his execution was so tremendous in a close that the face of Langan was changed, and both went down.

Second round, Langan was very bad, in fact he was unnerved his heart was as good as ever but his energy was reduced, he however got away from a hit, Spring now sent in so tremendous a facer; that it was heard all over the ring. Langan was bleeding at the mouth.

And after fighting 77 rounds, in one hour and 55 minutes, Spring was declared the Victor, Langan quite insensible;

part of the county took place in a field near Chichester between the reigning English champion, Tom Spring, and John Langan, an Irishman, on Tuesday 8 June 1824.

Six months earlier, in January, both men had previously fought for the championship on Worcester Race Course. Spring was declared the victor, but Langan called foul play and a bitter controversy followed. Langan accused the umpire of bias, claiming that the timekeeper was a friend of Spring and that it had been almost impossible to have a fair match as the ring had been broken. They had to fight in the middle of a crowd 'pushing, kicking, and striking with whips and sticks ... whenever Langan attempted to throw Spring, the rascals that were within the ropes gave Langan every obstruction ... Langan's loins and back had the impressions of the toe of a shoe....'

To settle the matter once and for all Spring agreed to a return match. Articles of agreement were drawn up at the famous sporting rendezvous, the Castle Tavern in Holborn, for a fight 'within 100 miles of London'.

The venue was not finally settled until two days before the match, a common practice as these fights were illegal gatherings in the sight of the law. As ever there was much confusion. Warwick Race Course was the first choice, to where thousands of the Fancy – the nickname for the followers of prize-fighting – were headed on the Saturday morning.

Langan, meaning to catch the *Leamington* coach, 'true Paddylike' according to one report, set off from London on the coach to *Lymington* in Hampshire. Put right, with his brains now in the right place, he then eventually made for the Midlands. At the last minute the venue was changed to Chichester and he was hurriedly intercepted, arriving at his headquarters 'suffering from fatigue, want of sleep, and mental agitation', having travelled three hundred miles in just two days in getting down here from London.

The local paper, the *Hampshire Telegraph and Sussex Chronicle*, reported that 'In London, the moment it was generally known that Chichester was the centre of attraction, there was a simultaneous move to secure places in all the coaches travelling that road ... The fares were increased nearly double.... The whole of Monday vehicles of every description were seen on the gentle trot down the Sussex roads. Many ... undertook the journey on foot, and were walking the whole of the night ... Post chaise and carriages and four ... began to pour into the town ... Every inn was crowded to an overflow.'

All Chichester was said to be in commotion, Spring and his followers making their headquarters at the Swan in East Street, with Langan's party at the Dolphin in West Street. 'Buried at one extremity of the county ... this city has for years had a doubtful and amphibious existence. Disregarded by the sailors, laughed at by the mariners, unimproved by Cockney intercourse, its inhabitants have grown sleek and soft-headed in this monotonous existence, and an incident like a fight for the Championship was caught at as likely to raise them to importance, and give one feature to their dull annals ...' reported another source.

To prevent a repetition of the Fancy crowding the fighters as at Worcester, a raised stage above the ground was built. An outer ring of fifty-three farm wagons was then formed, with a temporary building erected as a grandstand. The newspaper says that the organisers actually brought down the grandstand from Epsom Race Course for the purpose. This is shown on the right side of the accompanying print. Race-course grandstands were far smaller than they are today.

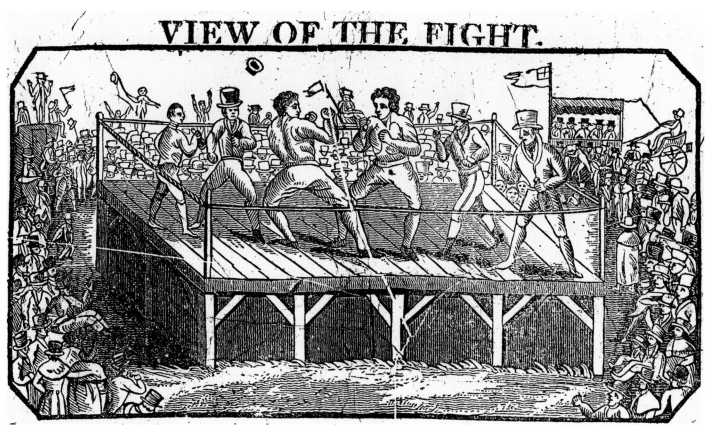

Chichester District Museum

*A souvenir lusterware jug commemorating the great fight*

Chichester District Museum

The match, in which Langan showed that he had 'neither weight, length or science' lasted a gruelling seventy-seven rounds. Rounds were not then fixed by time, but lasted until at least one fighter went down. No magistrates intervened to break up the fight, and Spring, after nearly two hours 'like a Roman hero', was once more declared the winner after what one racy report said was a 'gay blow on Langan's canister'. He had already had a vicious 'blow on the smeller ... on his pudding-bag' and a side-swiping 'left-handed nobber'. Langan was completely insensible. Spring claimed his prize money – a huge fortune of £500.

The Chichester match was a turning point in the history of prize-fighting. Spring retired from the ring and because of the successful prosecution of two prize-fighters in Surrey later in the same year, many supporters withdrew their patronage from the sport. This great Chichester match of 1824 was the end of the golden age of pugilism and one of the last of the great star bouts in England.

Where exactly did the fight take place? One source merely gives the place as 'near Chichester', but another is much more precise. It was 'In Goodwood Park' – but it never took place there. The Duke of Richmond, one of the district's most distinguished men of public affairs, a pillar of law and order, would never have indulged the Fancy in an illegal meet at Goodwood. This was all part of the subterfuge in dodging the magistrates.

The real clue is found in the local newspaper report. It says the spot was in a large ploughed field at 'Birkhambridge' – meaning Birdham Bridge which is where the Chichester – Witterings road (now the A286) crosses the Chichester Canal. More locally this is known as Cutfield Bridge, once a swing bridge across the canal.

Support for the Birdham bridge location comes from an unexpected source: the nineteenth-century Tithe Maps for Apuldram and Birdham. Both parishes held a portion of a large triangular field bounded by the main road, the canal and Wophams Lane. The Apuldram Tithe Map of 1838 shows the field as Spring Field, the undated but contemporary Birdham map as Springs Field. In the late eighteenth century the field was named quite differently.

The changed field name undoubtedly commemorates Tom Spring's famous victory as all-England champion in 1824, a curiously unusual derivation for the name of a farmer's field.

*Location of Spring Field commemorating Tom Spring's victory in 1824*
Ordnance Survey, one inch to one mile, 1945 (shown enlarged)

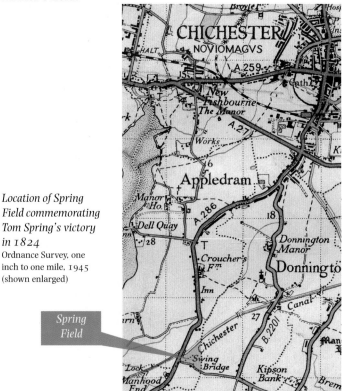

92

# THE
# GREAT FIGHT
## BETWEEN
# SPRING AND LANGAN.
### BY W. MITFORD.

TUNE—The Cuckoo's Nest.

Come all you milling coves, both of high and low degree,
Do'nt grumble at misfortunes, but listen unto me ;
It is of British courage I now intend to sing,
And the hero of my harmony's bold Winter Spring.

Now, the fame of this pugilist had reached the Irish shore,
When Langan prick'd his ears, and says he, I'll travel o'er,
I'll do my best to serve him out, and make old Ireland ring,
And I'll meet this English champion in Winter or Spring.

When he came up to London, he figur'd at the Fives,
He was quiz'd by the swells, as to bottom and to size :
When a match was soon agreed upon, that in a roped ring,
For two hundred gold Sovereigns he should fight Spring.

'Twas on a winter's morning to Worcester they drew,
They both look'd well, and shewing game, like Lions they set too,
When they got from semiquavers into semibraves to sing ;
And the battle terminated with it's Well done Spring.

Now Pat, though defeated, says he, my darling friends,
I'll meet the boy in summer, and I'll make you all amends,
Upon a stage, I'll him engage, not in a roped ring ;
And I'll turn the tune to Langan, boys, instead of Spring.

Oh, your bullying dear Pat, it shall never me confound,
I will meet you on those terms for five hundred pounds,
Within a hundred miles of town, your forces you may bring,
And so table down your blunt, I'm your man says Spring.

On the eight day of June, they to Chichester went down,
Attended by the Fancy both from country and town,
With looks as bold as Hercules they leapt into the ring,
This day must prove the best of us, says Langan to Spring.

For the first seven rounds, oh, they both made gallant play,
But Spring he stopt ; hit right and left, then quickly got away,
When he gave to him a facer, and floor'd him on the ring,
Which made the bets at two to one, with bravo Spring.

Now Langan strove to wrestle and to bring him to the ground,
And he fought, though piping weak, until the 77th round ;
When he coud'nt come up to the scratch, for time had taken wing,
And the laurel still adorns the brow of bold Tom Spring.

(Edgar, Printer.)

*Victory song for Tom Spring*

93

# VERY
# SUPERIOR AND FAST TRAVELLING
## BY SAFETY COACHES,
### TO
# LONDON,

**Shoreham, Brighton, Lewes, Newhaven, Horsebridge, Eastbourne, Battle, Dover, Arundel, Littlehampton, Bognor, Chichester, Emsworth, Havant, and Portsmouth,**

FROM J. SNOW'S SPREAD-EAGLE AND UNIVERSAL COACH OFFICE,

## No. 20, SOUTH STREET, WORTHING.

---

## TO LONDON,

THE SOVEREIGN and ACCOMMODATION, Safety Coaches, every Morning, at NINE o'Clock, to the Spread Eagle, Gracechurch Street, CITY, and Spread Eagle Office, 220, PICCADILLY, corner of the Regent Circus, and next door to Webb's Hotel ; from whence they return every Morning, at a Quarter before NINE.

Route—Through Horsham, Dorking, and Epsom.

Messrs. JOHN SNOW, HOWES, DAWSON, MITCHELL, HOLDEN, and W. CHAPLIN, Proprietors.

N. B. Parcels Booked to all parts of the Kingdom.

## TO BRIGHTON,
### PATENT SAFETY COACHES,

THE MAGNET, every Morning at Half-past NINE o'Clock, and returns from Brighton every Evening at FIVE.

THE ECLIPSE, every Evening at FIVE o'Clock, and returns from Brighton every Morning, at TEN.

The above Coaches go to the Spread Eagle Office, No. 18, Castle Square, Brighton, from whence the WONDER and HERO Coaches leave for HASTINGS every Morning (except Sundays) at NINE o'Clock.

## TO PORTSMOUTH,

THE DEFIANCE, through Arundel, Chichester, and Havant, every day at Half-past TWELVE precisely, and returns from the George Hotel, Portsmouth, every Morning at NINE o'Clock.

Passengers and Parcels Booked for the above Coach at the Norfolk Arms, Arundel, and the Dolphin Hotel, Chichester.

J. SNOW & Co. Proprietors.

---o---

## County Fire and Provident Life Office.

---o---

The London Daily and Weekly Newspapers to be had at the above Office, as stated on the other side.

# 20 Kings of the Road: Worthing Coaching Days

TODAY'S WORTHING TO LONDON express coach is timetabled to cover the off-peak journey in two-and-a-half hours. Back in the 1820s, the date of this coaching poster, the same distance of just on sixty miles took between six and eight hours, an average running speed of anything between seven-and-a-half and ten miles an hour. This is what the poster means by 'fast travelling'. But considering the road conditions then and now – even with today's congestion into London – the slower horse-drawn speed was pretty good for the period.

With galloping horses under the crack of the coachman's whip, the miniature engraving on the poster reinforces the notion of speed. Advertisements like this deliberately emphasised the superiority of the coaches.

... the horses, bursting into a canter at a smart crack of the whip, step along the road as if the load behind them: coach, passengers, cod-fish, oyster barrels, and all: were but a feather at their heels.... Another crack of the whip, and on they speed, at a smart gallop: the horses tossing their heads and rattling the harness, as if in exhilaration at the rapidity of the motion.... the coachman ... cracks the whip again, and on they speed .... The lively notes of the guard's key-bugle vibrate in the clean cold air.... And now the bugle plays a lively air as the coach rattles through the ill-paved streets of a country town ....

Charles Dickens, *The Posthumous Papers of the Pickwick Club* (1837)

There was intense rivalry between coach proprietors who chose forceful, exotic names for each machine. From Worthing, *The Defiance* ran through Arundel and Chichester, there was *The Eclipse* to Brighton, and from there *The Wonder* and *Hero* went on to Hastings. They were meant to sound like kings of the road, and, to remove all doubt, one London-bound coach was even called *The Sovereign*.

Marketing more modern vehicles of the road with personalities suggested by elemental forces or symbols of power – like Ford's *Zephyr*, Sunbeam's *Rapier*, Lamborghini's *Diabolo* – is a deeply-rooted tradition going back to these old coaching days.

Rivalry between coaching establishments was so great that at times road racing seems to have been of more importance than safety. Racing, and not the mere conveying of passengers,

*The Accommodation in 1830 – the Worthing to London 'safety' coach run by Mitchell and Howes: watercolour by C.A. Morris*

*Opposite: Worthing coaching poster, c.1828*

became the real interest of so many high-spirited coach-men. Fatal accidents were all too common.

In 1810 two rivals raced their coaches from Worthing to Brighton. With no regard for the protesting passengers, the two drivers raced neck and neck to the Sussex Pad in Lancing, first one and then the other taking the lead. But at Buckingham Farm, Shoreham, the leading coach took the corner too sharply, overturned, and the driver was thrown off and killed.

Other more cautious and reputable proprietors, fearing for loss of business, had to give emphatic assurances that this type of thing was officially discouraged. A slow Sussex coach, *The Life Preserver*, was even put on the London road to win the support of the old ladies and more timorous travellers.

What slowed Sussex coaches down was the appalling state of the roads. Wheels came off, axles broke and coaches overturned with depressing regularity. One eighteenth-century writer described Sussex as 'extreamly Dirty, insomuch that it is better measured by Days Journies than by Miles. Hence it is that in the Order for regulating the Wages of Stage-Coachmen at such a Price and Distance from London, Sussex was excepted, as deserving better Pay for shorter Way.'

Chalk Pit Lane from East Lavant up to Seven Points by the Trundle gives a good idea of what a main road could have been like. This rutted, uphill climb was part of the main Chichester – London coaching route before the road was turnpiked through West Dean. The sixty-three miles took at least eight hours even under the best weather conditions. The dukes of Richmond, travelling between their houses in Whitehall and Goodwood, had a half-way house at Godalming so they could make the journey more comfortably in two days.

Bad weather could create a nightmare. Rain made the Wealden roads a vast sea of mud, in some places several feet deep where it had been churned up by wheels and the hooves of the struggling horses. A heavy fall of snow could cut off whole districts for days on end. In the annals of stage-coaching the great snowstorm of Christmas 1836 was almost without parallel. So deep was the snow at Worthing that all roads came to a standstill, and although the Worthing-bound coach from London reached the top of Washington Bostal, there it stuck for nearly a whole week.

*Chalk Pit Lane from East Lavant over the Trundle to Singleton was the old Chichester–London coach road before the turnpike opened through West Dean. Poor surfaces and deep ruts were a frequent cause of accidents on many coaching routes.*

This was the famous storm that produced Sussex's only recorded avalanche – at Lewes – commemorated by the Snowdrop inn. The snow not only blocked all road communications but also flattened cottages, killing eight people and injuring many more.

Fast driving, poor roads and bad weather made road travel hazardous. A glance at local newspapers of the time shows that coach accidents were frequent. Bearing in mind the fewer road vehicles on the road, it's quite possible that there was a far greater proportion of accidents then than now. No wonder coaching posters often added the caution that the journey would be completed 'if God permits'.

## BRIGHTON AND CHICHESTER ROYAL MAIL,

### WITH A GUARD,

SETS off from the Blue Coach Office, No. 44, East Street, Brighton, every morning *precisely* at seven o'clock, and arrives at Chichester in five hours; from which place it returns every afternoon at half past one o'clock, and arrives at Brighton at seven in the evening Performed by the public's obedient servants,

KIRBY, Chichester.
CROSWELLER,
ALLEN, and Co. } Brighton.

N. B Will not be accountable for any parcel above the value of five pounds, unless entered as such, and paid for accordingly.

☞ Coaches and Waggons from the above office, every morning and evening to Piccadilly, Cheapside, and Holborn.

---

## WORTHING, BRIGHTON, STEYNING, HENFIELD AND HORSHAM ACCOMMODATION COACHES, TO LONDON.

SET out from the Nelson's Hotel, and Worthing, and the Star and Garter, Brighton, every day, (Sunday excepted,) at Seven o'clock in the morning; arrive at the Swan and Crown Inns, Horsham, at ten o'clock; passes through Warnham, Capel, Dorking, Leatherhead, Ashtead, Epsom and Ewell, and arrives at the White Hart Inn in the Borough; White Bear, Piccadilly; Hope Tavern, Charing Cross; Bell-Savage Inn, Ludgate Hill; George and Gate Inn, Grace Church Street, at five o'clock in the afternoon: returns from the above Inns every day except Sunday, at seven o'clock in the morning, arrives at Horsham at half past one o'clock, and at Worthing and Brighton at seven o'clock in the afternoon.

☞ Calls at the Elephant and Castle, and the Red Lion, Westminster Bridge, going in and coming out of Town.

| | | |
|---|---|---|
| Inside, from Worthing to London | £1 | 0 |
| Outside, Ditto, | 0 | 11 |
| Inside from Steyning, | 0 | 18 |
| Outside, Ditto, | 0 | 10 |
| Inside from Horsham to London | 0 | 12 |
| Outside, Ditto | 0 | 7 |

Intermediate places in proportion.

### Performed by

### JAMES, SOUTH, LOXLEY, & Co.

Places and parcels booked at Stafford's circulating library, Worthing; at Pattenden's Coach Office, Brighton Place; at the Swan and Crown Inns, Horsham; at the White Bear, Piccadilly; Hope Tavern, Charing Cross; Bell-Savage, Ludgate Hill; George and Gate, Grace-Church Street; and at the White Hart Inn, in the Borough.

N. B. No parcels accounted for above Five Pounds value, except entered and paid for accordingly.

☞ Small parcels moderately charged.

---

*Left: coaching times and ticket prices in 1806: Brighton Herald, 25 October 1806*

*Right: carriers' carts, rather than passenger coaches, were the usual means by which bulky parcels and goods were sent by road. From Worthing – as shown by this invoice of 1837 – carriers operated to London and neighbouring Sussex towns. Like the coach services, the principal carriers had offices in South Street.*

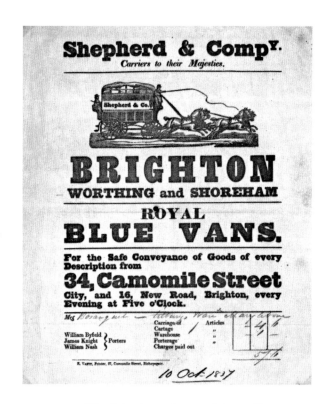

*The Norfolk Arms, Arundel, a stage-stop for coaches between Worthing and Chichester*

For many years Worthing's main coaching offices were centred in South Street, one of the principal being at number 20, run by John Snow, who is advertised on the Worthing poster. It also refers to stage-stops at the Norfolk Arms, Arundel (where the original coach entrance and courtyard still survive) and Chichester. Here the main coaching stop was the Dolphin in West Street, then described as an inn, hotel and coffee house. Its rival, the Anchor, stood next door and the two were only united as one business in 1910. The old entrance to the coach yard has been made into an architectural feature for the bookshop occupying these premises today.

## BATH TO LEWES, THROUGH SALISBURY, SOUTHAMPTON,
### CHICHESTER, ARUNDEL, WORTHING, AND BRIGHTON, WITH BRANCHES TO FROME,
### CHRISTCHURCH, GOSPORT, AND PORTSMOUTH.

| Left column | From Lewes | Route | From Bath | Right column |
|---|---|---|---|---|
| JUNCTION OF THE ROAD to Bishop's Waltham. Before, Bittern Manor House, Mrs. *Hall*; and Bittern Grove, *James Dott*, Esq. | 61½ | Titchfield | 70¾ | COWSFIELD. Melchet Park, *unoccupied*; Broxmore Park, *R. Bristow*, Esq.; Landford House, *unoccupied*; and Landford Lodge, Rev. *G. F. Everett*. |
| | | *To Gosport 7 m.* ☞ | | |
| TITCHFIELD, 1 m. beyond, Blackbrook, *G. Purvis*, Esq. | | *Bath to * GOSPORT 77¾ m.* | | ROMSEY. Emley Park, Sir *Thomas Freeman Heathcote*, Bart.; and Broadlands, Lord Viscount *Palmerston*. |
| FAREHAM, before, Uplands, Admiral *Halkett*; and Roch Court, *W. Thresher*, Esq. | 59¼ | *FAREHAM* | 73 | |
| | | *To Gosport 6 m* ☞ | | JUNCTION OF THE ROAD to Winchester. Shirley House, Lady *Rich*; and 1 m. farther, Freemantle, Sir *George Hewett*, Bart. |
| WIMMERING, 2 m. distant, Southwick Park, *Thos. Thistlethwayte*, Esq. | 56¾ | Porchester | 75½ | |
| | 55¾ | Palsgrave | 76½ | |
| COSHAM, 1 m. distant, Purbrook House, *G. Morant*, Esq. | 54¾ | Wimmering | 77½ | JUNCTION OF THE ROAD to Bishop's Waltham. Chissel House, Lord *Ashtown*; and Merry Oak Farm, Mrs. *George Ede*; Ridgeway Castle, *James Ede*, Esq.; 1 m. farther on the right, Woolston House, ———; and near it, on the Southampton Water, Weston Grove, *Wm. Chamberlayne*, Esq.; near to which are the ruins of Netley Abbey; ½ m. lower down the Southampton Water, Netley Lodge, ———; and 1 m. farther, Sydney Lodge, Sir *Joseph Yorke*. |
| | 54¼ | Cosham | 78 | |
| BEDHAMPTON, before, Belmont Castle. | | ☞ *to Petersfield 13½ m.* | | |
| HAVANT, 1 m. distant, Leigh House, Sir *George Staunton*, Bart. | | *To Portsmouth 4¼ m.* ☞ | | |
| | | *Bath to PORTSMOUTH 82¼ m.* | | |
| EMSWORTH, 2½ m. distant, Woodlands, *C. Short*, Esq. and Stanstead House, Rev. *Lewis Way*. This was formerly the seat of the Earl of Halifax, was bought by the late Richard Barwell, in 1781, for the sum of 102,500*l.* and after his death sold to the present proprietor. It enjoys one of the most delightful situations in the kingdom; the windows commanding a complete view of Portsmouth, the Isle of Wight, and the shipping at Spithead, together with an extensive sea prospect. The principal front of the house, which is of brick, faces the west, and consists of a centre, a quadrangular building, connected with the two wings by a low open colonnade of the Ionic order: in the middle of the building is a balcony, sustained by two stages of Ionic columns, and on the summit is a small observatory, crowned with a cupola. The wings are handsome quadrangular structures, ornamented with a pediment in the middle of each side, and likewise surmounted by light open cupolas. | 50¾ | Bedhampton | 81½ | BURSLEDON BRIDGE. Bursledon Lodge, *Rd. Trench*, Esq.; beyond, Brooklands, *Robert Shedden*, Esq.; and Holly Hill, — *Henning*, Esq. |
| | 50 | *HAVANT* | 82¼ | |
| | | ☞ *to Petersfield 11½ m.* | | TITCHFIELD, before, Abshot, Capt. *Lyon*; West Hill, Lord *H. Paulet*; and St. Margarets, Mrs. *Delmé*. At Titchfield, Hallam House, *J. Anderson*, Esq.; and Crofton House, *T. Naghten*, Esq. |
| | 48 | *Emsworth* | 84¼ | |
| | | ☞ *to Petersfield 12½ m.* | | |
| | 46½ | Nutbourne, *Sussex* | 85¾ | FAREHAM. Cams Hall, *H. P. Delmé*, Esq.; and 2 m. distant, Fleetland House, ———. |
| | 44 | Broadbridge Mill | 88¼ | |
| | 43 | Old Fishbourne | 89¼ | PORCHESTER. Porchester Castle. This is undoubtedly a very ancient fortress, having been possessed successively by the Britons, the Romans, the Saxons, and the Normans. In its present state it is a noble pile, in form quadrangular, and surrounding an area of near five acres: it exhibits specimens of various styles of military architecture, and is in sufficient preservation to be appropriated to the purposes of a military prison, for which use it was rented by government of the proprietors, and during the last war 5000 persons were secured here at one time. |
| | 42 | Fishbourne ⛩ Turnpike | 90¼ | |
| | 41 | *CHICHESTER, Cross* | 91¼ | |
| | | ☞ { *to Midhurst 11¼ m.* / *to Petworth 13¼ m.* | | |
| | | *To Bognor 7½ m.* ☞ | | |
| | | *Bath to * BOGNOR 98¾ m.* | | |
| BROADBRIDGE MILL, 1 m. distant, Oakwood, the beautiful seat of Sir *George Barlow*, Bart.; farther to the left, Ashling House, Mrs. Gen. *Fraser*; at Funtington, Sir *James Duff*; and 2 m. distant, Stoke House, *C. S. Dickens*, Esq. | 39½ | West Hampnet | 92¾ | HAVANT is a neat respectable town, consisting, principally, of two streets crossing each other at right angles. In the centre of the town stands the church, built in the form of a cross, with a tower rising from the intersection. In October 1764, two distinct shocks of an earthquake were felt in this town, which continued from two to three minutes, each accompanied with a tremulous motion, spreading great alarm, but no damage was done. Market on Saturday. |
| | 39 | Maudling | 93¼ | |
| | | ☞ { *to Halnaker 1¾ m.* / *to Petworth 12¼ m.* | | |
| OLD FISHBOURNE, Berkeley Cottage, Hon. Capt. *F. F. Berkeley*. | 36½ | Crocker Hill | 95¾ | |
| | | *Near Ball's Hut,* | | |
| | | ☞ { *to Petworth, by Eartham, 10¾ m.* | | |
| FISHBOURNE TURNPIKE, 1 m. distant, North Lands, Gen. *Crosbie*; and Salt Hill, *Zadick Levin*, Esq.; beyond which is Sennicots, *C. Baker*, Esq.; and Densworth Cottage, Sir — *Brisbane*. | 34¾ | Ball's Hut | 97½ | |
| | | *To Eastergate 1½ m.* } ☞ / *To Bognor 6½ m.* } | | |
| | 33¼ | Avisford Hill | 99 | |
| | | *To Yapton 2 m.* } ☞ / *To Bognor 7½ m.* } | | |
| MAUDLING, 2 m. distant, Goodwood, Duke of *Richmond*; and 1½ m. beyond, at Boxgrove, The Priory, Rev. Archdeacon *Webber*. | 30¼ | *ARUNDEL, Bridge* | 102 | FISHBOURNE. At this place, see Chichester Harbour. |
| | | ☞ { *to Petworth 11½ m.* / *to Pulborough 11¼ m.* | | |
| | | Cross the ⛵ river Arun | | |

*Bath to Lewes through Chichester – Arundel – Worthing – Brighton, giving distances, turnpike gates, river crossings, direction signs and notable sites. From Edward Mogg's* Paterson's Roads *(18th edition, c.1831).*

## BATH TO LEWES, THROUGH SALISBURY, SOUTHAMPTON, CHICHESTER, ARUNDEL, WORTHING, AND BRIGHTON, WITH BRANCHES TO FROME, CHRISTCHURCH, GOSPORT, AND PORTSMOUTH.

CROCKER HILL, beyond, Aldingbourne House, Lady *Henry Howard.*

BALL'S HUT, near, Slinden House, Countess of *Newburgh;* and Eartham, Rt. Hon. *W. Huskisson.*

AVISFORD HILL. Avisford House, Lieut. Gen. Sir *W. Houston.*

ARUNDEL. Arundel Castle, Duke of *Norfolk.* (*See description below.*)

POLING, beyond, Mitchell Grove, *Richard Watt Walker,* Esq.

OFFINGTON HOUSE is the seat of *John Theophilus Daubuz,* Esq.

LANCING, near, at Sompting, *E. Barker,* Esq.; and at Lancing, Lancing House, *J. M. Lloyd,* Esq.

BUCKINGHAM HOUSE is the seat of *Henry Bridger,* Esq.; and beyond Buckingham House, at Portslade, Portslade House, *John Hall,* Esq.

ARUNDEL CASTLE. This was a place of great fame and strength in the earliest periods of English history; it became alternately the property of different individuals, and underwent two sieges during the civil wars of the 17th century, from which period it continued little better than a mass of ruins till the late Duke of Norfolk undertook to restore it to its ancient magnificence. Arundel Castle occupies an elevated situation, and commands a fine view over the sea as far as the Isle of Wight; it is embosomed in a luxuriant grove, and presents a singularly beautiful, imposing, and majestic appearance. The building is in the Gothic style, of free-stone, that was carefully selected so as to assimilate in colour with the remains of the ancient fabric. The internal arrangements and decorations of this superb residence are eminently calculated to exhibit the talent and taste of the late noble proprietor; and among the many specimens of the arts with which it is adorned, are several curious paintings of the Howard family, and a large window of painted glass in the dining-room, executed by Egginton, representing the late Duke and Duchess in the characters of King Solomon and Queen Sheba, at a banquet. Arundel Castle enjoys the peculiar privilege of conferring the dignity of Earl on the possessor, without any patent or creation from the crown, a privilege not enjoyed by any other place in the kingdom.

| From Lewes | | From Bath |
|---|---|---|
| | *¾ m. beyond Arundel, To Little Hampton 3¼ m.* ☞ | |
| | *¼ m. farther,* ☜ *to Storrington 8 m.* | |
| 28¼ | Poling, *Cross Roads* | 104 |
| | *To Poling ¾ m.* ☞ | |
| | ☜ *to Burpham 2½ m.* | |
| | *1¼ m. farther, To Angmering 1 m.* ☞ | |
| 25¾ | Patching Pond | 106½ |
| 22½ | Offington House | 109¾ |
| | *To Tarring 1 m.* ☞ | |
| | ☜ { *to London, thro' Horsham, 53½ m.* | |
| 22 | Division of the Road | 110¼ |
| | *Forward to Lancing, through Sompting, 2¾ m.* | |
| 21½ | *To* Broadwater ☞ | 110¾ |
| 20¼ | * *WORTHING* | 112 |
| 18 | Lower Lancing | 114¼ |
| 17¼ | Upper Lancing | 115 |
| | Cross the river Adur, by Shoreham Bridge. | |
| 15½ | Old Shoreham *T. G.* | 116¾ |
| 15 | Cross Roads | 117¼ |
| | *To New Shoreham ¾ m.* ☞ | |
| | ☜ *to Steyning 4½ m.* | |
| 14½ | Buckingham House | 117¾ |
| | *1 m. farther, To Kingston by Sea ¾ m.* ☞ | |
| 12¼ | The Turning to Portslade | 120 |
| 8¾ | Brighton Old Church | 123½ |
| 8¼ | * *BRIGHTON, The Pavilion* | 124 |
| | * *LEWES, page 31* | 132¼ |

CROCKER HILL, beyond, Westergate Cottage, Rev. *W. Bayton.*

AVISFORD HILL, ½ m. distant, Walberton Place, *R. Prime,* Esq.

PATCHING POND, beyond, Goring Castle, *unoccupied.*

WORTHING. From an obscure village, the town of Worthing has, within the short space of a few years, risen to its present height of popularity and elegance, which deservedly rank it among the most fashionable sea-bathing places; and, to those who prefer retirement, Worthing is considered superior to Brighton, or any of the more numerously frequented watering places on the coast. The facility it affords for bathing, even in the most stormy weather, and the accommodations in general, together with its vicinity to Brighton, give Worthing a just claim to attention; and that it has not escaped public notice, is clearly evinced by its numerous and respectable visitors during the season. It possesses the advantage of a fine firm level sand, which makes bathing here extremely pleasant; and also affords opportunities for the invigorating exercises of riding or walking, thereby enjoying the advantage to be derived from the sea-breezes, rendered temperate at all times by the lofty range of the Sussex Downs, which exclude the chilling blasts from the north and east. Worthing has a convenient daily market, a neat little theatre, and commodious baths.

OLD SHOREHAM. Hoker Lodge, Baron *Hochepied.*

BUCKINGHAM HOUSE, 1 m. beyond, at Southwick, *Wm. Gorringe,* Esq.

BRIGHTON. The Pavilion, a magnificent palace of *His Majesty.*

## BATH TO LYMINGTON, THROUGH SALISBURY.

WHADDON. 2 m. beyond, Brickworth House, *Thomas Bolton,* Esq.

LANDFORD, near, Landford House, *unoccupied.*

BRAMSHAW. Bramshaw House, Col. *Daniel.*

| From Lyming. | *From* | From Bath |
|---|---|---|
| 65½ | * BATH, *Somerset., to* | |
| 23¾ | Whaddon, *Wilts., p. 369* | 41¾ |
| | *2½ m. farther,* ☜ *to Romsey 9¼ m.* | |
| 20½ | Newton | 45 |
| 18 | *To* Landford ☞ | 47½ |

WHADDON, 2 m. beyond, Broxmore Park, *Robert Bristow,* Esq.

NEWTON, 1 m. distant, New House, Mrs. *Eyre.*

BRAMSHAW. Warrens, *George Eyre,* Esq.

From Chichester the single fare to Brighton around 1800 was ten shillings (50p), and in 1806 a one-way ticket between Worthing and London was being advertised at £1 for inside travel and eleven shillings (55p) for an outside seat in all weathers. These were far from cheap fares when seen against the wages of a farm labourer of the time earning on average one shilling and sixpence (7½p) a day. Coach travel was certainly not only for the intrepid but for the better-off.

The great days of stage coaching were between about 1820 and 1840, so this Worthing coaching poster helps capture something of the essence of this golden age.

It was the railways that killed the road coaches. As soon as the new iron roads came to Sussex in the 1840s their days were numbered. Just before the railway line from Shoreham to Worthing was opened in 1845, giving direct rail access to London, via Brighton, the last Worthing to London coach, *The Accommodation*, was taken off the road. In the following year, when the line was extended westwards to Chichester, the cross-country coaches were then finally put out of business. The coaching office at number 20 South Street became a grocer's shop. Coaching from Worthing was over.

In *The Uncommercial Traveller* (1869), Dickens gives a good picture of the commercial decay that fell on a stage-coaching town after 'the ruthless railways had killed and buried it'. The stage-coach inn fell apart. Everywhere 'expressed past coachfulness and present coachlessness'. The harness-makers and corn dealers had shut shop, the coachmaker's workshop was desolate. Symbolically a once-proud post-chaise, less wheels and its axletree, was dumped among a ragged growth of vegetables, patched and mended with old tea-trays, scarlet beans trained up its sides, a knocker put on the passengers' door. It was now a little house. And so had passed a bit of old England.

This is exactly what must have happened in so many Sussex towns and villages, places like Cuckfield and Lindfield, once on main coaching routes to Brighton, their road business now lost to the railroad through Haywards Heath.

There must have been hundreds, possibly thousands, of coaching posters circulating in Sussex during the coaching era. Where are they all now? West Sussex Record Office has just one original local poster, this Worthing example, a type of document classified as ephemera, originally just produced for passing use, like a ticket, a programme, a leaflet. As most get thrown away the few that do survive become extremely scarce. The Record Office is always interested in acquiring local ephemera. Can you help save some history? Even today's rubbish can become tomorrow's treasure.

*The iron road reaches Arundel – competition from the railways killed the coaching industry*

# 21 Blubberhead the Beadle: Troubles in the Workhouse

BLUBBERHEAD THE BEADLE – see overleaf – might have stepped straight from the pages of *Oliver Twist*. Dickens penned his novel in the 1830s to expose the horrors of the new workhouse system revealed through Oliver, the orphaned 'little bag o'bones' versus Bumble the beadle, that arch-symbol of vicious officialdom. 'Bumbledom' is officiousness in the name of the law and its regulations, the jobsworth of the petty tyrant, the law and its compassionless enforcement.

Blubberhead is bumbledom in all its glory, presiding over this little one-act drama of Dickensian proportions.

This grotesque figurehead came to Horsham in the 1830s, at least fictitiously in paper form, as give-away street literature. He was used as propaganda to whip up agitation against the implementation of the new poor law. There were riots in the streets of Horsham and armed troops had to be called in.

So what exactly was going on in Horsham to draw in Blubberhead's interference? The leaflet originated in London where it was printed and published for mass circulation throughout the whole country. What was going on in Horsham was far from unusual. There were troubles everywhere.

The Horsham rioters were protesting about changes to a poor law with roots going back over many centuries.

In medieval times the poor, beggars and vagrants, were seen as a threat to law and order, so much so that legislation was more aimed at social control than philanthropy. In 1388 two principles were enacted that were to live long in the English poor law. The poor were not to move from their home areas without authority and to be categorised into two distinct divisions: those unable to work by reason of bodily or mental incapacity, and those too lazy and indolent to support themselves. The 'can't work' and the 'won't work' were clearly distinguished. The 'won'ts' were either imprisoned or shamed in the stocks. By an act of 1531 all beggars found to be capable of work were 'to be tied to the end of a cart naked and . . . beaten with whips. . .'.

It was from legislation passed between 1598 and 1601, collectively known as the Elizabethan poor law, that a

*The monstrous Blubberhead – 'bumbledom in all its glory'*

mechanism emerged that lasted until the 1830s. This made each parish responsible for its own poor, each empowered to make payments in support of genuine cases of need for the sick and elderly. This was called outdoor relief and was the generous and charitable side of the poor law, in stark contrast to indoor relief for the able-bodied and idle poor who were forced into houses of correction to work at productive labour. These houses of correction eventually became known as workhouses.

All these controls might have been successful in regulating the menace of the poor, but the downside was that each parish had to pay the price by collecting a poor rate from every property owner. This parish tax was the start of rating in this country. Today we now pay for a multitude of services from the rates, but originally they were used just to support the poor.

Throughout the seventeenth and eighteenth centuries a stream of poor laws poured from parliament. Every pauper was to wear a badge of shame, a pauper's badge bearing the letter P. The iniquitous law of settlement rigorously restricted a pauper's movements and their place of residence, sending thousands and thousands of poor men and women on long journeys back to their native parishes on which they were to become a charge. And it was the same for 'lewd women who have bastards' – a potential liability to the parish – and parents abandoning their children so that they fell on the parish rates. They were all to be committed to the magistrates for judgement.

The war with France from 1793 brought in its wake all manner of social troubles, especially in rising prices. Wages didn't keep pace with the day-to-day cost of living. Many labourers applied to their parishes for relief to keep themselves and their families alive. In Berkshire, at Speenhamland next to Newbury, magistrates devised the simple expedient of making up the deficiency in wages from the poor rate, according to a sliding scale based on the price of bread and the number in each family. When they adopted the same system at Midhurst in 1817, they insisted that all paupers in receipt of relief attend Sunday church and that they destroy or get rid of their dogs.

# The English
# POOR LAW BILL
# In Force.

It is all round the country there is a pretty
    piece of work,
All around the country against poor people's
    will;
  If feeble and borne down with grief,
  And you ask the parish for relief,
They will tell you to go home and try to
    learn the poor law bill.

Now if a man has got a wife and several
    children starving,
  If distress should only seize him, and he's
    got no work to do,
  If to the overseers he'll go,
  Borne down with sorrow, grief, and woe,
The answer he will get is now, begone you
    worthless crew.

Spoken.) Now Blubberhead the
beadle fetch in the overseers and
church-wardens 12 bottles of the best
port wine. —Yes sir. —And Blubberhead, is there any vagabonds to
be examined? —Why sir there is a
wonderful lot of people outside, and
I think there all bones sir, for there
is very little flesh on them —Very
well they will all make skeletons then
our workhouse is now completed, so
we will begin our labours, and send
off some of our deserving poor to the
tune of—

    All round the country, &c

Now Blubberhead, open the door
and let in one of the rascals.—Here
he is sir.—Why he has got no body
at all: what is your name old man?
—Bill Fast-a-month.—Well I expect

you will have to fast 3 months; how
old are you? —122 next Friday week
—What do you want — Relief.—
Where's your wife? — Dead sir —
Why dont you die too, you good for
nothing old son of w—u. — Cause
noboddy wont kill me —Blubberhead.—Yes sir.—Get a barrow and
tie this old fellow by the legs to it,
and tell Tom Sweatwell to drive him
to the new workhouse 16 miles off
and tell him to put him in 1247 ward,
and when he comes back, he must
have 6d. for his trouble.
    So its round, &c.

Blubberhead.—Yes, sir.—Let in
another, what are you pray?—Why
I am John Pineaway, who has been
ill 17 long months; my wife is con-
fin'd and I have 8 children starving.—
Well what is that to me? go home &
sell your bed. —I have no bed, sir,
I sleep on straw.—Well I pity you,
when had you any food?—Last Saturday, sir. — Blubberhead. — Yes,
sir. —Get a truck and put this man
and his family into it, and have them
removed to the great house; put
the man into No. 116 cell and the
woman in 394 ward, and send the
children to the barn 12 miles from
there, and give the governor strict
orders not to let them see each other
dead nor alive for 18 months, & that
must be through iron bars 24 yards
distant.    So its all round, &c

Mr. Blubberhead. — Yes your
honour.—Is there any likelihoods of
a riot outside?.. Yes, sir, there is old
Betty Skin-and-bones, and old Peter
Brokenback grumbling... Put them
in the stocks side by side till tomorrow at 11 o'clock, & they shall have 3
months each at the treadmill... Now
let in another, who are you marm?
I am Betsy Bigenough.—So it seems,
have you got the dropsy? —Why,
why, why, why.— Why dont you
speak out?—Sir, I am, I am, I—

What are you?.. I am in the family
way sir .. The devil you are... Yes
I am sir... Arnt you ashamed of
yourself?..No sir... The devil you
arnt... Who is the father?.. Blub-
berhead the beadle sir...Is this true
Blubberhead?..Perhaps so sir.....
Then turn her out, & Blubberhead.
..Yes, sir... What is your pay?—
One pound one a week sir... Well
then you shall have 30s a week now.
..Thankee sir... Let in another...
Yes sir.—Who are you marm?..
Jenny Frolicksome. .. And you appear to be in a frolicksome way.—
Yes sir, I am very queer. .. So it
seems, who is the father?..Blubber-
head the beadle —The devil he is.
Where did he get it?—Beh'nd the
tomb stones in the church-yard sir.
..Kick her out Blubberhead, and in
future your salary shall be two
guineas per week.    So its, &c

Now Blubberhead let in another,
who are you Mrs.?..Why sir, my
name is Mary Never-fret..What do
you want?.. Why sir, my husband
is very ill, and I have nine children
starving..Who sent you here?..
The magistrates sir..Mr. Blubberhead, send all the paupers and wag-
gabones outside to their homes, and
tell them to come to-morrow, and
those that have got no homes can
sleep in Farmer Snufflenose's cart-
house, and take this woman and her
husband and nine children in our
dung-cart to the new workhouse,
put the man in the cellar unde-
ground, put the woman in 367 ward,
and send the children six miles from
there, and let them see each other
once in 2 years, for we must enforce
the regulations of the bill.
    So its all round, &c.
    John Morgan.

Printed by W. Taylor, 14, Waterloo-road,
Sold by Hillatt and Martin, 13, Little
Prescott-street, Minories.

*Rabble-rousing street literature circulating in Horsham in the 1830s*

As an emergency measure this overall approach to the problem certainly had its humanity (perhaps not quite at Midhurst), but as a long-term solution it was a disaster. Knowing that the parish would pay, farmers weren't encouraged to pay a living wage. It destroyed the

*'The Skeleton at the plough'*

independence and self-respect of many wage earners, creating friction between employer and employee. In increasing the poor rates it caused anger and resentment amongst the ratepayers as costs soared. In 1784 poor relief

in England and Wales cost some two million pounds. By 1818 this had quadrupled to eight million.

The nation was scandalised. So much money being spent, yet so much trouble being created. The problem of the poor became the biggest political hot potato of the new century. After endless debate, enquiries and a poor law commission report, the government took drastic action by passing the most draconian reform of the poor law ever seen: the Poor Law Amendment Act of 1834.

Its twin tenets were economy and efficiency. The old parish-based system with all its handouts was condemned as far too soft and far too generous. From now on the new system was to be directed by poor law commissioners in London empowered to control, audit and document every move made by the local guardians of the poor. Local deviance from the new law was not to be tolerated. A vast, centralised bureaucracy emerged, spending money to save money.

Thousands of parishes throughout the land had each been operating their own workhouses. Wasteful duplication, said the political economists bent on reform. And so one by one they were closed down. Many can still be seen today like the old workhouse cottage in Mouse Lane, Steyning. They were small and on a human scale.

# THE OLD-STYLE PRE-1834 PARISH WORKHOUSE
*'small and on a human scale'*

*Steyning Workhouse in Mouse Lane (now a private house)*

*Rustington Workhouse by East Preston church (demolished)*

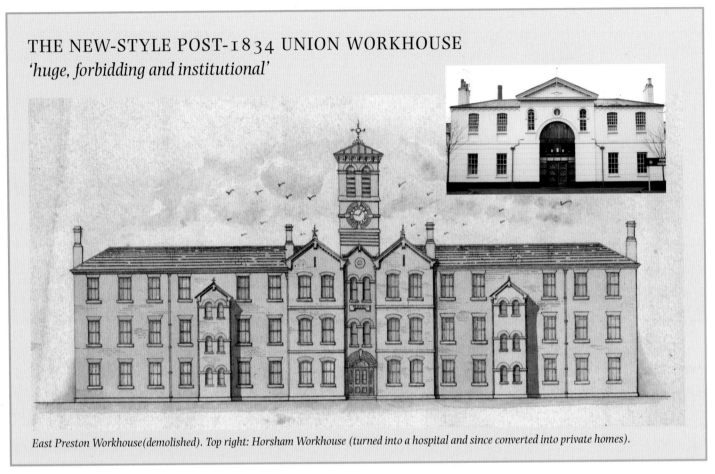

# THE NEW-STYLE POST-1834 UNION WORKHOUSE
*'huge, forbidding and institutional'*

*East Preston Workhouse (demolished). Top right: Horsham Workhouse (turned into a hospital and since converted into private homes).*

By contrast the new ones were just the opposite. Parishes were forced to unite into 'unions' and ordered to build huge union workhouses, generally to serve anything from ten to twenty parishes. No longer could paupers find relief in their local cottage workhouse just up their own familiar village street. Now they were forced into a grim monster, huge, forbidding and institutional, miles away from where they belonged. A journey of ten miles to the local union for a nineteenth-century pauper could be a long way and seem so very far from home.

These daunting-looking workhouses were the first large-scale institutional buildings put up in this country, all part of a new way of thinking with which we are so familiar today: closing down the small and personal and centralising into the big and impersonal whatever the human cost.

Inside each of these new union workhouses the regulations were enforced with the utmost rigour. Husbands were separated from wives, children from their parents.

Food – with plenty of gruel – was deliberately inadequate and work both hard and degrading. The new workhouses were harshly administered and made as unattractive as possible, contrived to discourage paupers from taking up residence. At Cuckfield in 1836, at the height of one of the severest winters in living memory, one hundred and eighteen able-bodied labourers went to the workhouse for relief, hoping for a free handout of food, not incarceration. Offered a stay in the dreaded workhouse as the only option, only six accepted to go inside, one hundred and twelve went away empty-handed. To those operating the system this was the measure of success, economy and efficiency in action.

The new act of 1834 and all its horrors were first widely exposed in *Oliver Twist*, first published in 1837. Dickens tells about the old workhouse system: 'The poor people liked it!' But Oliver faced the new system when 'all poor people should have the alternative . . . of being starved by a gradual process in the house, or by a quick one out of it'.

*'Welcome to the Workhouse . . .'*

As in Oliver's story, everything that happened in Blubberhead's little show caricatures the very essence of the new law as the vagabonds were examined. The fate of John Pineaway typifies the situation: ill for seventeen long months with eight starving children and another on the way. His fate: removal to the new workhouse – 'the great house' sixteen miles away, separation from his wife, the children to be sent 'to the barn 12 miles from there'.

The Blubberhead cases were all shock-horror stories meant to stir up trouble against the new legislation. Wherever there was fear for the future then this sort of propaganda would fall into receptive hands. This was exactly the case in and around Horsham.

There the act authorised the creation of the Horsham Union, made up of Horsham itself, plus Ifield, Itchingfield, Lower Beeding, Nuthurst, Rusper, Shipley, Slinfold, Warnham and West Grinstead, with a new union workhouse to be built along the Crawley road in Horsham. Compared with the little cottage buildings of the old poor law, the new workhouse was overpowering and grim, its front entrance more resembling a Victorian prison, highly appropriate as paupers were treated like criminals. The original building survives, but is now converted into comfortable homes.

In 1835 a Home Office official addressed a large meeting in Horsham Town Hall to explain the benefits of the change. Few were won over and when the poor law guardians met later in the same year a great mob appeared

brandishing bats and clubs, trading insults and hurling stones. The chairman's coach was attacked.

Sixty-six special constables were sworn in and armed troops were drafted in from Brighton. It was an ugly situation.

One grievance was the plight of some orphaned children. Before the new union workhouse could be opened in 1839 it was decided to concentrate all the children from the newly-united parishes into the old Shipley parish workhouse before it was finally closed down. It had a terrible reputation, with a 'Black Hole' – a dark room – for punishment. There were rumours that children sent to Shipley were being spirited away to the factories of the industrial North.

So when a group of orphans was forcibly removed from Warnham to Shipley, the poor law officers were threatened with such violence by the enraged mob that they were forced to fall back and call in the dragoons to drag the children away.

It was a tense situation all around Horsham, just the right place with just the right mood for planting a day in the life of Blubberhead, the infamous beadle.

*'Please, sir, I want some more.' Oliver Twist's plight in the workhouse – 'desperate with hunger, and reckless with misery' – was Charles Dickens' attempt to expose the horrors of the new poor law in the 1830s.*

# 22 'I would not go back to England on no account': Emigration to Canada

THE LANAWAYS' PERSONAL LETTER to their friend William Thorp in Petworth went far beyond their original intention in sending news back home. It got caught up in the publicity drive encouraging emigration to Canada in the 1840s.

Their letter was printed and published as a leaflet by the Petworth Emigration Committee. This was a charitable body responsible for sending nearly two thousand men, women and children to the colony in the 1830s and '40s. The emigrants didn't just come from Petworth, but from all the surrounding parishes and even further afield such as Brighton, Dorking, Wiltshire and the Isle of Wight. In all nearly a hundred parishes were involved in the scheme. The committee's influence and sphere of operations were considerable.

These emigrants were part of a huge mass movement of more than a million settlers escaping the bleak economic conditions of England for new opportunities and challenges in British North America in the first half of the nineteenth century.

Many similar letters were published by the committee, not only as leaflets as in this case, but also as pamphlets and booklets. Others appeared in the local press. In total they form a quite remarkable series of letters from a class of working people who otherwise would have left few traces of their lives behind them.

On the surface they tell us much about pioneer life in Canada: about conditions at home and at work, with great stress on their financial circumstances and a great deal about their hopes and expectations. But between the lines the letters give so many clues about what the emigrants left behind them, the crippling burden of high prices and problems of being out of a job constantly in the background.

The letters are also a fascinating source of information about the trans-Atlantic sea passage that took up to nearly fifty days from Portsmouth to Quebec, and anything up to sixteen days further on to Toronto. Seasickness was a major problem – a surprising number wrote home that bacon had been a good remedy. Many were excitedly distracted at seeing porpoises, whales and distant icebergs 'as big as the whole of the buildings on your farm'.

## Emigration to Canada.

*From James Lanaway, who emigrated with his wife and family from Petworth, Sussex, in the year 1838.*

Woodstock, September 24th. 1840.

I have taken the liberty of writing you these few lines, to let you know that I am in good health at present, hoping this will find you, and all my acquaintances, the same. I have wrote two letters, one to Mrs. Thorp, and another to Mrs. Luff, to both of which I have not received any answer, of which I hope you will not forget to write me an answer to this, and let me know the state of the country, and how are all my old acquaintance, since I left England. I must now tell you, that we are doing well : there is plenty of work in this country, the wages for a labourer is 3s. sterling per day. Provisions are cheap, flour is 10s. per cwt., pork is 3d. per pound, tea is 3s. 6d. per pound. I have also to tell you, that we have five acres of land, and two cows, with a good comfortable house : we have 50 bushels of oats, and a sufficient quantity of potatoes, with other vegetables. I have to mention to you, that vegetables grow here the same as they do in England. I have also to tell you, that the children are all well, Joseph, Rachel, Leah, Sarah, and Lucy we have had in this country. The oldest of the children is often talking about you, Mrs. Hill, Mrs. Baxter, Mrs. Luff, Mrs. Smith, and Mrs. Thorp, and William. We send all of us our love to you all. You will be so good to let me know how James's brothers and sisters ; and James wants to know how is Joseph Richardson, and Mr. Edwards the coachmaker.

This is a good country for a poor man : he can get a good living, if he is industrious. I have also to mention to you, that the winter is a little colder, and the summer is a little warmer than in England. The winter commences in December, and ends in April. We commence making sugar in the month of March, and generally continues for about 5 weeks. I make my own yeast, and bake my own bread. I also make my own soap, which, if I should go back to England, I should be a little more used to, than when I came away. The children never had any sickness since we came to this country. I have also to mention to you, that you will remember us to Mr. and Mrs. King. I have also to mention to you, that all the emigrants that came here two years ago is doing very well. This is a good country, I like it very much, I would not go back to England on no account. I can earn with the needle from 10s. to 15s. per week. I have nothing more particular to mention to you at present, but our blessing to you all, and all enquiring friends.

JAMES and SARAH LANAWAY.

When you write, you will address James Lanaway, Woodstock, Brock District, Upper Canada.

To Mr. WILLIAM THORP, Pound Street, Petworth.

*'That others might follow . . .': Petworth Emigration Committee propaganda*

**The Emigrant's Last Sight of Home** (*1858*) *by Richard Redgrave* (*1804–88*)

*The family are leaving a village near Dorking in Surrey from which area over a hundred and fifty emigrants left for Canada under the Petworth scheme. The father anxiously waves to friends, whilst his family, sad and wistful, wait for the wagon to take them away from home for ever.*
Tate Gallery, London

The Petworth Emigration Committee was financed by the third Earl of Egremont who lived at Petworth House. With some hundred and ten thousand acres (44,000 hectares) – thirty thousand of them (12,000 hectares) in West Sussex – he was one of the wealthiest men in the kingdom. His philanthropy and vision in supporting so many improvements and good causes around his Petworth estate villages and further afield in the county were legendary.

Egremont's general factotum and personal chaplain, and whom he appointed rector of Petworth, was Thomas Sockett, the committee's prime mover. The two of them made a formidable pair. Egremont's money and Sockett's administrative skills guaranteed the success of the emigration scheme. As a model of its type it was famed far beyond Petworth for the quality of its organisation.

Sockett negotiated the charter of the ships, selected those of 'approved character' as emigrants, sorted all the finances

**The Last of England** (*1855*) *by Ford Madox Brown* (*1821–93*)

*The couple's apprehension and sense of loss is heightened by what the artist describes as 'the circle of love' – he holds her gloved hand as she clutches her tiny baby's hand under her cloak. Note the vegetables for the voyage, hanging in the salt spray in the hope of keeping them fresh.*
Birmingham Museums and Art Gallery

# THE LONG VOYAGE TO CANADA

*The British Tar left Portsmouth with its Petworth-sponsored emigrants on 17 April 1834, arriving at Montreal on 5 June after a 50-day voyage. Before its 150 emigrants were allowed to land, the boat had its first contact with Canadian officialdom at the Grosse Island Quarantine Station for medical inspections and fumigation.*

## 4

I immediately formed the people into messes, amounting to twenty in number, and issued the following Regulations:

*Spithead, 17th April, 1834.*

RULES AND REGULATIONS OF J. M. BRYDONE, TO BE OBSERVED BY THE EMIGRANTS ON BOARD THE BRITISH TAR.

1st.—The Bread and Water will be issued daily, between six and seven in the morning.

2nd.—The beef or pork, on Sundays, Mondays, Thursdays, and Saturdays, at ten in the forenoon; and on these days, brandy, or rum and water, at two in the afternoon.

3rd.—The flour, raisins, cheese, and butter, on Mondays, Wednesdays, and Fridays, at ten in the forenoon.

4th.—The tea, or coffee, and sugar, on Saturdays, at four in the afternoon.

5th.—One man to be selected from each mess, to draw the provisions and water. Four of the young men, in daily rotation, to assist the cook in getting up the provisions, coals, and water, fill the water cisterns, and keep the upper deck clean and dry.

6th.—John Gamblin, William Green, and William Martin, to attend the issuing of the provisions and water, in daily rotation, to see that the messes occasion no delay, and that justice is done to all.

7th.—The heads of the messes, in the fore steerage; Perring, Snelling, Voice, and Warren, in the middle steerage; Bassam, Coleman, Ditton, and West, in the after steerage; to see that the berths and deck of the ship be properly cleaned every morning, before *nine*, the deck swept up, after every meal, and the water cistern kept constantly supplied with water, by the young men in rotation; who are also requested to give some assistance to the families, if required by the superintendent to do so.

8th.—John Gamblin, William Green, and William Martin, to visit the berths daily, and when clean, report to the superintendent for his inspection, in the forenoon.

9th.—All the parties before named, to prevent smoking between decks, swearing, or improper conduct of any sort: and all are required to refrain from such acts as may tend to disturb the comfort and harmony of the whole.

10th.—No person to remove, or take a light from the lamps, or move the lamps from their position, unless directed by the superintendent, or master of the ship to do so; and all complaints, or causes of complaint, to be submitted to the superintendent, who will immediately enquire into them, and as far as in his power, cause them to be removed.

### SCALE FOR THE ISSUING OF PROVISIONS.

| | |
|---|---|
| Daily, | Bread, ½ pound; water. ½ gallon. |
| Sunday. | Beef, 1 pound; potatoes, 1¾ pound; rum and water, ½ pint. |
| Monday. | Flour, ½ pound; raisins, ¼ pound; cheese, ½ pound; butter, ¼ pound. |
| Tuesday. | Pork, 1 pound; potatoes, 1¾ pound; brandy and water, ½ pint. |
| Wednesday. | Flour, ½ pound; raisins, ¼ pound; cheese, ½ pound; butter, ¼ pound. |
| Thursday. | Beef, 1 pound; potatoes, 1¾ pound; rum and water, ½ pint. |
| Friday. | Flour, ½ pound; raisins, ¼ pound; cheese, ½ pound; butter, ¼ pound. |
| Saturday. | Pork, 1 pound; potatoes, 1¼ pound; brandy and water, ½ pint. |
| Weekly. | Tea, 2 oz., or coffee, 4 oz.; sugar, 1¼ pound. |

When required, vinegar, mustard, and soap.
Preserved meat, and porter, for the use of the sick.

*Rules and Regulations of J.M Brydone, surgeon-superindendent on board the British Tar. 1834*

---

## THE
# British Tar,
### A 1. coppered and copper fastened,
### 383 TONS registered Burthen,
### is engaged by
### *The Petworth Emigration Committee,*
### to sail from
# Portsmouth,
### FOR
# Montreal, direct,
### On THURSDAY, APRIL 17th.

A few first and second Cabin Berths may be had, by *early* application, and further Particulars known of the PRINTER,

**J. Phillips, Petworth.**

**March 18th. 1834.**

---

April 29th.—A violent gale, the wind blowing very hard from the west, from the attention however, of Captain Crawford to the ship, and still more, from the qualities of the ship herself, we rode safely, and triumphantly, through the storm; and the people suffered but little comparative inconvenience. From this period, the winds continued alternately adverse, and favourable.

Finding that all the people, more especially those affected by sea sickness, were suffering much from thirst and cold, during this tempestuous weather; and that the latter, was increasing as we approached Newfoundland, and knowing, from experience, that the water on board of a ship, is, at no time, a very palatable beverage, I procured some peas from Captain Crawford, and caused to be made for every person a pint of excellent soup, which was so generally liked, that I was induced to continue it, every Tuesday and Saturday, until we reached the river St. Lawrence.

April 30th and May 1st.—A strong gale from the west.

May 4th. (Sunday.)—Whether there be any thing clerical in my manner or appearance, I cannot pretend to say, but certain it is, that this day, Mrs. Ditton's husband came to me, and gravely requested to have the child, born on Monday last, baptized.

May 8th.—At 4 A. M. A most beautiful morning, the wind S. S. W., and the sea as smooth as glass. At noon cold, lat. 43.9; long. 50.27. At 2 P. M. passed within one hundred yards of an ice berg, about 100 yards long, 30 yards broad, and 10 or 12 yards high. At 5 P. M. passed another ice berg, and at 9 P. M. a third.

May 9th.—Obtained soundings on the grand bank of Newfoundland in 50 fathoms. Long. 54.32. Passed three brigs at anchor, fishing.

*From the diary of J.M. Brydone. 1834*

and arranged for the reception and care of the newly arrived – and no doubt nervous – settlers in Canada. He even wrote the sermons to be read on board ship on Sundays. He was tireless in publicising the work and in choosing and organising the printing of the letters to advance the cause.

Egremont paid for chartering the ships and the full-cost of the one-way fare for all emigrants coming from parishes where he owned all the land. (These were Duncton, Egdean, Northchapel, Petworth and Tillington.) Emigrants from parishes where he was only a part-owner received a part-contribution, hopefully with contributions from the other landowners, with the parish authorities making up the rest from the poor rate. In 1832 the adult fare from Petworth to Toronto was set at £10 to cover food, supervision and medical care during the long journey.

Each parish was expected to pay for all the clothing and the basic essentials they were expected to take. This was called 'the outfit' and was to cost £5 for each adult.

*The emigrants' sponsor: the imposing life-like, full-sized sculpture of the third Earl of Egremont (1751–1837) by Edward Baily in St Mary's parish church, Petworth*

Families were recommended to take bedding, pewter plates or wooden trenchers, cutlery, tea-kettles and saucepans and working tools – 'A large tin Can or watering Pot would be useful'. They had to cook for themselves on board ship.

Labourers were advised to take a fur cap, a greatcoat, various 'trowsers', a 'flushing jacket' (a rough and thick woollen cloth), a 'duck frock' (a smock of strong linen or cotton, lighter than canvas), plus two 'Jersey frocks' (possibly close-fitting vests), shirts, stockings, shoes, a Bible and a prayer book. They were told that everything could be bought in Petworth.

The case of Sarah and James Lanaway is slightly different to many others who left for Canada. James had been a groom and night coachman at Petworth House, working for Lord Egremont. His death in November 1837 was felt widely, no more so than in the Lanaway household as Egremont's son and heir immediately decided to cut his expenses, including reducing his staff. James was given three months' notice in the following month. So he wasn't one of the long-term unemployed depending on poor law handouts.

So it was natural that he and his wife Sarah, who worked as a needlewoman, should have turned to the emigration committee for help. They left Petworth in 1838 and landed up at Woodstock, near Toronto, where many previous arrivals from home had clustered. They were the only Petworth people sponsored by the committee in that year as Canada suddenly became unpopular for a while because of civil disorder.

Their letter is typical of so many sent back home. Letter after letter enthusiastically repeats that there is plenty of work – but it's *hard* work – and that the cost of living is so much cheaper than in England. Sarah, who actually wrote the original letter, sums up the situation:

*This is a good country for a poor man: he can get a good living, if he is industrious ... I would not go back to England on no account.*

It has been said that these colonial emigrants – just as with economic migrants and refugees today – were amongst the most vulnerable and helpless people in the world. Only the strong and hardy survived and prospered.

James Lanaway was certainly a survivor, alive and still working in Woodstock in 1871, aged sixty-seven, some thirty-three years after quitting Petworth.

The Lanaways proved that out of the bleak prospects of Petworth and Sussex in the 1830s there could still be a land of hope and promise. In this way they, and millions of others, made their own little contribution to the growth of the British Empire in the nineteenth century.

*'Land ho!' – on board an emigrant ship. When the Petworth emigrants neared the coast of Newfoundland on the* British Tar, *Superintendent Brydone noted that 'The People were rejoiced at the sight of land, but nothing flattered by its snow covered mountains. . . . The people enjoying themselves dancing on deck, to the violin'.*

# 23 Noah's Ark Days: Sundays in Sussex

SHUT UP – LOCKED – CLOSED. That was Sunday, day of prohibition in Victorian England. In protecting this day of worship for the godly, centuries of tradition, acts of parliament and moral censure all conspired to make this day of rest one of unrelieved gloom for those of more earthly persuasions.

The clergy of the Rural Deanery of Horsham added the weight of their opinion to the furious debate that polarised nineteenth-century society. Their message, rigid and inflexible, was firmly grounded in the scriptures: 'Remember the sabbath day, to keep it holy . . . in it thou shalt not do any work'. Exodus chapter 20 gives the commandment, the scriptural precedent for keeping this one day as holy and free from labour. The Horsham clergy's seven resolutions of 1842 pinpoint the troubles facing the early Victorian church in trying to maintain this biblically-ordained sabbath. The troubles were from what they called 'worldly traffic', from shopkeepers, beer shops, carriers and cattle drovers who were all treating this day as if it were any other in the week.

But the ungodly and seekers of freedom sought other ways for their one day released from the shackles of work. 'Thou shalt not . . .' was not part of their agenda. Their trips to pleasureland, their descent into drink, were seen as blasphemies flying in the face of this God-given sabbath. That churchmen felt their special day threatened found expression in the Lord's Day Observance Society, established in 1831. From public platforms and church pulpits it thundered its message: the desecration of Sunday was the devil's route to hell and perdition.

Attempts to control life for religion on one day in seven go back deep into history, to the earliest days of the church. Two thousand years of Christian history are crowded with decrees, ordinances and acts of parliament: through canon law in attempts to ring-fence this holy day for the Lord; through civil law always alive to issues of morality and social stability. Unfettered freedom on this day of no-work was seen as a threat to the very fabric of society. And no more so than in the first half of the nineteenth century under the shadow of riots and insurrection.

Sunday falling apart was all part of this bigger picture. Keeping Sunday special was a major key to the problem. Had not parliament heard damning evidence of the crime and moral degradation sweeping the country because workmen were deprived of the religious benefits of the Lord's Day?

Victorians in search of Sunday observance found a great deal of historical precedent for all their campaigning. Centuries before, the laws were severe. They involved financial penalties and – importantly – they were enforced.

A law passed in 1558 ruled that everyone 'shall diligently and faithfully . . . resort to their parish church or chapel . . . every Sunday . . . upon pain of punishment by the censures of the church, and also upon pain that every person so offending shall forfeit for every such offence twelve pence'. The seventeenth-century statute book was littered with prohibitions: no boots and shoes to be sold on a Sunday (1603); no meetings for sports and pastimes such as bull- and bear-baiting and going to the theatre (1625); no travelling on business with wagons and carts and droving cattle (1627); no tradesman and workman to go about their usual worldly labour (1677).

*Puritan intolerance – burning 'the Boocke of Sportes'. Sunday games and pastimes were banned by Cromwell and the Puritans in the seventeenth century. This engraving shows the ceremonial burning of* The Book of Sports *(1618) that had permitted, 'after the end of Divine Service . . . dancing . . . archery . . . leaping, vaulting, or any such harmless recreation'.*

# OBSERVANCE OF THE LORD'S DAY.

**At a Meeting** of the **Clergy** of the **Rural Deanery** of **Horsham**, held at the **Vicarage**, on Wednesday, 18th May, 1842, under the sanction of the Lord Bishop of the Diocese, and of the Venerable the Archdeacon of Chichester, it came under the consideration of the Clergy assembled whether something could not be done towards ensuring a stricter observance of the Lord's Day in their respective Parishes, and a more general attendance on the ordinances of religion,

It was accordingly resolved,

1.—That, by God's help, *we* will *ourselves* exhibit to our respective flocks a uniform example of sanctifying *His* day by personal and domestic observance of the fourth commandment;

2.—That all Shopkeepers, and Dealers of whatever kind, be recommended strictly to abstain from all worldly traffic on the Lord's day;

3.—That the Gentry, Farmers, and others, from whom the Labouring Classes derive their means of subsistence, be requested to pay their labourers their wages, as far as in them lies, on Friday instead of Saturday night or Sunday morning;

4.—That the Gentry, Farmers, and respectable Householders, be earnestly invited to co-operate with the Churchwardens in preventing or dispersing all idle or noisy persons lounging about the streets and thoroughfares, especially in the approaches to Church, on the Lord's day; and in promoting by their own example, and by the best means their judgement suggests, a regular attendance on the Church Services, and the scriptural observance of the Sunday in their respective Parishes, among those over whom they have authority or influence;

5.—That the Churchwardens be reminded of their duty to visit, more frequently than is commonly done, the Public Houses and Beer Shops in their several Parishes, during the hours of Divine Service; and that the Constables and Headboroughs be called on to pay due attention to such houses at other times of the day; and especially that they be closed in the evening at the time prescribed by the late Act of Parliament;

6.—That the keepers themselves, of such houses, be requested to use their utmost exertions, that no just offence may be taken at their conduct in these respects; assured that the diligent observer of the Lord's day generally thrives in this world; and the neglecter of it, very seldom, throughout the whole of his life; and above all, that "Them that honour God, He will honour;"

7.—That all persons engaged in the public conveyance of Goods, and driving of Cattle, on the Lord's day—as also persons sending off their Waggons and Teams in the evening of that day, be strongly urged to abstain from such sinful conduct; and that they and all our parishioners be affectionately solicited to forbear in future from all unnecessary employment of their horses, needless journeys, and such and every profanation of the day of sacred rest.

## BELOVED BRETHREN,

We, the appointed ministers of Christ to you, commend to your serious attention the above suggestions, hoping they will be received as they are given, in a spirit of kindness. And that God's Holy Spirit may incline and enable you to carry them into effect, to *His* honour, who is the Lord of the Sabbath, and our only Saviour, is the earnest prayer of

Your sincere friends and servants, for Christ's sake.

JOHN FISHER HODGSON, *Vicar of Horsham, Rural Dean.*
EDWARD ELMS, *Rector of Itchingfield.*
GEORGE BLAND, *Rector of Slinfold.*
GEORGE MATTHEWS, *Vicar of Rudgwick.*
JAMES WOOD, *Vicar of Warnham.*

WILLIAM ADAMSON, *Curate of Slinfold.*
HENRY ALLEN, *Chaplain of the Gaol, Horsham.*
ALEXANDER H. BRIDGES, *Minister of St. Mark's, Horsham.*
JARVIS KENRICK, *Curate of Horsham.*

*Horsham Deanery's Seven Sunday Resolutions, 1842*

Seventeenth-century sabbath-breaking was a way of life in country districts like Sussex. Farming had to go on, its seasonal work dictated by weather, not the day of the week. So when the law was rigidly applied, offences multiplied. In the 1620s Robert Hogsflesh of Up Marden was charged with 'turning of pease in his field upon a Sabbath day in harvest'; Thomas Pilfold of Horsham 'for labouring on the Sabbath ... the said Thomas did ted, gather and cocke hay'. John Hargood, farming on Thorney Island, had to watch the tides in his harvesting. He was accused of 'bringing his cart and horses over the water uppon a Sabbath day in the morning, about the begining of harvest ... he being constrayned thereunto by necessity, the tide falling out so that he could not possibly passe over uppon the Saturday by reason of fowle weather'.

As one sympathetic commentator on these Sussex cases has said: 'where those technically guilty are both church-goers and conscientious workers on the land, the offence seems pardonable in every sense except the legal'. But such were the tortuous ways of life enforced by puritanical rigid dogma. These farmers' predicaments give the local worm's eye view of this troublesome period leading to civil war, with law enforcement that in all its perversity shows a world gradually turning upside down.

The extent to which sabbath law went in paralysing everyday life can be illustrated by a few more examples, again of Sussex men charged in the 1620s:

| | |
|---|---|
| Burpham | Robert Wadlington – *for carrying of wood upon the Sabbath* |
| Felpham | Richard Hall – *miller, hath bin twice presented already for grinding on the Sabbath ... nor doth he refrayne* |
| Tortington | Richard Manning – *for driving of beasts and bringing them uppon the Sabbath day from Chichester to Tortington ... being the day before Arundell fayre* |
| Wisborough Green | John Haler – *whoe kepeth an alehouse about a mile from our parryshe church, where many have prophaned the Sabbath day by unlawfull games and drinking* |

In those days there would have been no need for a voluntary society to compel church attendance. The law did the job because the law was enforced. But by the early

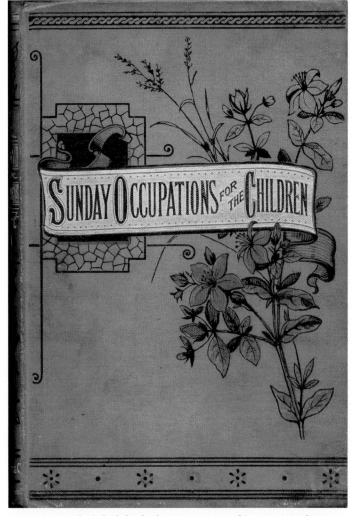

*Mrs H.M. Barclay's little book of c.1892 suggested 'occupations that may be found to promote the pleasure and profit of the little ones. . . . to teach our children to look upon the Sabbath as the happiest day of the week. . . .' The children's lives were far from dull when scripture was taught by Aunt Myra around the family table with drawing, games and stories such as 'The Heavenly Railroad'.*

nineteenth century, enforcement was in the past. The 1558 act for compulsion might still have been on the statute book – it was only repealed in 1846 – but by then it was unenforceable. In three hundred years the world had moved on. Freedoms had loosened up. That's why the Lord's Day Observance Society was founded in 1831 and precisely the reason why the clergy of Horsham Rural Deanery felt it so necessary to try and tighten up in their own parishes.

Significantly their resolutions have no reference to the law, except in number five about public houses and beer

"Sunday Occupations for The Children."

*Everything was bolted and barred that could by possibility furnish relief to an over-worked people ... Nothing to see but streets, streets, streets. Nothing to breathe but streets, streets, streets. Nothing to change the brooding mind, or raise it up. Nothing for the spent toiler to do, but to compare the monotony of his seventh day with the monotony of his six days, think what a weary life he led, and make the best of it. . . . There was the dreary Sunday of his childhood, when he sat with his hands before him, scared out of his senses by a horrible tract which commenced business with the poor child by asking him in its title, why was he going to Perdition? . . .*

*There was the sleepy Sunday of his boyhood, when, like a military deserter, he was marched to chapel by a picquet of teachers three times a day, morally handcuffed to another boy . . . There was a legion of Sundays, all days of unserviceable bitterness and mortification, slowly passing before him. . . .*

Just how far life at home could be affected by Sunday has been well shown by Alison Uttley (1884–1976) – best remembered today for her 'Little Grey Rabbit' books. She recalled her late Victorian life on this very special day, but she didn't complain, she actually enjoyed the differences in the tempo of life, different food, different clothes and different treats, like being allowed to play with her 'religious' toy, her Noah's Ark. The following lines are taken from her autobiographical *Ambush of Young Days*:

*'And of every living thing of all flesh, two of every sort shalt thou bring into the ark . . .'* (Genesis 6:19)

shops, simply because the law had lost its hold on other spheres of life. Powerless, except by moral persuasion, all they could now do was 'recommend' to the shopkeepers, 'request' the gentry, farmers and respectable householders, and 'urge' those engaged in the public conveyance of goods and driving cattle. This was a very far cry from the threats and punishments of the 1620s.

At Warnham the vicar was intent on driving home his parishioners' commitment to these resolutions. He got them to publicly promise their good intentions by signing an undertaking of support. Thus amongst the parish records we have a list of all the local shopkeepers who promised to keep their shops closed for the entire day.

'Closed' was the touchstone for the Victorian Sunday, so well captured by Dickens' description of the gloomy London suffered by Arthur Clennam in *Little Dorrit*:

*There was no knitting or sewing or cleaning. It was wrong to use a pair of scissors, or a needle. The newspaper was hidden out of sight, the work-box was put away, the scissors gleamed as they hung on their hooks, and I looked up at them as if they were enemies. No wood was chopped or hay cut from the stacks. . . .*

*On Saturday nights all toys were tidied away till Monday morning, and I put my dolls in the carved oak box under the pantry bench and said good-bye for a whole day . . . I joined my brother in his special Sunday game. It was Noah's Ark, kept in the Dark Passage all the week, and brought out only on Sundays. . . . We only played Bible games with these animals. . . .*

Interestingly another writer, reminiscing about her childhood in Edwardian Sussex, at Fernhurst, called her own precious ark her 'Sunday toy'. Such Noah's Ark days, when people even spoke in hushed tones with 'Sunday voices', could be baffling beyond belief to so many young children caught up in all the restrictions. Taken by her aunts to the priory church at Easebourne in the 1890s, one little girl found it 'only tolerable by the weaving of fantasies in all I saw. The organ pipes were prison bars, behind which naughty choirboys were held. Then fairies and imps leapt about on the astonishing hats of those days. . . . I do not know how we were expected to spend the long hours of the day, but how I did spend them was to draw and paint. Then

## CHAPTER IX.

### ANIMALS.

I WISH we might have my Noah's Ark this Sunday," said little Bertram.

"Oh, Aunt Myra, let us have it, and find all the animals mentioned in the Bible!" exclaimed Amy.

"Then I can set up the animals as you find them," said Bertram, putting his ark down on the table before him.

"A dove," said Evelyn; "one went out of the ark."

"A dove was one of the birds offered in sacrifice," said Arthur.

"The Holy Spirit came down in the form of a dove," said Amy.

"Let us take the animals, to-day, and the birds next Sunday," said Nelly, "I think that would be a better kind of order. I choose a very small one— the ant; one of the four things Solomon says are exceeding wise."

*From* Sunday Occupations for the Children

indeed I was free. Hundreds of fairylike creatures filled every corner of the sheets of paper. . . .'

So fantasy became at least an escape from childhood monotony and boredom from a Sunday world so tight and unyielding, light years away from the bustling commerce of our own times. The loosening of the Sunday trading and licensing laws has all but obliterated the old-style day, but the Lord's Day Observance Society still keeps up its work, the churches battle on with their mission. Today we each take our choice, a far cry from the punitive days when a Burpham workman could be fined for being caught carrying a load of wood all those years ago in the seventeenth century.

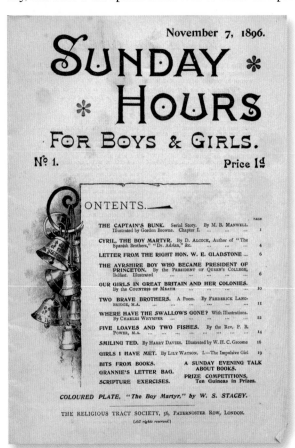

24 Pages, in Cover. Price One Penny every Week. And in Monthly Parts, Sixpence.

PUBLISHED EVERY SATURDAY. SUNDAY HOURS FOR BOYS AND GIRLS.

"SUNDAY HOURS" will aim at being *the Best Pennyworth* of Sunday reading for Boys and Girls.

# 24 A Penny a Week: Victorian Schools

BEFORE THE GOVERNMENT BEGAN controlling education in the late nineteenth century, the provision of schools was entirely dependent on voluntary effort. Private individuals and the church were crucial in this work.

One of the most momentous advances in this voluntary field was the foundation of the National Society for Promoting the Education of the Poor in the Principles of the Established Church in 1811. By 1870 they assisted nearly nine thousand voluntary schools throughout the country.

It was to the National Society that the new school at Compton was officially affiliated in 1848. Here, in what was then a remote downland village, several prominent land-owners got together to raise funds for a school for 'the lower orders', led by a retired naval man, Admiral Sir Phipps Hornby. He donated a plot of land from his local estate for the school close to Compton church. It was also to serve the neighbouring parish of Up Marden.

As lord of the manor, described in *Kelly's Directory* as 'chief owner of the soil', Hornby owned the big house in the area, Lordington. When he retired from the Admiralty he came to live in his other property, Little Green, now turned into a special school. In these days it was local men of substance like this that played such a vital role in providing for the poor.

Hornby, incidentally, had seen distinguished service around the world, and in his younger days had served under Captain Bligh of *Bounty* fame and under Nelson on HMS *Victory*. He became Controller General of the Coast Guard.

These school rules, drawn up in 1847, show not only the very strict control required by the national body in its supervision of one of its members, but also convey something of the organisation and atmosphere of a typical Victorian church school.

*The former Compton and Up Marden National School*

# RULES OF THE
# COMPTON AND UP-MARDEN
## NATIONAL SCHOOLS.

1.   THE Schoolmaster and Schoolmistress will be required to educate the Children in strict conformity with the Rules and Regulations of the National Society for promoting the Education of the Poor in the Principles of the Established Church.

2.   They will also be required to attend the Sunday Schools, under the superintendence of the Minister of the United Parishes.

3.   Any Person wishing to have a Child admitted into either School, must apply to the Minister as Superintendent of the School, or in his absence to his Curate.

4.   The Parents and Friends of Children admitted are expected to send their Children to School punctually at the appointed hours, (except when leave of absence has been obtained from the Master or Mistress) and to submit to all the Regulations of the School for the discipline and correction of the Children.

5.   All complaints are to be made to the Superintendent, or to the Committee ; and no Parent will be allowed to make any complaint to the Master or Mistress, or to interfere with the management or discipline of the School.

6.   One penny for each Child is to be paid in advance regularly every Monday Morning ; and Children whose payments are in arrear will be liable to be dismissed.

7.   The Children are expected to come to School clean—with their hair well combed, and their clothes properly mended when necessary.

8.   No Child will be admitted into the School with a sore head—measles—or other infectious disorder ; nor from a family where any such disorder exists, without previous leave from the Superintendent.

9.   THE SCHOOL HOURS ARE AS FOLLOW—

**Morning, from 9 to 12**
**Afternoon, from 2 to 4½ in Summer.**
**———— from 2 to 3½ in Winter.**
**Saturday will be a Holyday.**

10.   Every Child admitted into the Weekly Schools will be required to attend the Sunday Schools, regularly and punctually ; or to give a satisfactory excuse for absence to the Superintendent.

11.   The Hours of attendance on SUNDAYS will be—when the Service in COMPTON Church is in the Morning :—

**Morning, from 10 till Church Time.**
**Afternoon, from 2 till 4.**
**Evening, from      till**

When the Service in COMPTON Church is in the Afternoon :—
**Morning, from 10 to 12.**
**Afternoon, from 2 till Church Time.**
**Evening, from      till**

12.   The Superintendent will have the power of suspending the attendance of any Child at the School, until the next Meeting of the Committee, in whom will rest the power of dismissal.

13.   Any Child guilty of ill behaviour at Church, disrespectful conduct to the Master or Mistress, or of any other gross misconduct, either in or out of School, will be subject to the loss of Tickets and Rewards, confinement after school hours, and to such other punishment as may be judged necessary for the correction of the offending Child, and for an example to the School.

14.   Children dismissed from the School, or taken from it without due notice and sufficient reason, will forfeit all rewards and other advantages to which they would otherwise have been entitled, and can only be re-admitted by order of the Committee.

15.   The Girls will be employed every afternoon in plain and useful needle-work.  Parents will be permitted to send their own and their Children's clothes to be made or mended at the School every Friday, and on other days upon leave obtained from the Mistress ; but whatever is sent must be perfectly clean.

*By order of the Committee.*

## W. TYNER,
Chariman.

Compton, November 23rd, 1847.

MINCHIN, PRINTER, ATLAS PRESS, PETERSFIELD.

*this? . . . God had placed them just where they were in the social order and given them their own special work to do; to envy others or to try to change their own lot in life was a sin. . . .*

From our own standpoint these rules suggest a most severe and authoritarian regime, its educational fundamentals as much based on emphasising children's guilt, and its correction and punishment, as they were on the hard-biting religion taught by so many nineteenth-century schoolmasters and clergymen.

The Compton and Up Marden National School worked on a six-day-a-week timetable involving compulsory church

The teaching of the scriptures was given the highest priority in the curriculum, and by a National Society ruling was under the strict control of the local parson who would usually make a daily visit.

Flora Thompson's classic book about her Victorian childhood, *Lark Rise to Candleford*, gives first-hand memories of such visits to her own school. She vividly remembered being taught more about her own lowly place in the world than about a God of love:

*Every morning at ten o'clock the Rector arrived to take the older children for Scripture. He was a parson of the old school . . . as far as possible removed by birth, education, and worldly circumstances from the lambs of his flock. He spoke to them from a great height, physical, mental, and spiritual. 'To order myself lowly and reverently before my betters' was the clause he underlined in the Church Catechism, for had he not been divinely appointed pastor and master to those little rustics and was it not one of his chief duties to teach them to realize*

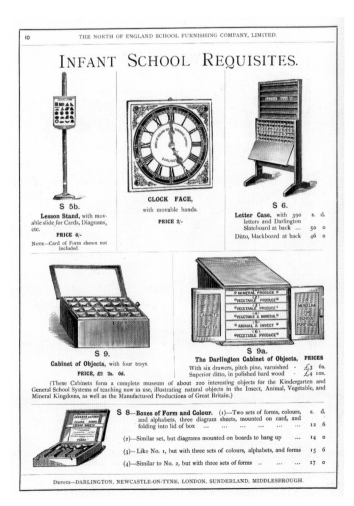

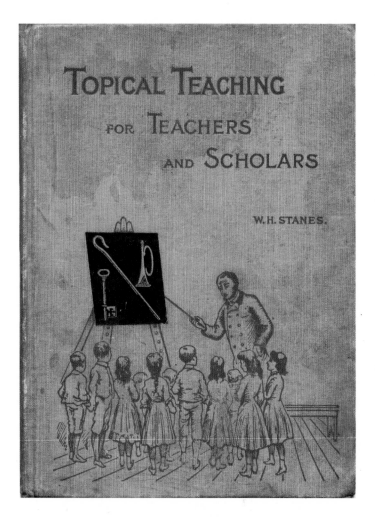

salaries of the teaching staff. In 1854, out of a total annual income of £119 10 shillings and 1 penny (£119.50½), the pupils' fees only amounted to £11 10 shillings and 5 pence (£11.52). The combined salaries of the schoolmaster and mistress alone amounted to £65. In the early days of the school there was thus the need for a heavy subsidy from the local community until state aid, particularly in the form of 'payment by results', was introduced in 1862.

Since the days of these school rules we have seen change – and yet more and more change – in education. The first really radical national shake-up to affect Compton took place when the church lost its exclusive control over its own schools by the Balfour Education Act of 1902. For the first time West Sussex County Council became the local education authority with ultimate powers over the voluntary sector in finance, secular instruction in the classroom, teachers' appointments and inspection. By this measure the non-church schools – known as board schools – were taken over by the County Council and hence became known for many years as council schools.

The authority assumed its new powers in the county on 1 April 1903. The West Sussex Education Committee then had its very first meeting on 3 April in Horsham Town Hall – there was no County Hall in Chichester then. So we are now approaching the centenary of what up to then had been the most radical change in management and control to have been experienced by these schools. [This article was originally published to coincide with the centenary in 2003.]

The little school amongst the Downs, whose rules give us such an insight into Victorian education, survives to this day – in modern premises – as the Compton and Up Marden Church of England Primary School, with a roll of just seventy-six children in 2002.

attendance on Sundays, all for the price of one old penny (½p), 'to be paid in advance regularly every Monday Morning'.

From the rules, the obvious maxims were punctuality, cleanliness and respectful conduct, standards that could be enforced by the ultimate sanction, dismissal. That dismissal could be used at all to enforce discipline is significant.

One old Sussex clergyman, the rector of Berwick, thought that regularity and punctuality only became a problem after attendance became compulsory from 1870: 'The most effectual punishment for a child ... for irregular attendance, or any serious fault, was to strike the name off the books, and thus I have kept a child away from school for three months, with good effect, not only to the child, but also in the example to the others. But such a punishment would not now be allowed' he wrote in 1912.

The penny a week fee would not even have covered the

# COCKING NATIONAL SCHOOL
*– highlights of the year*

## 1880

**19 Feb** — *Very wet this morning. Many children from Bepton & Linch were so wet on reaching school that they were sent home again.*

**18 March** — *Geo. Lambert sent home for his sister's money. Returned with a note from his mother as follows: 'You can't get a shirt off a naked man. I will send it as soon as I can'.*

**2 June** — *The Rev. R. Drummond Ash visited . . . and distributed rewards to those children who successfully passed the three R's in the recent examination.*

**8 Oct** — *Geo. Woodford punished for committing a dirty trick on another boy's head . . .the same boy punished this afternoon for writing indecent words on his slate.*

**3 Nov** — *Several children applied for leave to purchase clothing through the Clothing Club.*

**10 Nov** — *Several boys absent cover-beating for General Paxton's shooting party.*

## 1881

**21 Jan** — *There has been but one day's School this week owing to the severe snowstorm which commenced last Tuesday morning. On that morning only 10 children presented themselves; the next day 4; the next 2; and the next none at all. [Average attendance in early February was 88.]*

**13 June** — *A monitor is appointed to throw a bucket of water down the boys' urinal every day. . . .*

**20 July** — *Fanny North was required to carry her father's dinner some distance: and leaving school early on that account, her attendance for this morning was cancelled.*

**2 Aug** — *Flora Burroughs was dismissed from the Monitorship of the 3rd Standard as she was eating apples whilst in charge of the class.*

**8 Aug** — *As not more than a dozen of the elder children came to school this morning, harvesting being now very general, the school was closed for harvest & hopping vacation.*

# NOTICE.

**WHEREAS** frequent complaints have been made to us of the assemblage of many idle and disorderly persons on Sundays, who molest and otherwise annoy females passing along the Highways of this Parish, and who also play at marbles and other unlawful games thereon, to the great Nuisance of the Public.

## *Now we do Hereby Give Notice,*

that all persons found so offending *will be punished with the utmost severity of the Law.*

**W. NORRIS FRANKLYN,**
**FRANCIS WELLS,** } Churchwardens.

*WARNHAM*, 18th May, 1850.

Kennett and Breads, Printers, Bookbinders, Stationers, &c., West Street, Horsham.

# 25 'Idle and Disorderly': Public Nuisances in Warnham

THIS VICTORIAN NOTICE TAKES us back to the days when there was no county police force in West Sussex. This wasn't formed until 1857. Apart from small town forces such as in Arundel and Chichester, law and order elsewhere relied on untrained, unpaid constables who were under the jurisdiction of the parish churchwardens. This was all part of a system of local government based on the parish dating back to the Tudor period. It was a system in which the churchwardens were responsible for all sorts of local life, both ecclesiastical and secular.

In the parish of Warnham we see the two churchwardens threatening the 'many idle and disorderly ... *with the utmost severity of the Law*'. Churchwardens then had considerable local powers extending far beyond the church. They were also in overall charge of the local workhouse, roads and bridges and even the killing of vermin in the parish.

In this case the specific offence was a breach of the Highways Act of 1835, making it unlawful to 'play at Football or any other Game on any Part of the said Highways, to the Annoyance of any Passenger or Passengers'. Technically these 'idle and disorderly persons' were causing an obstruction. They were liable to a fine up to £2, approximately just over three times a labourer's weekly wage of twelve shillings (60p) in mid-nineteenth century Sussex, an enormous sum to pay for playing marbles on the street. But compounding the whole issue was the menace posed to females and the morality of all this trouble disturbing the Victorian Sunday. In today's terms the fine of £2 would be equivalent to over £900 for any worker on a weekly wage of £300.

So the churchwardens' threats reveal desperation. In these troubled times there was no county police, no village

*An age-old problem – the menace of the idle and disorderly*

street lighting, and no instant communications to bring help when there was any trouble. The threat of the mob in the first half of the nineteenth century was very real, the feeling that under a very thin veneer of law and order were the makings of riots, maybe even of social collapse. Authority had to take a firm stand, resorting to threats of the most severe penalties and dire warnings. In this way public announcements – as printed notices – came into their own as instruments of public control. Thousands upon thousands of similarly-intentioned notices were issued throughout the length and breadth of the land during the nineteenth century, warning and threatening evil doers and makers of mischief.

Warnham's notice is couched typically in exalted phraseology with its lofty sounding lead-in – its mightily authoritative 'WHEREAS' opening the preamble, culminating in bombastic crescendo: '*Now we do Hereby Give Notice*' in threatening '*the utmost severity of the Law*'. Here were just two country churchwardens – local farmers – investing themselves in the full and intimidating majesty of the law, and, by such high-flown legalese, adopting 'the resounding language of the throne room', according to Maurice Rickards, the historian of the public notice.

The question remains – just how many of Warnham's 'idle and disorderly' were actually able to read any of these mighty words in 1850, some twenty years before the law made schooling compulsory? But illiteracy disguised as ignorance would have been no mitigation in any court of law.

What this notice does challenge is the idea about cosy, stress-free village life in the past. Some of today's community problems were certainly alive and well in Queen Victoria's reign.

# 26 Exotic Groves: Lady Dorothy Nevill at Dangstein

DEEP IN THE WEST SUSSEX countryside lived an extraordinary woman, as much famed for her part as a brilliant society hostess as for the exotic groves of her remarkable country garden. She was Lady Dorothy Nevill (1826–1913) whose country estate was at Dangstein, between Midhurst and Petersfield.

Lady Dorothy came of a most distinguished family. A Walpole, her great-grandfather was the first Earl of Orford, otherwise more notably the eighteenth-century prime minister, Sir Robert Walpole. She married Reginald Nevill, grandson of the first Earl of Abergavenny, whose seat was at Eridge Castle in East Sussex where the family had an estate of some ten thousand acres (4,000 hectares).

With this blue-blooded background she was to move effortlessly in the most exalted circles. She became a leading political hostess, her London *salon* a roll-call of the great and the good in high society. The Tory's Primrose League originated around her luncheon table.

When noticing her eightieth birthday in 1906 the *West Sussex Gazette* commented that:

> She belongs to that brilliant period of the Victorian era which seems to have no parallel in our own. She was the originator of those Sunday luncheon-parties which, before the days of motors and week-ends, were so much the vogue, and her house in Charles-street [London] became the recognised meeting place for the greatest intellects of the day. For more than half a century, in fact, Lady Dorothy has known almost everyone of political, social or intellectual distinction in the country. Lord Beaconsfield, Cobden, Darwin and Huxley, were only a few of the distinguished men whom she knew.

Dangstein, her place in the country, was an extraordinary spot as a result of all the improvements and building work carried out after its purchase in 1851. It lay at the centre of a two-thousand acre (800 hectare) estate sprawling across five parishes: Chithurst, Rogate, Terwick, Trotton and Woolavington. Reginald set about improving the farmland and forestry with new drainage and new planting, his wife concentrating on the domestic arrangements in the house, and in the gardens indulging her passion for the exotic.

The imposing mansion, built in the Greek Corinthian style in the early nineteenth century, was noted for its massive heating system installed by Lady Dorothy, quite unusual for its time. Its huge circular furnace was over

*Lady Dorothy Nevill in 1846 by Robert Thorburn (1818–85)*

sixty feet (18 metres) in circumference, built like a giant octopus, its tentacles a maze of subterranean pipes. The massive domed and galleried hall was so big that the furnace had to be stoked for three days before the freezing air could be dispersed. Such a house required a huge labour force.

Immediately around the big house was Lady Dorothy's very special place, her extensive and exotic gardens. A great army of labourers was employed to sculpt the former woodland into dells, ponds, sunken lawns and terraces, the setting for rare plants from all over the world. There were seventeen greenhouses, a magnificent domed palm house, orchid houses, a peach house, a fernery and a hundred feet (30 metres) of forcing pits, all heated by hot air and water.

*This view of the house is from an undated postcard franked 1908; the description above from the 1879 sale particulars*

*The galleried hall*

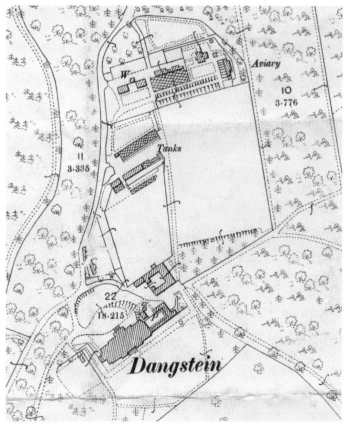

*House, gardens, glasshouses and pleasure grounds in 1896*

# RANGE OF HOT AND ORCHID HOUSES

119ft long by 13ft wide; comprising Three Vineries and Two Orchid Houses, heated by Hot Water.

## A WALLED PEACH HOUSE,

28ft by 13ft; Two Rain-water Tanks.

# RANGE OF FORCING PITS

(21 Lights), 84ft by 12ft.

Mushroom House and Stoke Hole, Tool House Shed, Potting Shed, Seed Room with Cellars under for Roots, Orchid House, Tank for Rain-water, capable of holding 5,000 gallons, a ditto by Stabling, holding 4,000 gallons,

# RANGE OF PITS

Heated by Hot Water with Tanks, 103ft by 24ft.

# RANGE OF HOUSES,

138ft by 24ft, heated by Hot Water, and comprising Orange House, Orchard House, Orchid House and Succulent House, Two Tanks,

## A MAGNIFICENT PALM HOUSE,

### WITH DOMED ROOF,

80ft by 50ft, heated by both Hot Air and Water, Potting Shed and Bothy, Rain-water Tank under, capable of holding 11,000 gallons, Stoke Hole and Coal Shed.

CONSERVATORY (heated by Hot Water), 50ft by 32ft with a 5,000 gallon Tank and cool Fern House communicating with

**FERNERY,** 50ft by 26ft, heated both by Hot Air and Water, opening to

## A SMALL MUSEUM

And Potting Shed with a 4,000 gallon Tank under, Stoke Hole, &c. Two cool Brick Pits, one with Ten and the other with Eleven double Lights.

### GARDENER'S COTTAGE AND GARDEN,

**DOUBLE AVIARY,** Pheasantry in six compartments with Two Pigeon Lofts over, and Wash-house at back, Small Lean-to, and a Small Aviary.

# CHARMING PLEASURE GROUNDS,

Laid-out in Lawns and Flower Beds, Terrace Walks, Winding Broad Gravelled Paths, tastefully disposed and adorned with fine specimen Wellingtonia, rare Conifers, and choice Shrubs, a PINETUM and HARDY FERNERY, and

## A PRETTILY TIMBERED UNDULATING PARK,

*Lady Dorothy's exotic interests – from the 1879 sale particulars*

*The sunken garden*

Lady Dorothy's collection of rare plants brought her into contact with some of the most famous botanists, scientists and explorers of the day, including the great Charles Darwin whom she helped with her observations on orchids and insectivorous plants. She was said to have gathered the finest collection of exotic plants outside Kew, whilst her lifelong friend, politician and prime minister Benjamin Disraeli, said that she had 'without doubt the finest pinetum and conservatories and collection of rare trees in the world'.

The exotic extended far beyond plants at Dangstein. In the grounds she even had her own little museum and there were aviaries of rare and colourful birds. Loving the unusual, she was sent some pigeon whistles from China for her aerial orchestra. Clipped to pigeons' tails, the little whistles

*The surviving aviary in 2007*

*Chinese pigeon whistles, made from lightweight gourds and reeds, were attached to the tail feathers by a fine copper wire so that when the birds flew they produced 'music in the skies'*

winged their way across the lawns, delighting guests with their heavenly music. She was one of the first society ladies to own Siamese cats direct from the court of Siam, and also one of the first to be seen with a new type of lap dog, a 'lion dog of China' – a Pekinese – introduced into Britain in the 1860s. Also of Chinese origin were her silkworms, bred so successfully that from her Dangstein stock worms were sent to create silkworm studs in South Africa and Australia. Her friend, the second Duke of Wellington, was so captivated by her work that he too became a silkworm enthusiast.

A quite extraordinary woman, her life faced tragedy when her husband Reginald died in 1878 and the Dangstein estate was hit by the agricultural depression in the late 1870s. Forced to sell, Lady Dorothy moved to

*Lady Dorothy Nevill at home*

smaller premises near Heathfield in East Sussex. Many of her plants were sold off, the tropical palms taken to Monte Carlo for planting around the casino. In the next century the mansion fell into decay; by 1926 it was put up for sale for demolition and then pulled down, replaced by a new and far from imposing house built in the 1930s. Around its grounds just a few relics of her exotic paradise survive, but much, like the Victorian aviary, are in sad and gentle decay. [Since this article was written the estate was gifted to the National Trust, and then put up for sale in 2007. The future for Dangstein and its grounds should look brighter.]

Lady Dorothy's world more vividly survives in several published memoirs. The following passages are from *The Reminiscences of Lady Dorothy Nevill* (1906) and *Under Five Reigns* (1910) when she looked back to her time at Dangstein between the early 1850s and late '70s. She certainly wasn't too good at local geography, having the confusingly irritating habit of repeatedly saying she lived in Hampshire because postally her address was Dangstein, *near* Petersfield. Even her reminiscences about her life in Sussex were headed 'Our Life in Hampshire'. Dangstein stands firmly in West Sussex.

## THE REMINISCENCES OF LADY DOROTHY NEVILL

ENGLISH COUNTRY LIFE at that time still retained many of its old characteristics. Rustic mummers at the proper season used to come and enact the quaint play of 'St George and the Dragon' in the grounds of the local gentry, where they were always sure of some pecuniary renumeration as well as a hearty meal. Mr Nevill took great interest in his estate, whilst I devoted a great deal of time to my garden, which became quite a show-place in the county. We had seventeen hot-houses, and employed a good many men. Most of the tropical fruit-trees were there as well as orchids without number, and few plants of any rarity were lacking in the hot-houses....

The second Duke of Wellington took a great interest in my horticultural experiments, and I used always to keep him informed of any botanical wonders which I might chance to discover....

There were a great many curiosities of different sorts in my garden, one of which, I think, was absolutely unique, having never been seen or, rather, heard anywhere else in England. I had sent me from China a number of pigeon-whistles made out of gourds, which were something like small organ pipes, and could be attached with great ease to a pigeon's tail. The effect produced by the flight of these birds with whistles attached was extremely pretty, resembling Æolian harps, the whistles being all of a different note. People used to be considerably astonished at such heavenly music, and their bewilderment and puzzled faces afforded me great amusement. No one but myself, I believe, has ever organised such a winged orchestra, but should anyone care to make the experiment, I can assure them they will be well rewarded for their trouble.

## UNDER FIVE REIGNS

Besides my garden I had many other things with which to pass my time, including a model farm with a Dutch dairy, situated amidst the lovely surroundings. In a little wooded hollow, not far from the house, stood a fair-sized cottage, and here I established a model laundry, where a certain number of poor girls were trained for domestic service, not always, I am bound to say, with very satisfactory results. The recollection of one matron, who was anything but fond of supervision, lingers with me yet. She was always anxious as to when we were going to return to London, and in honeyed though anxious tones would inquire, 'I hope we are not going to lose your ladyship yet?'...

When we first went to live in Hampshire, the beautiful country close to us on the borders of Surrey was far more wild and rural than is to-day the case. Liss, where now are multitudes of villas, was quite a tiny place, and parts of the district remained in much the same condition as they had been in for centuries. On the other side of us loomed the restful outlines of the South Downs, between which and our home, called Dangstein, the gently undulating country abounded in peaceful-looking homesteads, well-farmed fields, and delightful woods, here and there intersected by the swift flowing Rother, in places the most picturesque of streams. The countryside was wrapped in the peaceful semi-slumber which had prevailed with but short interruptions since the advent of the Conqueror's knights, many of whom slept their last long sleep beneath the stones of the quaint old village churches, as yet little affected by the destructive craze for the most part miscalled 'restoration'.

Alas! as the nineteenth century began to wane, sinister signs of destruction began to manifest themselves in most of the village churchyards, which became encumbered with sheds and tool huts, whilst workmen hammered and hacked the old churches according to the whims and fancies of iconoclastic architects.

Rogate Church near us (in its untouched condition an ideal old English village church) was almost completely stripped of its picturesqueness by such vandals, who, in addition to robbing the church of much that was interesting to the lovers of the past, also contrived to mingle the gravestones of those buried in the churchyard in such inextricable confusion that the tombstones of one family were in some cases either re-erected over the graves of others or, worse still, lost altogether. This gross carelessness naturally produced much irritation amongst surviving relatives of the dead.

Many old ways and customs still prevailed in the neighbourhood, and as late as June 1859 the town of Midhurst witnessed the somewhat brutal sight of 'a man in the stocks' for six hours, for non-payment of the trumpery fine of five shillings for being drunk. The culprit was rather noisy at the commencement of his durance vile; but, as the hours wore on, his enjoyment of exposure – forced and fixed – to an easterly wind, although accompanied with sunshine, did not increase. The stocks were placed in the market-place, in order that the exhibition should be as public as possible. In justice to the occasional bystanders, it was reported that they appeared to enjoy the spectacle as little as the offender himself.

The clergy, though many were kindly and earnest men, were quite different to the energetic clerics of to-day. They had, however, very queer parishioners to deal with in those days, before universal education was thought of. A certain vicar, whom I remember, whose spiritual activity was rather ahead of his age, was upbraiding one of his rustic parishioners for lax attendance at church, whilst holding up another yokel who chanced to be standing by as an example.

'You always come to church, Tommy, don't you?' said the good man.

'Yes, sir, indeed I do. It's just beautiful, for when I gets there I puts my feet upon the bench and thinks a nothing.'

*Dangstein stained glass*

# 27 'Grinding the Wind': Hard Labour in Petworth Prison

Q  *How many hours at a time are the men kept upon the wheel?*
A  *They are employed now about nine hours daily at the wheel.*
Q  *Is the treadwheel applied to productive labour?*
A  *Not at all.*
Q  *Is it ever used for any productive purpose?*
A  *No, for nothing but punishment.*

The exchanges droned on one April day in 1863 as their lordships on the Select Committee on Prisons – which numbered the Duke of Richmond from Goodwood – examined Governor William Linton on how he ran Petworth Prison.

The prison treadwheel was the most feared of hard-labour punishments: 'the absence of any human sound – the dull, soughing voice of the wheel, like the agony of drowning men – the dark shadows toiling and treading in a journey which knows no progress – force on the mind involuntary sensations of horror and disgust'. The humanitarian response to the terrors it held echoed throughout the penal system until these 'walking wheels' were finally outlawed in 1898.

As a form of punishment the wheel was first recommended by the Penitentiary Act of 1779, directing that prisoners be kept 'to labour of the hardest and most servile kind, in which drudgery is chiefly required ... such as treading in a wheel'. The idea was probably inspired by the example of ancient treadwheels in which men or donkeys raised water from deep wells or hauled stone into lofty buildings – power was generated *within* the wheel, as in a mouse or hamster wheel. But as eventually developed in the nineteenth century, these punishment wheels were worked from *outside* the machinery.

*Petworth Jail from the Tillington Road.*

# THE PETWORTH TREADWHEEL

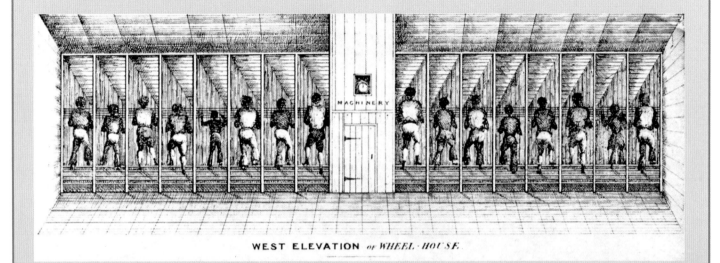

WEST ELEVATION of WHEEL·HOUSE.

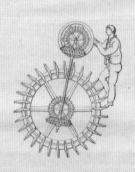

*View and sections through the Petworth treadwheel from the prison commission reports of 1835 (top) and 1863. The measurement of the 'work' performed by Mance's Ergometer – in the box marked 'MACHINERY' – was regulated according to the table reproduced below from the Petworth rule book of 1853.*

## SCALE OF TREAD-WHEEL AND CRANK LABOR REFERRED TO.

| Months. | TREAD-WHEEL LABOR. | | | | | | CRANK LABOR. | | How recorded with precision. |
|---|---|---|---|---|---|---|---|---|---|
| | The number of Hours the Prisoners are to Work per day. | The number of Prisoners the wheels will hold at one time. | The height of each step. | The number of steps per minute. | The ordinary proportion of Prisoners on the Wheels to the total number employed. | The number of feet ascent per day to be performed by each Prisoner. | The number of Prisoners the Cranks will employ at one time. | The ordinary velocity of the Cranks per minute. | |
| January February November December | 7 hours. | 16 | 9 inches. | 48 steps. | 3-4ths. | 11,340. | 30 | 32 | Mance's Ergometer and the key is to be kept by the Governor. |
| March October | 8¾ hours. | 16 | 9 inches. | 48 steps. | 3-5ths. | 11,340. | 30 | 24, and 840 over in the course of the day. | |
| April May June July August September | 10 hours. | 16 | 9 inches. | 42 steps. | 3-5ths. | 11,340. | 30 | 22, and 240 over in the course of the day. | |

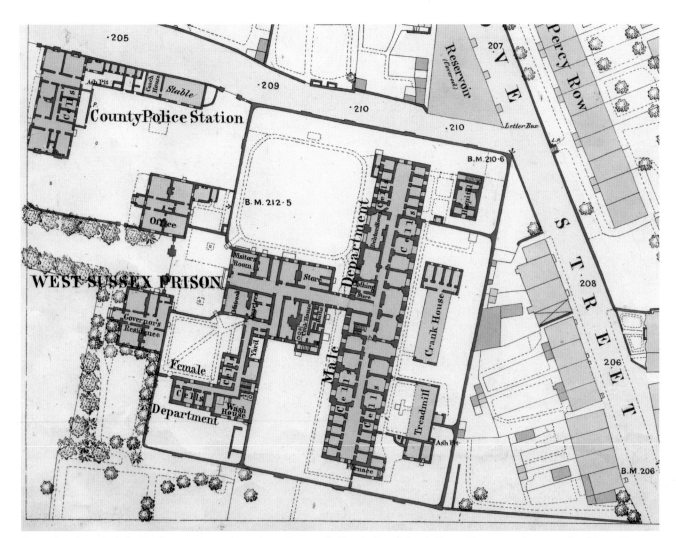

*Room plan, from an Ordnance Survey map made in 1874, showing the Treadmill and Crank House. The site, on the west side of Grove Street, has since been redeveloped with housing.*

To its advocates charged with devising methods for keeping discipline, the beauty of the wheel was both in its simplicity and efficiency. Some wheels even raised an income for the prisons, turning millstones for grinding flour or working a saw-mill. Others, as at Petworth, did nothing but 'grind the wind', as contemporaries said. It was useless toil, to break a man's spirit.

As with similar devices elsewhere, the Petworth wheel was designed as a long drum, thirty-two feet (about 10 metres) in length, in this case to house sixteen prisoners at a time. The circumference was made in the form of steps, looking something like the floats on a paddle wheel. The prisoners walked as if going upstairs. But instead of going up, the steps dropped down beneath them. The actual 'work' wasn't so much in turning the wheel as in lifting the body each time the steps fell away underneath.

Governor Linton claimed that the subsidiary handwheel was unique to Petworth. This additional mechanism ensured that there was no stationary fixture on which to grip. Until they had learnt to balance, prisoners would be in a state of instability. With both wheels in action it must have been a most curious and frightening sensation. To prevent slipping, or serious injury, total concentration was needed all the time. Many legs were mangled in careless moments. And if legs weren't crushed and broken, prisoners turned into medical cases with severe weight loss, varicose veins and and heart complaints.

The treadwheel and its human cargo operated to precise

mechanical measurements. Rules decreed that it turn at forty-eight steps per minute, and that each prisoner stepped 11,340 feet (3,456 metres), or just over two miles a day. This was the rough equivalent of climbing Snowdon three times daily, six days a week. The distance had to be achieved within a precise time limit: ten hours in the summer, seven in the winter. Speed was encouraged in the colder months.

The revolutions and variable times were carefully recorded at Petworth on a dialled instrument called 'Mance's Ergometer', Mance being a former governor, and its inventor, in the 1830s. The dial showed the amount of labour to be performed hourly and daily over a period of seventy-eight days. When the prescribed amount of labour had been recorded each day the ergometer rang an alarm bell. To the despairing inmates, the hands must have moved so slowly. The wheel wasn't called 'the everlasting staircase' for nothing.

So if the severity of the physical punishment was bad enough, the regime that underpinned the hard labour sentence was purposely designed to make things worse. Many inmates were driven to insanity or attempted suicide.

The Silent and Separate Systems both operated at Petworth. All communications between prisoners by word, gesture or sign were forbidden and as far as possible they were kept apart at all times. On the wheel, though close to one another, prisoners were separated from each other by partition walls, enclosing each man in an individual compartment. In this way each was forced in upon himself, to reflect and suffer. The underlying belief was that this was not only punishment, but a way of breaking a man. From being broken and crushed a man might then be reformed and improved. At least this was the theory.

As well as the wheel – for men – Petworth had one other hard-labour machine called the crank – for men and women. Thirty prisoners at a time each had to turn a handle against a resisting pressure, another humiliating sensation of labouring hard to achieve nothing but a daily ration of revolutions – 13,200 in a ten-hour day.

The Petworth treadwheel and crank were both being used until 1878 when the prison was finally closed down. The prison was demolished in 1882.

Oscar Wilde, who suffered so much within the hell of another Victorian prison, lived in constant fear of going out

## WEEKLY DIETARY.

| Description of Prisoners. | Good Wheaten Bread. | Meat, including Bone, before being cooked. | Potatoes. | Soup. In which the meat is boiled, containing a portion of Oatmeal, Pepper & Vegetables. | Gruel. |
|---|---|---|---|---|---|
| | lbs. | lbs. | lbs. | Pints | Pints |
| **DEBTORS.** | | | | | |
| TABLE 1.—Poor Debtors wholly supported by the County ...... | 10½ | 1¾ | 3½ | 7 | { 1¼lbs. of Oatmeal and 3½oz of Sugar for Gruel. |
| TABLE 2.—On the Days they partly support themselves........ | 1 | ,, | ,, | ,, | ,, |
| TABLE 3.—Debtors for contempt of Court, &c., &c. .......... | 10½ | 1¾ | ,, | 7 | 10½, made with 3½lbs. of Flour and Salt. |
| **CRIMINALS.** | | | | | |
| TABLE 1.—Persons whose Sentences do not exceed 14 Days...... | 7 | ,, | ,, | ,, | ditto. |
| TABLE 2.—Persons whose Sentences do not exceed One Calendar Month ...................................... | 10½ | ,, | ,, | ,, | ditto. |
| TABLE 3.—All Persons for Trial and for Re-examination, from the day of their being received into the Prison, and those under Sentence from and after the first Calendar Month of their Imprisonment ............. | 10½ | 1¾ | ,, | 10½ | ditto. |
| TABLE 4.—All Persons from and after the third Calendar Month of their Imprisonment ...................... | 10½ | 1¾ | 7, or 3½d. worth of other Vegetables. | 10½ | ditto. |

*Feeding the Petworth prisoners, from the 1853 rule book*

## FORM A.

State of the Prisoners in PETWORTH House of Correction, on the *18th* day of *February* 1837

| OFFENCES AND SENTENCES | | | Tread Wheel Labour | Crank Labour | Making Linen & Woollen Articles, &c. | Shoemaking | Tailoring | Carpentering | Painting | Bricklayering | Whitewashing | Blacksmithing | Washing, &c. | Wardsmen | Cooking | Stoker | Sick or Infirm | Nurses | Solitary Confinement | Refractory Cells | Rolling the Yards | Factory, by order of the Surgeon | Not employed | TOTAL IN CUSTODY |
|---|---|---|---|---|---|---|---|---|---|---|---|---|---|---|---|---|---|---|---|---|---|---|---|---|
| **UNDER SENTENCE — To Hard Labour — MALES** | | Of Death | | | | | | | | | | | | | | | | | | | | | | |
| | | Transports | | | | | | | | | | | | | | | | | | | | | | |
| | | Felons | 7 | 2 | | | | | | | | | | | | | 1 | | | | | | | 10 |
| | Misdemeanors | Soldiers | | | | | | | | | | | | | | | | | | | | | | |
| | | Excise and Customs | | | | | | | | | | | 1 | 1 | | | | | | | | 2 | | 4 |
| | | Game Laws | 8 | 6 | | | | | | | | | | 1 | 1 | | | | | | | 1 | | 17 |
| | | Other Misdemeanors | 1 | 4 | | | | | | | | | | 1 | | | | | | | | | | 6 |
| | | Vagrant Act | 3 | 1 | | | | | | | | | | | | | | | | | | | | 4 |
| **FEMALES** | | Felons | | | | | | | | | | | | | | | | | | | | | | |
| | | Misdemeanors | | | | | | | | | | | 1 | | | | | | | | | | | 1 |
| | | Vagrant Act | | | | | | | | | | | | | | | | | | | | | | |
| **To Simple Imprisonment — MALES** | | Felons | | | | | | | | | | | | | | | | | | | | | | |
| | Misdemeanors | Soldiers | | | | | | | | | | | | | | | | | | | | | | |
| | | Excise and Customs | | | 1 | | | | | | | | | | | | | | | | | | | 1 |
| | | Game Laws | | | | | | | | | | | | | | | | | | | | | | |
| | | Other Misdemeanors | | | 3 | | | | | | | | | | | | | | | | | | | 3 |
| | | For want of Securities | | | | | | | | | | | | | | | | | | | | | | |
| **FEMALES** | | Felons | | | | | | | | | | | | | | | | | | | | | | |
| | | Excise or Customs | | | | | | | | | | | | | | | | | | | | | | |
| | | Misdemeanors | | | | | | | | | | | | | | | | | | | | | | |
| **FOR TRIAL** — Felons | | Males | | | 10 | 1 | | | | | | | | | | | | | | | | | | 11 |
| | | Females | | | | | | | | | | | | | | | | | | | | | | |
| Misdemeanors | | Males | | | | | | | | | | | | | | | | | | | | | | |
| | | Females | | | | | | | | | | | | | | | | | | | | | | |
| Incorrigible Rogues | | Males | | | | | | | | | | | | | | | | | | | | | | |
| | | Females | | | | | | | | | | | | | | | | | | | | | | |
| Witnesses for the Crown | | | | | | | | | | | | | | | | | | | | | | | | |
| Further Examination | | | | | | | | | | | | | | | | | | | | | | | | |
| **Total Males** | | | 19 | 13 | 14 | 1 | | | | | | | 1 | 3 | 1 | | 1 | | | | | 3 | | 56 |
| **Total Females** | | | | | | | | | | | | | 1 | | | | | | | | | | | 1 |
| Children with their Mothers | | | | | | | | | | | | | | | | | | | | | | | | |
| **GRAND TOTAL** | | | 19 | 13 | 14 | 1 | | | | | | | 2 | 3 | 1 | | 1 | | | | | 3 | | 57 |

In Custody on the *18th* Day of *February* 1836 .. 105
Ditto *18th* Day of *Ditto* 1837 .. 57
~~Increased~~ or Decreased .. .. .. .. .. .. .. .. .. .. .. 48.

*John Mance*

**KEEPER.**

*There were other categories of more useful work besides the unproductive labour of the treadwheel and crank. The employment of the prisoners and their sentences were recorded by the prison governor – called the 'keeper' here in this report of 1837.*

of his mind. His outburst in *The Ballad of Reading Gaol* (1898) is an insight into its terror:

> *. . . every prison that men build*
> *Is built with bricks of shame,*
> *And bound with bars lest Christ should see*
> *How men their brothers maim.*
>
> *With bars they blur the gracious moon,*
> *And blind the goodly sun;*
> *And they do well to hide their Hell,*
> *For in it things are done*
> *That Son of God nor Son of Man*
> *Ever should look upon!*

At Petworth the 'bricks of shame' all went with the demolition of the prison in 1882. But its horrors still live on in the mountains of documents that once steered the punitive regime of the likes of Mance and Linton towards its cruelly-mechanical efficiency. Their papers, accounts, rule books and reports, with page after page of the condemned, by name, offence and punishment, are all preserved in West Sussex Record Office.

*Above: the main prison office, built in 1835, survived the demolition in 1882 and is now a Grade II listed building*

*Right: prison uniform button*

*Below: prisoners leave their mark - scratched bricks in a wall on the edge of the former prison, photographed in 2008*

# 28 Mouse-trap Man: Colin Pullinger, Selsey Inventor

'MOUSETRAPS DO NOT at first sight seem the most promising material out of which to raise up a temple of fame.' Quite so, but this was being written about Selsey – mouse-trap capital of the country – where life has always been a little different. At least this was the opinion given in a series of articles about Sussex industries published in the *Sussex Advertiser* in the 1880s.

Isolated, 'almost surrounded by the ocean', its locals had several peculiarities. And there was none more unusual than Colin Pullinger whose mouse traps took the name of Selsey around the world. Unique in design and operation, the trap was entirely his own invention.

But it wasn't just mouse traps that were made in what he called his 'inventive factory' in Selsey's High Street.

Pullinger's trade card was quite extraordinary, more like a complete directory of trades in itself. The wonder was that all these skills belonged to just one person. He was a jack-of-all-trades, Selsey's Pooh Bah, a man of so many parts that he can hardly be categorised.

His skills and knowledge covered all the essential household and building trades and a lot more, from repairing umbrellas, cleaning clocks, mending china and glass, trading in groceries, fish and bread, farming the land, building boats, teaching navigation, inventing and selling farm implements as well as mouse, rat and mole traps. He even advertised himself as a bell hanger. If all these trades weren't enough he also measured land, acted as a house agent and accountant, wrote peoples' letters if they couldn't do it for themselves – before compulsory education, illiteracy was high – and was employed as the local tax collector, as well as being clerk to the Selsey

Sparrow Club. The club paid a bounty for all dead sparrows as they were seen as pests and vermin. He was even the village undertaker. Another of his advertisements lists his 'improved Meat Safe', his 'Sulphur Blower, to destroy mildew on vines [and] flowers' and 'A Swing Washing Machine, with which two boys can with ease wash any amount of dirty clothes clean'.

## COLIN PULLINGER,
### SELSEY, NEAR CHICHESTER,
**Contractor, Inventor, Fisherman, and Mechanic,**

FOLLOWING THE VARIOUS TRADES OF A
BUILDER, CARPENTER, JOINER, SAWYER, UNDERTAKER,
*Turner, Cooper, Painter, Glazier, Wooden Pump Maker,*
PAPER HANGER, BELL HANGER, SIGN PAINTER,
**BOAT BUILDER,**
CLOCK CLEANER, REPAIRER OF LOCKS, AND KEYS FITTED,
Repairer of Umbrellas and Parasols, Mender of China and Glass,
Copying Clerk, Letter Writer, Accountant, Teacher of Navigation,

**GROCER, BAKER, FARMER,**

Assessor and Collector of Taxes, Surveyor, House Agent, Engineer, Land
Measurer, Assistant Overseer, Clerk at the Parish Vestry Meetings,
Clerk to the Selsey Police, Clerk to the Selsey Sparrow Club,

*Has served at Sea in the four Quarters of the World, as Seaman, Cook,
Steward, Mate and Navigator.*

---

THE MAKER AND INVENTOR OF THE FOLLOWING :

**AN IMPROVED HORSE HOE, AN IMPROVED SCARIFIER,**

A newly-invented Couch Grass Rake, a Machine to Tar Ropes, Model of a
Vessel to cut asunder Chains put across the Mouth of a Harbour,

## A CURIOUS MOUSE TRAP,

*Made on a scientific principle, where each one caught resets the trap to catch
its next neighbour, requires no fresh baiting, and will catch them by dozens,*

**A Rat Trap on a peculiar Construction,**

*That will catch and put them into the trap,*

An improved Mole Trap, an improved Velocipede, Model of a fast-sailing
Yacht on an improved construction, 2ft. long, and challenged to sail
against any Boat of the same length in the world, &c., &c., &c.

---

CRABS, LOBSTERS, AND PRAWNS SENT TO ANY PART OF ENGLAND.

**MOUSE TRAPS LET ON HIRE.**

*Pullinger's Inventive Factory. Colin Pullinger holds one of his mouse traps; the barn on the left is decorated with the name-board of a ship from Barcelona – possibly from a wreck.*

This master of invention, Colin Pullinger (1814 – 1894), was born at Ivy Lodge in the High Street, his father and grandfather both carpenters. But he left home to strike out on his own, wanting to be something quite different. So he went off to Brighton to work for a law stationer and then as a copy clerk in a lawyer's office. Wanting adventure he sailed the world, for as his trade card says he 'served at Sea in the four Quarters of the World, as Seaman, Cook, Steward, Mate and Navigator'. Many were the dangers and hair-breadth escapes he faced, once nearly being lost overboard by an insecure rope, another time shipwrecked in a great storm off the Australian coast.

Pullinger later recounted that this near fatality was the turning point in his life, leading him to reflect seriously on the direction of his future. 'If fear of death ... so terrifies the conscience, why not, while life is spared, strive to do what a good man can ... I left following a sailor's life ... and returned to my native village, Selsey, there to pursue the same trade as my father – a carpenter – determined to carry out the resolution made during the storm at sea, and to use as much as possible the talent with which Providence had entrusted me – an inventive mind.'

On the death of his father, William, in 1847, Pullinger inherited the family home and its neighbouring carpenters' workshops, timber yard and some six acres (2.4 hectares) of adjoining farmland. He settled down to his inventive life.

When he had to fill out official forms, Pullinger had to forget the way he described himself in his encyclopaediac trade card. In the Selsey parish registers, when his six children were baptised, he called himself just 'Farmer' in the first three entries between 1847 and 1850, then 'Fisherman' in 1852, back to 'Farmer' in 1854, and then 'Carpenter & Builder' in 1856. By the 1861 census he was then referring to himself as 'Inventor & Maker of the Automaton Mouse Trap and Farmer of 6 acres'. It was as the mouse-trap maker that he became so well known.

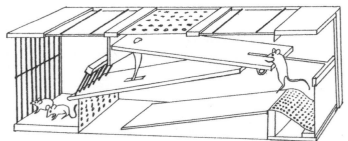

*Pullinger's Automaton Mouse Trap redrawn from an advertisement of 1860*

*Colin Pullinger's 'Curious Mouse Trap, Made on a scientific principle', c.1880–5*
Chichester District Museum

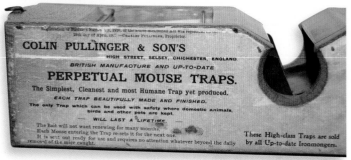

*Label on one of the last Pullinger mouse traps ever made, c.1920s*
Chichester District Museum

There were several designs to the traps, but their essence was that they were humane – quite different from the modern spring-loaded back-breaker – and they were self-setting in that many mice, one after another, could be accommodated before the trap was full and had to be emptied.

Attracted by the bait, the mouse entered an enclosed box, stepping onto one end of a see-saw mechanism that directed it down through a one-way inner door into a holding compartment. This action ingeniously allowed the next mouse to see-saw itself into the other holding compartment at the opposite end of the box; this in turn re-opened the other end of the trap, and so on. Hence it

became known as a 'Perpetual' trap, its name after a design modification in 1861.

The mouse traps were made in Pullinger's factory workshops by the side of his house where, in 1861, he was employing just three men and fifteen boys. The boys varied in age from ten to sixteen. At one time it was said there were upwards of forty men and boys working there.

Possibly one reason that young boys could be employed was that the workshop was so automated that nothing was left to the workmen's eyes or initiative. The machines were all pre-set so that each part of the trap was sawn and drilled to the exact size, depth and shape. The motive power to drive all the machinery came from a horse gin (a horse-driven engine) powering two circular saws and four drills.

At full production the Selsey factory produced nearly a thousand traps a week. They sold all over the country and beyond, promoted by being shown at national and international exhibitions. Pullinger was a great publicist. They were shown at the International Exhibition in 1862 and recommended at the Royal Society for the Prevention of Cruelty to Animals' exhibition in 1864. In 1870 he won silver medals at the Workmen's International Exhibition and in 1876 won a medal at the International Exhibition in Philadelphia. He well knew the value of advertising and putting his stamp on the trap trade, so much so that he is the first *identifiable* mouse-trap inventor in the world, according to David Drummond in his American-published book – *Mouse Traps: A Quick Scamper through their Long History*.

Pullinger died in 1894 aged seventy-nine. The business was then carried on by his son Charles into the 1920s. By then the Pullinger traps had several imitators in both the United States and this country. Probably the last copy of a Selsey trap was one made by a Midlands company and advertised by the Army and Navy Stores in its 1925–6 catalogue as 'The Colin Pullinger Mouse and Vole Trap'. Very few of the Selsey traps survive today. Three are in Chichester District Museum.

The site of the workshop is now marked by a blue plaque outside Selsey Town Council's office in the High Street.

*Pullinger's advertisement of 1882*

# SUSSEX MOUSETRAPS

## AND OTHER INVENTIONS.

——

# COLIN PULLINGER,

## Of SELSEY, near CHICHESTER,

### Inventor & Manufacturer of many useful Articles,

AS exhibited at the late Industrial Exhibition at Lewes; at the International Exhibition, London; International Exhibition, Philadelphia; Royal Counties' Show at Brighton; Workmen's Exhibition, London, and many other places. Many medals and other prizes have been awarded.

The following is a list of some of the most important Articles :—

An AUTOMATON MOUSETRAP on a scientific principle, 5s.

A PERPETUAL MOUSETRAP—always set and baited, 2s. 6d.

An improved BEETLE and COCKROACH TRAP—catch hundreds in one night, 1s.

An improved SELF-ACTING CINDER SIFTER, £1 1s.

A ROCKING CINDER SIFTER, 5s. and upwards.

An improved CASK STAND, 9s.

A TAPPING MALLET, 1s.

An improved MEAT SAFE, from 18s. upwards.

SULPHUR BLOWER, to destroy mildew on vines, flowers, 2s.

A SWING WASHING MACHINE, with which two boys can with ease wash any amount of dirty clothes clean.

An improved TRAP FOR CATCHING RATS, 5s.

———

*Visitors to Selsey are respectfully invited to inspect the Factory, where all the Inventions will be cheerfully shown and explained.*

———

**Illustrated Catalogues forwarded, post free, on application.**

# 29 'The Sussex Aboriginal': Stories from Harting

IS FATHER-IN-LAW'S PASSION was 'underground-ology' – geology to us – and he ate rodents and insects, once even part of a puppy, keeping a bear and a jackel for pets. His brother-in-law, possessed of similar gastronomic curiosity, cooked a rhinoceros pie and made elephant's trunk soup. Less bizarrely, he himself gathered stories of the peculiar habits and superstitions of the Sussex peasant – 'the Sussex aboriginal' he called him – retelling his tales of witchcraft, the black arts and even of the day it rained hot flints from the Downs.

He was the Reverend Henry Doddridge Gordon (1833–97), best remembered today for his *History of Harting* published in 1877, one of the most remarkable Sussex parish histories of the nineteenth century. What made the book unusual for a parish history of its time was Gordon's collaboration with two other writers, a professional geologist and amateur naturalist, thereby giving a three-dimensional view of the *whole* parish, its history set against its geological landscape and natural history. Here are not only the rocks, fossils and human history of Harting's past, but also all the birds and animals of the parish, even its slugs and snails, earwigs, frog-hoppers, cudworms, a migratory locust and the most extraordinary fungus, *Phallus impudicus*. There is a warning against eating rook pie made out of baby rooklings, swarming with parasites if taken from the nest 'while yet warm'. This is a book teeming with life, from the aristocracy high up on their hill above the village at Uppark, right down to the lowliest creatures in the depths of the parish. The story told is far from dry-as-dust as in so many Victorian parish histories.

THE HISTORY OF HARTING,

BY THE

REV. H. D. GORDON, M.A.,

*Rector and Vicar of the Parish;*

With a Chapter on the Geology of the District,

BY THE LATE

SIR RODERICK IMPEY MURCHISON, BART., F.G.S.,
ETC., ETC., ETC.,

AND SOME NOTICE OF ITS FAUNA AND FLORA,

BY J. WEAVER.

LONDON:
PRINTED FOR THE AUTHORS BY
W. DAVY & SON, 8, GILBERT STREET, W.
1877.

*Harting – the village street*

Henry Gordon was both rector and vicar of Harting from 1864 until his death in 1897, with a reputation as a strong pastoral clergyman who really got out amongst his people. He knew not only every inch of his parish, but everyone who lived there. Hence the ease by which he collected so many local stories. Once asked about his Harting flock, he replied: 'Most of them are nature's gentlemen. The rest are on their way to becoming so. The progress they make I regard as the best and severest test of my ministry.' Through his mother he was descended from an eminent eighteenth-century divine and prolific hymn-writer, Philip Doddridge. A close cousin was Richard Doddridge Blackmore of *Lorna Doone* fame, and through his wife Elizabeth's family, he was related to Thomas Arnold, the great reforming headmaster of Rugby, and his son, the poet Matthew Arnold. Elizabeth, an amateur artist, had been a pupil of John Ruskin. The world of the Gordons of Harting touched a rich seam of Victorian society.

*Henry Gordon married into an extraordinary family. His Buckland in-laws lived amongst skeletons, stuffed animals, fossils, and a huge and noisy menagerie – snakes, toads, frogs, hawks and owls. Examining some of their treasures are Professor and Mrs Buckland and, under the table, their young son, Frank, who in later life greatly influenced Gordon's wildlife studies around Harting.*

Like so many Victorian clergymen balancing their life as men of God with research, scholarship and the world of letters, Gordon had a keen interest in natural history, the landscape and antiquarian pursuits. He observed and investigated the local countryside, researched in libraries and amongst the parish records, wrote and lectured, notably on Harting's history and local bird life and migration. In 1886 he was contributing a column about birds to the *West Sussex Gazette*. He was elected a fellow of the Royal Historical Society and a vice-president of the influential Selborne Society, founded to save the life of rare birds and plants. And on top of all this he led his church congregation.

His most distinguished father-in-law, William Buckland, similarly embraced wide interests, both as a pioneer geologist and as one of the earliest researchers into dinosaurs – particularly the Megalosaurus – as well as later becoming a leading churchman: he was the first Professor of Geology at Oxford, and then Dean of Westminster, an extraordinary transition. So he found himself at the sharp-end of the great Victorian controversy, trying to equate the new science of geology with the Bible and creation – evidence for Noah's Great Flood he said could be found in a cave in North Yorkshire. A renowned eccentric with an inquisitive palate, he claimed to be eating his way through the animal kingdom. He once tried mice in batter and said that the most disagreeable creatures he ever tasted were mole and bluebottle! His son, Gordon's brother-in-law, Frank Buckland, was a noted nineteenth-century populariser of natural history – he has been called the David Bellamy of his day – and was a great influence on his studies. The rector/vicar of Harting, his life thus woven into a web of astonishing Victorian intellectuals, had extraordinary connections.

With all his own wide-ranging interests and contacts Gordon was a busy, happy man, much loved in the village of Harting. Two memorial windows in the church commemorate his life. His grave, under a memorial cross, surrounded by those of other members of his family, Gordons and Bucklands, is at the top of the church-yard bank by the western end of the church.

Gordon's wide-ranging researches closely parallel those of that great eighteenth-century parson-naturalist from just over the Hampshire border, Gilbert White of Selborne. Interestingly White had considerable lands in Harting which he frequently visited and from where he collected much data on the South Downs for his studies. So in his local investigations Harting's parson was treading in some famous footsteps. It was no mere coincidence that Gordon was a vice-president of the Selborne Society. What Walter S. Scott wrote of White could equally apply to Gordon: that he was 'a sort of localised Pan who knew every inch of his tiny kingdom'. Gilbert White and Henry Doddridge Gordon were indeed Selborne and Harting personified.

One particularly valuable part of Gordon's work was in the gathering of local traditions and stories told by his elderly parishioners – 'cottage tales' he called them.

*Victorian rustics – still going strong*

*Gordon's 'Sussex aboriginals' of the 1870s were still hale and hearty in the 1930s, the date of these photographs by George Garland. Jimmy Ifold aged 90 worked at West Lavant (above) and Jimmy Puttick with the hayfork, aged about 80, at Balls Cross, near Petworth.*

## COTTAGE TALES

An old man, aged 82, now living, gives the following graphic picture of a Harting labourer's work and fare at harvest time, at the end of the last century:– 'Out in morning at four o'clock. Mouthful of bread and cheese and pint of ale. Then off to the harvest field. Rippin and moën (reaping and mowing) till eight. Then morning brakfast and small beer. Brakfast – a piece of fat pork as thick as your hat (a broad-brimmed wideawake) is wide. Then work till ten o'clock: then a mouthful of bread and cheese and a pint of strong beer ('farnooner', *i.e.* forenooner, 'far-nooner's-lunch' we called it). Work till twelve. Then at dinner in the farm-house; sometimes a leg of mutton, sometimes a piece of ham and plum pudding. Then work till five: then a *nunch* and a quart of ale. Nunch was cheese, 'twas skimmed cheese though. Then work till sunset: then home and have supper and a pint of ale. I never knew a man drunk in the harvest field in my life. Could drink six quarts, and believe that a man might drink two gallons in a day. All of us were in the house (*i.e.*, the usual hired servants, and those specially engaged for the harvest): the yearly servants used to go with the monthly ones.

'There were two thrashers: and the head thrasher used always to go before the reapers. A man could cut according to the goodness of the job, half-an-acre a day. The terms of wages were £3 10s. to 50s. for the month.

'When the hay was in cock or the wheat in shock, then the Titheman come (came): you didn't dare take up a field without you let him know. If the Titheman didn't come at the time, you tithed yourself. He marked his sheaves with a bough or bush. You couldn't get over the Titheman. If you began at a hedge and made the tenth cock smaller than the rest, the Titheman might begin in the middle just where he liked. The Titheman at Harting, old John Blackmore, lived at Mundy's (South Harting Street). His grandson is blacksmith at Harting now. All the tithing was quiet. You didn't dare even set your eggs till the Titheman had been and ta'en his tithe. The usual day's work was from 7 to 5.'...

The Sussex swain is, however, not without certain talents of his own. His womankind have unusually quick powers of utterance, and he himself though but a trifle slower, is often a wonderful mimic; and thus his yarn is broken up into a constant parenthetical drama, very cleverly acted, while the nimble tongue casts off the historical appendages of, 'says he,' 'said I,' and the alteration of tone and gesture carries at once the speaker's personality. In this respect he has almost the vivacity and imitative powers of his neighbour the French peasant. On the other hand, one of the Teutonic elements is much wanting: he has very few proverbs, no native songs, such as the Celt delights in – absolutely no literature or trace of cultured conversation, and hence unusually few local traditions. He is a much-enduring, passive, easy-going, home-loving specimen of humanity; and if we consider the crowded hovels and wigwams that for centuries he has inhabited, and the constant intermarriage of which he is the result, it is a wonder that his nineteenth century appearance is so good as it is. Mr. Phillips told me that on his arrival at Harting some fifty years since, there were but six families in the place, so compact was the affinity, though the population was over 1,200. There are two views of the place, the outside one, 'never come near it': the inside, 'never leave it'. The truth is of course between the two; but it may be said that nine out of ten emigrants catch the Harting fever in their absence, and return. . . .

With regard to the black arts, local tradition still declares that hot flints were rained at East Harting House (now Mrs Luff's) in Squire Johnny Russell's time by a fortune-teller. This lady was discoursing to a servant girl about her destiny, when, being summarily ejected by the mistress, she in retaliation witched the girl, and broke all the windows by hot flints rained from the Downs.

Item, that old Mother Digby (*née* Mollen), who lived at a house in Hog's Lane, East Harting, had the power of witching herself into a hare, and was always, like Hecate, attended by dogs. Squire Russell of Tye Oak always lost his hare at the sink-hole of a drain near by the old lady's house. One day the dogs caught hold of the hare by its hind quarters, which escaped down the drain; and Squire Russell, instantly opening the old beldame's door, found her rubbing that identical part of her body in which the hound had seized the hare!. . .

The superstitions of the Sussex aboriginal have generally some sensible tendency. For instance, it is supposed to token death within a year to you if you gather apples from a tree that has a blossom upon it: the object here being to protect the unripe fruit from young hands. Also to bring May-blossom (white thorn) into the house is forbidden, the object again being to save the fruit for the coming winter for the birds, a lesson of humanity that may have come from the Monks. In like manner, if your plough turns up a mouse's nest, you must stop it, or be undone. The Humane Society would doubtless support this last superstition. Some years ago a man, grubbing a fence near Compton down, pulled up an ash stump that disclosed a nest of silver pieces of the time of Queen Elizabeth, no doubt hidden there in the time of civil war. He ran away in terror, for to find a treasure signifies that you belong to Mercury, the god of death as well as the god of luck in the old pagan creed. Recovering himself he told the cause of his fear to another, who at once accompanied him to the spot, and the two soon shared the spoil. The love of money is stronger than any superstition.

# 30 'Sleepy Hollow': Late-Victorian Chichester

*Dr Francis Pigou, Dean of Chichester, 1888–91*

Dr Francis Pigou spent three disagreeable years as Dean of Chichester between 1888 and 1891. There was so much of city and cathedral life he didn't like. Just how much comes out very strongly in his autobiographical *Phases of My Life*, first published in 1898. The dean's stinging barbs, so widely publicised – the book went through at least four editions in three years – must have animated many an after-dinner conversation in cathedral society.

Chichester was stagnant, restricted and drowsy. How much he agreed with his predecessor, Dean Burgon, who addressed his letters from 'The Deanery, Sleepy Hollow'!

Of French Huguenot descent, Pigou – his name rhymes with 'true' – was used to stimulating and lively company. Born in Baden-Baden in 1832, he was partly educated in Germany, and well travelled on the continent from his earliest years. In the ministry he served in Paris and then at the very heart of fashionable London in churches at Kensington and Regent Street where he said that his distinguished congregation was probably one of the most wealthy and influential in town. Prime Minister Gladstone, members of royalty, the royal household and a glittering cross-section of Victorian aristocracy made up his worshippers. He revelled in London life, its social gatherings, lectures, concerts and bookshops.

A noted preacher, Pigou was invited to speak in virtually every cathedral in the country, preached at least a dozen times before Queen Victoria at Windsor, as well as conducting parochial missions and religious retreats as far apart as New York, Italy and Germany.

When offered preferment as Bishop of Nassau, Pigou wisely decided to check on the climate, so one summer he had himself locked up in the tropical banana house at Kew. Emerging the worse for wear from the bananas he declined promotion.

Pigou then took off in a totally different direction to widen his ministerial experience. By invitation he became vicar of Doncaster and then later of Halifax. Whilst finding Yorkshiremen warm-hearted and hospitable, their bluntness was a great strain, as was the climate, so severe and harsh after the south. Halifax played havoc with Pigou's health and so after nearly twenty years in the industrial West Riding, the vicar readily accepted promotion as Dean of Chichester in 1888.

Hence his great relief in coming south to Chichester, and gratitude that the move saved his health. But the place lacked the stimulus and sharpness he craved for after years in much more challenging environments. 'I yearned for a fuller life and for more opportunity than Chichester afforded.' The place was 'a very by-word for torpor'.

And so Pigou's discomfort in Chichester led to a parting of the ways and resignation after just three years. He was offered the Deanery of Bristol where he once more thrived. The *West Sussex Gazette* (17 December 1891), reporting on his Bristol installation, noted his 'signs of vigour, physical and intellectual'. Clearly Chichester's dullness quickly wore

*Chichester Cathedral, late 19th century, according to Pigou 'a very by-word for torpor' (note the gravestones, long since removed)*

off as he was soon flourishing again. Pigou remained at Bristol for twenty-five years until his death in 1916. He said that the only thing he missed about Chichester was the Deanery garden.

But the dean did leave one enduring legacy here in his restoration of the cathedral cloisters – described as decaying and a discredit both to the cathedral and the diocese. Pigou oversaw the appeal for funds and the rebuilding, thereby ensuring their long-term survival. All who enjoy the peaceful walk through the Chichester cloisters today have Pigou to thank for their rescue a little over a century ago.

The following extracts from Pigou's autobiography are a good measure of his feelings for Chichester. One little story is included, told at Dean Burgon's expense. Certainly the solemn Burgon wasn't usually described quite like this!

The book is rich in this sort of clergy humour, putting it in a class apart from so many unreadable dry-as-dust Victorian memoirs. Pigou, a twinkle in his eye, offended many a stuffed-shirt in Chichester.

But before giving the Chichester paragraphs, here's just one Pigou anecdote of a death-bed scene where a bishop started to read from the scriptures. Whilst he was reading the man suddenly dived under the bed, brought out a cake and began to eat it. ' "What are you doing?" said the Bishop. "I came to see you, hearing you were dying." "Oh, I'm not dying," he said. "My old woman thinks I am dying, and she goes out to get funeral-cakes, and I eats them. . . . She thinks it be rats, when she finds them gone, as has taken 'em, *but I'm the rat*. Go on." '

## SLEEPY HOLLOW

SHORTLY AFTERWARDS we moved to Chichester. How great the contrast from the stir and busy life of a West Riding manufacturing centre to the quiet of a Cathedral city! The Cathedral is on the borders of the Diocese, and can never hope to be made the home and centre of the spiritual life of the Diocese. The fact, again, that there are no less than *nine* distinct parish churches and a Cathedral, to a population of about 10,000, sufficiently accounts for the confessed 'dead alive' condition of Chichester. This my two immediate predecessors, Dean Hook and Dean Burgon, keenly felt. I doubt if there is a city in England that can compare with the general drowsiness and sleepiness of Chichester. Dean Burgon is credited with having said that 'Half its citizens were fast asleep, and the other half walked on tiptoe so as not to awake them'. He dated some of his letters from 'Sleepy Hollow'. This was quoted to me by one of its citizens, who interviewed me, and asked me what I thought of Chichester. My reply was: 'Your motto should be, "as it was in the beginning, is now, and ever shall be, world without end".' What with its deep-rooted Conservatism, favoured by three or four great neighbouring landlords, the absence of the quickening influence or active rivalries of Non-conformity, the want of room or space for real Church life, and the soft air of Sussex, Chichester is a very by-word for torpor. Morning Service in the Cathedral, lasting from 10.30 to 1, is the most sleep-inducing I have ever had to attend. . . .

The City was much divided on the question of *drains versus cesspools*. Chichester in my time was honey-combed with cesspools, and there was much to be said in favour of them. The citizens used to speak of this as a local 'burning' question. I preferred, whenever I had occasion to allude to it, to call it an 'unsavoury' question. A large Meeting was held one evening to discuss the advantages of cesspools *versus* drains. The excitement was great, as both methods had their advocates. The excitement must have been great, inasmuch as a strong partisan had occasion to write to me after attending the Meeting – I have his envelope – 'The Very Rev. the Dean, the *Drainage*, Chichester.' Whenever the citizens complained of my absence, I produced this envelope, and said that if my house was to be the centre of all the drains of Chichester, I felt fully justified in frequent absence. . . .

*Left: The Deanery in the 1880s*

*Above: The Dean's study in the 1880s*

*Right: The way to the Deanery – Sleepy Hollow's Canon Lane in the 1880s*

*Lower House of Convocation,*
*Jerusalem Chamber,*
*Westminster, S.W.*

THE DEAN

THINKING ABOUT DODO.

*Dean Burgon's stiff exterior belied his warm-hearted impish humour, treating children as his playmates and decorating his letters to them with grotesque figures. He drew this cartoon for a little girl who lived in the Vicar's Close in Chichester, nicknamed 'Dodo' (because of her fascination with the dodos on the gateposts of Pallant House).*

It is generally allowed that Dean Burgon was out of his element as Dean of Chichester. The change must have been great from the life and intellectual atmosphere of Oxford to the quiet and stagnation of 'Sleepy Hollow'. There are many good stories about Burgon. He was devotedly fond of children. He went to pay a visit at one of the Scarsdale Villas, expecting to find some children there, his pockets filled with bonbons. These villas are, outwardly, precisely alike. It is said that a dog, let out in the morning, thoughtfully put a stone on the steps that he might know to which to return. Burgon was shown into the drawing-room, and enveloped himself in a tiger-skin which was used as a rug. Hearing footsteps, as the door opened, he roared like a tiger for its prey. A grave and aged couple entered, very much surprised to find the Dean of Chichester thus arrayed and thus behaving himself. He had mistaken the house. . . .

The soft air of Sussex has also its soothing and debilitating effect. But for all that there is a certain grace and charm about the 'City of Gardens', and though, from a ministerial point of view, it does not offer much opportunity, yet I owe Chichester a debt of gratitude which I never can pay. My general health was re-established; I gained an insight into Cathedral life of the 'Old Foundation' that was of great value to me. It brought me into contact with many throughout the diocese, whose friendship I cherish. It brought happiness to one of my dear children in her married life. It enlarged my experience. And so, Chichester Citizens, forgive me for saying anything you do not quite like, and think kindly of your quondam Dean, who thinks kindly of you. . . .

# 31 A Snob's Guide:
## Augustus Hare in Sussex

HAYWARDS HEATH WAS FULL of cockney villas, Petworth House overcrowded by the uninterested and uneducated, Selsey dreary and treeless and being eaten up by the sea, Worthing so ugly that visitors were advised to take excursions to get away from the place.

These were just a few of the biting asides by Augustus Hare (1834–1903) that give a bit of spirit to his guidebook *Sussex*, first published in 1894.

To collectors of old guides, Hare's books on England and Europe – and his multi-volume autobiography – are always so distinctive: uniformly presented in black cloth imprinted with four red horizontal lines from front to back, with gilt spine lettering. The Sussex volume bears the arms of the city of Chichester – inaccurately represented – against a castellated background, all blocked in gilt. If the gilt and red are still bright and clean then this is a distinguished looking addition to any bookshelf. But whatever its state the guide is a fascinating dip into late Victorian Sussex well worth seeking out.

According to his young protégé, Somerset Maugham,

*Augustus Hare in about 1858*

Augustus Hare was always deeply conscious of his roots. He was the last surviving representative of the Hares of Herstmonceux, a noted county family in their day, claiming descent from Edward I.

The family's position in Sussex was laid in the eighteenth century by Francis Hare as Bishop of Chichester between 1731 and 1740, and then by his son's acquisition of Herstmonceux Castle. One of the uncles of Augustus was Julius Hare, noted Cambridge academic and theologian, rector of Herstmonceux and Archdeacon of Lewes. It was through uncle Julius that the young Augustus met many of the leading intellectuals and writers of the day, people such as Matthew Arnold, Southey and Wordsworth. Another uncle – another Augustus – renowned for his eccentricity, might have been an inspiration for Lewis Carroll's mad March Hare. They were an extraordinarily odd family.

On his mother's side Augustus prided himself on his descent from the earls of Strathmore, a family link shared by Alice Liddell – the original *Alice* – giving another link with Lewis Carroll and his curious world.

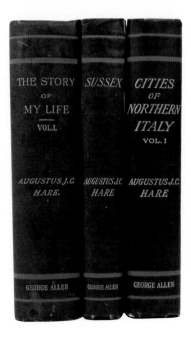

*Herstmonceux Castle, c.1909, once owned by the Hare family and now, sadly in the lifetime of Augustus, desolate and in decay, its 'mouldering walls . . . much overgrown with ivy' he wrote in his Sussex guidebook*

Well and interestingly connected he might have been, but this didn't save him from the most unimaginable suffering as a child. The spine-chilling story of his childhood seems unbelievable in its cruelty, a cruelty masquerading as religion and even more improbable than anything created by Dickens.

Born in Rome where his feckless parents were wintering – they moved restlessly throughout Europe in search of high society – they abandoned baby Augustus at seventeen months old into the keeping of his aunt Maria who assumed the role of adoptive mother. For her, a clergyman's widow, self sacrifice and deprivation were the only way to heaven for small boys. Comfort and pleasure led to ungodliness, virtue went hand-in-hand with suffering.

No toys, and no children other than cousins, were allowed to play. Aunt Maria would summon uncle Julius from his rectory next door with orders to flog the little boy with a horsewhip at her slightest whim. In his autobiography Augustus said that 'In the most literal sense, and in every other, I was "brought up at the point of the rod"'.

For his birthday he asked that a family from the village be invited to play and have tea 'but the mere request was not only refused, but so punished that I never dared to express a wish to play with any child again'. Aunt Maria invented a form of dietary torment. At mealtimes she and her friends would talk temptingly about the most delicious puddings, and then having set one on the table, ordered Augustus to remove it and take it to some poor person in the village. Next door, his aunt Esther, wife of uncle Julius, was even more savage. Anything that Augustus loved must be taken away. So that when she realised his love for Selma,

his pet cat, he had to hand her over. Selma was hanged from a tree, Augustus made to witness its quivering body. Aunt Esther was the 'Inquisition in person'.

Eventually sent away from Herstmonceux to several boarding schools where the deprivation and cruelty were not much better, Augustus contemplated suicide.

But he found escape and release in solitary walks,

*Augustus, the little schoolboy so cruelly treated by his family*

getting away into the countryside to discover old buildings and ruins. Their peace and tranquillity gave the young boy a respite from the terrors at home and school, their history an escape into distant realms. These were excursions that laid the foundations for his passion for travel and sightseeing that remained with him for the rest of his life. He started sketching the sights he saw. Thus were born interests that later flourished in his life's work as an artist and writer of guidebooks.

Despite all her cruelty, Augustus stuck to aunt Maria after finishing his education at Oxford. Her money gave him the freedom to travel, socialize and write. They both eventually left Herstmonceux when Maria bought a house just outside Hastings called Holmhurst which Augustus inherited and where he died, unmarried and the last of his line, in 1903. He was buried back in Herstmonceux.

*'Huz' and 'Buz', the two clipped yew trees standing guard at the entrance to Holmhurst, Augustus Hare's home at Hastings*

*In Herstmonceux churchyard overlooking the marshlands of the Pevensey Levels: the grave of Augustus Hare planted with a rare Zizyphus Spini Christi, more commonly found in Jordan. As a symbol of suffering – literally the 'thorn of Christ' in allusion to the crown of thorns at the crucifixion – this biblical thorn tree aptly memorialises the brutal upbringing of Hare as a young boy.*

Between 1856 and 1900 he wrote just over thirty books. A few were guides to some of the English counties and London, the majority on European cities and countries. There were biographies and his massive six-volume autobiography. All were immensely popular, his *Walks in Rome* going through twenty-two editions and still being published fifty years after its first appearance.

When invited to write his first guidebook, the publisher John Murray reminded Hare that it was to be a reference book of facts without personal opinions and sentiment. As he was at the start of his writing career, he had to obey. And after all he had been schooled in obedience from his earliest days. But thirty or so years later, and with another publisher, George Allen, Augustus could clearly indulge himself in freely expressing what he thought about parts of Sussex in his 1894 guide. As Somerset Maugham has said, he was an undoubted snob, and so we find him objecting to

Victorian villadom – hence his dislike of Haywards Heath – 'a colony of cockney villas' – and surges of uneducated tourists as they poured through Petworth House. His likes and dislikes come over very strongly, even in the index to the Sussex guide when it came to inns and hotels.

In the index he tells us that in Chichester the Dolphin was better than the Anchor (the two were not united until 1910), the Brambletye Castle inn at Forest Row was 'clean and good' and at Haywards Heath, his *bête noire*, all the inns were 'indiffererent, a better inn at Cuckfield'. The Tiger and Red Lion at Lindfield were 'very humble'. An extraordinary index from a consummate snob.

Here are some of Augustus Hare's comments about the county, some provocative, others chosen to give a sample of some of the more curious places he recommended on his local travels:

## SUSSEX IN 1894

### HAYWARDS HEATH

Here, till recently, was a wild heath with fine groups of fir trees. The land has been cut up and sold in small portions by the Sergisons, and is now a colony of cockney villas, and the roads both to Lindfield and Cuckfield are lined with lamps.

'a colony of cockney villas. . .'

### LOWER BEEDING

with a tall modern churchyard cross 'to the unknown dead'. At *Leonardslee* (Sir Edmund G. Loder, Bt.) kangaroos have been acclimatised and breed in the woods, and beavers have a lodge. There is a famous Alpine garden here.

### WORTH

*Crabbet Park* is a modern Georgian house, built from the admirable design of its mistress, Lady Anne Blunt, the African traveller and granddaughter of the poet Byron. The place has become celebrated for its breed of Arab horses and their sales. The owner of the house, Mr. Wilfrid Blunt, has insisted on a wild piece of land, covered with rubbish heaps and brushwood – 'the African desert' – being left in front of the house door, in curious contrast to the well-kept lawns and pleached alleys a little farther off.

Crabbet Park

## ST. LEONARD'S FOREST

takes its name from a chapel of the saint. It belonged to the great family of De Braose and the Dukes of Norfolk, who succeeded them, but reverting to the Crown, has for more than two hundred years been held by several owners. The principal avenue was called *Mike Mill's Race*, from a runner for a wager who fell dead there in the moment of victory; but this has been recently cut down, with many other of the finest trees. Many picturesque legends linger around the forest. Dr. Andrew Borde, writing in the XVI.c., says of the nightingale, 'The bird wyl syng round about the forest, but never within the precinct of the forest'. This is because they once disturbed the devotions of a forest hermit, who cursed them.

'Adders never stynge
Nor nightingales synge,'

is an old distich. If a man rides through the charmed precincts at night, a headless figure is apt to vault up behind him and accompany him to the limit of the forest: this figure is 'Squire Paulett'. St. Leonard himself fought in the recesses of the wood with a mighty dragon, and, though the saint was victorious in the end, the combat was terrible. Wherever the blood of St. Leonard, drawn by the monster, dropped upon the earth, masses of lilies of the valley sprung up, and are still to be seen in proof of the authenticity of the story. As late as 1614 an account of 'a strange monstrous serpent' haunting St. Leonard's Forest, was published by one John Trundle.

'There is always left in his track or path a glutinous and shine matter (as by a small similitude we may perceive in a snail's) which is very corrupt and offensive to the senses. The serpent is reputed to be 9 feete, or rather more, in length,

and shaped almost in the forme of an axeltree of a cart, a quantitie of thicknesse in the middest, and somewhat smaller at both ends. The former part, which he shootes forth as a necke, is supposed to be an elle long, with a white ring, as it were, of scales about it. There are likewise on either side of him discovered two greate bunches as big as a large foote-ball, and, as some think, will in time grow to wings; but God, I hope, will so defend the poor people in the neighbourhood that he shall be destroyed before he grow to fledge.'

## SUSSEX IN 1894

### COWFOLD

In the parish ... is the modern monastery of S. Hugh, Parkminster (1886), with a large church. All the thirty-six silent fathers have little houses of their own. The monastery was built upon the general expulsion of religious orders from France, and in the fear that the famous monastery of the Grande Chartreuse would be confiscated, its most precious relics were brought here, including a piece of the True Cross given by S. Louis, a bone of S. Peter, and a Veronica napkin, in splendid monstrances. The white-robed monks of Parkminster are a great feature of this country-side. They never eat meat, and observe rules of silence.

### WORTHING

Worthing rose, with Brighton, from a fishing village to a considerable town in the time of the Prince Regent. It is a very ugly, uninteresting place, with a relaxing climate; but pleasant excursions may be made from it. Worthing wheatears – 'the English ortolan' – are a well-known dainty, and are taken in great numbers on the Downs in rude traps excavated in the turf.

*'The white-robed monks . . . are a great feature of this country-side'*

COWFOLD. No 21.

*'a very ugly, uninteresting place . . .'*

New Parade, Worthing

They are so abundant that one man sometimes takes a hundred in a day...

Hence, by lanes, we may reach *Highdown Hill*, with a camp (300 ft. by 180) enclosing 'the Miller's Tomb', with verses composed by the eccentric John Oliver, who had a mill here, and erected his tomb thirty years before his death. He died 1793, and was carried to his grave by a procession of maidens in white, followed by all the surrounding country-side.

'Mr. Warter, the vicar of West Tarring, has testified to the prevalence among the peasantry thereabouts of such superstitions as the following:– Pills made of spiders' webs are prescribed by unqualified practitioners as a remedy for ague. Warts are charmed away by pronouncing a magic formula. Evil spirits are exorcised. It is believed that to cure a child afflicted with hernia you must pass it through a split sapling ash nine times before sunrise on the 20th of March, and, in the event of the tree's closing up, the patient will be healed; but should the tree dwindle, so will the life. Horse-shoes are nailed over doors to avert witches. On the occurrence of death in a household the bees belonging to it are 'waked' to prevent the same fate befalling them. "Funeral biscuits" are baked especially for those who visit the house on the day of interment.' – *Nineteenth Cent[ury]*, August 1884.

*Foxes-brewings*
*'a mist which rolls among the trees . . .'*

## COCKING

'A curious phenomenon is observable in this neighbourhood. From the leafy recesses of the layers of beech on the escarpments of the Downs, there rises in unsettled weather a mist which rolls among the trees like the smoke out of a chimney. This exhalation is called "Foxes-brewings", whatever that may mean, and if it tends westward towards Cocking, rain follows speedily. Hence the local proverb:–

> "When Foxes-brewings go to Cocking,
> Foxes-brewings come back dropping."'

*M.A. Lower*

## SELSEY

Day by day the land here is still continually carried away, and the small proprietors lie in their beds, and know that the storm which they hear is bearing their acres and their subsistence out to sea, no one attempting to save them.

*'the land here is still continually carried away . . .'*

It is a dreary, ugly road which leads across *the Manhood* (Manwode, Main-Wood) from Chichester to Selsey. . .

*Selsey on Sea* is a most dreary, treeless little place, with a very fine air, which causes its scattered lodging-houses to be frequented in summer. In fine weather the Isle of Wight is visible on the west.

## PETWORTH

. . . at a door in the street close to the church, visitors should apply to visit *Petworth House* (Lord Leconfield), which was built by Charles, Duke of Somerset, at the end of the XVII. c. Magnificently uninteresting in itself, it contains the most important private collection of pictures in the kingdom (above six hundred in number), and one of the finest collections of family portraits in the world. The statues, purchased through Gavin Hamilton for the third Earl of Egremont, are of no great merit.

The house is shown with great liberality (no fees being intended) at 11, 12, 2, and 3. Visitors are admitted in parties as the clock strikes, after which a very rapid walk through the rooms occupies exactly an hour. There is no time or possibility of examining or enjoying any special picture, but, with the crowds – chiefly uninterested and uneducated – who have to be herded along, no other system is possible. No casual visitor can carry away more than a confused jumble of beautiful impressions.

# 32 Chichester: 'as human as home and as lovely as heaven'

H E DIED OVER SIXTY YEARS AGO, but television still uses his work between programmes each day. Examples of his creativity can be found all over the country, covering buildings great and small. He was one of the major English artist-craftsmen not just of his own generation, but of the twentieth century, whose work persists as part of the backdrop of life today.

He honed his skills and gathered his influences from his boyhood and youth in Brighton, the town that repelled him with its urban, shapeless sprawl, and – in complete contrast – Chichester with its 'beauty having unity, proportion and clarity'. The city was 'a revelation' of how things should be in the civilised world.

His name was Eric Gill (1882–1940), sculptor, engraver, letter-cutter and designer of typefaces.

*Eric Gill, Self Portrait (1927)*

Number 2
North Walls

The BBC's corporate logo – three simple bold letters on three spaced building blocks – is from a printer's font called Gill Sans, one of the many alphabets Gill designed in the 1920s and '30s, still in use today with its timeless simplicity and directness. He produced lettering for the Army and Navy Stores, W.H. Smith and the London and North Eastern Railway as some of the earliest specimens of commercial house-styles in which he had such a formative influence.

In London, Gill's massive architectural sculptures adorn the BBC's Broadcasting House in Langham Place (Prospero and Ariel) and the Underground's offices above St James's Park station (the wind sculptures). More locally in West Sussex, at Harting, the Great War memorial in the church-yard is by Gill.

The youthful Eric Gill first came to Chichester in the late summer of 1897 when his father was studying at the Theological College.

Gill's family moved from Brighton to live at number 2 North Walls, part of a short terrace of houses demolished in 1963 for road widening near the end of West Street. Eleven children and two adults crowded into the tiny house, said to

*The Gill family home at 2 North Walls, photographed in the 1950s and since the 1960s the site of the Westgate roundabout. The position can be located by the partly- shown house on the extreme right – 8 North Walls – as this old south-facing wall of this rebuilt property is still recognisable today.*

'... that little squashy house ... was a distinct lowering of our standard of living. There was no bathroom; there were innumerable black beetles in the kitchen. There was no "tradesman's entrance". Our bedroom window looked onto the neighbour's backyard. The front door (which was also the back door) opened straight on to the pavement, and you went down two steps into the entrance passage ... Domestically, we were pretty well crowded in – but it was an improvement on 'Preston View' [in Brighton] and it was sufficient for me that we lived in Chichester.'

*Eric Gill in his Autobiography*

be not only rather inconvenient – putting it rather mildly – but unhygienic as well. The young Eric always said that he was haunted by the thought of big black beetles crawling all over their kitchen.

Although the Gill family only lived here for two years, it was the aesthetics of his surroundings rather than health at home that had such a profound effect on the fifteen-year old boy. Chichester's influence set the course for much of Eric Gill's life's work.

It was in Chichester where he first studied art – at the Technical and Art School in Crane Street where he was introduced to lettering that was to become such an important part of his life and work – and here he also gained his first awareness of the meaning and relationship of buildings. Some of his earliest architectural drawings were of Chichester views. What delighted him so much about the city was its small human scale, its tidy street layout centred on the Cross, all neatly enclosed within its ancient walls.

As Fiona MacCarthy has written: 'Chichester was so important to Eric … in teaching him something he had never comprehended in the shapeless and soulless sprawl of Brighton: that towns could in themselves have character and meaning. It was also to become a lasting symbol of perfection, the ideal of the good city, human, decorous, coherent. The vision of Chichester always remained central to Gill's passionate urge to achieve an integration of life and art and worship. . . .'

Although Gill moved from North Walls in June 1899 when his father became curate of St John's in Bognor, he continued his studies at the Art School in the city until he left the Bognor family home in April 1900 for London.

Here he was articled to W.D. Caröe, architect to the Ecclesiastical Commissioners in Whitehall. During this London period Gill took his first steps in stone carving by attending classes in masonry, and then met the calligrapher Edward Johnston who was to prove the greatest single influence on his artistic life.

*Chichester Doorways by Eric Gill: drawings submitted for a national competition by the young Gill in 1900*

Chichester.

F. BERG.

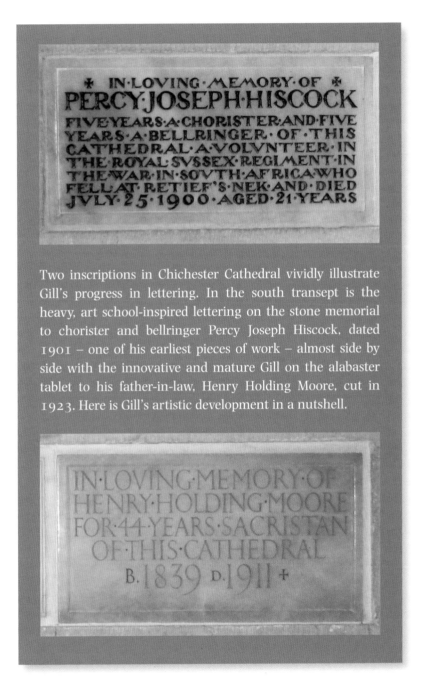

Two inscriptions in Chichester Cathedral vividly illustrate Gill's progress in lettering. In the south transept is the heavy, art school-inspired lettering on the stone memorial to chorister and bellringer Percy Joseph Hiscock, dated 1901 – one of his earliest pieces of work – almost side by side with the innovative and mature Gill on the alabaster tablet to his father-in-law, Henry Holding Moore, cut in 1923. Here is Gill's artistic development in a nutshell.

*Left: West Pallant, Chichester, by Eric Gill, 1900*

But although life was rapidly changing, Eric Gill never forgot Chichester and what it had meant to him. Even forty years later its memory inspired some of the most lyrical passages in his autobiography. Its beauty was not in its 'picturesqueness' but in its planning and order as 'the human city, the city of God, the place where life and work and things were all in one and all in harmony. . . . Here was something as human as home and as lovely as heaven.'

'Harmony' and 'Order' were Gill's two watchwords in understanding what it was that gave visual delight and pleasure in the Chichester streetscape of his day.

Gill wrote letters to the *Chichester Observer* in 1901 and 1903 about the proposed restoration of the city's Cross, pointing out the absurdity of trying to renovate in fake medieval masonry rather than do a good honest repair, pouring scorn on the idea of moving it either to Jubilee Park or into the cathedral precincts.

In 1904 he married Ethel Moore in the subdeanery church of St Peter in West Street. She was the daughter of the cathedral's head-verger. By 1907 he was considering a move back to the city, this time with Edward Johnston where they might set up a Chichester scriptorium. But instead he left London for the more rural life of Ditchling in East Sussex where he eventually gathered a community of craftsmen on Ditchling Common.

Chichester's crucial position in Gill's development is now reflected by its importance for research into his life and work as it is the home of the Eric Gill Collection in West Sussex Record Office in Orchard Street. Started by his widow and Walter Shewring, his literary executor, it includes an extensive collection of his published writings, engravings, drawings, some small sculptures, personal papers and even some of his working tools and equipment. Every Gill scholar must come to Chichester.

Eric Gill's short but influential stay in Chichester is now marked by a commemorative blue plaque unveiled in 1997 near the site of his old family home in North Walls. The plaque, sadly not in any Gill lettering, is on the brick wall on the north-east side of Westgate roundabout.

The following extracts, comparing Brighton with Chichester, are taken from Gill's autobiography, first published in 1940:

## BRIGHTON AND CHICHESTER – A SHAPELESS MESS ... AND ORDER

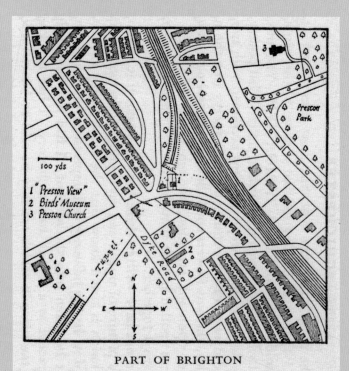

PART OF BRIGHTON

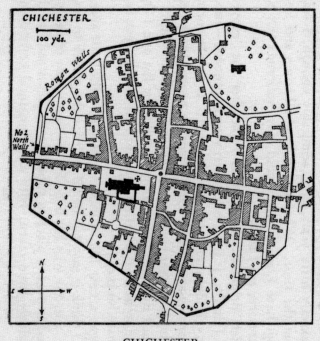

CHICHESTER

*Maps used by Eric Gill in his* Autobiography *to illustrate the plan of Chichester with its 'unity, proportion and clarity' and the contrasting speculative builders' 'shapeless mess' around the Brighton railway. Pinpointed is 1 'Preston View', the Gill family home near Preston Park before they moved to Chichester.*

AND, BY GOING TO CHICHESTER, I for the first time, saw Brighton. For, however little I put it in words or even into articulate thought at the time, suddenly – and indeed it was quite suddenly, for it happened all in one day – I saw Brighton for what it was – a shapeless mess. Perhaps if we had lived somewhere near the old Aquarium or in one of the superb Regency Squares by the West Pier or on the Marine Parade, I should have been able to think differently of my native town. There are many fine things about Brighton, many dignified old early Victorian houses and squares, and the almost majestic sweep of its long 'parade'. But we lived a long way from these things and we thought of Brighton only from the back and from our suburb above Preston. Brighton was not for me a Regency watering-place nestling in the junction of downland valleys; it was the Western Road and North Street, the Dyke Road and the Dyke Road Drive. It was Preston Park and the railway viaduct, the Seven Dials and the mass and mess of unplanned slums round Edward Street. All this will be pretty meaningless to the reader who knows not Brighton but that is all to the good, for it is its meaninglessness that I am wanting to convey to him.

I saw Brighton for what it was, and suddenly, almost directly I saw Chichester. It had simply never occurred to me before that day that towns could have a shape and be, like my beloved locomotives, things with character and meaning. If you had been drawing 'engines' for years and were then suddenly taken to such a city, you would instantly see what I mean. I had not been training myself to become an engineer, I had been training myself to see Chichester, the human city, the city of God, the place where life and work and things were all in one and all in harmony. That, without words, was how it seemed to me that day. It was not its picturesqueness; for Chichester is the least picturesque of cathedral cities. It wasn't its antiquity; for I had learned no history and age meant little to me. It was a town, a city, a thing planned and ordered – no mere congeries of more or less sordid streets, growing, like a fungus, wherever the network of railways and sidings and railway sheds would allow. That, I discovered, was mainly what Brighton was to me. A railway, with a sort of nondescript encampment crowding round it. For the railway from London to Brighton had been built in the days when the town was only the Regency watering-place. But since then the population had spread inland up all the valleys and the builders had perforce been obliged to get in where they could, in between the railway lines. And nineteenth-century speculative builders were not concerned with towns or cities, with plan and order, they were only concerned to build houses, as many and as quickly as possible. I did not know the economics of all this then; I only knew that Chichester was what Brighton was not, an end, a thing, a place, the product of reason and love. For love too was visible. Here was no dead product of mathematical calculation, no merely sanitary and convenient arrangement. Here was something as human as home and as lovely as heaven....

*Tower Street, Chichester, by Eric Gill, 1900*

Now began a new life, a miraculous life, a life as it were in fairyland. I think it may not be difficult for the reader to understand this. Anyone who has lived for the first ten or fifteen years of childhood in such a place as suburban Brighton and has then, almost suddenly been taken, with all the natural enthusiasm of childhood for green field and pastures new, to live in such a truly noble town as Chichester will understand; and I think even those who have not had such an experience will see that the contrast must have been almost frightening in its violence. For even if a Brighton suburb is not more than usually shapeless, not more shapeless than all such nineteenth-century towns are and must naturally be – for they are the product of nothing nobler than the speculative builder's appetite for money – on the other hand the 'ancient and loyal' city of Chichester is more than usually serene and orderly. And it owes its quality not merely to the civil and religious exuberance of the medieval world but, more fundamentally, to the military and civic order of Rome....

Though not at all mathematically symmetrical the plan of Chichester is clear and clean and rational – a thing of beauty having unity, proportion and clarity. The small modern growth of the town outside the walls was, forty years ago, almost negligible. Over more than half the length of the Roman wall (a great part of which is thick enough to form a broad footpath along the top) you could look straight out into the green fields. A town, a city, of ten thousand persons, with the Cathedral, the Bishop's and canons' houses, ten parish churches and twice as many 'public' houses – four straight, wide main streets dividing the city into nearly equal quarters and the residential south-eastern quarter similarly again divided by four small streets and these almost completely filled with seventeenth- and eighteenth-century houses – and all this almost immediately obvious and clear.

# 33 Pure Nostalgia: E.V. Lucas in Sussex

*Midhurst ... unmodernised and unambitious ... being on no great high road is nearly always quiet. Nothing ever hurries there. The people live their own lives, passing along their few narrow streets and the one broad one, under the projecting eaves of timbered houses, unrecking of London and the world. Sussex has no more contented town.*

THEN, BY DEVIOUS ZIGZAGS, we are led through 'the heart of an unpopulated country ... by way of one of the pleasantest and narrowest lanes that I know, rising and falling for miles through silent woods' eventually to reach feudal Petworth. 'The town seems to be beneath the shadow of its lord ... it is like Pompeii, with Vesuvius emitting glory far above ... Petworth must be the very home of low-pulsed peace.'

Moving us gently across the county, our guide throws in a rich store of anecdotes picked up on the way: of the lady sick with the mulygrubes (fits of ill-tempered grumbling); of Lord Thurlow who laid an egg; of the cunning 'peasants' and their furniture swindle, tempting the unwary into their cottages with their 'Ginger-beer sold Here' notices to sell fake antiques made old with artificial wormholes – 'the profession of wormholer, is now, I believe, recognised'.

This Sussex was such a world away from ours. It was the world of E.V. Lucas who shared his enthusiasms for the county in *Highways and Byways in Sussex*, first published in 1904, now a classic of Sussex writing.

His Sussex was quite different from ours today as there were so few motor cars on the road. None of the delicate pen and ink illustrations of roadside scenes by artist Frederick Griggs, drawn in the summer of 1903, gives a hint of these new-fangled machines. His picture of sheep

*Highways and Byways in Sussex*

BY E. V. LUCAS
WITH · ILLUSTRATIONS · BY
FREDERICK L. GRIGGS

London
MACMILLAN AND CO., LIMITED
NEW YORK : THE MACMILLAN COMPANY
1904
*All rights reserved*

*Almshouse at Petworth.*

*Petworth: 'the very home of low-pulsed peace' – Somerset Hospital in North Street*

across the main road at Pulborough suggests a scene long since gone. A drawing by Griggs was always such a nostalgic vision into the past, so happily matched with the mood of Lucas's text. Spotting a car in the early years of the new century was still enough to create a stir. So when off-the-beaten-track places were 'discovered' it wasn't by car. Going west from Cuckfield, Lucas was able to comment that 'Before the days of bicycles Bolney was practically unknown'. It was the cycle that liberated the countryside explorer.

When Lucas gives advice on how best to explore Sussex he lists all the options: by carriage, bicycle or on foot with just occasional assistance from the train. What he liked best about the train system was its single-line branches as they 'always mean thinly populated country'.

As much as he loved the quiet places of the county, he equally loved London with its theatres, clubland and good living. London eventually

*At Pulborough.*

*The road through the rocks*

gave him his living as a journalist, writer, film reviewer and publisher. It was the mix of lifestyles that he needed, the one energising the other. He was constantly flitting between his Sussex homes and London.

Edward Verrall Lucas (1868–1938), essayist, man of letters and publisher, was born into a Quaker family in Kent. Like many of their persuasion they were successful business-men who either banked or brewed. His parents moved to Brighton when he was a young boy. His

*E.V. Lucas*
*man of letters, essayist and publisher*

education was a mixed-up affair, nine schools in all, its most beneficial part being his own personal reading. Bitten by the book bug before he could even read, his boyhood saw books occupying every spare minute of his time. Writers became his gods and he yearned to write like the best of them. His dream world was literature and what he didn't want was a commercial career like his forebears.

But any hopes of pursuing a literary or classical education were soon dashed by his removal from school at sixteen, but at least the work was in a bookshop. He was sent to Brighton's best-known booksellers, Harry and Charles Treacher. Some of the mundane duties he hated intensely. Denied higher education himself, what galled him most was having to go up to Brighton College 'to see what new guides to knowledge the young barbarians were needing'. The young Edward was deeply envious of their public school lot.

*Rudgwick.*

*'with the most comfortable looking church-tower in Sussex'*

What cheered him most was that the bookshop had its own lending library with an enormous stock of books, many dating from the eighteenth century. He read voraciously. Then he started to write for the local newspapers. They didn't pay, but the most memorable moment of his life so far came when the *Globe*, a famous London evening paper, printed some of his verses on its front page, actually sending him a postal order for fifteen shillings (75p). 'Never can one know again such rapture as accompanies the opening of the envelope containing the first payment for literary work' he wrote in his reminiscences.

The young Lucas, the bookshop apprentice, was overwhelmed. Writing for a profit opened up new worlds. He left the shop for a regular salary from writing when he became a staff reporter on the *Sussex Daily News*. It wasn't exactly exciting stuff – police courts, inquests, flower shows and weddings – but he honed his skills, did a bit of book reviewing and learnt about deadlines.

Things got better when an uncle gave him £200 so that he could study, giving him the freedom to read English at University College, London. He was now twenty-four, and at last able to make up for a lost formal education. He sat at the feet of men of literature, freelanced for the press, explored London, haunted bookshops and widened his contacts in literary and journalistic circles. Everything now seemed to be opening up for him. As a regular contributor to the *Globe*, responsible for its 'Literary Gossip' column, he found himself at the very centre of the world he loved best. His friends were the literary giants of the day: James Barrie,

Arnold Bennett, Joseph Conrad, G.K. Chesterton, John Galsworthy, Rudyard Kipling, A.A. Milne. In his world he knew everyone that mattered.

Books and articles poured from his pen. There were nearly a hundred books in all: a major biography of Charles Lamb, novels, poetry, anthologies, volume after volume of essays, children's stories, books on art and travel. He contributed to *Punch*, and for the publishing house of Methuen he worked up from author to reader to chairman. As a major figure in the world of letters, Lucas was awarded honorary doctorates from Oxford and St Andrew's universities, and in 1932, the ultimate accolade, a Companion of Honour for his distinguished contribution to literature.

Ever since living in Brighton, he thought himself a Sussex man. For the rest of his life he kept a place in London, but was always drawn back to Sussex. So, once financially secure, he saw the fulfilment of his long-held dream in 1908, a solid Sussex home under the Downs.

This was Kingston Manor, three miles into the country from Lewes, 'a jumble of periods' according to his daughter Audrey: 'The back ... Queen Anne ... With a roof of

*Cottages at Slinfold.*

*'a little quiet village'*

*Bramber.*

*'a pleasant village, but when the dust flies it is good neither for man nor beast'*

Horsham stone; the front, white and very trim, suggesting occupation by one of Jane Austen's less wealthy characters'. Here he rode and walked, played at being squire – not too well received by the locals – and entertained the great and the good from the literary establishment.

He sold up in 1912 – we don't know why – and London became home for a bit. But forever hankering for Sussex, it wasn't long before he bought the old village school on Coates Common near Fittleworth, an odd choice as it was so small, just serving for weekends and holidays. Family and guests all slept and ate in the local pub at Fittleworth. It was the walking that was so attractive, a favourite excursion being 'to see the Emu' at Coates Castle 'whose purpose in life was to provide the local inhabitants with the necessary incentive for taking Sunday walks'.

Then, by the time war broke out in 1914, the family made their third and final Sussex move, this time to Tillington, to Tillington Cottage. Because of a sign just beyond the gate announcing a DANGEROUS CORNER, Lucas insisted on taking the warning as the name of the house and even had it printed on his notepaper.

Lucas's celebration of the county he loved was *Highways and Byways in Sussex*, so popular since it was first published in 1904 that it was reissued at least eight times in his lifetime. It was part of the *Highways and Byways* series published by Macmillan from 1897. The series – there are thirty-six volumes in all – has long been cherished and collected by lovers of the countryside. The text is always

accompanied by exquisitely-drawn pen and ink illustrations revealing an image of towns and villages as they were before the motor car had done its worst. Reading their pages is pure nostalgia.

By the 1930s the Sussex volume ranked among the three best-selling Sussex books. Whilst the book is largely a compilation of what others had already written before, Lucas's great contribution was in bringing them all together in one handy volume, 'made more readable by the genius of one who was a journalist and master anthologist', according to his publisher friend Arthur Beckett, founder of *The Sussex County Magazine*.

In *Highways and Byways* we are never far from the Downs. Between Midhurst and Chichester we climb to the heights, pausing for reflection:

*The Downs are the symbol of Sussex. The sea, the Weald, the heather hills of her great forest district, she shares with other counties, but the Downs are her own. Wiltshire, Berkshire, Kent and Hampshire, it is true, have also their turf-covered chalk hills, but the Sussex Downs are vaster, more remarkable, and more beautiful than these ... They are the smoothest things in England, gigantic, rotund, easy; the eye rests upon their gentle contours and is at peace.... There is a hypnotism of form: a rugged peak will alarm the mind where a billowy green undulation will lull it....*

*Chanctonbury Ring.*

*'the monarch of the range'*

*The Downs have a human and historic as well as scenic interest. On many of their highest points are the barrows or graves of our British ancestors, who, could they revisit the glimpses of the moon, would find little change, for these hills have been less interfered with than any district within twice the distance from London. The English dislike of climbing has saved them. They will probably be the last stronghold of the horse when petrol has ousted him from every other region.*

The Downs lead on to 'the most imposing town in Sussex', Arundel. 'I know of no town with so low a pulse as this precipitous little settlement under the shadow of Rome and the Duke. In spite of picnic parties in the park, in spite of anglers from London, in spite of the railway in the valley, Arundel is still medieval and curiously foreign. On a very hot day, as one climbs the hill to the cathedral, one might be in old France, and certainly in the Middle Ages.' (Curiously he refers to the cathedral years before it achieved this status.)

'The Barons of the Exchequer' in the castle keep, from an engraving of 1846

age in 1859.' They were such a feature of the castle that when Queen Victoria visited in 1846 the Duke organised 'A Conynge and Ryghte Solempne Masque' presented by a chorus of actors-turned-owls, led by the 'Owl called ye Chancellor' – that is, Lord Thurlow – dancing 'a stately pavan' and hooting their lines 'Who-whoop! whoo-whoo-here's a to do/ ... We're all eyes and ears/ In wonders and feares...'. Five of these Barons of the Exchequer, dead and stuffed, still perch around the castle today.

If you want a time-machine to go back a hundred years, then enjoy E.V. Lucas's *Highways and Byways in Sussex*. Its images, in words and drawings before the 'modern' age, make for an enchanting read, so evocative of times past.

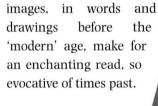

*Arundel.*

'one might be in old France'

*Exploring the countryside: Edwardian explorers needed a good road map to follow in the footsteps of E.V. Lucas's tours in* Highways and Byways in Sussex

Arundel is where Lord Thurlow lived, not with his lordship, but in the castle keep. He was actually an owl, an American Eagle Owl, known for its big ears – and female at that – one of several named after Barons of the Exchequer by the eleventh Duke. '"Please, your Grace, Lord Thurlow has laid an egg", is an historic speech handed down by tradition. Lord Thurlow, the owl in question, died at a great

# 34 The 'dream that comes to men in hell': Sussex and the Great War

AFTER FOUR YEARS AND THREE MONTHS the guns fell silent. It was the eleventh hour of the eleventh day of the eleventh month, eighty-five years ago next Tuesday: Armistice Day 1918. [This article was originally published a few days before the commemoration of Armistice Day, 2003.]

The agony of the Great War was at last all over and with it nearly one million British, colonial and dominion troops lay dead, wiping out almost an entire generation, exceeding all previous wars in the scale of its casualties.

They lie at rest in their serried ranks across the now silent battlefields – Mons, Ypres, the Somme and elsewhere – towered over by some of the most extraordinarily moving war memorials in the world. At Thiepval, Lutyens' massive multi-arched monument records the names of some seventy-three thousand men killed, but missing, with no known grave. Near Verdun, the Ossuary – or bonehouse – of Douaumont lies across the forested hilltop, a spectacular art deco cylinder of concrete holding the remains of some hundred and thirty thousand unknown soldiers.

These appalling statistics of death can be multiplied many times over in wartime cemeteries across the whole of the Western Front. They pepper the French and Belgian landscapes in their hundreds. There are very nearly six hundred military cemeteries in the Ypres Salient alone.

In Sussex there are pockets of soldiers' graves of the wounded who made it home to military hospitals, but who didn't survive their gruesome injuries. Over a thousand are concentrated in burial plots maintained by the Commonwealth War Graves Commission in East Sussex cemeteries at Bexhill, Brighton, Eastbourne, Hastings, Newhaven and Seaford.

In West Sussex the only concentration of Great War graves is in Chichester Cemetery at Portfield with around ninety burials: soldiers, sailors and airmen from regiments and bases all over the country, and from Scotland and Ireland as well as Australia and Canada, men who had been drafted back to Graylingwell War Hospital where they died of their wounds. Fifty-six of this number – mostly in their twenties, one aged just seventeen, another eighteen – are gathered together under a stark Portland stone cross, known as a war cross. Incorporating a sword and wreath of laurel, it is the work of Sir Reginald Blomfield, the architect who also designed the Menin Gate memorial at Ypres.

*First World War Cemetery, Chichester*
*Right: grave of a boy-soldier aged 17*
*Far right: the war cross*

Better known by far than these Sussex Great War graves are the county's parish war memorials on which Remembrance Sunday is focused. Restrained and simple in design they are in marked contrast to the elaborate theatricality of those across the Channel in French towns and villages. West Sussex's most unusual Great War memorial must surely be the magnificent lion with its pendulous tail guarding the road junction at Eastergate.

In its turn the Royal Sussex Regiment's call to arms took it a stage further by not only appealing to this same ideal of King and Country, but also working on local pride: 'Will you Come Forward Or must Recruits be obtained outside the County? We are confident you will help to uphold the honor of the County of Sussex.'

It was posters like this that led the campaign of persuasion, a medium of advertising that the Great War transformed into such a powerful propaganda tool. In a world without radio and television, and where newspapers were still the preserve of a literate minority, the poster was the big instrument of mass communication.

*Lion War Memorial, Eastergate*

The county's own regiment, the Royal Sussex, suffered heavy casualties in so many theatres of activity: just over seven thousand Sussex officers and men died. Most, but not all, of this number, are named on panels in the regimental chapel in Chichester Cathedral. Their stories can be pieced together from the regimental papers, personal letters and diaries now in the care of West Sussex Record Office.

The first urgent need at the beginning of the war in 1914 was to recruit on a massive scale. As Secretary for War, Lord Kitchener's first military decision was to appeal for a hundred thousand troops – 'Your King and Country Need YOU'. At this time all were volunteers. There was no conscription until 1916.

*Recruits outside the Drill Hall, Bognor, September 1914*

*Below: 'fifty commandeered horses were assembled in Waterloo Square'*

COMMANDEERING -HORSES -AT- BOGNOR. AUG '14

At first recruitment was brisk as men responded to the call. By 25 August, just three weeks after the declaration of war, the first hundred thousand had joined up. By the end of the following month the number stood at half-a-million. Volunteers poured into the recruiting centres. On one morning at Chichester Barracks an army of Shippam's paste workers joined forty men from the village of Boxgrove, many of them Goodwood Estate workers.

As well as manpower, there was a massive compulsory round-up of horses for pulling the guns and ammunition. Stables and farms were raided by War Office officials all around Chichester, and at Bognor, fifty commandeered horses were assembled in Waterloo Square. Drivers of vehicles were stopped and had their horses removed, with vehicles reported as 'standing about in the vicinity of the Pier minus the means of locomotion'. If the horse could stand it was taken.

As the war grew longer, the early euphoria for joining up lost its momentum, so more and more ways of persuasion had to be devised. Persuasion became intimidation. Posters were merciless in unsettling and disturbing those not facing up to their duty. One featured a post-war sitting room, with father being quizzed by his child – 'Daddy, what did YOU do in the Great War?' This was psychological warfare on the home front.

An open letter in the *Bognor Observer* was addressed to 'Bognor's Young Men', urging the local girls to 'Give the cold shoulder to all the men till they don the Khaki, and show what stuff they are made of '. The anonymous writer suggested that Bognor girls do what 'the girls of another watering-place are doing; band together and give a white feather to every able-bodied young man we meet'. (The watering-place was Folkestone where the Great War's white feather movement started.) One writer in the Midhurst parish magazine emphasised that 'there should be no one left in the town but old people, women and children'.

*Psychological warfare on the home front*

*Daddy, what did YOU do in the Great War?*

*Mud – that other enemy of the frontline: horse transport during the third battle of Ypres, 16 December 1917*

Once at the Front the troops dug themselves into their labyrynthine trench system to face the shells, gas and war's indescribable horrors. It was the beginning of the long nightmare, all too terrible to put into words and convey to loved ones back home. So a typical trench letter was light and cheerful, about the weather and quite everyday things. The art was to fill the page by saying nothing in the maximum number of clichés, a favourite being to say the writer was 'in the pink of condition, so please don't worry'.

One of the Royal Sussex's Great War VCs – there were four in all – was Company Sergeant-Major Nelson Carter. His letter home to his wife in Sussex is a perfect specimen of this unflappable formula:

*Just a few lines to let you know that I am in the pink of condition. . . . This is a lovely place. . . . I am getting as fat as a little pig & as happy as a little dog with two tails. . . .*

Another of his letters is of quite everyday matters, enquiring about the weather back home, what the weather was like at the Front, about letter writing and then 'Well Duck, I have a devil of a lot to do before we move off tonight so I suppose that I must draw to a close'. This was his last letter home before he went over the top for the last time.

One outstanding phenomenon of the Great War was its poetry. Every trench seems to have produced its own poet. There were the great names that personify the war itself – Sassoon, Owen, Blunden, Brooke – but behind their immortal lines are the verses of well over two thousand published poets alone, now nearly all forgotten, many never dignified by inclusion in the host of anthologies of war poetry that have regularly popularised the predictable few.

One of these unknown soldier-poets was 'Field Officer', the anonymous and unidentified Royal Sussex poet, author of *A Soldier's Sonnets*.

His beautifully constructed poem, 'A Soldier's Dream', is loaded with poignant contrast, captured sharply in the stark picture accompanying the poem: two symbols – peace and war – in juxtaposition. There is the soldier at war and the cosy cottage back at home; the idyllic and threatening; home and abroad linked by a dream in a lonely trench – the 'dream that comes to men in hell'.

A SOLDIER'S SONNETS.     41

## ❈ A Soldier's Dream. ❈

IT was a dream at midnight, when, in the lonely trench
I saw a vision, sweet with beauty rare,
And fragrant with the scent of summer's dawn.
Like dream that comes to men in hell
When parted from the light of radiant earth
They see the forms of those in life so dear,
Or hear the sighs of all who mourn.
A sun-kissed cottage nestling in a vale of peace
Where verdure cooled the torrid heat of day
And garden rich with nature's many charms
So near in dreams, in distance far away.
Roses and rue and jasmine's fragrant scent
With open windows breathing in the sun,
And lilies clad like seraphims in purity of white
Kissing with grace the scented stocks of night
And marguerites I saw, like children's innocence,
Bending their heads before a gentle zephyr's breeze.
Beyond the house an old and mossy orchard told
Where trees in root and wisdom knarled
Gave forth the fruits of earth that to my parched tongue
Were like the draughts of Tantalus of old
While all was peace, peace in stillness of the day
In English countryside far from hosts or crowded way,
'Tis twilight now, and lowering kine in meadow sweet
Have sought their quiet rest and ease, before the stars
Shed white effulgence on this radiant scene
Where all to God and Mother Nature yield
Their thankfulness of joy in rest serene
That knows no anguish of a blood-stained field.
I hear the birds in evening anthems sung to God,
Skylark and nightingale with notes that greet
The passing of the western sun when bathed in tender light
It hails the dawning of the Queen of night.
Inside the cottage shines so soft the evening lamp,
And near the smouldering embers is my Mother's chair.
My Mother! Has she visions too, of one so far away
Who dreams of peace but knows not fear?

# 35 Magical Landscapes: Eleanor Farjeon's Sussex

SUSSEX IS RICH IN MAGICAL LANDSCAPES where place, folklore and fairy tales together weave their powerful spells. It was Rudyard Kipling who told the world about the Sussex fairies around his home at Burwash in *Puck of Pook's Hill* (1906) and *Rewards and Fairies* (1910). Puck, 'the oldest Old Thing in England' – the last of the fairies – casts his spell through centuries of Sussex history in these two much-loved books.

And just as Puck is to East Sussex, so is Martin Pippin to West Sussex, another fantasy story-telling figure who brought both fame and fortune to his begetter, Eleanor Farjeon. She became one of the most prolific and most popular children's writers of her day. Through Martin Pippin and her other writings she added her own special brand of magic to the county's literary landscapes.

She loved all Sussex, but the part most particularly sweet to her was the Arun valley from Billingshurst down through the Wildbrooks to the top of the Downs. This is 'Eleanor Farjeon Country' – her own very special arcadia. In a letter to her lover, George Earle, in 1920 she described how she felt about the Downs above Amberley:

*I can't imagine why the Downs are always deserted, even on a day like this.... Perhaps they aren't deserted but have the power to make their lovers and wanderers invisible and so keep themselves to themselves. They are so much beyond human beings to me that I can almost not talk of it – I don't mean I love them more, and yet in a sense I think perhaps I do. Anyhow, I'm theirs, and if ever I vanish from the face of the earth it will be because they've drawn me in, and if you walk there any green hummock or shadow in a great round dimple in their sides, or tuft of thyme, or breath of the wind that is perpetual on them, might be me. They've healed me more, and given me more strength and certainty and peace, than any other living thing.*

*On Amberley Mount: Eleanor's 'deserted' Downs*

Eleanor Farjeon (1881–1965) was born with books and theatre in her blood, her father a successful novelist, her mother from an American acting family. She always said that her childhood with her three brothers was so happy with 'its tremendous imaginative stimulus from the actors and authors, painters and musicians who were our parents' friends ... Father told our Nursery Governess to teach us nothing that we didn't want to learn.' So she had no formal education, but instead devoured the mountains of books cramming their Hampstead home, eight thousand of them:

*In the home of my childhood there was a room we called 'The Little Bookroom'. True, every room in the house could have been called a bookroom. Our nurseries upstairs were full of books. Downstairs my father's study was full of them. They lined the dining-room walls, and overflowed into my mother's sitting-room, and up into the bedrooms. It would have been more natural to live without clothes than without books. As unnatural not to read as not to eat. ... That dusty bookroom ... opened magic casements for me. ...*

*Eleanor, aged 11*

Edward Ardizzone

*Eleanor 'devoured the mountains of books cramming their Hampstead home, eight thousand of them'*

And as soon as Eleanor could guide a pencil she was writing little poems and short stories, drawing on her fabulous store of book knowledge, Greek myths, Norse legends, fairy tales, Shakespeare and the Bible. She was just ten when her first article about her pet sparrow, Pop, was published in a magazine. For years, well into her twenties, she stayed at home in the retreat of her little attic room, reading and writing, with an awful lot of day-dreaming in between. She was nearly twenty-eight when her first book came out in 1908, *Pan-Worship and Other Poems*.

Getting this far had been a slow start, but the next fifty and more years of her life were to bring as yet unimagined success, with eighty books and nearly twenty musical works to her name. To her own bewildered amusement, Eleanor became one of the leading figures in children's literature, her books found in children's libraries all over the world.

If success in her own lifetime bewildered her, then her latter-day acclaim would have astonished her. Six years after her death in 1965, her hymn 'Morning has Broken', rocketed to stardom when pop singer Cat Stevens took it into the Top Twenty.

The book that first made her famous was *Martin Pippin in the Apple Orchard*, published in 1921, and now, over eighty years on, still in print. Six fairy tales are told by Martin, a wandering minstrel, to win the release of an imprisoned

*Down Mucky Lane, Houghton, where Eleanor lived and watched the children skip beneath her window*

*Eleanor outside The End Cottage, Mucky Lane*

maiden. The magic of these tales is woven against a Sussex background of real place-names and real landscapes.

Eleanor loved the sound of these little places hidden away in the Sussex countryside, places like Open Winkins, Pilley Green, Tegleaze, Gumber, High and Over, Poverty Bottom, Smock Alley. Searching maps and exploring lanes and byways she found a rich store of real-life names, conjuring up romantic visions for her playful imagination. They were a magic carpet into a mysterious past.

She took special delight in the little village called Adversane, such an intriguing name in which to enfold Martin's adventures in the sunny orchard where 'the blossom blows for happiness on the apple-trees'. It's here, in this ancient place astride the old Roman road, that Martin's tales open and close, 'the prettiest hamlet I ever had the luck to light on in my wanderings'.

She knew the place well, for just over a mile across the fields lived her writer brother, Joe, and his family, with whom she and her mother lodged for safety during the Great War, escaping the Zeppelins over London. Their refuge was Joe's Gillmans Cottage on the edge of Billingshurst. Today there's no property bearing this exact name, just Great Gillmans and Little Gillmans, but according to Wendy Lines, Billingshurst's local historian,

the cottage is almost certainly the old weatherboarded farmhouse in the fields called Great Gillmans. Here, in sheer delight, Eleanor wrote of how farmer Gillman and his six milkmaids were foiled by the silver-tongued Martin Pippin.

Eleanor's mother eventually went back to Hampstead, Eleanor staying in Sussex. Now, well into her thirties, she had found a place of her own: a tiny two-up, two-down thatched home by the Arun at Houghton. It was the first place of her own and although she was only here for two years, she felt that these may have been the most important of her life.

The cottage was along a deeply-rutted cart track leading down to the river, then appropriately known as Mucky Lane, now called South Lane. Annabel Farjeon, writing the biography of her aunt, *Morning has Broken*, said that 'As a child she had feared almost everything: death, illness ... ghosts...'. Now she taught herself to be alone. '... she walked the downs at all hours of the day or night ... and here she wrote and went to bed leaving doors and windows open. It seemed to her an almost perfect way of living, filled with natural and necessary things, like collecting wood and fir cones, picking flowers and mushrooms from the fields, watching the seasons change, learning to grow vegetables, and above all learning to lose fear.'

Whilst learning to be fearless in the lonely little riverside cottage, she was finishing the Martin Pippin book and storing away more colourful memories and ideas for its sequel, *Martin Pippin in the Daisy Field*, published years later in 1937.

Dedicated 'To the children of Sussex who skipped in my lane', Martin tells six more fairy tales, again steeped in a Sussex background, this time bedtime stories for six little girls playing in a daisy field: 'It spread to the far foot of the Downs, like a green tablecloth full of crumbs ... Overhead the sky was going green, and the stars were making pin-pricks where the green was deepest, and the moon a yellow hole where it was palest, along the shoulder of Rackham Hill, and the dome of Amberley Mount.'

*The Arun valley under the dome of Amberley Mount – where the daisy field ended – Eleanor's own very special arcadia*

Apart from the adventures of Selsey Bill who sailed to the Spanish Main from Worthing City, all the other stories are deeply embedded in the Sussex landscape. Two were directly inspired by her time at Houghton.

'Elsie Piddock Skips in Her Sleep' came out of Eleanor's huge delight in watching Houghton children skipping along the lane and singing old rhymes handed down for generations. One old lady of eighty, reminiscing in the 1960s, remembered Eleanor joining in with the children in these far-off days: 'She didn't walk, she danced down the lane, and all the children danced after her'. The best skipper of all was Elsie Puttick whom Eleanor slightly re-named and by magical geography made Houghton into the village of Glynde which stands under the hill called Caburn, near Lewes. No mortal or fairy could touch her at skipping as she saved Mount Caburn from its greedy landlord. The real Elsie was still living in Amberley in the 1960s.

'Tom Cobble and Ooney' was firmly set in and around Houghton – called 'Southways' in the story – and the Duke of Norfolk's park on the edge of which Tom lived in one of the lodges. The three caves where Ooney lived were the three old lime-kilns where the real Elsie Puttick used to play. The little shop selling

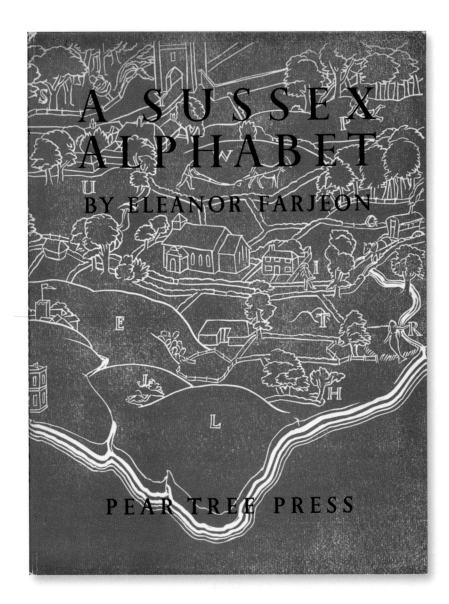

brandy balls once really existed in the now shopless Houghton. So fantasy and reality were thus intermingled, as though the fantastic might even be true.

Magical kingdoms are all about confusing the senses, so when Martin Pippin exhausts his tales to the little girls in the daisy field, he adds yet more confusion with his mixed-up time, when 'in the future the present will be the past'.

The book prized by Farjeon collectors is also a most prized Sussex item, as well as being from a private press whose work is eagerly sought by connoisseurs of fine printing. This is Eleanor's *A Sussex Alphabet*, limited to just two hundred and twenty copies on hand-made paper. Printed by James Guthrie's Pear Tree Press at Flansham, near Bognor, in 1939, it was originally published in *Tunes of a Penny Piper* in 1922, but in this edition with only one illustration, and bears no comparison with the striking map cover and crisply printed lino-cuts of the 1930s made by Sheila Thompson of Middleton-on-Sea, who acted as Guthrie's assistant at the press.

Another Farjeon/Sussex gem also came from the Guthrie family, Eleanor's very first little collection of Sussex verse – *All the Way to Alfriston* – illustrated and printed by James Guthrie's sixteen-year-old son, Robin and published by his very own Greenleaf Press in 1918. Eleanor never understood why he drew her 'as a sort of H.G. Wellsian tramp in check knickerbockers'. His somewhat naïve drawings and the floral wallpaper in which he covered each copy give considerable charm to this celebration of Eleanor's adopted county:

*All the way to Alfriston,*
*From Chichester to Alfriston,*
*I went along the running Downs*
*High above the patchwork plain. . . .*

Walking across the Downs was pure joy to Eleanor. One day she set off for Chichester with D.H. Lawrence. They started early 'in one of those white Sussex mists which muffle the meadows before sunrise ... The low-lying sun began to melt the mists as we climbed, unpacking the world from its lamb's-wool.' Eleanor strode ahead, Lawrence lagging behind. 'I must teach you to walk like a tramp', he said. They breasted the steep slope of the Downs, Lawrence in child-like mood admiring her green silk mackintosh on which they lolled every two miles. They sang snatches of songs and Lawrence cried 'We must be springlike!', sticking green leaves into their hats. Somewhere near Eartham they got lost, Lawrence cursing civilisation when he suddenly saw East Dean down in the valley.

Just like her books, so Eleanor's life was packed with fun and zest. She first met Lawrence when he was staying at Greatham, near Pulborough. Here Humphrey's Homestead was a vibrant literary colony as much as a home to writers Alice and Wilfrid Meynell. Sir Shane Leslie, who knew the place well, spoke of the Greatham Group in much the same breath as the Bloomsbury Group, for here, gathered for lazy summer weekends of charades, croquet and cricket, were

*Humphrey's Homestead at Greatham, the seventeeth-century farmhouse where Eleanor first met D.H. Lawrence in 1915*

key writers of the day, people like Edward Thomas – with whom Eleanor had a very special relationship – Wilfrid Blunt, Francis Thompson, Bertrand Russell and others. Lawrence took it all in and made it the inspiration for his *England, My England*, and it was here, in a converted cowshed they all called Shed Hall, where he completed his controversial – and banned – novel *The Rainbow* and where Eleanor helped type up the manuscript for publication.

These were exhilarating days full of energy and excitement for Eleanor. Her stories kept her young and kept her going into a good old age. As her niece Annabel has written: 'She never gave up wanting life to be a glorious feast of love and enjoyment'.

*Shed Hall at Humphrey's Homestead, where D.H. Lawrence completed* The Rainbow. *Long and narrow, he said it was 'like the refectory of a little monastery'.*

# 36 Mr Punch in Sussex: Humour from the Sussex Countryside

SUSSEX HAS LONG ATTRACTED an extraordinary range of creative talent, its writers, artists and musicians a roll-call of many of the most outstanding and influential people in their field.

So what did Malcolm Muggeridge (Robertsbridge), E.H. Shepard (Lodsworth), A.A.Milne (Hartfield), Basil Boothroyd (Cuckfield), E.V. Lucas (Brighton), Rowland Emett (Henfield and Ditchling), A.A. Willis (Harting), Mark Lemon (Crawley) and E.V. Knox (Balcombe) all have in common?

The answer is that they were either writers, illustrators, or editors of that great British institution, the humorous magazine *Punch*, born 1841, died 1992. It was always a great favourite in doctors' and dentists' waiting rooms.

There was Emett who made a weird and wonderful world of derelict railways and crazy machinery, like the Far Tottering and Oyster Creek Railway and who designed comic machines for the film *Chitty Chitty Bang Bang*. Willis, better known by his pen name, Anthony Armstrong, won the war in the air with his Pilot Officer Prune, the RAF's legendary World War Two dimwit. The hero of official aircrew training manuals, Prune demonstrated how *not* to do it, in a bizarre and yet effective teaching twist. 'A.A.', as

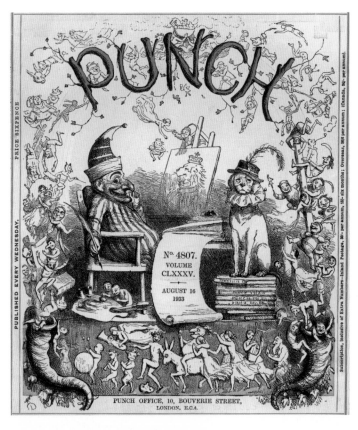

*A great British institution: the once-famous* Punch *cover, first designed in 1849 and still going strong in 1933 – a patriotic symbol is on the artist's easel: the smug-looking crowned lion*

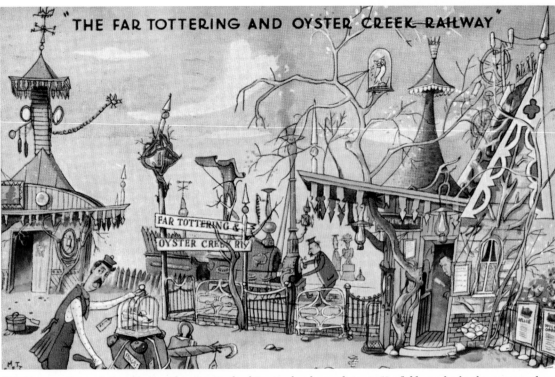

*This bizarre railway, designed by* Punch *artist Rowland Emett when he was living in Henfield, was by far the most popular attraction of the 1951 Festival of Britain Pleasure Gardens in Battersea Park*

Punch Cartoon Library

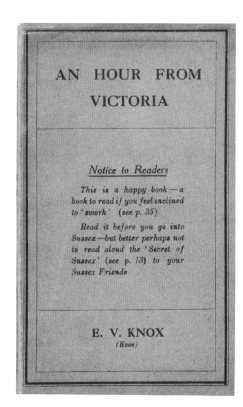

*Dull cover – enticing invitation . . .*

*E.V. Knox – 'Evoe' – editor of* Punch *1932-49*

he was known to *Punch* readers, also wrote a delightful quintet of books (published 1936–53) about West Sussex country life around his Harting home. Then there was Milne's and Shepard's world of Winnie-the-Pooh and friends in Ashdown Forest. *Punch's* trail of Sussex connections is full of endless delight.

The Sussex book featured here was written by former *Punch* contributor, and later its editor, E.V. Knox. In 1924 he put together a little book called *An Hour from Victoria* as a light-hearted dig at Sussex country ways. To Knox there was a joke in every situation and it wasn't too difficult to find a real Sussex native for some gentle fun.

Edmund Valpy Knox (1881–1971) was the eldest of a remarkable foursome of brothers, the sons of the Bishop of Manchester. All were brilliant, scholarly and quick-witted.

Dillwyn was a classicist and later cryptographer who worked on cracking the German Enigma code at Bletchley

Park; Wilfred, a theologian and mystic; Ronald, a man of many parts: Roman Catholic priest, translator of the New Testament (the 'Knox Version', 1945), as well as a writer of detective fiction and a newspaper columnist, dubbed by the *Daily Mail* in 1924 as 'the wittiest young man' in England.

Their brother Edmund, a classical scholar at Oxford, first went into schoolmastering, but as his daughter, the writer Penelope Fitzgerald, remarked 'he wanted to write, and suffered, as generations of authors have done, at the stuffy and inky boredom of the classroom'. After a number of attempts, some of his verses were accepted by *Punch* in 1905, the beginning of his lifetime's association with the magazine. For years he freelanced, writing under the pen name 'Evoe', winning the ultimate accolade in 1932 when appointed its editor. He reigned for seventeen years, bringing fresh flair and vigour to the somewhat stultifying atmosphere of his predecessor. His gifts revitalised the ageing periodical he steered safely through the difficult years of the war. Under his editorship some of the best work it ever published appeared in its pages.

Evoe's *An Hour from Victoria* was one of the fruits of his few brief years living in Sussex in the early 1920s. He left London wanting a place in the country, yet within a train's ride of the office, a place where his family could keep hens, grow vegetables and put up a swing for the children. They found Balcombe, on the main London line, settling at Trent House overlooking the village school and little green.

*Trent House, Evoe's family home in Balcombe, the village he called 'Bittleigh'*

*'In the 1920s and '30s . . . there was a new freedom in the air . . . people going in search of old places and old ways . . . .'*

The book is mainly made up of little conversation pieces about village and country life in and around Balcombe. Most had previously appeared in *Punch*.

Balcombe is disguised as 'Bittleigh'. The daily goings on here, and in the Sussex countryside, are glossed with Evoe's gentle humour. His gifts were in parody and caricature – enlarging the ordinary and everyday into something special and noteworthy.

'The Secret of Sussex' is a perfect specimen of Evoe's style of parody. He investigates what a real Sussex local thinks about the beauty of his own county.

In the 1920s and '30s there was a lot of interest in holding a magnifying glass to what was going on in the countryside. The war was over, there was a new freedom in the air – exploring by car, rambling, camping, picnics, people going in search of old places and old ways, looking for a return to nature and a lost arcady. The Society of Sussex Downsmen (planning open-air dancing and old-fashioned suppers in Sussex inns), *The Sussex County Magazine* (celebrating the history and heritage of the county), the Youth Hostels Association and the Ramblers Association, were all founded in these liberating days.

Similarly, the contemporary rural novel expressed this passionate interest in life in the countryside. Sheila Kaye-Smith's many novels embody this passion within a deeply-felt Sussex background. Then, with Kaye-Smith partly in mind, Stella Gibbons mocked this type of writing in her classic *Cold Comfort Farm* (1932), partly written in Sussex, at Alfriston.

The intensity of this gusto for rural backwaters was also the subject of many jokes by *Punch* cartoonists, neatly illustrated by the send-up of the motor tourist and the oldest inhabitant, and the patronising stranger coming across an 'ancient relic' of a farm labourer out in the fields. What was happening out in the country gave rich pickings to artists and writers.

TOURIST. "Well, I must be off to the next village."
YOKEL. "Will 'ee take Oi in the car? I be oldest in'abitant there too."

PATRONISING STRANGER. "Nothing ever changes, I suppose, in this out-of-the-way place?"
ANCIENT RELIC. "Oh, don't it? These 'ills bain't what they wos when I first started shiftin' of 'em."

*'this gusto for rural backwaters'* – Punch *sends-up the craze for country life*

Unlike Bittleigh, the place Evoe called 'Twitteringly' – featured in the following lines – can't be positively identified, but is possibly Ardingly. The choice of the jokey place name ending in 'ly' is quite deliberate as a way of sorting locals from 'vurriners'. Like 'Ardingly', it's pronounced to rhyme with 'lie', not 'lea'.

## THE SECRET OF SUSSEX

'But what I want to do is to get right to the heart of this Sussex charm, to pierce its secret to the core. I suppose you know every inch of your native shire?'

'Pretty nearly,' he agreed.

'Then can you tell me,' I asked him, whispering so that the other Sussex men might not hear, 'the remotest and quietest spot in it, some place where the natives stay in Sussex all the week round. I want to know how this beauty appeals to men like that.'

'Ah,' he said, 'you ought to go to Twitteringly.' And he told me where Twitteringly lay, buried and forgotten in a tiny nook between the Downs and the Weald. . . .

When we reached Twitteringly after a rather complicated journey . . . we found it to be a small, silent and straggling village with a tiny church. The place was as quiet as the grave. It seemed difficult to believe that any stranger had visited it since the Jutes.

There was a little inn, and on one of several benches outside it, under a large fig-tree, was seated a very old man in corduroys. I hastily finished the list of quotations I had been making in my note-book, and we left the car. Sitting down on a bench near him, we called for beer. When it came, I addressed the old man.

'I want to ask you a few questions,' I said.

'First of all, have you been a Sussex man all your life?'

It appeared that the old man was very deaf. When the question had been repeated three times, and each time in a louder voice, he slowly nodded his head.

'Ah,' I said, opening my note-book, "then you are the man I am looking for. Have you ever walked in the high woods with the men who were boys when you were a boy, walking along with you?'

We shouted this also three times, very loudly, but the old man made no reply.

'I will try something else,' I said to my friend.

'What do you think,' I bellowed in stentorian tones, making a funnel with my two hands, 'of the wooded, dim, blue goodness of the Weald?'

But there was still no response.

'Have you ever found,' I began again, my voice now breaking and going off into a shriek, ' "peace upon your pasture-lands

Where grazing flocks drift on continually
As little clouds that travel with no sound
Across a windless sky?"'

The old man remained as silent as a little cloud.

'But has not Sussex,' I wailed, in a last despairing agony, '"ever cried to you from primrose lags and brakes:

Why do you leave my woods untrod so long?"'
Apparently she had not.

'Look here, my dear old friend,' I said huskily, 'you have lived all your life amongst these glorious scenes, in this wealth of beauty, gazing at your Downs, your sea, your Weald, and they seem to awaken no responsive echo in your heart. Tell me at least what you think of your own native home of Twitteringly, Twitteringly, Twitteringly.' On the last 'ly' my voice reached its highest register.

A faint gleam now shone in the old man's dim, blue eyes, a glint as it were of that laughter which I am assured that Sussex men get from the loud surf, and of the faith that comes to them from their sister the Spring; and he spoke:

'Be a tar'ble pleace vur vurriners, Twitteringly,' he said.

I turned to my friend.

'I think we will go now,' I told him. 'All the same, I have formed a great resolution. I am going to live in Sussex, and be a Sussex man.'

'Are you going to live at Twitteringly?'

'As near to it as I can,' I said.

'And what are you going to do?'

'I shall write,' I said, 'a book.'

Two months later I had taken a house at Bittleigh. It lies much nearer the main road than Twitteringly, and the big motor-cars hum through it all day long. But it is quite a little village, and full of Sussex men.

# 37 'Great arterial roads very broad and straight': The London – Brighton Motorway

THE COUNTRY'S FIRST PAY-AS-YOU-GO motorway – the twenty-seven-mile M6 Toll around Birmingham – is due to open within the next year. [Written in 2003.] On the continent motorists have been paying to use motorways there for years, but what might seem a new idea for Britain could well have come to fruition years ago, with major repercussions for Sussex.

For the new M6 is not the first toll motorway to have been planned for England.

Two abortive attempts were made to build a London-Brighton Motorway, one as early as 1906, the other in 1928. This would have been Britain's first motorway, putting Sussex and Surrey well to the fore in road modernisation. But it was left to the rest of Europe to pioneer motorway development.

The very first European motorway designed for the exclusive use of motor traffic, with controlled access, a central reservation between carriageways, and ferro-concrete flyovers, was the Avus Autobahn in Berlin, some six miles long and opened in 1921. A decade later Hitler made the autobahn network a major priority, so that Germany had a total of over two thousand miles of these new super highways by 1939. The Italians started their programme under Mussolini with the Milan – Varese Autostrada in 1924, the first inter-urban motorway.

So Britain was well behind when its own first motorway was opened to traffic in December 1958. This was the eight-mile section of the M6 in Lancashire, the Preston Bypass. At its opening, Prime Minister Harold Macmillan promised it as 'a token of what was to follow, the symbol of a new era of motor travel'. Then the following year, in November 1959, the southern section of the M1 was opened. Its novelty caused a sensation, with weekend sightseers picnicking on the approaches.

But although we were late in the field, it was in England that motorways were first seriously advocated in the very earliest days of motoring.

As early as 1900 the Treasury urged the need for 'great highways constructed for rapid motor traffic and *confined* to motor traffic'. Agitation from the newly-founded Road Improvement Association sparked heated discussion on 'trunk thoroughfares' against a background of alarming statistics. In 1904 there were some seventeen thousand private and commercial vehicles in use. By 1910 this stood at just over a hundred thousand, a six-fold increase in as many years. By 1930 this shot up to one-and-a-half million and then almost doubled again by 1939. Even then the road traffic problem seemed to be spiralling out of control with dire consequences: accidents, congestion and stress.

PLAYER'S CIGARETTES

WOLSELEY 25 SUPER SIX SALOON

*Popular cars seen on British roads in the 1930s when car ownership doubled*

*Price £340*

PLAYER'S CIGARETTES

STANDARD 12 SALOON

*Price £229*

PLAYER'S CIGARETTES

AUSTIN SEVEN RUBY SALOON

*Price £125*

## ROAD SAFETY

Bumper to bumper: the perils of driving in the Sussex countryside: right, on the A29 near Slinfold in the late 1920s; and below, a Whit-Monday traffic jam in Crawley High Street in 1930. Croydon, Redhill and Crawley were notorious bottle-necks on the road to the Brighton seaside.

Motorways were not the only answer to the problems of motor traffic increasing at an alarming rate. In 1931 the Ministry of Transport launched its first *Highway Code*. In his foreword to the second edition, Leslie Hore-Belisha, Minister of Transport from 1934 – and best remembered for his introduction of pedestrian crossings with their 'Belisha Beacons' and the compulsory driving test – emphasised that its provisions were 'to prevent that kind of mistake or thoughtless action which may result in some one's bereavement or suffering.... Respect for the Code and for the spirit underlying it is so much a moral duty that its practice should become a habit and its breach a reproach.'

The new Code warned of the effect of alcohol and fatigue, gave just ten traffic signs and several pages of hand signals to be given by drivers of cars and horse-drawn vehicles and cyclists – hand signals were an essential part of the new driving test.

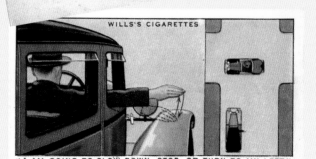

*The Minister of Transport commended Wills for its cigarette cards first issued in 1934 to reinforce* The Highway Code *– 'the traveller's code of honour'*

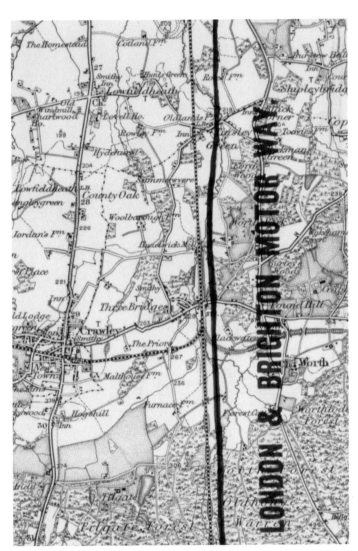

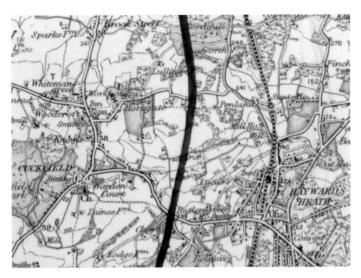

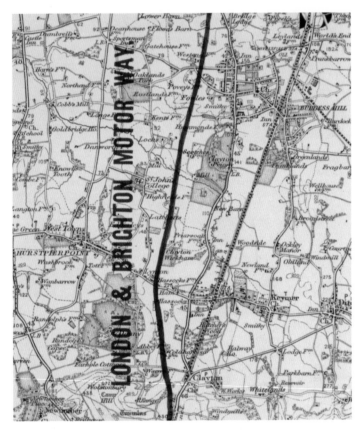

*Communities divided – cutting a swathe through the Sussex countryside:*
*Sussex sections of the proposed London to Brighton Motorway of 1906 –*
*to be Britain's first motorway*

It is against this background that the road lobby agitated as early as 1906 with a private bill promoted in Parliament as the London and Brighton Motor Way Bill for the construction of a forty-mile route. It was to start from the west of Croydon, aim to the east of Merstham and Redhill and thence into what was then East (now West) Sussex, through Worth and Balcombe and then, heading southwards again, driving a wedge between towns and villages on its route – a ribbon of fast and noisy motorway between Three Bridges and Pound Hill, Haywards Heath and Cuckfield, Burgess Hill and its westernmost parts, then Hassocks and Hurstpierpoint. The terminus was to be at Patcham, just short of Brighton and the coast. It was to be a dual carriageway – 'a special road for automobiles' – from which all animal-drawn vehicles and foot passengers were to be excluded. Tolls were to be paid, as with the earlier turnpikes. Existing roads and railway lines were to be crossed either over or under the motorway by fifty-three new bridges. Opposition there was in plenty, its major opponents from the landed interest whose estates were to be cut up, with big names like Sir Weetman Pearson – later Viscount Cowdray – who had extensive estates amongst the forestlands at Paddockhurst and Balcombe, Major Stephenson Clarke who was to lose parkland on the Borde Hill Estate and Colonel William Campion who was to see his Danny lands under the Downs covered in cars rather than sheep. The London, Brighton and South Coast Railway Company felt threatened. The bill was killed.

With increasing numbers of cars on our antiquated road system the road lobby despaired at their lack of foresight. And there was no more distinguished agitator for new roads than Sussex's own Hilaire Belloc who lived at Shipley. His ideas for reforming the roads were curiously prophetic.

In 1923 his book *The Road* argued the case for 'circular ways round the towns' as well as 'great arterial roads very broad and straight with a special surface, confined to motor traffic alone'. He outlined their necessary features: avoidance of sudden curves, great width, crossings either over or under, and easy gradients. By the time he wrote his *The Highway and its Vehicles* (1926) he was stressing the need for new roads – he called them 'motor ways' – to 'drain' the traffic away from the country's 'charming, narrow, hedged, tortuous lanes' that simply were not made for the motor car.

Belloc's 1936 book, *The County of Sussex*, spelt out some of the perils facing the county's survival. Its very identity was at stake from a combination of factors, not least the car. 'The internal combustion engine ... strikes with peculiar force at the ancient spirit of this county ... it has killed quiet and with quiet all dignity: there is peace nowhere ... Of a week-end the roads from north to south are like a city street....'

Sadly he was never to see his ideas for new roads materialise, as he died in 1953, just five years before Britain's first motorway was opened.

But the failed 1906 proposal for a London – Brighton Motorway was certainly not the last Parliament was to hear of the matter; it was revived again in 1928, led by pioneer motorist Lord Montagu of Beaulieu who tabled The Southern Motor Road Bill. This involved a new, slightly shorter, route down to Brighton. Its prospectus – a rare

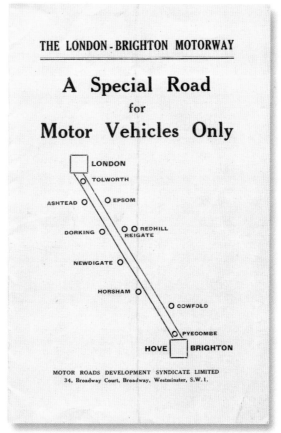

*The second attempt to build a motorway through Sussex – the proposal of 1928*

copy of which survives in the parish records of Rusper, as one of the parishes to be affected – sets out the need for urgent construction.

'The roads between London and Brighton are an outstanding example of ... dangerous congestion', notoriously at weekends. The volume of traffic heading for the coast was growing at an 'astonishing rate; probably in excess of the average rate of increase for the whole Country which has been shewn by official census figures to be 21 per cent per annum ... Visualise what this means, the traffic on the main roads to Brighton doubling itself in about three years.'

The prospectus quoted the National Housing and Town Planning Council's opinion that 'The present stream of motor traffic represents only a rivulet compared with the river which will flow a quarter of a century later. Those best qualified to speak are concerned that the next twenty years will witness such a great increase in the volume of mechanically propelled vehicles using the main roads as will compel the State to undertake the complete reorganisation of our national roads.'

The projected Brighton Motorway was planned to start at Tolworth on the Kingston Bypass. It would sweep through the Surrey and West Sussex countryside, avoiding all centres of population. Its thirty-seven-mile route southwards was to take the road between Epsom and Ashtead, then between Reigate and Dorking, crossing into West Sussex just north-west of the village of Rusper. Passing east of Horsham and Nuthurst, it would then cross the present A272 west of Cowfold before veering south-eastwards to a point between Albourne and Hurstpierpoint. The terminus was to be at Dale Hill, Pyecombe, giving easy access to Brighton and Hove.

The full and unhampered development of motor traffic can only proceed satisfactorily if adequate accommodation is provided on *roads specially constructed for the purpose*. In congested areas something more than our Highway Authorities have so far envisaged is being urgently demanded. It is suggested that the chief requirements of the country would be met by constructing the following arterial scheme of Motorways :—

1. London to Brighton and Portsmouth, bifurcating at Horsham.

2. London to Birmingham and Liverpool, with a branch line to Manchester.

3. Hull to Birmingham and the West, bifurcating at Gloucester and running both to Bristol and Cardiff.

4. Liverpool to Hull, running north of Manchester and south of Bradford and Leeds.

The London to Brighton Motorway will be the first, and most necessary, step in the direction of providing motor vehicle owners with the type of road they require.

## SUMMARY OF ADVANTAGES.

(1) **Motor Traffic Only.**—The road would be reserved entirely for mechanically-propelled vehicles using rubber tyres.

(2) **Cross Traffic.**—No cross traffic ; delays avoided ; danger eliminated.

(3) **A Straight Road.**—Necessary curves so gradual that motorists will always have a clear view a quarter-of-a-mile ahead.

(4) **A Level Road.**—Hills avoided, the steepest gradient being only 1 in 40.

(5) **A Smooth, Hard Road.**—Reinforced concrete surface, hardened by special treatment with silicate of soda and rendered practically dust and rain proof.

(6) **Congestion.**—No congestion due to bottle-necks, corkscrew turns and sudden corners. No pedestrians, cyclists, cattle or horse traffic.

(7) **Financial Relief.**—Damaging traffic, such as heavy vehicles, would be induced to use the road, thus reducing expenditure on the upkeep of the ordinary roads.

*Extracts from the 1928 prospectus*

There would be no steep gradients, with a tunnel to be built through the North Downs near Headley in Surrey. The motorway's alignment would follow gentle curves, avoiding any sharp bends, giving 'practically a level road with an uninterrupted view for some distance ahead'. Like railways, the motorway would be fenced, and carried over or under existing roads or railways. Access junctions would be built 'in such a way that motor vehicles would have to join the Motorway just as a tributary flows into a river, that is, *in the same direction as the stream of traffic is flowing*'.

The road, with a concrete surface, was to be wide enough to accommodate four lanes of traffic, with a slow and fast lane in each direction.

As the whole enterprise was the scheme of a private company – the Motor Roads Development Syndicate – its investment was to be recouped through a toll charge, so arrangements were designed to collect money on entering the approach roads.

But whatever the pressing need, the project once again failed to achieve the necessary backing and the idea was abandoned. Interestingly, when the Ministry of Transport announced its post-war highways policy for 'National Routes' in 1946 – anticipating the M25 with a 'London

Orbital Road' – the existing route from London to Brighton was only to be upgraded rather than replaced by a completely 'new motor road' of the type planned for elsewhere in the country. In the event it was not until the M23 was built that Sussex had its first, and so far only, glimpse of a motorway, and this for only just under eight miles into the county as far as Pease Pottage, near Crawley. It opened in December 1974, nearly seventy years after the very first scheme was put to Parliament in 1906. And that early scheme would have at least taken a motorway to the very outskirts of Brighton. As it is, the 'Brighton' motorway still falls short of its south coast destination by some twenty miles.

# 38 Escape to Bognor: R.C. Sherriff's *The Fortnight in September*

THE PUBLIC WENT FOR THE STORY like hot cakes: ten thousand copies went as fast as they were printed, then it was twenty thousand within the first month. In the first three months there were five reprints, two the following year, with at least six more still to follow up to 1974. 'A little masterpiece' declared the *Daily Express*. 'Enchanting' said another reviewer. An American publisher had it out in record time. Translations were made for Germany, France, Scandinavia, Italy and Spain. It was a phenomenal success.

One New Yorker wrote to the author that she read it every morning on the ferry that took her across the Hudson River to work in the city, saying it made her feel so warm and free and happy.

And the book? Just a simple and very gentle tale of a family holiday spent by the seaside at Bognor – *The Fortnight in September* – first published in 1931.

And the author? This was R.C. Sherriff who just three years earlier had written one of the great stage classics about the Great War, *Journey's End*, the famous play still performed today that made his name a household word.

Although from Surrey, Sherriff found much pleasure and relaxation on the Sussex coast, with holiday homes at Selsey and then at Bognor. He knew this area of West Sussex intimately.

Robert Cedric Sherriff (1896–1975), playwright, novelist and scriptwriter, went to Kingston Grammar School in Surrey where he was something of a big shot as captain of rowing and cricket. From that heroic period it was a demoralising come-down to junior clerk sticking stamps on envelopes and running errands. As both his grandfather and father had always worked for the Sun Insurance office it was taken for granted that he would follow in their footsteps. Father worked there for forty-five years. It was a good steady job.

But the young Sherriff, stuck in that London office, hated

Wills's Cigarettes

R. C. Sherriff

the hopeless monotony of it all. He looked out of the windows at the smoke-grimed suffocating buildings opposite and dreamed of escape. With no qualifications for a better job he felt doomed to sit in that musty old office until he was a worn-out old man.

And conditions at home weren't that much brighter. A shabby little house with loose window-frames rattling every time a tram went by and a railway embankment at the bottom of the garden didn't add up to much. He could dream.

So when the Great War broke out with its ravenous appetite for young men, Sherriff saw this as a merciful release, little realising that out of all its horrors were to come fame, fortune and a permanent place in the annals of the stage.

Demobbed, he returned to the insurance company, but this time not stuck in a dingy old office but as an 'outdoor man' as he called it, working the Thames Valley from Putney to Windsor. It was all routine and predictable, but at least he had the freedom of the road.

Sherriff joined the Kingston Rowing Club. They were always strapped for cash and in 1921 desperately needed money for new boats. So the rowers organised entertainments, Sherriff writing some short plays. All seats were a sell-out and the club was saved. Sherriff the playwright was born. Rowing and writing in his spare time went well together.

Then, with no idea of the box office, but just to fill empty evenings with a nostalgic journey into the past, Sherriff began writing about his wartime experiences, of the men in the trenches with all their wretchedness and longing for home. All his previous plays had been about imaginary people in imaginary situations. Now he was actually writing about men he had lived with and knew so well that every line they spoke came straight from them. The play almost wrote itself. Exhilarated, he sent it off for a professional opinion. The rest is theatrical history.

*Journey's End* opened in the West End in January 1929 to rapturous audiences, the admiration of Winston Churchill and rave reviews: 'the greatest of all war plays.... English theatre at its best' according to that most feared of all critics, Hannen Swaffer in the *Daily Express*.

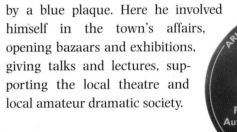

*The Theatre Royal could guarantee packed houses when* Journey's End *played on Sherriff's home ground in 1937*

It was nothing but sensational, with the biggest ticket agency deal ever known for the West End. By the end of 1929 Sherriff's royalties added up to more than a staggering £48,000 and the published version of the play sold over a hundred and seventy-five thousand copies, an all-time record for a new play. From London it travelled the world, to Broadway and into twenty-seven languages.

To Sherriff, 'Journey's End was like Aladdin's Lamp. You rubbed it, and what you wanted was yours.' He could now buy the house of his dreams in Esher with its magnificent panelled library, 'a far cry from the poky little room I had worked in at the old house, with its spluttering gas-fire, solitary dangling light and loose window-frame'.

These new riches gave Sherriff the opportunity to enrol as a mature student at Oxford – he was now aged thirty-four – to read history at New College. He loved history with a passion, and this was pure indulgence.

But even in cloistered academia he wasn't free from the lure of the entertainment moguls. On the strength of *Journey's End*, Universal Studios in Hollywood invited Sherriff to do the screenplay for *The Invisible Man* (1933), H.G. Wells' science-fiction horror story set in West Sussex. He proved a natural for the film industry and so a new lucrative career opened as scriptwriter to the stars. Three of his most outstanding successes were for British studios: *Goodbye Mr Chips* (1939), *The Four Feathers* (1939) – the original novel was by A.E.W. Mason of Petworth – and *The Dam Busters* (1954). They brought him untold wealth. In the 1930s the money from screen-writing poured in at the rate of £500 a week.

From the proceeds Sherriff bought a Rolls, a farm in Dorset and a fine new holiday home in Bognor, a green-pantiled residence in King's Parade overlooking Marine Park Gardens called Sandmartins, today marked by a blue plaque. Here he involved himself in the town's affairs, opening bazaars and exhibitions, giving talks and lectures, supporting the local theatre and local amateur dramatic society.

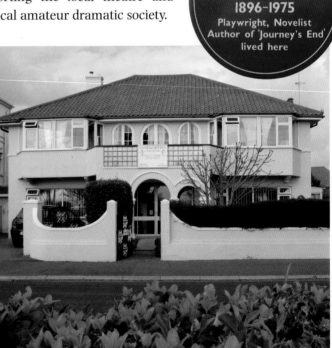

In his autobiography, *No Leading Lady* (1968), Sherriff recalls that just as *Journey's End* made Oxford possible, so Hollywood gave the opportunity to gratify a yearning that began years ago as a schoolboy when he had first seen Roman ruins at Silchester. He fell for the excitement of archaeology and now, with money and time to spare, approached Mortimer Wheeler to see if there was a dig he could sponsor. Yes, there was: a Roman site at Angmering, known for years through pottery fragments ploughed up year after year, but never systematically investigated.

So in the 1930s Sherriff leased the field from the Duke of Norfolk and paid for a team of diggers to search. He himself worked tirelessly with wheelbarrow and shovel to uncover the long-lost villa. And out of it all came a BBC radio play about Roman life at Angmering – *The Long Sunset* – with stage versions played at the Birmingham Rep and London's Mermaid, as well as becoming a set book for schools to study. Again, another tremendous success for Sherriff.

Sherriff's first novel – he wrote seven in all – was *The Fortnight in September* – the book that gave Bognor so much fame in the early 1930s soon after George V had given the town its ultimate accolade in 1929 with his award of 'Regis', following his successful convalescence from serious illness at nearby Craigweil House. On 'The Royal Road to Health and Happy Holidays' proudly boasted the new town guide in 1931. This was a golden age for the little seaside resort to which Sherriff and his mother came for their holidays.

The idea for the book happened when they went to the promenade just to watch the crowds go by. 'I began to feel the itch to take one of those families at random and build up an imaginary story of their annual holiday by the sea.' He took a small suburban family, the Stevens, on their fortnight's holiday at

*Watching the world go by – on Bognor's seafront in the 1920s. It was here, whilst promenading with his mother and watching the holidaymakers, that Sherriff first came up with the idea of writing his novel about a family holiday in Bognor.*

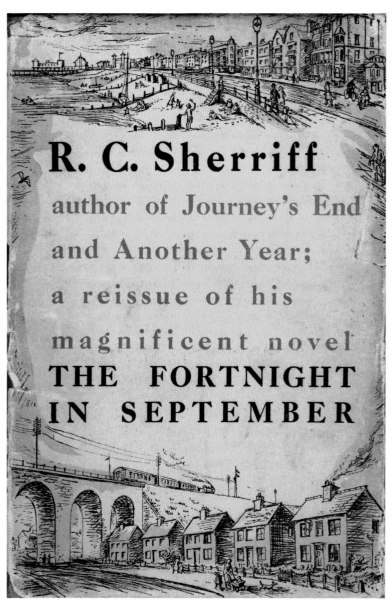

*The cover of this 1949 reissue, symbolising the Stevens' escape from drab suburban surroundings to the Sussex seaside. It echoes Sherriff's own personal journey – from a tiny house with a railway at the end of the garden to riches and freedom enjoyed at Bognor.*

Bognor. It was a day-by-day account of their time here. How every morning they came out of their shabby boarding house – £3 10 shillings a week plus a shilling 'for cruet' – and went down to the sea; how the father found hope for the future in his brief freedom from his humdrum office work; how the children found romance and adventure as an escape from their tedious jobs; and how the mother, scared of the sea, tried to make the others think that she was enjoying it.

There's little plot, it's more an exploration of personal relationships, about family values, loyalty and respect. Sherriff could write the book with so much feeling and sincerity – and this was why it was such an enormous success, because, as with *Journey's End*, it was rooted in his own experience. He knew the townscape and atmosphere of boarding-house Bognor of the 1920s and '30s so well. He had suffered the anguish and lifestyle of the Stevens as well.

He himself came from a humdrum drab background, from a tiny house with a railway embankment at the end of the garden and a dead-end job, just like the Stevens. Sherriff needed to escape from its boring soul-destroying monotony, just like the Stevens escaped for their annual fortnight to Bognor as they had been doing for the last twenty years. Sherriff knew their problems and their feelings and he applauded them for their decency and goodness.

From a humble background himself, he was always overwhelmed and nervous about meeting important people. Likewise the poor Stevens who all get dragged into the vacuous arrogance of the wealthy Mr Montgomery,

*Boarding-house Bognor: the Stevens paid £3 10 shillings a week plus a shilling 'for cruet'*

manufacturer of the famous Montgomery Butter Nuts, with his brand new home of bright red brick and dazzling white stucco on Bognor's Aldwick Road. Vulgar and overbearing, he made the Stevens writhe with pain and embarrassment. Dick Stevens, the older son, saw through it all:

*His father was just a clerk, struggling proudly and silently on a few pounds a week: this other man had thousands . . . all round lay signs of careless wealth . . . yet what was it all worth? . . . He would not exchange his father for a thousand fat Montgomeries, or the things his father thought and did for a million jars of Butter Nuts. . . .*

The book was written some seventy-five years ago. The Bognor setting and style may be dated, but it's still a fable for our own times. *The Fortnight in September* is worth searching out.

*Deckchairs, sun and sand, by Sunny Snaps in 1934 – just the way the Stevens family enjoyed their Bognor holiday. After London 'Everything . . . was so unutterably fresh and clean: bronzed faces – open shirts – bare legs – blue sky'.*

# 39 'The smallest port in England': Dell Quay

*Dell Quay in the late 1920s or early '30s: loading grain onto one of the last coastal steamers to use the harbour*

*The jetty across the mud: Dell Quay in 1938*

6 'PERHAPS THE SMALLEST PORT IN ENGLAND.... a house or two, a shed or two, and a small jetty.' In these few words Arthur Mee dismisses this tiny place in 1937 in his well-known Sussex volume in the King's England series. Then he would have seen just a few cargo steamers berthing here each year, but not for much longer now, for as a commercial quay it was in terminal decline. And nowadays its chugging steamers and their trade have all but been forgotten, replaced by a backdrop of very different craft, the white sails of the dinghies making the harbour as busy as ever in the summer months.

This 'smallest port' was Dell Quay, just two miles from Chichester. The photograph, dating from either the late 1920s or early '30s, is one of the very few known to exist showing the quay still in commercial use, a coastal steamer tied alongside as sacks of grain are wheeled onboard.

The old seaman in the other photograph, dated about 1940, is George Haines, a much-loved local character and man of many parts in Chichester Harbour. His family ran the Itchenor boatyard as well as the ferry across to Bosham. One of his vital jobs was acting as harbour pilot, taking commercial sailing craft and steamers up the shallow channel from Itchenor to Dell Quay. Shoals and sandbanks have always made navigation into the harbour mouth and up through the narrow creeks a haphazard business for bigger craft. George knew the channels like the back of his hand. His grandson, also George, has recalled that as a little boy going up to Dell Quay in the big boats with his grandfather, he was so terrified because of all the bumping and scraping over the harbour bottom as they drew so much water over the shallows. The older George Haines was the last pilot to take cargo steamers up to Dell Quay in the 1930s. These must have been sad days for George as he was seeing the last commercial freight through here, a trade that went back over many centuries.

## GEORGE HAINES OF ITCHENOR

Now to introduce you to the man who can tell you most about Itchenor. Turn left after leaving the village and you will come to a long wooden jetty which takes you to the ferry and thence over the water to Bosham.

Seventy-six years old George Haines, harbour-master, ferry-man, and scores of other official posts, was just tying up his ferry boat – a small rowing boat – on to the side of the jetty. Nearby, was the *Tinamu*, the biggest yacht in the harbour, and it seemed to dwarf the ferry boat into insignificance.

Somehow, George does not look like a seafaring man, despite the fact that he spent 16 years roughing the oceans. Rather small in stature and slightly thin, he has a handsome bearded face. He was wearing the traditional sea-man's clothes.

'Things have changed,' he told me. 'I was born at Portsmouth and spent 16 years at sea and I have been in Itchenor for 45 years. It is only during the last few years that all these yachts have come into the harbour. When I was a boy there were only a few coal boats.'

*George Haines in about 1940*

I asked George to tell me some stories about his sea life, but he would say nothing more than that he was once shipwrecked after a fierce gale which lasted four days without ceasing.

George lives in a quaint little cottage near the ferry and he told me that this was once Itchenor's inn. Indeed, one could imagine the carefree sailors entering that little place when it had a thatched roof that nearly touched the ground. Next door is the old customs house and this receives a thorough washing during winter gales when the sea lashes up against its walls.

George's house is named 'Ferryside' and above the entrance is a door. 'This often puzzles people,' said George, with a chuckle, 'but we use it for storing all sorts of things to do with the boats.'

George likes to look back on the days when he was a sea-man. 'It was a hard life' he said, 'but it was a good one. Things are all quickness to-day. Yes, and in ten years time men won't know how to splice a wire.'

*Southern Weekly News*, 4 July 1936

*'Del Key' – the Port of Chichester in 1795*

Early traders must have come this way from time immemorial. Certainly the Romans passed by on their way to Fishbourne, and the Normans building Chichester Cathedral landed their stone from France and elsewhere somewhere along these shores, the nearest they could come by water to the city itself. Chichester Harbour has been a waterway to history over all these centuries, its long fingers of water inviting invaders and settlers deep into its protective waters.

What we now know as Itchenor Reach leading up to Fishbourne Channel was once known as 'La Delle' in thirteenth-century documents, and on Saxton's map of Sussex of 1575 it is called 'Delle flu', from the Latin flumen, meaning flow or river. Place-name specialists have suggested that the Dell element might refer to the slight depression along the channel here that made navigation possible.

For centuries Dell Quay has enjoyed a status out of all proportion to its size. For long it was the main wharf for goods entering and leaving the harbour and at one time

was the only one legalised for carrying on foreign trade within what was technically known as the Port of Chichester.

Although an inland city without direct access to the sea – until 1822 when the Chichester Canal was opened from Birdham to the basin at Southgate – Chichester ranked legally as a port since the 1270s. This was when Edward I established a customs service operating through a dozen or so ports to raise extra revenue for the crown and to cut down on smuggling. In this way Chichester joined a small group of customs ports throughout the country. By 1312 there were only five along the whole of the southern coast: Sandwich, Winchelsea, Chichester, Southampton and Exeter. In 1353 Chichester became a Staple Port, legally empowered to deal in the export of wool, the basis of England's medieval wealth and a carefully controlled commodity. Then, over the centuries, Chichester saw a wide range of goods pass through the port. Apart from wool, some of the main exports were cloth, grain, malt and timber. Wine came in from France, Spain and Portugal, salt

*Mills of Chichester Harbour – left: Birdham tidemill in 1931, right: Fishbourne windmill by the water in 1896*

from the Bay of Biscay, coal mainly from Newcastle. Much of these cargoes went through Dell Quay, although around the harbour there were a number of licensed creeks authorised to trade. Emsworth became Dell Quay's great rival.

Throughout the seventeenth and eighteenth centuries the whole harbour buzzed with commercial activity. The port became the leading Sussex exporter of wheat and barley. One famous writer came through these parts in the 1720s, when he wrote about the prosperous grain trade hereabouts. This was Daniel Defoe (1660–1731) whose *Robinson Crusoe* (1719) created one of the most enduring and famous adventures in English literature. As well as a novelist he was a businessman, pamphleteer and government agent, gathering information and testing the political climate to relay back to the politicians. For this he travelled widely, publishing his *Tour Through the Whole Island of Great Britain* in three volumes between 1724 and 1726.

With his own background in business, Defoe was always keen to note matters of trade and commerce. He described how grain merchants around the harbour had built large granaries 'near the Crook, where the vessels come up', by which he meant Dell Quay, 'and here they buy and lay up all the corn which the country on that side can spare; and having good mills in the neighbourhood, they grind and dress the corn, and send it to London ... by Long Sea, as they call it', rather than as previously sending it by road to Farnham in Surrey 'the greatest corn-market in England, London excepted'.

The success of the local grain trade through these Dell Quay granaries was closely linked to the numerous corn mills dotted around the harbourside. Reflecting the rich cornlands of the coastal plain, these mills were signs of considerable prosperity, pointing to a golden age in farming during the eighteenth and nineteenth centuries.

A few were windmills by the water's edge, as at Bosham and Fishbourne. One was built at Dell Quay, probably sometime in the 1780s. It was taken down around 1870, with its roundhouse incorporated into Dell Quay House.

But most of the mills around the harbour were water-powered, the most unusual of these being the tidemills, the Chichester area having one of the largest concentrations in the country. By the nineteenth century there were seven working tidemills in the area.

The incoming water operated the mill wheel as it rose to its full height, the sea water being impounded until released by the falling tide. So they were as reliable as the daily tides, unlike ordinary watermills that might stand idle for lack of water in a dry summer, or be totally useless in a district where streams were seasonably intermittent. The Lavant, dry for much of the year, at one time powered four watermills, one right by the harbour at Apuldram.

The tidemills were at Birdham and Nutbourne, with two each at Emsworth and Fishbourne, and another at Sidlesham. Sidlesham's mill might have been geographically in

Rules, regulations and
port dues that operated
from 1872

Pagham Harbour, but it was legally within the Port of Chichester. This was because the port's boundaries in 1680 were defined as between the county boundary at Hermitage by Emsworth in the west to the eastern extremity of the parish of Felpham in the east. So all the Selsey, Pagham and Bognor coastline fell within the old port's jurisdiction (see map, page 41).

The development of these mills in the eighteenth century changed the pattern of trade within the harbour as less and less grain went out in favour of milled and dressed flour. Each of these tidemills had its own wharf that in their day brought sailing barges to the top of the creeks. Going to the foot of Mill Lane in Fishbourne today and seeing the creek full of reeds, it doesn't seem possible that this was once a busy working quay.

The eighteenth century was full of expansion and development around the harbour. At Dell Quay this was reflected in the road improvements made as far as the waterfront by the building of the turnpike. This changed

Date 2 July 1872

# RULES & REGULATIONS

To be observed by Masters of Ships and
Vessels coming to load and unload at

# DELL QUAY.

1.—Before coming alongside Masters shall apply to the Quay Master for a berth, and shall anchor, moor and place the Ship or Vessel as the Quay Master may direct.

2.—All Ships and Vessels coming to load or unload at the Quay shall take their turn in regular rotation of arrival, and if required by the Quay Master shall shift their berths when partly unloaded and remove to other Quay berths, or lie in a second or third tier when the Quay Master shall deem it absolutely requisite.

3.—Masters and their mates lying at the head of the Quay shall at high water time be ready when required to slack their chains and wharfs, and to have their jib and mizen booms and running bowsprits rigged close in to allow free egress and ingress to the side berths,

4.—Immediately a Cargo is discharged Masters shall haul out from the Quay berths, unless specially allowed to remain by the Quay Master or compelled by stress of weather.

BY ORDER,

## S. SIMMONDS,
Quay Master.

# SCHEDULE

*Of the Dues, Duties, Customs, Petty Customs, Measurage, and ~~Discharge~~ Anchorage, due and payable to the Mayor, Aldermen, and Citizens of the City of Chichester, for all Goods and Merchandize and Vessels within the Port of Chichester.*

| | s. | d. | | s. | d. | | s. | d. |
|---|---|---|---|---|---|---|---|---|
| Bacon, a last or thirty flitches .. | 1 | 8 | Hops, the bag or poke .. .. | 0 | 2 | Timber or Plank, the load (4 ton) | 0 | 2 |
| Barrels, to wit, ten barrels .. | 1 | 8 | Iron, Wrought, the ton .. | 0 | 2 | Tar, the barrel .. .. | 0 | 0½ |
| Butter, the last or ten firkins.. | 1 | 8 | Iron, Cast, the ton .. .. | 0 | 3 | Wine, the tun .. .. .. | 0 | 4 |
| Bales of Cloth, the pack .. | 0 | 6 | Lead, the fother or ton weight.. | 0 | 4 | Wood, the cord or one hundred billits .. .. | 0 | 2 |
| Barrel Boards, per thousand .. | 0 | 6 | Leather Hides, the dicker or ten hides .. .. | 0 | 5 | | | |
| Bank Fish, per hundred .. | 0 | 4 | | | | Vinegar or Verjuice, the tun .. | 0 | 4 |
| Canvas, the pack mayled .. | 0 | 4 | Metal, Brass, Pewter, and Copper, the cwt. | 0 | 1 | Trenchers, the pack .. .. | 0 | 1 |
| Calves' Skins, the dozen .. | 0 | 4 | | | | Deal Boards, the hundred .. | 0 | 4 |
| Cards for Wool, the pack .. | 0 | 4 | Mackerel, the thousand .. | 0 | 4 | Sea Coal, the chaldron (3 ton) | 0 | 4 |
| Cards for Playing, the dryvat .. | 1 | 0 | Oil, the hogshead .. .. | 0 | 2 | All other Merchandize not herein mentioned, the ton | 0 | 4 |
| Cheese, per hundred weight .. | 0 | 1 | Oil, the barrel .. .. .. | 0 | 1 | | | |
| Cloth, the piece, full length .. | 0 | 1 | Oade, the ton .. .. .. | 0 | 4 | For Anchorage of every Vessel coming in or going out of the said Port .. | 0 | 4 |
| Cod Fish, the burthen or 21 fishes .. .. | 0 | 1 | Oysters, every boat .. .. | 0 | 2 | | | |
| | | | Mill Stones, the pair .. .. | 0 | 1 | | | |
| Glass, the case .. .. .. | 0 | 1 | Quern Stones, the pair.. .. | 0 | 4 | Malt, 20 quarters { Freemen | 0 | 8 |
| | | | | | | { Foreigners | 1 | 6 |
| Hoops, the hundred dozen .. | 0 | 4 | Tombstones, the pair .. .. | 0 | 2 | | | |
| Herrings, White, the last or ten barrels .. | 0 | 10 | Grindstones, the pair .. .. | 0 | 6 | Wheat, Barley, Salt, { Freemen or any other { grain, per qtr. { Foreigners | 0 | 0⅓ |
| | | | Purbeck Stones, the ton .. | 0 | 4 | | 0 | 1 |
| Herrings, Red, the card or barrel | 0 | 1 | Shovels, the hundred .. .. | 0 | 5 | | | |

the legal status of the road, meaning that tolls could be taken to pay for road improvements. Significantly the turnpike road from Surrey through Midhurst and on to Chichester, dated 1749 – one of the earliest of these types of road in the county – was extended to have its terminus at Dell Quay, rather than in Chichester. This would have eased the land carriage of goods to and from the harbour.

Other signs of commercial prosperity around the harbour at this time were in the shipbuilding yards at Emsworth and Bosham. At Itchenor a number of small to medium-sized warships and two East Indiamen were built. Not far from here the third Duke of Richmond (1735–1806) had his yachting lodge at Itchenor House. He had his own private dock from which his cargo sloop *Goodwood* operated. In West Sussex Record Office are the master's accounts for operating the sloop in the 1780s and '90s when Goodwood House was being enlarged. Much of the stone for these works came in through his Itchenor dock for onward transit to Goodwood. In 1787 the sloop brought in over a hundred tons of Swanage stone; other voyages saw her bringing stone and bricks from Plymouth and the huge lengths of pink granite from Guernsey for the decorative columns in the main entrance hall of Goodwood House.

*Itchenor waterfront in 1802: warships and East Indiamen were built here on the shores of the harbour in the 18th century*

There were those who took advantage of these isolated creeks and channels of the harbour for their own nefarious activities – the free traders, or smugglers – who landed their illegal cargoes here. On the Hampshire side of the harbour, on Hayling Island, they dug 'caves' on the beach where goods could be hidden until it was safe to move them inland. One amusing story from the early nineteenth century is told about Dell Quay, which had its fair share of cargo-running:

One day a smart French yacht came to the jetty with her flag flying at half-mast. She was met by a hearse and mourning carriages, and of course mourners. In the presence of a sympathetic crowd of customs officials and villagers the weighty coffin was received with all due solemnity. The cortège, once clear of Chichester, developed a suspicious briskness and disappeared over the Downs. Too late did the infuriated customs officials realise that they had let a cargo of contraband pass right under their very noses.

The harbour is full of tales, legends and history so that it is more than appropriate that Dell Quay is now home to Chichester Harbour Conservancy's Education Centre where the story of this wonderful watery environment is told. In conjunction with Dell Quay Sailing Club its work is expanding here with the opening of more exhibition space in the recently-restored old grain store. Under the Conservancy all is very much alive and well at Dell Quay today, a far cry from the days when George Haines bumped over the harbour with the last of his cargoes seventy to eighty years ago.

*Dell Quay in 1897: most of the coastal shipping using Chichester Harbour before the end of the 19th century was made up of small wooden sailing vessels of less than 100 registered tons – an engraving by Dr Arthur Evershed of Fishbourne*

# 40 'Can Sussex Endure?': Hilaire Belloc on Threats to the County

*Wills's Cigarettes*

*Hilaire Belloc*

'A GREAT MASTER of the English language has died in ripe old age. Through half a century of continuous and enormous creative energy, in poems, essays, biographies, histories, novels, satires, and light verses, Mr Hilaire Belloc added, year by year ... to the riches of English prose and verse.' So ran *The Times* obituary. The socialite-chronicler Lady Diana Cooper judged that he was, 'perhaps with Winston Churchill, the man nearest to genius I have known'. And she knew all the great men of the time.

Fortunately for lovers of Sussex, Belloc put his genius to work in extolling the county in prose and verse. No Sussex anthology is complete without lines from Belloc. And significantly when J.B. Priestley wanted to celebrate the magic of the English landscape in *Our Nation's Heritage* (1939) he chose for its introductory essay Belloc's 'The Mowing of a Field', set in a Sussex downland valley at Slindon.

What is so special about this month and this year to lovers of Belloc is that the great man –forever associated with Sussex – died fifty years ago, on 16 July 1953. [This article was originally published in July 2003.] He was buried at West Grinstead, in the Catholic churchyard. So this year has been marked by a programme of special events throughout West Sussex. It will culminate in next Sunday's unveiling of a commemorative plaque – in National Trust green – to celebrate his birthday on 27 July at a remote downland spot called Gumber. Belloc always loved solitary places.

Hilaire Belloc was born in 1870, just outside Paris, his father Louis being French, his mother Bessie, English. After Louis' death in 1872 the widowed Bessie came back to England, to Westminster, to enjoy an energetic time in intellectual, literary circles. When her investments crashed she was forced to find an alternative lifestyle.

So it was that Bessie, Hilaire and his sister Marie forsook the capital for the countryside. Through a great friend they came to Slindon in 1878, renting Slindon Cottage (now the Dower House) in Top Road for £10 a month. But even this proved too much and so they all went down Church Hill by the village pond to Newlands for just £4 a month. Bessie, ever the romantic, renamed the house the Grange, with its more historic overtones.

*Slindon Cottage – Belloc's first boyhood home in the village from 1878*

## GUMBER

*Lift up your hearts in Gumber, laugh the Weald*
*And you my mother the Valley of Arun sing.*
*Here am I homeward from my wandering,*
*Here am I homeward and my heart is healed.*
*You my companions whom the World has tired*
*Come out to greet me. I have found a face*
*More beautiful than Gardens; more desired*
*Than boys in exile love their native place.*

*Lift up your hearts in Gumber, laugh the Weald*
*And you most ancient Valley of Arun sing.*
*Here am I homeward from my wandering,*
*Here am I homeward and my heart is healed.*
*If I was thirsty, I have heard a spring.*
*If I was dusty, I have found a field.*

Hilaire Belloc

Belloc first discovered Gumber as a boy when living in Slindon, around where his great love for Sussex was first nurtured. He never forgot this remote little place deep in the hills, the very heart of a landscape which was to nourish and feed his soul for the rest of his life.

THE NATIONAL TRUST
TO COMMEMORATE
**HILAIRE BELLOC**
1870 - 1953
WRITER, POET & WALKER
"LIFT UP YOUR HEARTS IN GUMBER"
WEST SUSSEX COUNTY COUNCIL

The young Belloc loved the village and its countryside and from these early years grew his lifelong love of Sussex. Up its chalk lanes, through the beech woods and then on to the heights above Gumber, the sparkling sea on the distant horizon, the green tapestry of the Weald rolling away on the other: this was a landscape with history underfoot that couldn't fail to leave a deep impression on the sensitive boy. He had to leave all this for boarding school, the Oratory at Edgbaston, to be taught by Cardinal Newman, an education that not only deepened his faith but also left him with a lifelong love for the classics. Holidays were spent back in the Sussex countryside.

Leaving school, Belloc drifted in and out of a variety of jobs, including working at Manor Farm, Bury, near Arundel. But concerned that he was getting nowhere, his mother and sister encouraged him to try for Oxford, to follow his academic bent at Balliol in 1893. Here his impact was both immediate and pronounced, gaining intellectual friendship, academic distinction and election as President of the Union. To this day his portrait presides over all the great debates in the Oxford Union.

Soon after graduating with first class honours, Belloc married his American love, Elodie Hogan, in California, returning to set up home in Oxford and working as an extension lecturer. A move to London followed, but, as with his mother before, money troubles loomed. They needed a cheaper place to live and so Belloc returned to Slindon, this time to live at Bleak House in Top Road in 1903 – today

marked by a blue plaque. From here they could see hills and sea, a great emotional comfort expressed in so many of his writings. Two years later the family – by now there were five children – moved to the much bigger Court Hill Farm just outside the village. Enfolded by downland on all sides, here there was a protective warmth that stirred Belloc's heart. At Court Hill he put the finishing touches to one of the finest collections of his essays, *Hills and the Sea* (1906).

These Slindon houses were rented. What he really wanted was a Sussex home of his own, a stake in the county to which he was so deeply attached. So in 1906 the family moved to King's Land at Shipley, to an old rambling house with five acres and a windmill.

*King's Land in Shipley, c.1907, where Belloc lived from 1906 until his death in 1953. In front are his five children and in the background stands the mill. Here was his own little bit of heaven on earth, bringing him (according to his son-in-law, Reginald Jebb) 'peace of mind and a sense of permanence'.*

By then Belloc had started to carve out his reputation as an author. His first two books came out in 1896. One was poetry – *Verses and Sonnets*, a very rare book to find now, curiously printed on cardboard pages – the other *The Bad Child's Book of Beasts*, the first of his nonsense books for

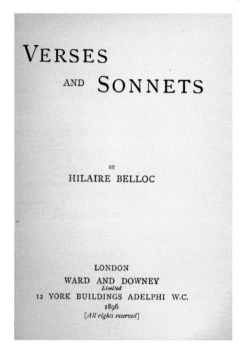

*Belloc's first two books: throughout his life he wrote over 150. Belloc suppressed the issue of this first attempt at publishing his poetry – probably destroying the books – surviving copies today are scarce. Children – and adults – loved his comic 'Beasts'. In the first three months four thousand copies were sold and the book has been kept in print ever since.*

children which came to include *Cautionary Tales for Children* (1907) with its immortal stories of sad Jim 'Who ran away from his Nurse, and was eaten by a Lion' and poor Matilda who 'told such Dreadful Lies' that she was burned to death. Still in print today, these tales are admired by 'children' from eight to eighty.

What was amazing about Belloc as a writer was his sheer versatility. One moment writing for the young with such a light fun-touch, then turning to weighty studies of politicians, military strategies, the Catholic church, travel, walking and topography, as well as a whole clutch of fiction. Not only versatile, he was prolific. By the end of 1910, aged forty, he had published some forty books in just fifteen years, and to top it all he was a Liberal MP between 1906 and 1910. And he had done so many other unusual things by now, like walking alone across dangerous terrain from Toul in northern France to Rome, some seven hundred miles in just twenty-seven days. This incredible achievement he retold in *The Path to Rome* (1902). His energy and endurance were legendary.

The year 1906 had yet another significance, as it was the year that he produced his first book on the county, simply called *Sussex*, and for a reason never explained, without any acknowledgement to its author, but just to the artist of its seventy-five watercolour plates, Wilfrid Ball.

Typically Bellocian, this is a ground-breaking book in both its scope and robust opinions. There had never been another Sussex book quite like this in dealing with its geography and history, and perhaps more importantly, about its own special identity, its 'Individual Character' as he calls it. Firstly he looks at the character of its people, the real Sussex inhabitants and their 'resistant quality' and then turns to the Sussex landscape. But even in 1906 he senses the dangers that Sussex people and places faced:

> *It will be of interest to watch the near future and to see if his characteristics can be retained as the county gets better and better known, and more thoroughly spoiled by the advent of what is called the leisured class.*

On the landscape, even in 1906, Belloc senses blotches, with places like Haywards Heath ('like a London suburb') and the coast ('dreary' and 'heart-breaking' with its 'red brick and boarding houses, and esplanades and tin bungalows'). But he remained optimistic:

> *The great spaces of landscape which Sussex can afford have never changed and never can. No man will ever build largely upon the Downs ... No mere extension of buildings or further cultivation will destroy the distant aspect of the Weald.*

But some thirty years later, in 1936, he was not so sure. Asked to rewrite his original book, Belloc took the opportunity to bring the text up to date with his views on what was happening between the two world wars. And it was disaster. 'Sussex is in peril of dissolution' he wrote in its preface. Parts of its last few pages, reproduced here, end on a sombre note. This time the book has a slightly fuller title, *The County of Sussex*, and at last credits the author on its beautifully-illustrated dustwrapper by Rowland Hilder.

Belloc feared for the future of Sussex in his book of 1936, warning of the effects of 'The internal combustion engine .... it has killed quiet and with quiet all dignity .... The new engines climb the Downs; they invade every corner', shown graphically by this 1920s postcard (below) advertising 'The Sussex Garden City of the South Downs' – Peacehaven.

PEACEHAVEN:
Looking towards Brighton.

And on top of this threat was yet another: the blight of 'alien building ... having no fellowship with the county at all ... meaningless new watering places ... suburban blotches'. The stampede to build was on....

· HOUSE · & · LAND · AGENT ·
· A · LIBRARY · TOO ·

Miss E. C. HARDING
(Sole Resident Agent).

Telephone : Swandean 153.

Downs Estate Office,

High Salvington,

Nr. Worthing.

In the grounds of CRAIGWEIL HOUSE

Backed by SUSSEX DOWNS

Fronted by the SEA

Freehold prices from £1,000 to £2,775. Sites from £300 for houses built to accepted plans and houses available for renting. Bathing huts available on private beach.

CRAIGWEIL-ON-SEA BOGNOR REGIS
Inspect also the Company's Inland Estate at Newberries, Radlett.

PEACEHAVEN
THE SOUTH COAST RESORT ALMOST FIVE MILES IN LENGTH FACING THE SEA

Free Gift
of a £1,125
FREEHOLD HOUSE
and LAND

Write to-day for full details of our Offer sent Post Free
PEACEHAVEN ESTATES LTD Dept. T.
Peacehaven, Sussex.
Only a short Bus ride from the Aquarium, Brighton.

## CAN SUSSEX ENDURE?

THERE REMAINS AFTER ALL this an anxious question which every man who knows and loves the county puts to himself. Can Susssex endure?

No man knows the answer to that question, but in measuring the chances we of the county must admit that they are heavily against our survival. It would seem that the forces making for the destruction of this county, its traditions, its personality, are too powerful to be withstood. Moreover, they are working at such speed that our own generation may well see the end of the land we knew.

It is, in a sense, the coming of a new mode of transport which thus threatens us. The internal combustion engine, which has revolutionised the world, strikes with peculiar force at the ancient spirit of this county, on account of its situation between London and the sea. . . .

Side by side with all this mechanical change has gone a spiritual change which destroys our powers of resistance. Men have lost their doctrines, and therefore their manners and morals, and the passing of all the ideas that made our civilisation is due more to this loss of standards than to any material causes.

In the midst of so much evil the passing of Sussex would seem a small thing, but to us it is a great one.

Which of us could have thought, when we wandered, years ago, in the full peace of the summer Weald, or through the sublime void of the high Downs, that the things upon which we had been nourished since first we could take joy in the world would be thus rapidly destroyed in our own time, dying even before we ourselves should die? Yet apparently it has come. In the old days when the huge amorphous mass of London, more numerous than many a state, was only linked with the sea-coast by the railway, we feared for the future, but did not despair of it. The coast might become a line of alien building, and here and there upon the main arteries across the Weald some suburban thing having no fellowship with the county at all would grow up round a station; but Sussex as a whole remained untainted by the intrusion. The contrast between the meaningless new watering places, the suburban blotches and the ancient plough land, woodland, downland, was only the stronger.

Then came the change: London broke out like a bursting reservoir, flooding all the ways to the sea, swamping our history and our past, so that already we are hardly ourselves. Of a week-end the roads from north to south are like a city street. The new engines climb the Downs; they invade every corner. You may hear the machine-gun fire of a motor bicycle on the greensward of Chanctonbury Ring. There is no retreat wherein you can escape the blind inhuman mechanic clatter. How could any organism survive this ubiquitous thrusting into its substance of alien things? . . .

There is only one consideration which may lighten somewhat the burden of what seems inevitable. It is this: that, just as we could not foresee the sudden tidal wave which has swept over us, so the future, even the immediate future, may check the ruin of our home, of our most ancient life. Some incalculable further change may stop the further process of disintegration. It is not conceivable – but often enough the inconceivable happens. Disaster and decline might destroy machines and so save, before they had disappeared, the last stocks and found some new repose wherein they might strike root again. But as things now stand there would seem to be no prospect of survival through the coming years; nor will there be any Sussex any more: *Ubi Troja fuit.*

How could Belloc face a further rewrite of his book today, seventy years later? Words would hardly describe his reaction to those intent on concreting the county as their legacy to its well-being, to those destroying its soul.

In the end – for himself – he would have found comfort for his own soul in the words of the moving crescendo to his *The Four Men* (1912):

> *. . .if a man is part of and is rooted in one steadfast piece of earth, which has nourished him and given him his being, and if he can on his side lend it glory and do it service . . . it will be a friend to him for ever. . .*

# Money and Measurement – Old and New

All sums of money and measurement of length, area, weight and capacity are quoted with their original historic values, i.e:

pounds, shillings and pence for money
inches, feet, yards and miles for length
acres for area
pounds (abbreviated to lbs) and tons for weight
gallons for capacity

*In most cases* conversions have been given in brackets in the text.

**Money**

Since decimalisation in 1971, shillings and pence have been replaced by new pence. Thus 1 shilling became 5 new pence and 20 shillings became 100 new pence = £1.

Nevertheless these conversions are meaningless without an appreciation of the real value of money at any one period: the relationship of earnings to the cost of living must be taken into account.

A useful guide is Lionel Munby's *How Much is that Worth?* (Phillimore/British Association for Local History, 1989).

**Length**

12 inches = 1 foot = 0.3048 metre
36 inches = 3 feet = 1 yard = 0.9144 metre
39.37 inches = 1 metre

**Area**

1 acre = 0.4 hectare

**Weight**

1 pound (lb) = 454 grams
14 lbs = 1 stone = 6.350 kilograms
1 ton = 1.016 tonne

**Capacity**

1 gallon = 4.55 litres

# Sources

## Abbreviations:

| | |
|---|---|
| *SAC* | *Sussex Archaeological Collections* |
| *SCM* | *Sussex County Magazine* |
| *SIH* | *Sussex Industrial History* |
| *SNQ* | *Sussex Notes and Queries* |
| SRS | Sussex Record Society |
| *VCH* | *Victoria County History: Sussex* |
| WSCC | West Sussex County Council |
| *WSG* | *West Sussex Gazette* |
| *WSH* | *West Sussex History* |
| WSRO | West Sussex Record Office |

All books cited have been published in the UK unless otherwise stated. References to most of the documents and illustrations used in the text are given below; those without references are from private collections. All Ordnance Survey maps cited are held by WSRO.

———

Endpapers (front): WSRO, PM 106; (back): WSRO, PM 65.
Page vi: WSRO, PM 83.
Page ix: WSRO, PM 104.

## 1 'Loathsome and Noysome': Tudor Chichester

The Chichester street plan is an enlargement of an inset to John Norden's Sussex map of 1595. Only one original copy is known, held by the Royal Geographical Society. For a reproduction of the whole map see WSRO, PM 24 and Harry Margary (ed.), *Two Hundred and Fifty Years of Map-Making in the County of Sussex: A Collection of Reproductions of Printed Maps published between the years 1575 and 1825* (Harry Margary/ Phillimore, 1970), f. 3. See also David Kingsley, *Printed Maps of Sussex 1575–1900* (SRS 72, 1982), pp.13–16.

Norden's street plan is described by David Butler in *The Town Plans of Chichester 1595–1898* (WSCC, 1972), pp.4–5.

The scale of Norden's original county map is approximately one inch to four miles. The area around Chichester is reproduced here at an enlarged scale.

Evidence for the city's ruin and decay in the 16th century is quoted from three major sources: Roy R. Morgan, *Chichester: A Documentary History* (Phillimore, 1992), pp.22

(health); 37 (the streets and neglect); 64 (housing); and for the cathedral, W.D. Peckham (ed.), *The Acts of the Dean and Chapter of the Cathedral Church of Chichester 1545–1642* (SRS 58, 1959), especially pp.138–42, and Andrew Foster's paper 'The Dean and Chapter 1570–1660' in Mary Hobbs (ed.), *Chichester Cathedral: An Historical Survey* (Phillimore, 1994), pp.85–100.

The gift of the market cross for the use of 'the poore peple' in 1501 is described by Francis W. Steer in *Bishop Edward Story and the Chichester City Cross* (Chichester City Council, Chichester Papers 1, 1955). (His name is more usually spelt Storey today.)

The conjectural view of East Street, Chichester, in the early 16th century is by Mike Codd and reproduced from the original painting in Chichester District Museum, and the engraving of Chichester Cross – 'Crux Cicestriae' – is dated *c.*1743 – WSRO, PD 216.

The 1570 grant of arms to the city of Chichester makes it clear that the arms were not new but a confirmation of their use from 'auncyent tyme'. See Francis W. Steer, *Chichester City Charters* (Chichester City Council, Chichester Papers 3, 1956), pp.4, 22–4 and plate 12. The grant is part of Chichester City Archives in WSRO – ref. B/2 – and a copy is displayed in the Council House in North Street.

## 2 Bohemia to Arundel: Wenceslaus Hollar

For an original copy of Hollar's etching of Arundel of 1644 see WSRO, PD 1367.

For some of the significant detail on this print see G.W. Eustace, *Arundel: Borough and Castle* (Robert Scott, 1922), pp.51, 75, 80, 134. Hollar's Arundel etching and other Sussex prints – Bramber Castle (four views), Chichester Cathedral (two views), Old Shoreham (1645), Pevensey Castle, Wiston Place and Rye (on a 1659 map of Kent) and his map of Sussex by Richard Blome (1668), are described by Richard Pennington in *A descriptive catalogue of the etched work of Wenceslaus Hollar 1606–1677* (Cambridge University Press, 1982). One of the Bramber views is reproduced in one of the best selections of Hollar's topographical work: in Richard T. Godfrey's *Wenceslaus Hollar: A Bohemian Artist in England* (Yale University Press, New Haven, USA, 1994), p.151. A brief review of his work in Sussex is given by John Farrant in *Sussex Depicted: Views and Descriptions 1600–1800* (SRS 85, 2001), pp.11–12, 169.

The hero of this Arundel article is the subject of Gillian Tindall's biography *The Man Who Drew London: Wenceslaus Hollar in Reality and Imagination* (Chatto & Windus, 2002).

The career of Hollar's patron, Thomas Howard, Earl of Arundel, is described in 'The Collector Earl' in John Martin Robinson's *The Dukes of Norfolk: A Quincentennial History* (Oxford University Press, 1982), pp.97–116. See also 'The Arundel Collection' in a special edition of the arts magazine *Apollo* (August 1996), and Michael Vickers, *The Arundel and Pomfret Marbles in Oxford* (Ashmolean Museum, 2006).

## 3 – 11 When Sussex Travellers Groaned: Tours with Richard Budgen in 1724

Budgen's pioneer map is reproduced in full, and commented upon, by R.A. Skelton in the Margary/Phillimore folio of Sussex maps, ff. 1,2, 5–9, and see David Kingsley's description in his Sussex carto-bibliography, pp. 57-63. For both these publications see p.199 above. For an original copy of this map see WSRO, PM 47.

The three scale bars are enlarged from Robert Morden's map of Sussex, WSRO, PM 106.

When Budgen published his map, the county was also being described by Daniel Defoe in *A Tour Through the Whole Island of Great Britain* (1724–6, republished, *inter alia*, in two volumes in Dent's Everyman's Library, 1962). His tour of western Sussex took in Shoreham, Bramber, Steyning, Wiston, Arundel, Petworth, Chichester and Stansted (1, pp.130–6).

The sources for the following subjects covered in these Budgen articles are listed below, with the tour number in which they occur in this present book given in brackets, or, in the case of roads, arranged under the tour numbers:

**ADUR, RIVER, AS A NAVIGATION (2):** Denis Hickman, 'The River Adur in Bygone Days' (*SCM* 18, 1944), pp.267–8; Henry de Candole, *The Story of Henfield* (Combridges, 1947), pp.32–9; Marjorie Carreck & Alan Barwick, *Henfield: A Sussex Village* (Phillimore, 2002), pp.25–6.

**ARUNDEL (7):** For the town as a port and shipbuilding centre see Tim Hudson, *A History of Arundel* (WSCC, 2000, abstracted from *VCH* V, part 1 (1997).

**BOGNOR, EARLY (I.E. PRE-SIR RICHARD HOTHAM) (7):** Insignificant in the early 18th century, little has been written about Bognor before its birth as a seaside resort except, most notably, in scattered references throughout Lindsay Fleming's *History of Pagham in Sussex* (the author, three volumes, 1949–50).

**BOUNDARIES (5):** Little fieldwork has been done in Sussex on parish boundaries and the county boundary itself. The Fernhurst Society has been walking its boundaries and recording its banks, ditches, hedges and marker stones as they stood at 2003–6, hoping to publish their findings in the future. The link between parish and manorial boundaries revealed by documentary and surviving evidence on the ground is exemplified by Robin Milner-Gulland in 'The Washington Estate: New Evidence on an Ancient Boundary' (*SAC* 143, 2005), pp.205–13. Angus Winchester's *Discovering Parish Boundaries* (Shire Publications, 1990) is the best introduction.

**BURGESS HILL (1):** Its early, pre-railway, history is well covered in Hugh Matthews, *Burgess Hill* (Phillimore, 1989), and see Heather Warne, 'The Place Names and Early Topography of Burgess Hill' (*SAC* 123, 1985), pp.127–43.

**CHICHESTER/CHICHESTER HARBOUR (6):** For Defoe's description see his *Tour* (1, pp.134–5) – for details of this book see p.200 above. The map showing the 1680 bounds of Chichester Harbour is from the Chichester City Archives, WSRO, AZ/2. For mills of the harbour see under MILLS, p.204 below, and for wadeways see under ROADS: Tour Six, p.206 below. The view of Chichester is from *The Modern Universal British Traveller* (1779); WSRO, PD 912 is an uncoloured version.

## COASTAL EROSION

Basil E. Cracknell's *'Outrageous Waves': Global Warming & Coastal Change in Britain through Two Thousand Years* (Phillimore, 2005), documents sea changes along the Sussex coast, pp.129–60.

**Charlton (7):** Lindsay Fleming's *Pagham* describes this lost village (for details of this book see under BOGNOR, EARLY, p.201 above).

**Cudlow (7):** Philip Mainwaring Johnston, 'Notes on an Early Map of Atherington Manor' (*SAC* 44, 1901) pp.147– 66, refers to the lost parish; the map, marking East and West Cudlow, is in WSRO, Add Ms 2031. See also Dr Carruthers Corfield's series of articles 'Cudlow and the Waters' in Rustington Church Magazine, June 1949–Jan. 1951 (copies in WSRO).

**Kingston (8):** The report on the decayed chapel in 1626 and its ruination by the sea in 1641 is quoted from Richard Standing's *Eastpreston & Kingeston parishes* (the author, 1994), pp.2–3, which includes his observations on its probable site, p.54. See also his *East Preston & Kingston: An Illustrated History* (Phillimore, 2006), pp.9–11.

**Middleton (7):** The map of 1606, showing land since devoured by the sea, is in WSRO, Add Ms 2030. The section reproduced here is a reduction from the original scale of 16 inches to 1 mile. The engravings and reports from *The Gentleman's Magazine* are from issues of May 1796 and September 1797. Charlotte Smith's much reprinted lines are taken from her *Elegiac Sonnets ... with Additional Sonnets and Other Poems* (1789), p.44 – WRSO, Crookshank 305. Her portrait is WSRO, F/PD 332.

For the changing coastline and destruction of the old parish church see Georgina Male & Winifred Abbott, *The Incoming Tide: Studies in the History of Middleton on Sea, West Sussex* (Felpham and Middleton Local History Workshop, 1995), pp.13–23, 41–8.

**Rustington/Shoreham/Worthing (8):** for encroachments along this stretch of coastline see H.C.P. Smail, 'Coast Erosion and the Port of Pende' (*SNQ* 17, 1968–71), pp.93–9.

**Selsey (6):** Its changing coastline and inundations are described in Frances Mee, *A History of Selsey* (Phillimore, 1988).

**COBBLESTONE BUILDINGS (8):** The possible connection between the beach-pebble buildings along the Sussex coast and cobblestone buildings of western New York State is investigated in a report on 'Cobblestone Buildings of America's Great Lakes Region, *c.*1825–60' by Robert W. Frasch of Rochester Museum and Science Centre, New York (1970–2); a copy is held by WSRO, MP 1218.

**COLONISATION (4):** The way in which the Weald was colonised from mother settlements in the south is featured, and illustrated with maps, by Peter Brandon in *The Kent & Sussex Weald* (Phillimore, 2003), pp.43–52, and see also his *Sussex* (Robert Hale, 2006), pp.32–6.

**CUCKFIELD (1):** For its former status as a town with a charter-market see Canon J.H. Cooper, *A History of The Parish of Cuckfield* (C. Clarke, 1912) and Maisie Wright, *Cuckfield – an old Sussex town* (Charles Clarke, 1971).

**DRAINAGE, LAND (6):** the maintenance of the low-lying lands around Chichester Harbour, Pagham Harbour and Selsey by an intricate network of rifes, ditches, drains and

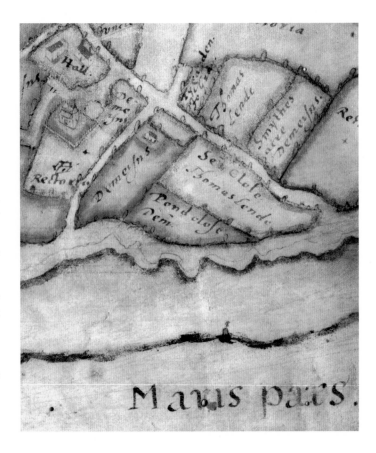

other means is described by David J. Butler in his introduction to *The Land Drainage Records of West Sussex: A Catalogue* (West Sussex County Council, 1973). In covering the historical geography of the Pagham area, Lindsay Fleming's *History of Pagham in Sussex* (the author, 1949–50), touches on ancient watercourses and bridges as features of the landscape in vol. 2, pp.362–9. The moody atmosphere of living in such watery flatlands is beautifully evoked in Graham Swift's novel *Waterland* (Heinemann, 1983). Although about the Fens of eastern England and its world of vast skies, flat landscapes and endless channels and dykes of water – where striving has always been 'against water' and where the drainers and reclaimers were 'plumbers of the land' – it might well be a universal statement about the dominant effect of landscape; his place a larger version of our own Sussex fens.

**EAST GRINSTEAD (1):** M. J. Leppard's *A History of East Grinstead* (Phillimore, 2001) covers the period of Budgen's map and local roads in chapter 8: 'The Parish in the Eighteenth Century', pp.54–9.

**HAMPSHIRE IN SUSSEX (4):** For North and South Ambersham as a detached part of Steep, Hampshire, see Kim Leslie & Brian Short (eds) in *An Historical Atlas of Sussex* (Phillimore, 1999), pp.v, 142.

**HAYWARDS HEATH (1):** The site of the pre-railway town when it was more heathland than even a village is covered by Wyn K. Ford & A.C. Gabe in *The Metropolis of Mid Sussex: A History of Haywards Heath* (Charles Clarke, 1981).

**HORSHAM, PRONUNCIATION OF (2):** The quotation is from the anonymously written *Sussex* (Adam & Charles Black, 1906), p.150. The author was Hilaire Belloc.

**HUNDREDS AS ADMINISTRATIVE DIVISIONS**
**ALDWICK (7):** Numerous references are given in Lindsay Fleming's *Pagham* – for details of this book see above.

**ROTHERBRIDGE (3):** Peter Jerrome, *Petworth from the beginnings to 1660* (Window Press, 2002), p.16.

**IRON INDUSTRY, WEALDEN (3,4):** For the history and precise locations of furnaces and forges see Ernest Straker, *Wealden Iron* (G. Bell, 1931; reprinted by David & Charles, 1969) and Henry Cleere & David Crossley, *The Iron Industry of the Weald* (Leicester University Press, 1985). The drawing of the water-powered hammer is reproduced from *SAC* 46 (1903), opp. p.14.

**LADYHOLT, CARYLL AND POPE (5):** 'John Caryll of Harting III, the Squire and Friend of Pope' in Rev. H.D. Gordon *et al.*, *The History of Harting* (the authors, 1877, reprinted by Frank Westwood, 1975), pp.121–61. See also Ann Parry, *The Carylls of Harting: A Study in Loyalty* (Phillimore, 1976), and Peter Martin, *Pursuing Innocent Pleasures: The Gardening World of Alexander Pope* (Archon Books, New Haven, USA, 1984), pp.36–8. For brief details

of the house based on the only surviving view by John Baptist Caryll *c.*1760, in the British Library, Add Ms 28,250, f.563, sale particulars of 1767, and a copy of map of 1739 in WSRO, Add Ms 28,770, see article by T. J. McCann in John Farrant, *Sussex Depicted: Views and Descriptions 1600–1800* (SRS 85, 2001), p.242. The precise position of the demolished mansion has been located by excavation and an archaeological resistivity survey, described in a report by James Kenny issued by Southern Archaeology in 1998, available on the internet. For Pope's lines expressive of his closeness to the Carylls and his deeply-felt love of rural solitude – as he found at Ladyholt – see perhaps the best edition of his work in John Butt (ed.), *The Poems of Alexander Pope: A one-volume edition of the Twickenham text with selected annotations* (Routledge, 1989 reprint), pp.218, 265, 274–5, 278–9.

**LODSWORTH, LIBERTY OF (4):** The privileges of the bishops of London within this special jurisdiction are described by Martyn Hepworth & A.E. Marshall in their history: *Lodsworth: The Story of an English Village* (Weald and Downland Open Air Museum, 1995), pp.32–46, and in John Fellows(ed.), *The Parish & Liberty of Lodsworth: Notes to Accompany the Lodsworth Millennium Map 2001* (Lodsworth Map Group, 2001), pp.4–6.

## MILLS

**PUMPING ENGINES, WATER (3):** Coultershaw: J.E. Taylor, P.A. Jerrome & A.G. Alnutt, 'Petworth Water Supply' (*SIH* 9, 1979), pp.15–22. Budgen's 'Engine to Raise Water' at Burton Park has not been described, but what was possibly a similar installation at nearby Bignor is recorded by R.M. Palmer & A.E. Baxter in 'Water-Wheel Driven Beam Pump at Bignor Park (*SIH* 19, 1989), pp.11–21, with a gazetteer of other Sussex pumps. The copper-plate engraving of 'Mr Holland's Engine for raising Water' is reproduced from *The Universal Magazine* (August 1755).

**WATER (1, 3, 4, 6):** Derek Stidder & Colin Smith, *Watermills of Sussex Volume II – West Sussex* (the authors, 2001). For more details of the history of the mills around Chichester Harbour, especially tidemills, see 'Of Mills and Millers' in John Reger, *Chichester Harbour: A History* (Phillimore, 1996), pp.107–16.

**WIND (1, 6):** Rev. Peter Hemming, *Windmills in Sussex* (The C.W. Daniel Co., 1936) and Martin Brunnarius, *The Windmills of Sussex* (Phillimore, 1979).

## RIVER CROSSINGS

**ADUR (9):** Henry Cheal, *The Story of Shoreham* (Combridges, 1921), pp.40–2; Kim C. Leslie, *Old Shoreham Toll Bridge* [Southern Railway charities, 1971], commemorating its history when it finally closed to road traffic in 1970. The reference to riding across the Adur 'up to horses' bellies' is from Philip C. Yorke, *The Diary of John Baker ...* (Hutchinson, 1931), p.235. His diary gives much information about travelling around Sussex and elsewhere in the 18th century. The engraving of Shoreham church and bridge is WSRO, PD 1104, and the watercolour of these same features is from a postcard, *c.*1905, WSRO, PD 1589; the map, by Yeakell, Gardner and Gream (1 inch=1 mile) is from their survey of Sussex of 1795, WSRO, PM 46.

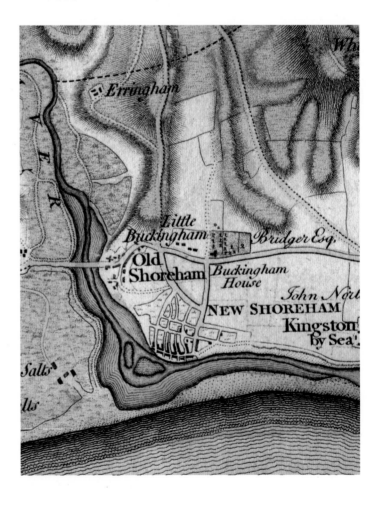

ARUN (7): H.J.F. Thompson, *The Littlehampton Story No. 2: The Swing Bridge Story* (the author, 1979). Includes the earlier ferry crossings.

## ROADS

For general articles on the state of 18th-century roads in the county see, for example, Robert Willis Blencowe, 'Paucity of High Roads in Sussex in 1731', (*SAC* 16,1864), pp.305–7; Rev. Edward Turner, 'High Roads in Sussex at the end of the seventeenth and at the commencement of the eighteenth centuries', (*SAC* 19, 1867), pp.153–69; J.L. André, 'Sussex Roads' [1725], (*SAC* 36, 1888), pp.245–6; Ivan D. Margary, 'Traffic Routes in Sussex, 1724, as shown by "Milestones" on Richard Budgen's Map', (*SAC* 109, 1971), pp.20–3; H.C.P. Smail & P.S. Benham, 'A Survey of Sussex Roads in 1719', (*SCM* 12, 1938), pp.330–9, 417; T. Ackermann & William C. Byron, 'When Sussex Travellers Groaned', (*SCM* 25, 1951), pp.170–3.

Specific references to roads in the articles are from the following sources:

### TOUR ONE

The coach road through Cuckfield, described as 'the Appian Way for the high nobility of England', is quoted from William C.A. Blew, *Brighton and its Coaches: A History of the London and Brighton Road* (John C. Nimmo, 1894), p.47.

The provenance of the two East Grinstead turnpike tickets is given by M.J. Leppard in *The Bulletin of the East Grinstead Society* (no. 53, Autumn 1993), p.11. Three other tickets for the area are also mentioned. Such tickets rarely survive.

The illustration of the tolls authorised for the turnpike road through East Grinstead is from the turnpike act series in WSRO, 4 Geo. II, c. 8.

### TOUR TWO

Burrell's road improvements are referred to by M.M. Hickman in *The History of Shipley* (no publisher given, 1947), p.25. Dr Burton's comments on the 'abominable' roads and the 'long-legged' are from W.H. Blaauw, 'Extracts from the "Iter Sussexiense" of Dr John Burton' (*SAC* 8, 1856), pp.254, 257–8. An overview of the growth of turnpike roads is given by Ivan D. Margary in

'The Development of Turnpike Roads in Sussex' (*SNQ* 13, 1950–3), pp.49–53, and for a useful map of Sussex turnpike roads see J.R. Armstrong, *A History of Sussex* (Phillimore, 3rd edn 1974), pp.132–3.

Burrell's portrait and the view of Knepp Castle are reproduced from Thomas Walker Horsfield, *The History, Antiquities and Topography of the County of Sussex* ( vol. 2, 1835), opp. pp.247–8.

### TOUR THREE

King Charles of Spain's journey to Petworth in 1703 is quoted from the Rev. F.H. Arnold, *Petworth: A Sketch of its History and Antiquities* (A.J. Bryant, 1864), p.76. The Archbishop's dispensation to permit a reduction in the frequency of church services held at Plaistow because of the poor state of the roads is documented in Kirdford's parish register as a memorandum in 1768: WSRO, Par 116/1/1/3, f. 35.

The diversion of the highway away from Rotherbridge, *c.*1800, is the subject of G.D. Johnston's article on 'The Rotherbridge' (*SNQ* 15, 1958–62), pp.296–303.

## TOUR SIX

Little has been written about the history of 'wadeways' as forms of 'roads' through tidal waters. For a few thoughts on the Thorney Island Wadeway see Richard Coates, *The Place-Names of West Thorney* (English Place-Name Society, 1999), pp.16, 26 and for the burial references to those drowned here in the 18th century see WSRO, Par 196/1/1/2. John Morley's *The Wadeway to Hayling – its history and origins* (Havant Borough Council, 1991) gives a more detailed history and description. For the Selsey Wadeway and Horseway see Edward Heron-Allen, *Selsey Bill: Historic and Prehistoric* (Duckworth, 1911), pp.279, 282, 293 and Frances Mee, *A History of Selsey* (Phillimore, 1988), pp.2, 45.

The map showing the Thorney Wadeway is an enlargement from the first sheet of a survey of Sussex, 1778, by Thomas Yeakell and William Gardner (2 inches = 1 mile), WSRO, PM48, and that of the Selsey Wadeway and Horseway is a reduction from a plan of Pagham Harbour, 1774, also by Yeakell and Gardner (20 inches = 1 mile), WSRO, West Dean 3315.

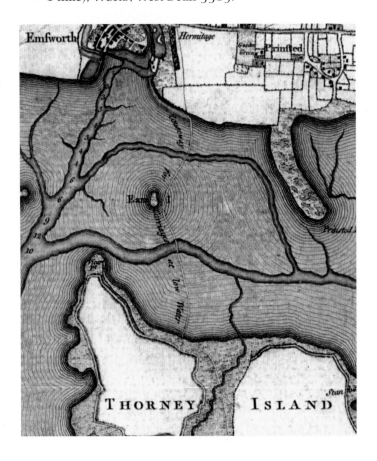

There were other wadeways within Chichester Harbour. Coates (see above), referring to the lost place-name 'funtewade', in West Wittering, suggests either a link with Thorney or Hayling, and also notes the causeway (still partly surviving) between Thorney and Pilsey Island and thence across to Cobnor in Chidham. At Emsworth, Fisherman's Walk (again surviving in part)) most likely gave access to the nearby oyster beds on Fowley Island and was possibly also used by fishermen to haul their vessels through the Emsworth Channel with the use of rope, a common practice known as 'warping'; see *Fisherman's Walk, Emsworth: Archaeological Assessment* (Maritime Archaeology Ltd, 2006). The road running between the waters of Chidham Creek and the pond – part of Chidham Lane – is still known locally as the Wadeway. South-east of here the feature known today as Mud Wall was named in the Apportionment accompanying the Chidham Tithe Map of 1846, WSRO, TD/W30, as 'the Harbour Bank leading to Bosham', another partly surviving low-tide trackway, in this case that followed the top of a dyke. It was used by wheeled farm traffic and by Chidham children to attend Sunday School in Bosham. See Angela Bromley-Martin, *Bosham . . . a village by the sea* (Hughenden Publications, 2006), pp.14–16. The one wadeway still regularly in use – and the most safe to walk in the harbour – crosses School Rithe in Bosham.

Yet another type of routeway across low-lying parts on the Manhood Peninsula – a 'stakeway' – is perhaps suggested by the several 'stakeway' parcels of land in Sidlesham (Stakeway 4 Acres, Stakeway Croft etc.) shown on the parish Tithe Map of 1846 in WSRO, TD/W109. The Sidlesham Stakeway would possibly have given a dry passage across marshy ground on either side of the Keynor Rife, 'probably . . . built by driving tree trunks (stocks or stakes) into the mud, and this may have given rise to the name . . .' – see Rev. H.W. Haynes, *Sidlesham Past and Present* (Southern Publishing Company, 1946), p.45.

## TOUR NINE

The influence of roads on the seasonal location of Sussex Assizes is commented on by William Albery in his mine of information about the county: *A Millennium of Facts in The History of Horsham and Sussex 947–1947* (Horsham Museum Society, 1947), p.591.

The problems of the coastal road between Worthing and Lancing are highlighted by Henfrey Smail in *The Worthing Map Story* (Aldridge, 1949), pp.79–83.

The colour-wash drawing showing the Henfield to Brighton turnpike crossing the Downs at Poynings, made in 1780 by S.H. Grimm, is reproduced from the original in the British Library, Add Ms 5672, f. 22.

**'ROTTEN BOROUGHS' (9):** For 18th-century political corruption see, for Bramber, Defoe's *Tour* 1, pp.130–1 – for book details see p.200 above; for Steyning see Thomas Cox, *Magna Britannia et Hibernia, Antiqua & Nova* (1730), pp.476–7; for Shoreham, Cheal, pp.207–13 – for details of this book see under RIVER CROSSINGS p.204 above. The print of Bramber Castle, originally drawn in 1760 and published in 1775, is WSRO, PD 903.

**SEA-WATER CURE (8):** Dr. Russell and his advocacy of this cure is featured in Edmund M. Gilbert's *Old Ocean's Bauble* (Methuen, 1954), pp.56–62 and Clifford Musgrave's *Life in Brighton* (Faber and Faber, 1970), pp.50–60. In *Georgian Brighton* (Phillimore, 2005), pp. 12–18, Sue Berry puts the town's emergence as a resort in context by showing that there were other towns around the coast of England where bathing in the sea was practised *before* Russell's time, at places like Scarborough, Whitby and Liverpool.

**'SEVEN GOOD THINGS OF SUSSEX' (7):** Admiral Chambers, 'Gastronomic Sussex: Being a Dissertation on the "Seven Good Things" and Some Others' (*SCM* 10, 1936), pp.18–22.

**SMUGGLING (8):** A much-quarried text on 18th-century smuggling is by an anonymous 'Gentleman of Chichester' (possibly the 2nd Duke of Richmond), *A Full and Genuine History of the Inhuman and Unparalled Murders of Mr William Galley, A Custom-House Officer, and Mr Daniel Chater, a Shoemaker, by Fourteen Notorious Smugglers, with the Trials and Execution of Seven of the Bloody Criminals, at Chichester* first published in 1749 and reprinted several times since. The engraving showing the Hawkhurst Gang whipping Richard Hawkins to death at Slindon is reproduced from the undated 6th edition in WSRO, and that of the gibbeting by the seashore is from an article by William Durrant Cooper, 'Smuggling in Sussex' in *SAC* 10 (1858), pp.69–94. The document about brandy smuggling at Goring is from WSRO, Goodwood Ms 156, f. 74. The best overview is by Mary Waugh, *Smuggling in Kent & Sussex 1700–1840* (Countryside Books, 1985).

**WATER POET, THE (JOHN TAYLOR) (8):** The journey of the indomitable poet who rowed along the Sussex coast in 1623 is described in [Henfrey Smail (ed.)], *The Worthing Parade Number Two* (Aldridge, 1954), pp.33–8 and John Chandler (ed.), *Travels Through Stuart Britain: The Adventures of John Taylor, The Water Poet* (Sutton Publishing, 1999), pp.111–12.

**WOOLLEN INDUSTRY (4):** There is no single study for this Sussex industry, but for an overview of some of the local centres, including Midhurst, see *VCH* II (1907), pp.255–7.

## 12  Bound for Botany Bay: Transportation to Australia

Unlike all the other articles in this book, this is the only one not published in the *WSG*. It is an abridged version of a paper originally published as 'The Australian Bicentennial, 1788–1988: Sussex, Australia and the First Fleet' (*WSH* 40, May 1988), pp.1–12.

Robert Hughes' description of the First Fleet as 'this Noah's Ark of small-time criminality' is from his epic study *The Fatal Shore: A History of the Transportation of Convicts to Australia, 1787–1868* (Collins Harvill, 1987), p.74.

The First Fleet convicts have been extensively documented by John Cobley in *The Crimes of the First Fleet Convicts* (Angus & Robertson, Sydney, 1970) and Mollie Gillen in *The Founders of Australia: A Biographical Dictionary of the First Fleet* (Library of Australian History, Sydney, 1989). Much of the information about the Sussex three is derived from this source. Other sources are quoted in the extensive footnotes accompanying the *WSH* article referred to above.

A well-illustrated account of the voyage drawn from original journals and diaries is in Jonathan King's *The First Fleet: The Convict Voyage that founded Australia, 1787–1788* (Macmillan, Melbourne, 1982).

John White's background is based on research by E. Charles Nelson, 'From the Banks of Erne to Botany Bay: John White (c.1756–1832), Surgeon-General of New South Wales' in *Familia: Ulster Genealogical Review* (2,no.3, December 1987), pp.72–81. A copy is in WSRO, MP 2856.

White's burial on 27 February 1832 is recorded in the Broadwater burial register: WSRO, Par 29/1/5/1, p.133.

Thomas Rowlandson's pen and wash drawing of convicts embarking for Botany Bay is reproduced from the original in the National Library of Australia, Canberra – ref. nla. pic – an5601547.

The two watercolour sketches of the First Fleet off the Isle of Wight and sailing into Botany Bay by William Bradley are reproduced from the originals in the Mitchell Library in the State Library of New South Wales, Sydney – refs. ML Safe 1/14, opp. p.13 and opp. p.56 respectively.

## 13 'The bones that had laughed and had cried': Midhurst Highwaymen

The Drewett's 'last dying speech' – WSRO, Add Ms 14,861(17) – is highlighted by Arthur Beckett in '"Catnachery" in Sussex: Bad Ballads of Forgotten Crimes' (*SCM* 1, 1927), pp.106–13, with a follow-up communication in 13 (1939), pp.501–2.

Catnach broadsheets, including many examples of these so-called 'last dying speeches', were collected together by Charles Hindley of Brighton in *Curiosities of Street Literature* (1871). Divided into two volumes and with a new introduction by Leslie Shepard, it has been republished by The Broadsheet King of London (1966).

The work of the Catnach Press is set in its historical context by Louis James in *Print and the People 1819–1851* (Allen Lane, 1976).

The crude woodcut of a public hanging, a popular stock-block used by several last-dying-speech printers, is reproduced from Charles Hindley's *The Life and Times of James Catnach (late of Seven Dials), Ballad Monger* (1878), p.186.

Another last-dying speech held by WSRO is incorporated into a broadsheet covering the trial, conviction and execution in Chichester of John Holloway for murder in 1818: Add Ms 29, 710.

The iron body cage made for gibbeting the body of John Breads in 1743 survives in Rye Town Hall. Shown to the public, and with his skull in place, his story is told endlessly, so much so that one American historian has made the wry comment that 'He is one of the last British criminals of the eighteenth century who is still being punished'. See Paul Kléber Monod, *The Murder of Mr Grebell: Madness and Civility in an English Town* (Yale University Press, New Haven, USA, 2003).

The map showing the gibbet near Rake is an enlargement from a Terrier of the Rogate Estate of 1803 by Thomas Poppleton (4.4 inches =1 mile), WSRO, Add Ms 2193.

'The Hand of Glory' in English and European folklore is well covered in many references on the internet.

The tragic story of the 18th-century Shoreham youth-turned-robber, told by Tennyson in his poem 'Rizpah', is recounted by Lewis T. Ackermann's article 'The Bones That Had Laughed' in *SCM* 22 (1948), pp.88–9.

David D. Cooper explores the gruesome practice of public hangings in *The Lesson of the Scaffold* (Allen Lane, 1976).

## 14 A Rough Horse: Petworth Prosecuting Society

Small-time crime of the type featured in this poster – WSRO, MP 866 – is the subject of George Rudé's analysis in his *Criminal and Victim: Crime and Society in Early Nineteenth-Century England* (Clarendon Press, 1985), a third of which concentrates on rural crime in Sussex.

Prosecuting societies have been largely ignored by historians; there is neither a national study nor much about them for Sussex, but one West Sussex society is the subject of an article by the Rev. R.A. Edwards, 'The Wisborough [Green] Prosecuting Society' in *SCM* 9 (1935), pp.231–6 and a dissertation by Jacqueline Golden – WSRO, MP 2018.

## FIFTEEN GUINEAS
### *REWARD.*

WHEREAS on the 27th of NOVEMBER laſt, JAMES PAGE fraudulently obtained from Mr. HENRY FORD, of *Midhurſt*, Suſſex, Malſter, at Horſham Fair, a handſome GREY GELDING, about 15 Hands high, 8 or 9 Years old, blind of the near Eye, Tail nicked, Head and Legs newly trimmed, but not the Tail; had ſeveral Saddle Marks, and Hoofs a little broke;---had on a very good Saddle, the Let-

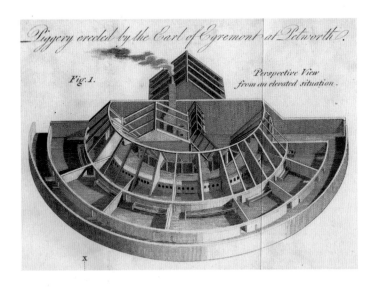

## 15  Petworth Porkers: Lord Egremont's Piggery

The engravings of the Petworth piggery are from between pp.377–8 of the Rev. Arthur Young's *General View of the Agriculture of the County of Sussex* (1808).

This is a major source for the Agricultural Revolution in Sussex as well as giving a great deal of information about the economy of Sussex generally including roads, canals, manufacturing, wages and the cost of provisions and the state of the poor. There are many references to Lord Egremont's work. His experiments in the feeding of pigs are described in the section on 'Hogs', pp.381–90.The book's reissue of 1813 was reprinted by David & Charles in 1970. For an appraisal of this work see John H. Farrant, '"Spirited and Intelligent Farmers": The Arthur Youngs and the Board of Agriculture's Reports on Sussex, 1793 and 1808' (*SAC* 130, 1992), pp.200–12.

The Ordnance Survey maps showing Egremont's piggery are from the first editions of 1874: that on the left is a reduction from the 25.344 inches to 1 mile map – Sussex sheet XXII:16, and the more detailed plan is a reduction from the 1 inch to 41.66 feet map – Sussex sheet XX:16:6 (WSRO, PM 121).

The remarkably fat pig in the coloured engraving was bred at Elsham Hall, Lincolnshire, and is from the original dated 1808 belonging to the Lawes Agricultural Trust, Rothamsted Research, Harpenden, Hertfordshire. (There are no known illustrations of the pigs bred experimentally at Petworth.)

The portrait of the 3rd Earl of Egremont by Thomas Phillips is from the original in the ownership of the National Trust at Petworth House – NT ref. 25893.

A survey of the pig as an essential part of country life in the past is given by Robert Malcolmson & Stephanos Mastoris in *The English Pig: A History* (Hambledon and London, 2001). They highlight Parson Trulliber's 'devotion . . . more to pig-rearing than to religion', pp.2–3. The source of the John Mills' quotation is Elspeth Moncrief *et al.*, *Farm Animal Portraits* – a magnificent series of paintings and prints – (Antique Collectors' Club, 1996), pp.233–4.

## 16  Smells, Filth and Flies: Chichester's Beast Market

WSRO holds Gilbert's original oil painting of the beast market in East Street of *c*.1813 – Fuller PD 478 – and the engraved copy of 1814 reproduced here – PD 2808. The photographs of the market in East Street and North Street are, respectively, WSRO, PH 9036 and PH 7445.

A copy of Canon Swainson's pamphlet exposing the grim state of the city in 1866: *A Few Words to those who have the welfare of Chichester at heart* is in WSRO, MP 784. His comments, and those from other writers in the same century, are collected together by Timothy J. McCann in *Restricted Grandeur: Impressions of Chichester 1586–1948* (WSCC, 1974).

The controversial drainage issue is pinpointed by the issue of a propaganda leaflet parodying Hamlet: *Shakespeare revised for the Non-Drainers* (c.1866); WSRO, MP 785 (copy).

Press coverage of the removal of the street market to new premises was given in the *WSG*, 11 May 1871. In the previous issue of 4 May is a nostalgic 'In Memoriam' letter from 'Eye Witness' about the old market, referring to Gilbert's East Street market picture made earlier in the century. The reminiscences by Thomas Gordon Willis are taken from his book *Records of Chichester: Some Glimpses of its Past* (T.G. Willis & Co., 1928), p.297.

## 17 Chichester's Charlies: The Watchmen's Patrol

Fleeting glimpses of the city's watchmen – and its street lighting – in the 1820s-30s can be found in three minute books of Chichester's guardians of the poor – WSRO, WG5/1A/3–5. 'The Regulations' poster of 1821 is pasted into WG5/1A/3 (between minutes of 17 and 28 September 1821).

The 1820 street plan of Chichester used to illustrate the routes of the watchmen's rounds is a reduction from a large-scale plan (2.15 inches to 300 feet) by Edward Fuller, WSRO, MP 51.

Lewes appointed town watchmen nearly thirty years earlier than in Chichester. In 1793 it was resolved 'to engage three Men at 7s. per week each, two of which are to perambulate the Streets, Lanes & Backways ... every Night, from Eleven o'clock in the Evening till six the next morning'. Costs were reduced by the three having to share equipment for two as they were only supplied with 'two warm great Coats, two Felt Hats, two large Horn Lanterns, and two Watchman's Ratchets'; see Verena Smith (ed.), *The Town Book of Lewes 1702–1837*, (SRS 69, 1972), pp.93–4.

For the regulations and duties of Brighton's watchmen, first appointed in 1810, see Gerald W. Baines, *History of the Brighton Police Force 1838–1967* (County Borough of Brighton Police, 1967), pp.14–15.

There is no major study of watchmen, but background details can be found in 'Under Watch and Ward' by William Andrews in *Bygone England: Social Studies in its Historic Byways and Highways* (Hutchinson, 1892), pp.1–16. The illustration of the sleeping watchman in his box is from this source. Their inadequacy comes out of evidence before the Select Committee on Police, 1817, on which a chapter, 'The Case of the Dangerous Subjects', is based, in Strathearn Gordon & T.G.B. Cocks, *A People's Conscience* (Constable, 1952). The lithograph of 1829 showing watchmen returning home is reproduced in this book.

How gas lighting affected night-time street life is investigated in some detail by Lynda Nead in *Victorian Babylon: People, Streets and Images in Nineteenth-Century London* (Yale University Press, New Haven, USA, 2000), and in Sussex, Judy Middleton has looked at changing provision in *The Lights of Brighton and Hove: Nineteenth Century Street Lighting* (no publisher given, 1982).

Brighton installed its first street lighting by gas in the Steyne in 1824, but even before then the private grounds of the Royal Pavilion were lit by gas from 1818. The gas lamp standards, the earliest street lights to survive in Sussex, date from the 1830s, and still stand in the grounds as listed structures. In Lewes, the Gas Light Company was established in 1822. See Timothy Carder, *The Encyclopaedia of Brighton* (East Sussex County Libraries, 1990), entry 176, and Rev. T.W. Horsfield, *The History and Antiquities of Lewes* (1824), pp.343–4.

## 18  Evils of Tea Drinking: William Cobbett's *Cottage Economy*

Many reprints of William Cobbett's classic book on self-sufficiency, *Cottage Economy*, have been published since it first appeared in 1822. One of the latest UK editions is by Verey & Von Kanitz Publishing in 2000. The preface to the 1926 edition published by Peter Davies includes a preface by G.K. Chesterton who is quoted in this article. The extracts quoted on Cobbett's diatribe about drinking tea in contrast to his enthusiasm for home-brewed beer is from this edition, pp.14–16, 19.

For the background to his eventful and controversial life see William Reitzel (ed.), *The Autobiography of William Cobbett: the progress of a plough-boy to a seat in Parliament* (Faber and Faber, 1967). The background to his *Cottage Economy* and its context is given in Ian Dyck, *William Cobbett and Rural Popular Culture* (Cambridge University Press, 1992), pp.107–24.

Cobbett gave his views on the state of the country in *Rural Rides*, first published in 1830 and still in print with a Penguin Classics edition of 2001. Through a series of tours, many of which took him through Sussex from his base at Worth, he pours out his views – and invective – on all the decay he found in 'the system' – in what he called 'the Thing'.

Cobbett's comment on his friend Mrs Brazier of Worth Lodge Farm where he stayed and wrote most of *Cottage Economy*, is taken from Reitzel, pp.187–8, where the farm is incorrectly called North Lodge. The Worth Tithe Map of 1839–40, showing the farm, is a reduction from the original scale of 26.6 inches to 1 mile, WSRO, TD/E155. Reitzel omits Cobbett's wish 'to raise a monument to her memory'. The source for the complete quotation is Cobbett's *Political Register*, 28 December 1833.

Her burial in 1833, and that of her husband in the following year, is recorded in the Worth parish register, WSRO, Par 516/1/5/1. Their grave and the unadorned facts it gives – almost certainly not the 'memorial' Cobbett wanted – is on the southern extremity of the churchyard. The Brazier's farm and their domestic economy was so significant to Cobbett that they deserve more research and recognition for the part they played in his life and work.

Cobbett's portrait, possibly by George Cooke, *c.*1831, is from the original in the National Portrait Gallery, London – ref. NPG 1549.

## 19  A 'blow on the smeller': A Great Fight near Chichester

Hazlitt's quotation is from his classic description 'The Fight' that took place on Hungerford Downs in Berkshire in 1821, and is quoted by Tom Sawyer in *Noble Art: An Artistic & Literary Celebration of the Old English Prize-Ring* (Unwin Hyman, 1989), pp.61–2.

Sawyer's book gives many references to Spring and Langan, but only with a brief mention of the Chichester match. This is much more fully described in John Hurley's *Tom Spring: Bare-Knuckle Champion of All England* (Tempus Publishing, 2002), pp.137–52, the source for W. Mitford's victory song for Spring, p.130.

The full story of the match was published in a little booklet entitled *History of the Great Fight between Spring & Langan for the Championship of England.* . . . It was summarised in a broadsheet. Both are in the Fuller collection (no. 59) in WSRO.

The newspaper report describing the fight was published in the *Hampshire Telegraph and Sussex Chronicle*, 14 June 1824.

The illustrations showing the fight – the engraving, from a Catnach broadsheet, the others on a commemorative jug – are from Chichester District Museum.

Another broadsheet, printed in Bristol, wrongly reporting that the match took place 'In Goodwood Park' and that it went to seventy-eight rounds rather than the accepted seventy-seven, is also in WSRO, Add Ms 28,752. Much of it was almost certainly written before the match took place, all part of the usual pre-match confusion and rumour when, because they were illegal, the locations were only declared at the last minute.

The clue to its exact location, corroborating other evidence, is given by the Apuldram and Birdham Tithe Maps showing the commemoration of the victor in the naming of Spring Field: WSRO, TD/W4, TD/W16. That the field was known by another name before the fight – suggesting therefore that it was not named after a water-spring – is indicated by a map of 1775: WSRO, Cap II/4/9/7.

Interestingly a similar commemoration was made at Smarden in Kent. Fight Field was named after a prize-fight that took place there in 1859 between Tom Sayers and Bill Benjamin. See Paul Jennings, *The Living Village* (Hodder and Stoughton, 1968), pp.17–18.

Although this Chichester match was one of the last great championship fights in England, just four years later, in 1828, a huge crowd of some seven to eight thousand gathered at Fisherstreet, on the county boundary with Surrey, to watch two London contestants fight for a wager. See Pamela Bruce, *Northchapel: A Parish History* (Northchapel Parish Council, 2000), pp.58–60.

## 20 Kings of the Road: Worthing Coaching Days

The Worthing coaching poster of *c.*1828 is in WSRO, MP 17.

Worthing is the best covered West Sussex town for its coaching history in two books by Henfrey Smail: *The Worthing Road and its Coaches* (1943) – in which the watercolour of the London-Worthing coach in 1830 reproduced here is printed – and *Coaching Times and After* (1948), both published by Aldridge.

Times for Worthing-London coaches are given by Alan Bates in *Directory of Stage Coach Services 1836* (David & Charles, 1969). Travelling the fifty-seven miles via Washington – Horsham – Leatherhead – Epsom – Morden – *The Sovereign* was timed for six hours, *The Accommodation*, a slower coach, for eight, p.55.

The 18th-century quotation about the bad state of Sussex roads is from Thomas Cox, *Magna Britannia et Hibernia, Antiqua & Nova* (1730), p.534 (a revised edition of the original book by William Camden of 1586). For other references see ROADS, pp.205–7 above.

Dickens' *The Posthumous Papers of the Pickwick Club* (1837) quotation is from chapter 28 'A Good-Humoured Christmas Chapter' and his classic description of a stage-coach town in decay is in chapter 24 'An old Stage-Coaching House' in *The Uncommercial Traveller* (1869).

The two 19th-century prints of Arundel, of the High Street showing the Norfolk Arms and the railway, are WSRO, F/PD 204.

The story of coaching throughout the country in its heyday is well described in R.C. & J.M. Anderson, *Quicksilver: A Hundred Years of Coaching 1750–1850* (David & Charles, 1973); Harry Hanson, *The Coaching Life* (Manchester University Press, 1983); David Mountfield, *Stage and Mail Coaches* (Shire, 2003).

## 21 Blubberhead the Beadle: Troubles in the Workhouse

The Blubberhead broadsheet – WSRO, Goodwood Ms 1582, f. 197 – was circulated widely throughout the country to stir up opposition to the new poor law. The same story was printed in at least one other format, with just minor variations, and is reproduced in Louis James, *Print and the People 1819–1851* (Allen Lane, 1976), p.132.

For a concise overview of the poor law between 1350 and 1948 see J.J. and A.J. Bagley, *The English Poor Law* (Macmillan, 1966). Developments from the reforms of the late eighteenth century to the abolition of the Board of Guardians in the twentieth century are illustrated through documentary evidence in Michael E. Rose, *The English Poor Law 1780–1930* (David & Charles, 1971).

The story of the resistance to the new poor law of 1834 – the Blubberhead theme – is told by Nicholas C. Edsall in *The anti-Poor Law movement 1834–44* (Manchester University Press, 1971).

Norman Longmate's *The Workhouse* (Temple Smith, 1974), and Trevor May's *The Victorian Workhouse* (Shire, 1999), describe the institutional conditions of these 'pauper palaces' caricatured in the Blubberhead broadsheet.

The background story to the Horsham poor law troubles in the 1830s is told by William Albery in *A Millennium of Facts in the History of Horsham and Sussex, 947–1947* (Horsham Museum Society, 1947), pp.579–86.

WSRO holds extensive series of official poor law documents relating to the old system based on parishes and the later unions. See the parish record catalogues and also Jane M. Coleman, Sussex *Poor Law Records: A Catalogue* (WSCC, 1960).

The Midhurst resolutions of 1817 are quoted from the town's vestry minute book, WSRO, Par 138/12/1, f. 106r. The severe rules of Shipley Workhouse, including confinement in 'the Black Hole', are enumerated in the vestry

minutes, 12 May 1830, WSRO, Par 168/12/1, ff. 16v–18r, and are the subject of a short article by M.M. Hickman, 'Rules for the Paupers in Shipley Poorhouse' in *SNQ* 10 (1944–5), pp.35–6. The pauper crisis at Cuckfield in the winter of 1836 and the cruel reaction of the authorities is told in Ian Anstruther's *The Scandal of the Andover Workhouse* (Geoffrey Bles, 1973), pp.30–1. A study of how poor law relief operated at parish level – at Hurstpierpoint – and how this was eventually affected by the new union workhouse at Cuckfield – is vividly described as a major thread throughout E. J. Colgate's *The Power and The Poverty: Life in a Sussex Village 1790–1850* (George Mann Publications, 2008).

The woodcut of the skeleton ploughing the field is from G. Mitchell, *The Skeleton at the plough* (1874).

The drawing of East Preston Union Workhouse, dated 1874, is from a series of architect's original plans in WSRO, WG9/56/3.

The 'Just-Starve-Us' illustration is from a Victorian music cover.

## 22 'I would not go back to England on no account': Emigration to Canada

The Lanaways' letter – WSRO, MP 320 – is one of 180 letters sent back home by Petworth Emigration Committee-sponsored emigrants reprinted by Wendy Cameron, Sheila Haines and Mary McDougall Maude in *English Immigrant Voices: Labourers' Letters from Upper Canada in the 1830s*. This is a companion volume to Cameron and Maude's *Assisting Emigration to Upper Canada: The Petworth Project 1832–1837*, both published by McGill-Queen's University Press, Montreal, Canada, 2000.

'Flying to a Distant Country' is a chapter in Sheila Haines' and Leigh Lawson's study of the prime mover behind the Emigration Committee's work in *Poor Cottages & Proud Palaces: The Life and Work of the Reverend Thomas Sockett of Petworth 1777–1859* (The Hastings Press, 2007), pp.155–67.

There is extensive documentation on 19th-century emigration in the Petworth House Archives and parish records held by WSRO.

Taking a wider view of emigration is Terry Coleman's *Passage to America* (Hutchinson, 1972), describing how more than two million men, women and children left England and Ireland for both Canada and the United States in the mid-19th century. Alexander Murdoch's *British Emigration 1603–1914* (Palgrave Macmillan, 2004) outlines the Petworth scheme (pp.94–6) in his chapter on assisted emigration.

'"If You Want To Live, Come Here": Emigration to the United States' is the subject of a section of Kim Leslie's *Roots of America* (WSCC, 1976), pp.32–48, documenting the experiences of West Sussex emigrants.

The rules and regulations and diary entry relating to the *British Tar* (from *Narrative of a Voyage, with a Party of Emigrants, sent out from Sussex, in 1834, by the Petworth Emigration Committee to ... Toronto ...* (1834), pp.4–6), and the poster advertising its sailing, are in WSRO, MP 320. A study of this shipment is in Sheila Haines (ed.), *'No Trifling Matter': Being an Account of a Voyage by Emigrants from Sussex and Hampshire to Upper Canada on board the 'British Tar' in 1834* (University of Sussex, 1990).

*The Emigrant's Last Sight of Home*, 1858, by Richard Redgrave is from the original in the Tate Gallery, London – accession no. TO2110 and *The Last of England*, 1855, by Ford Madox Brown, from the original in Birmingham Museum and Art Gallery – accession no. 1891P24. How these two artists and many others treated the subject of emigration in the 19th century is discussed by Susan P. Casteras in 'Oh! Emigration! thou'rt the curse ... Victorian Images of Emigration Themes' in *The Journal of Pre-Raphaelite Studies* 6 (November 1985), pp.1–23.

The engraving 'Land ho!' is from *The Illustrated London News*, 7 May 1870.

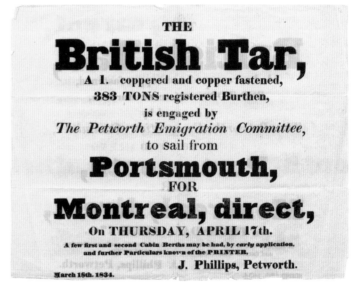

## 23 Noah's Ark Days: Sundays in Sussex

The poster publicising the Horsham Deanery's seven resolutions for observance of the Lord's Day is amongst the Warnham parish records – see WSRO, Par 203/7/9.

The cases of sabbath-breaking in the 1620s are quoted from transcripts printed in Hilda Johnstone (ed.), *Churchwardens' Presentments: Part 1, Archdeaconry of Chichester* (SRS 49, 1949). The specific cases quoted can be found by using the index in SRS 50. The original presentments are in WSRO.

The background to the enforcement of Sunday observance in this period is described by W.B. Whitaker in *Sunday in Tudor and Stuart Times* (Houghton Publishing, 1933).

The Victorian/Edwardian quotations used are from: Charles Dickens, *Little Dorrit* (1857), at the beginning of chapter 3 'Home'; Alison Uttley, *Ambush of Young Days* (Faber and Faber, 1937), pp.126,142,143,144 of the illustrated edition, 1951; Margaret Hutchinson, *A Childhood in Edwardian Sussex* (Saiga Publishing, 1981), p.105; 'Sunday voices' are in the diary of the Newhaven diarist, Caroline Waters, edited by Cecile Woodford as *Caroline's Kingdom: The Diary of a Victorian Lady* (Crown Quality Books, 1984), p.18; the Easebourne reminiscence is from 'A Little Girl Long Ago' by Mary Celia Reiss, an unpublished typescript, WSRO, MP 865, pp.16–17.

## 24 A Penny a Week: Victorian Schools

The history of Compton and Up Marden National School can be reconstructed from a fairly extensive series of documents in WSRO. The cash figures for 1854 quoted in this article are from the school's minute book, E56/1/1. The school rules of 1847, reproduced here, are pasted onto the flyleaf of this minute book.

The school was affiliated to the National Society; see H.J. Burgess & P.A. Welsby, A *Short History of the National Society 1811–1961* (National Society, 1961). A good concise overview of the history of education is given by George Berry, *Discovering Schools* (Shire, 1970) and see also Trevor May, *The Victorian Schoolroom* (Shire 1994).

Highlights of the school year for 1880–1 are taken from the log book for Cocking National School, WSRO, E53/12/1.

The 'Infant School Requisites' and other classroom equipment reproduced in this article are from two late 19th-century school equipment catalogues, WSRO, E125/8/2.

Steve Johnson and Kim Leslie document life in late Victorian schools from WSRO sources in *Scholars and Slates: Sussex Schools in the 1880s* (WSCC, 1989).

The Flora Thompson quotation is from her *Lark Rise to Candleford* trilogy, chapter xi: 'School' (Oxford University Press world's classic's edn, 1965), p.191. The rector of Berwick's ideas on exclusion as a form punishment are from the Rev. Edward Boys Ellman, *Recollections of a Sussex Parson* (Combridges, 2nd edn, 1925), pp.159–60.

## 25 'Idle and Disorderly': Public Nuisances in Warnham

The churchwardens flexing their law and order powers at Warnham, illustrated by this warning notice to the idle and disorderly – WSRO, Par 203/11/3 – emphasises the wide-ranging authority of parish officers in civil local government in the past. This is the subject of the classic work by W.E. Tate, *The Parish Chest: A Study of the Records of Parochial Administration in England* (Phillimore, 3rd edn, reprinted 2000). The parish constable and his work is examined, pp.176–87.

As unpopular as marble playing on Sundays might have been to the church authorities, it was one of the popular open-air games played in Victorian Sussex. That the annual World Marbles Championships are held in West Sussex – at Tinsley Green near Crawley – gives some measure of its deep-seated local popularity. See 'The Marble Players' in *Sussex Customs, Curiosities & Country Lore* by Tony Wales (Ensign Publications, 1990), pp.52–3.

The point about the ability of the 'idle and disorderly' – and indeed many others – to read this and other public warning notices (yet alone to understand them) before the introduction of compulsory education can be gauged by examining the ability of marriage partners and witnesses to sign the marriage register as a measure of literacy. In Warnham, in the ten years between 1845 and 1854, of the 229 people recorded as signatories at wedding ceremonies in the church, more than half could not write their name: 121 had to give their assent with their mark – by scribing an 'X'; WSRO, Par 203/1/3/2.

Maurice Rickards in *The Public Notice: An Illustrated History* (David & Charles, 1973), gives an authoritative account of this arm of law enforcement.

## 26 Exotic Groves: Lady Dorothy Nevill at Dangstein

Lady Dorothy Nevill's memoirs were edited by her son Ralph as *The Reminiscences of Lady Dorothy Nevill* (1906), *Under Five Reigns* (1910), *My Own Times* (1912) and *The Life and Letters of Lady Dorothy Nevill* (1919), the first published by Edward Arnold, the rest by Methuen. The extracts quoted in this article are from the first two books, pp.77, 78, 80–1 from the first, and pp.80–3 from the second.

With access to new sources (but not referenced) her biography has been written by Guy Nevill as *Exotic Groves: A Portrait of Lady Dorothy Nevill* (Michael Russell, 1984).

The extracts reproduced from the first edition of the sale particulars of 1879 are WSRO, SP 2726. (The second edition is SP 564.) They describe the Dangstein mansion and estate (2,120 acres – 848 hectares) as developed by the Nevills in some considerable detail. There are further sale particulars for 1919, 1922 and 1926 as SPs 2727–9. The Ordnance Survey map of the house and gardens is a reduction from a scale of 25.344 inches to 1 mile and is Sussex sheet XXI:5, 2nd edn survey made in 1896.

Lady Dorothy's 80th birthday notice was published in the *WSG* for 20 September 1906.

The story of her extraordinary 'aerial orchestra' is told by W.R. Trotter in 'Heavenly Harmonies: the Whistling Pigeons of Dangstein' in *WSH* 41, August 1988), pp.1–15.

## 27 'Grinding the Wind': Hard Labour in Petworth Prison

The questions and answers that introduce this article are from the *Report from the Select Committee of the House of Lords, on the Present State of Discipline in Gaols and Houses of Correction ... 1863*, p.385. A copy of this report is held by WSRO, giving an extensive examination of the Petworth Governor, William Linton, pp.383–405. The cross-sections of the Petworth treadwheel are from Appendix 1 of this

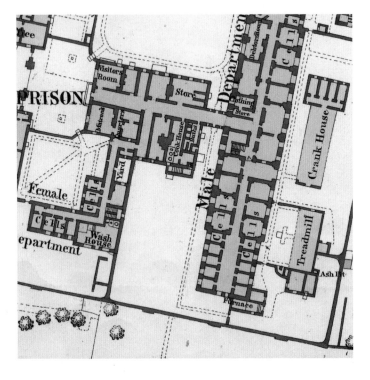

report (between pp.500–1), and the 1835 Report which is reproduced from *SCM* 16 (March 1942), p.76. The tables for 'Tread-wheel and Crank Labor' and 'Weekly Dietary' are from the *Rules for the Government of the Common Gaol and House of Correction at Petworth* (1853), WSRO, QAP/5/22/W7 and the 'State of the Prisoners' report, 1837, is WSRO, Goodwood Ms 1588, no.860. The mid-19th-century engraving of the prison from the Tillington Road is WSRO, PD 1660 and the detailed room plan is a reduction from the Ordnance Survey map of Petworth of 1874 at a scale of 1 inch to 41.66 feet – Sussex sheet XXII:16:12 (WSRO, PM 121).

Papers relating to Petworth House of Correction are also in WSRO as part of Quarter Sessions records, QAP/5.

The Petworth treadwheel and its operation, and how it was regulated (as well as the crank, another mechanised form of hard labour), are described in Michael Royall's *The Petworth House of Correction* (the author, 1999), pp.67–81.

The wider perspective on how prisons were administered at the time of the Select Committee's 1863 enquiry into conditions at Petworth can be appreciated from two quite different studies. *The Reform of Prisoners* (Croom Helm, 1987) by William James Forsythe focuses on the changing Victorian framework under which the whole system operated, whilst Philip Priestley's *Victorian Prison Lives: English Prison Biography 1830–1914* (Pimlico, 1999) draws on first-hand accounts from prisoners themselves.

One of those who suffered was Oscar Wilde whose haunting lines are quoted at the end of the Petworth article. His painful experiences, famously as prisoner C3.3, including the full version of 'The Ballad of Reading Gaol' are featured in Peter Southerton's *Reading Gaol by Reading Town* (Berkshire Books, 1993).

Bricks scratched with prisoners' names and dates (see p.133) that survived the 1882 demolition of Petworth Prison can still be seen (March 2008) on the west side of the north-south wall, just to the west of the letter box at the junction of Grove Street and Rosemary Lane.

## 28 Mouse-trap Man: Colin Pullinger, Selsey Inventor

Pullinger's trade card and the photograph showing him outside his mouse-trap works are in the Selsey WI Scrapbook – WSRO, Add Ms 53,617.

The story of Pullinger's escape from an Australian shipwreck and his determination to return to Selsey is based on a lost manuscript quoted in an unidentified and undated newspaper article also in this scrapbook.

The historian of mouse and rat traps is David Drummond who has published two papers on the Selsey traps: 'Colin Pullinger and his Perpetual Mouse Trap' and 'Colin Pullinger's Registered Designs' in *SIH* 24 (1994), pp.2–9, and 34 (2004), pp.36–7. The cross-section of the Automaton Mouse Trap is reproduced from the first of these. He puts Pullinger in a wider global and national context in his *Mouse Traps: A Quick Scamper through their Long History* (North American Trap Collectors Association, Galloway, Ohio, USA, 2005) and *British Mouse Traps and Their Makers* (Mouse Trap Books, 2008).

See also [H.W. Wolff], 'Selsey Mousetraps' in *Quaint Industries and Interesting Places in Sussex* (Sussex Advertiser, [1882]), pp.22–34 – copy in WSRO, Fuller no. 84, from which the opening sentence and the advertisement used in this present article are reproduced – and Frances Mee, *A History of Selsey* (Phillimore, 1998), pp.132–3.

Of six Selsey parish register entries for the baptism of Colin Pullinger's children between 1847 and 1856, four successively note Colin Pullinger with a changing occupation; see baptism records, WSRO, Par 166/1/2/2, pp.12, 18,22, 27, 33, 37.

## 29 'The Sussex Aboriginal': Stories from Harting

The quotations are from pp.212–14, 216, 218 of the Rev. H.D. Gordon's *The History of Harting.... With a Chapter on the Geology of the District by the late Sir Roderick Impey Murchison ... and Some Notice of its Flora and Fauna by J. Weaver* (the authors, 1877), republished in facsimile by the Petersfield Bookshop, 1975. The illustration of the village street at Harting is also from this book.

Gordon's collaborators were an interesting pair. Murchison (1792–1871), from Scotland, was Director General of the Geological Survey of the United Kingdom and one of the founding fathers of geological science after whom the Murchison Crater on the Moon and at least fifteen geographical locations in the world are named. His investigation into Wealden geology, on which his Harting chapter is based, was published as his first geological memoir in 1825. He got to know Harting well through marriage into the Hugonin family of Nursted House in the adjacent parish of Buriton in Hampshire. Joseph Weaver (1810–85), a much-loved upper servant at Uppark, where he lived for fifty years as a pillar of the household, was noted locally as a natural historian and man of learning. Like Gordon, he knew every inch of his parish. His brass memorial, at the west end of Harting church, records that he was 'Laid in the place of peace at Harting'.See Margaret Meade-Fetherstonhaugh & Oliver Warner, *Uppark and its People* (George Allen & Unwin, 1964), pp.100–1.

Gordon's thoughts about 'the best and severest test' of his ministry at Harting are quoted in a letter from Dr M.H. Gordon, 8 February 1951: WSRO, Par 98/7/11. It is amongst the papers of the late Horace Brightwell, a goldmine of information about Harting.

Besides his major work on Harting, Gordon's other publication was *Among the Birds of Harting* (Duplock and Woledge, 1886). His lecture to the Brighton Natural History Society was issued by them as *Birds and their Migrations* (1889). Copies are in WSRO, Par 98/7/7.

Something of the social/intellectual milieu in which country parsons like Gordon investigated their local natural history is explored by Patrick Armstrong in *The English Parson-Naturalist: A Companionship Between Science and Religion* (Gracewing, 2000).

The extraordinary world of his eccentric Buckland in-laws is revealed by Mrs Gordon (Elizabeth Oke Gordon, wife of the rector/vicar) in *The Life and Correspondence of William Buckland, DD,FRS* (John Murray, 1894) – from which the Buckland silhouette is reproduced – and Deborah Cadbury

in *The Dinosaur Hunters: A Story of Scientific Rivalry And the Discovery of the Prehistoric World* (Fourth Estate, 2000) and chapter 2 'The Genesis of the Modern Don – William Buckland' in Noel Annan's *The Dons, Mentors, Eccentrics and Geniuses* (HarperCollins, 1999). G.H.O. Burgess elaborates on Elizabeth Gordon's brother in *The Curious World of Frank Buckland* (John Baker, 1967).

Copies of letters to both Gordon and his wife Elizabeth at Harting are held on microfilm in the Devon Record Office, ref. MFC/97. That Elizabeth shared her husband's interest in historical matters is shown in this correspondence and also by her two major works published after she left Harting following his death: *Saint George, Champion of Christendom and Patron Saint of England* (Swan Sonnenschein, 1907); *Prehistoric London: its Mounds and Circles* (Elliot Stock, 1914). Her interest in Saint George is commemorated in Harting parish church by a window dedicated to her memory in the south wall of the nave.

The Reverend Gilbert White's work, including observations made around Harting, is distilled in his *Natural History of Selborne* (1789), one of the most famous books on natural history in the English language. Untold editions have been published and it is still in print. White has been

called 'a sort of localised Pan' by Walter S. Scott in *White of Selborne and his times* (John Westhouse, 1946), p.166, an apt description also of Harting's parson, who trod in White's footsteps.

The 1930s photographs of Jimmy Ifold and Jimmy Puttick are from the George Garland Collection in WSRO, N8830 and N4758. A tribute to Garland's work in recording such characters from the West Sussex countryside has been compiled by Peter Jerrome and Jonathan Newdick in *The Men with Laughter in their Hearts* (Window Press, 1986).

## 30 'Sleepy Hollow': Late-Victorian Chichester

Francis Pigou reveals his feelings about Chichester and cathedral life in his autobiographical *Phases of My Life* (Edward Arnold, 1898). The Chichester extracts quoted are from pp.357–9, 361, 371, and are taken from the third edition, 1899. His anecdote about the death-bed scene and the funeral cakes is from p.330.

That Pigou – and Burgon – were not the only deans to find Chichester a sleepy backwater is illustrated by Walter Hook who came from bustling, busy Leeds in 1859. He saw his Chichester days as ones of quiet retirement, so much so that it gave him all the time he needed to research and write his monumental eleven-volume work on the arch-

bishops of Canterbury. See Mary Hobbs (ed.), *Chichester Cathedral: An Historical Survey* (Phillimore, 1994), p.126.

Pigou's farewell sermon at Chichester is a significant pointer to his own apparent neglect. He ended the sermon by justifying his frequent absences from the cathedral and city, pointing out that the statutory duties of a dean were exceedingly light, and if the holder of the office simply performed them, and did nothing else, he would lead a life of indolence. To fill up his spare time he might have written a theological work and burden bookshelves with yet another book that would never be read. His answer had been to make himself useful around the diocese by helping parish clergymen who needed assistance. See *WSG*, 10 December 1891.

The photographs illustrating this article are in WSRO: Pigou – PH 12,024; Cathedral – PH 12,558; Deanery – Cap I/21/25 (Burgon's own album).

Details about Dean Burgon's drawing sent to his little Chichester friend 'Dodo' – 'THE DEAN THINKING ABOUT DODO' – are in Monica Maloney's article 'An Artistic Dean' in *Chichester History* 23 (2007), p.3.

## 31   A Snob's Guide: Augustus Hare in Sussex

The extracts quoted in this article are taken from Augustus J.C. Hare's *Sussex* (George Allen, 1894).

None of the illustrations accompanying the extracts from Hare's text was published in his book. The postcard

views used here, of a slightly later date than the text, are from a private collection. The cover of John Trundle's pamphlet about the 'Serpent' of St Leonard's Forest is reproduced from the only known copy in the Bodleian Library, Oxford, shelf-mark 4 R21(5) Art Seld. See Jeremy Knight and Jason Semmens, *Horsham's Dragon Containing True and Wonderfull – a Discourse Relating to a*

*Strange and Monstrous Serpent (1614)* (Horsham Museum Society, 2007).

Hare's endurance of one of the most extraordinarily cruel Victorian childhoods in one of the most bizarre of Sussex households is based on his own recollections in *The Story of My Life*, one of the longest autobiographies in the English language, published in six volumes in 1896 and 1900. An incomparable picture of privileged society at its best – and very worst – it lifted the lid on the gossip and scandal of his high-born contemporaries, causing yet more scandal in its frankness.

More accessible and manageable are Malcolm Barnes' abridgements of this massive work, the first three volumes as *The Years with Mother* (1952), the second three as *In My Solitary Life* (1953), both published by Allen & Unwin. A one-volume abridgement has been edited by Anita Miller and James Papp as *Augustus Hare, Peculiar People: The Story of My Life* (Academy Chicago Publishers, Chicago, USA, 1995).

So much of what has been written about Hare is based on what he wanted people to know about himself. An attempt to disentangle the real Hare from his own published memoirs has been made in Malcolm Barnes' biography, *Augustus Hare* (Allen & Unwin, 1985).

Hare, the consummate snob, emerges from novelist Somerset Maugham's intimate pen portrait 'Augustus' in *The Vagrant Mood* (William Heinemann, 1952), pp.1–50.

The possible link between the Hare family and *Alice's Adventures in Wonderland* is explored by Jo Elwyn Jones and J. Francis Gladstone in *The Red King's Dream or Lewis Carroll in Wonderland* (Jonathan Cape, 1995), pp.132, 136–7, 171–2, 195, 222, 226.

## 32 Chichester: 'as human as home and as lovely as heaven'

The extracts quoted on pp.156–7 are from Eric Gill's, *Autobiography* (Jonathan Cape, 1940), pp.76–7, 79–81. The description of 2 North Walls, Chichester, in the caption on p.152, is from p.123.

Symbolic of Chichester's importance to Eric Gill has been the gathering of a permanent collection of his works in the city, now preserved in WSRO. This is listed and described by Timothy J. McCann in *The Eric Gill Collection at Chichester: A Catalogue* (WSCC, 2nd edn, 1982). The collection includes his writings and drawings, some sculptures, wood-carvings and the tools he used for engraving. His self-portrait and sketches of Chichester doorways reproduced in this article are from this collection and numbered 190 and 30 respectively.

The sketches of West Pallant and Tower Street, are WSRO, PD 256 and 255 respectively. The photograph of the Gill family home at 2 North Walls is WSRO, PH 171.

Amongst the plethora of writings about Gill there are two major biographies: Malcolm Yorke's *Eric Gill: Man of Flesh and Spirit* (Constable, 1981); covering his Chichester years in much more detail is Fiona MacCarthy's *Eric Gill* (Faber and Faber, 1989).

The other Sussex place crucial to Gill's life and work was Ditchling. See Peter Holliday (ed.), *Eric Gill in Ditchling: Four Essays* (Oak Knoll Press, New Castle, Delaware, USA, 2002).

## 33 Pure Nostalgia: E.V. Lucas in Sussex

This article is based around extracts and drawings from *Highways and Byways in Sussex* by E.V. Lucas (Macmillan, 1904).

As much as the first edition evokes a great deal of nostalgia for a Sussex long gone, Lucas's preface to his revised second edition, dated 1935, makes salutary reading where he notes the effects of thirty years of change and the influence of the 'minatory car and the immanent aeroplane', new houses and scientific progress in the form of 'stark pylons'. Yet, in spite of 'feverish modernity', there was still much for which to be thankful: sealed tarmac was a vast improvement on the old dusty roads and 'Sussex has not really been harmed … the Downs … are still sacred and secure … the Weald has … its secluded coppices … most of the great landowners have survived…'. (But note the more down-beat Belloc surveying exactly the same period, see pp.196–7 above.)

The series, of which this Sussex volume forms part, has been reviewed by Richard Dalby in 'The "Highways and Byways" series' in *Book and Magazine Collector* 50 (May 1988), pp.34–41.

Lucas reviewed his life in his autobiographical *Reading, Writing and Remembering: A Literary Record* (Methuen, 1932). A year after his death the same firm published a short memoir by his daughter, Audrey Lucas, as *E.V. Lucas: A Portrait* (1939).

Three articles focusing on Lucas and Sussex, were published in *SCM*, all by Arthur Beckett, its editor: 'Mr E.V. Lucas on Sussex' (a review of the 2nd revised edn of

*Highways and Byways in Sussex*), 10 (1936), pp.148–9; 'The Sussex Side of E.V. Lucas' (a tribute on his death), 12 (1938), pp.495–7; 'E.V. Lucas in Brighton' (on the 10th anniversary of his death), 22 (1948), pp.70–2.

The success of *Highways and Byways in Sussex* owed much to its exquisite line drawings by Frederick Griggs. For an appreciation of his life and work as a topographical artist – 'the story of a neglected English visionary' – see Jerrold Northrop Moore, *F.L. Griggs (1876–1938): The Architecture of Dreams* (Oxford University Press, 1999, reprinted by the Antique Collectors' Club, 2008). See pp.42–4 for his work in Sussex collaborating with Lucas in 1903.

The engraving of the Arundel Castle American Eagle Owls is taken from *The Illustrated London News* of 5 December 1846, giving a detailed report of Queen Victoria's visit to Arundel, including seeing the owls in the keep and watching actor-owls hooting their lines as they performed their special 'Masque' for the royal party.

## 34 The 'dream that comes to men in hell': Sussex and the Great War

A wealth of information about the Great War of 1914–18 is held in WSRO. Official and personal diaries, field service papers and soldiers' letters are listed and described by Alan Readman in *Records of the Royal Sussex Regiment: A Catalogue* (WSCC, 1985). The recruiting poster illustrating this article

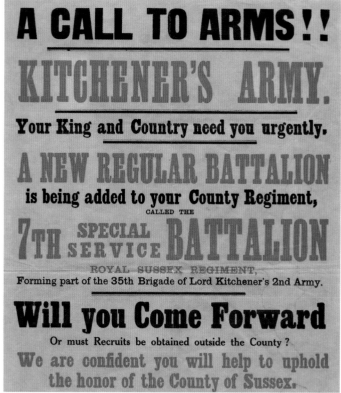

is catalogued as RSR Ms 7/5 and the photograph of the mud at Ypres as RSR PH 2/164. The two Bognor photographs are not part of the regimental collection and catalogued as PH 9603 (the horses) and PH 9604 (the recruits).

This present article is partly based on Kim Leslie's *The Great War illustrated by documents from the West Sussex Record Office* (WSCC, 1989), mainly using these regimental papers plus contemporary newspapers and parish records. It looks at the war through the home front, recruitment and the battlefield. WSRO sources quoted in this book are supported by a select bibliography of just twelve books from a vast and almost overwhelming field of literature. If two of these had to be chosen as key to the mind-set of those who endured this cataclysmic war they would be Paul Fussell, *The Great War and Modern Memory* (Oxford University Press, 1975) – a highly original approach about its expression in myth and literature – and Denis Winter, *Death's Men: Soldiers of the Great War* (Allen Lane, 1978).

The county's response and support for the war is treated comprehensively by Keith Grieves in *Sussex in the First World War* (SRS 84, 2004), with sections on recruitment and mobilisation; shore defences; active service; transportation and supply; aerial reconnaissance; ministering to the forces; mobilising the rural economy; morale and dissent; parish communities; county patriotism and war poetry; returning home and commemorating the fallen. Much information on the impact of the war on the county, particularly at Selsey, is in Brian W. Harvey and Carol Fitzgerald (eds), *Edward Heron-Allen's Journal of the Great War: From Sussex Shore to Flanders Fields* (SRS 86, 2002).

A torrent of poetry came out of the trenches. Apart from the usual roll-call of heroic names, like Blunden, Brooke, Owen and Sassoon, there were hundreds more, lesser known and forgotten. Indeed at least 2,225 Great War poets have been identified: see Catherine W. Reilly, *English Poetry of the First World War: A Bibliography* (George Prior, 1978). One of these listed (p.126) was the anonymous 'Field Officer' whose moving 'A Soldier's Dream' is quoted at the end of this article. His illustrated poem is taken from *A Soldier's Sonnets: Verses Grave and Gay* (Birdsall, [1916]), pp.40–1. The unidentified soldier was an officer of the 4th Battalion, Royal Sussex Regiment. A copy of his book is in the regimental library in WRSO, RSR 5/21.

## 35 Magical Landscapes: Eleanor Farjeon's Sussex

Her biographer was her niece, Annabel Farjeon, in *Morning has Broken: A biography of Eleanor Farjeon* (Julia MacRae Books, 1986). Eleanor's letter to her lover, George Earle, on the powerful effect of the Downs is quoted from p.138; her lonely 'but almost perfect way of living' in the cottage at Houghton from pp.130–1.

The vivid description of Eleanor's childhood home overflowing with books, with Eleanor deep into one of her story books portrayed by Edward Ardizzone, is from *The Little Bookroom* (Oxford University Press, 1955).

Her two Martin Pippin books of Sussex tales are *Martin Pippin in the Apple Orchard* (Collins, 1921) and *Martin Pippin in the Daisy Field* (Michael Joseph, 1937).

The background to the story of the skipping Elsie Piddock (in the second of these two books) was investigated in Denys Blakelock's *In Search of Elsie Piddock: An Echo of Eleanor Farjeon* (Favil Press, 1967) that took him to the site of her cottage in Houghton and in search of the original Elsie (as

Elsie Puttick and by then Mrs Elsie Daughtrey) living in Amberley. The story has since been republished as a stand-alone illustrated book, *Elsie Piddock Skips in Her Sleep* (Walker Books, 2000).

Much information on Eleanor, the Farjeon family and her many friends and Sussex connections, is given in her *Edward Thomas: The Last Four Years* (Oxford University Press, 1958). Republished by Sutton Publishing in 1997, a new introduction by Anne Harvey elaborates on the Farjeon/ Thomas relationship. Eleanor chronicles her friendship

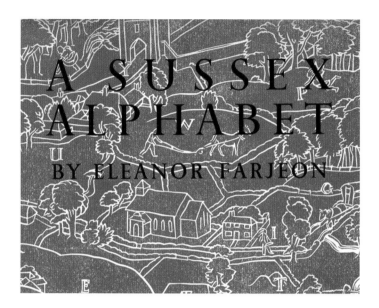

with James Guthrie – artist – writer – printer – who ran the Pear Tree Press at Flansham, near Bognor, where he printed *A Sussex Alphabet*. (See also the 'James Guthrie' issue of *The Private Library* (vol.9:I, Spring 1976.) Her downland walk from Rackham to Chichester with D.H. Lawrence is quoted from pp.134–7. They met as part of a literary colony centred on Humphrey's Homestead at Greatham – see also Kim Leslie, *A Sense of Place: West Sussex Parish Maps* (WSCC, 2006), pp.190, 275. Previously unpublished Farjeon writings will appear in Anne Harvey's forthcoming *Eleanor Farjeon's Sussex* (Book Guild Publishing).

## 36 Mr Punch in Sussex: Humour from the Sussex Countryside

E. V. Knox's parody of country life – 'The Secret of Sussex' – part of which is reprinted here – was published in *An Hour from Victoria and some other excursions* (George Allen & Unwin, 1924), pp.13–22 in which his own village of Balcombe masquerades as Bittleigh.

Knox's familiarity with popular Sussex verse is echoed in the questions put to the old man. The line about walking 'in the high woods with the men who were boys when you were a boy ...' echoes Belloc's 'The South Country' and the line about 'the wooded, dim, blue goodness of the Weald' is quoted from Kipling's 'Sussex'.

Knox's Balcombe phase is recalled by his daughter, Penelope Fitzgerald, in *The Knox Brothers* (Macmillan, 1977), pp.165–9.

His fame rested on his work for *Punch* as contributor and then editor. See R.G.G. Price, *A History of Punch* (Collins, 1957), especially pp.200–2, 238, 242, 256–62, 269, 299. Much of *An Hour from Victoria* had been previously published in the magazine as separate sketches or articles.

He used the opportunity to celebrate 'Balcombe's crowning hour' when the nation's eyes were on the village for a gathering of the royals for the wedding of Queen Mary's niece in 1931. His piece 'About Balcombe' (28 October 1931) adds a comic touch about village life and matters of 'profound importance ... over which Balcombe slumbered nor slept'.

The pull of the countryside as a recreational escape from towns and cities in the quest for a rural arcadia – a marked feature of the 1920s and '30s represented by Knox's little book and his taking up residence in the depths of Sussex and yet still close to his city office by train – is explored in Dennis Hardy & Colin Ward, *Arcadia for All: The Legacy of a Makeshift Landscape* (Mansell Publishing, 1984); Harvey Taylor, *A Claim on the Countryside: A History of the British Outdoor Movement* (Keele University Press, 1997); David Matless, *Landscape and Englishness* (Reaktion Books, 1998).

The two cartoons parodying the search for country characters first appeared in *Punch* and then were re-published in *Mr Punch's Country Manners* (Educational Book Co., n.d.), pp.88, 211.

The Sussex novels of Sheila Kaye-Smith as an expression of the interest in rural life in the 1920s and '30s and her identity with Sussex is touched on in Kim Leslie's introduction to the reissue of her two first published stories of 1905–6, *Kate All Alone & Paradise Park* (Northgate Press, 1993).

Rowland Emett's cartoon of 'The Far Tottering and Oyster Creek Railway' is reproduced from a postcard produced for the Festival of Britain in 1951.

## 37 'Great arterial roads very broad and straight': The London-Brighton Motorway

Information about the 1906 proposal to build 'The London and Brighton Motor Way', with maps, plans and sections, and a list of its supporters and opponents, is held by the Parliamentary Archives at Westminster: HL/PO/PB/3/plan 1906/L4.

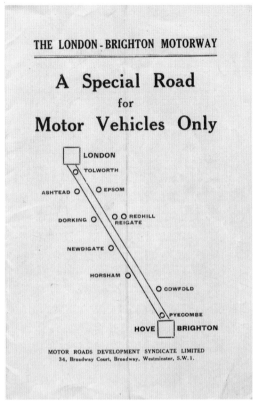

The next attempt to link London with Brighton by a motorway link, in the late 1920s, is based on a prospectus preserved in the Rusper parish records: WSRO, Par 163/54/5.

A map showing the overall route, together with the engineer's plans and sections, was deposited with West Sussex County Council in 1929: WSRO, QDP/W287.

The proposals of 1906 and 1928 are noted in Sir Peter Baldwin *et al*, *The Motorway Achievement: Building the Network in Southern and Eastern England* (Phillimore/Motorway Archive Trust, 2007), pp.4–8.

The wider context is given in Rees Jeffreys, *The King's Highway: An Historical and Autobiographical Record of the Developments of the past Sixty Years* (Batchworth Press, 1949); James Drake *et al.*, *Motorways* (Faber and Faber, 1969).

Hilaire Belloc argued the case for new types of road – bypasses ( he called them 'circular ways round the towns') and 'motor ways' in *The Road* (British Reinforced Concrete Engineering Company, 1923), chapter XIV, 'The Future' and in *The Highway and its Vehicles* (The Studio, 1926) in the chapter 'The Reaction of the Highway upon the Vehicle'.

Belloc's concerns for Sussex at the mercy of the motor car are expressed in *The County of Sussex* (Cassell, 1936), pp.201, 203.

The photograph of the Crawley traffic jam in 1930 is in WSRO, PH 21, 649.

Tim Harding's *Motoring Around Sussex: the first fifty years* (Tempus, 2004) uses a wealth of previously unpublished photographs to survey the history of motor traffic on the county's roads up until 1939.

The developing awareness of road-safety issues in the twentieth century is traced in *The Original Highway Code: Reproductions of Highway Code booklets from the Thirties, Forties and Fifties* (Michael O'Mara Books, 2008).

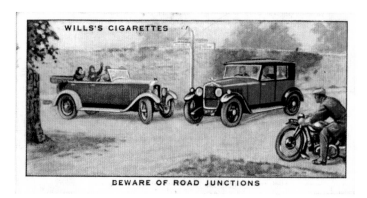

WILLS'S CIGARETTES

DEWARE OF ROAD JUNCTIONS

## 38  Escape to Bognor: R.C. Sherriff's *The Fortnight in September*

The Stevens' escape to the seaside in R.C. Sherriff's *The Fortnight in September* (Gollancz, 1931) has been most recently republished by Persephone Books in 2006. The book cover in this article is from the 1949 edition published by William Heinemann.

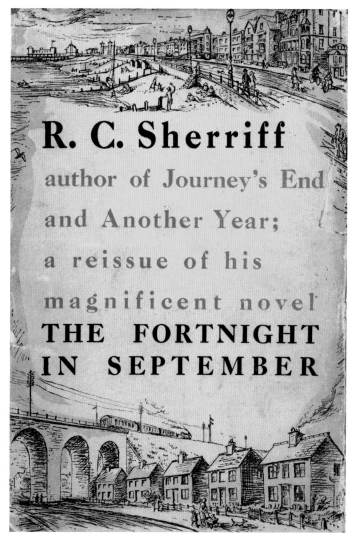

For information about Sherriff's life see his *No Leading Lady: An Autobiography* (Victor Gallancz, 1968) and his obituary in *The Times*, 18 November 1975.

An insight into Sherriff's involvement in Sussex archaeology with the Roman villa at Angmering is given by Oliver J. Gilkes, 'Amateurs and professionals: the excavation of Angmering Roman Villa 1935–1947' (*SAC* 136, 1998), pp.67–80.

The advertisements for Chatsworth House and Lilianet boarding houses are from the *Official Guide to Bognor Regis* (1931).

A lively and well-illustrated view of Bognor in the 1930s is given by Michael Alford in *The Paradise Rocks: A 1930s Childhood in Bognor and a Little Local History* (Phillimore, 2002).

## 39 'The smallest port in England': Dell Quay

The position of Dell Quay as the Port of Chichester is told by John Reger in *Chichester Harbour: A History* (Phillimore, 1996), touching on its status, its trade and traffic within the wider context of the harbour and its economy including all the mills: water, tide and wind. See also J.H. Andrews, 'The Port of Chichester and the Grain Trade, 1650–1750' (*SAC* 92, 1954), pp.93–105; John H. Farrant, 'The Seaborne Trade of Sussex, 1720–1845' (*SAC* 114, 1976), pp.97–120; John H. Farrant, *The Harbours of Sussex 1700–1914* (the author, 1976).

Information about the Duke of Richmond's sloop *Goodwood* is from the vessel's account book of 1782–98: WSRO, Goodwood Ms 250.

The map showing Dell Quay in 1795 is an enlargement from a map of Sussex by Yeakell, Gardner and Gream (1 inch = 1 mile), WSRO, PM 46. The later map is a same-size reproduction from the 6-Inch Ordnance Survey, surveyed in 1938 and published in 1945 – Sussex sheet LXV:SW.

The etching of Dell Quay in 1897 is by Dr Arthur Evershed of Fishbourne (1836–1919), WSRO, PD 286, the drawing of Fishbourne windmill is WSRO, PD 1016, and

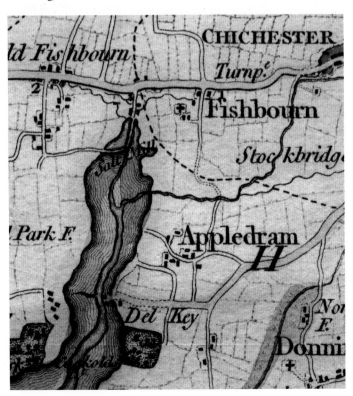

the engraving of Itchenor waterfront is from *The Gentleman's Magazine* (September 1803), WSRO, PD 1033. Three photograph are also from WSRO: George Haines and the steamer being loaded with grain are Accession 14,727 (uncatalogued), and Birdham tidemill, PH 8.

The Dell Quay rules and regulations and the schedule of Chichester port dues, both of 1872, are from Chichester Harbour Records in WSRO, HC/8/2/1.

Two recent publications include information about Dell Quay and associated interests: Monika Smith, *Chichester Harbour: An informal look at the last hundred years* (2004) and *Chichester Harbour: A Reference Guide* (2006), both published by Chichester Harbour Conservancy.

---

**RULES & REGULATIONS**

To be observed by Masters of Ships and Vessels coming to load and unload at

**DELL QUAY.**

1.—Before coming alongside Masters shall apply to the Quay Master for a berth, and shall anchor, moor and place the Ship or Vessel as the Quay Master may direct.

2.—All Ships and Vessels coming to load or unload at the Quay shall take their turn in regular rotation of arrival, and if required by the Quay Master shall shift their berths when partly unloaded and remove to other Quay berths, or lie in a second or third tier when the Quay Master shall deem it absolutely requisite.

3.—Masters and their mates lying at the head of the Quay shall at high water time be ready when required to slack their chains and wharfs, and to have their jib and mizen booms and running bowsprits rigged close in to allow free egress and ingress to the side berths.

4.—Immediately a Cargo is discharged Masters shall haul out from the Quay berths, unless specially allowed to remain by the Quay Master or compelled by stress of weather.

BY ORDER,

**S. SIMMONDS,**

Quay Master.

MOORE, PRINTER, CHICHESTER.

## 40 'Can Sussex Endure?': Hilaire Belloc on Threats to the County

The question is Belloc's and was asked provocatively in *The County of Sussex* (Cassell, 1936), p.200 and then answered in the last few paragraphs of the book (pp.201–4) which have been reprinted at the end of this article. The two Belloc quotations about the dangers faced by Sussex in 1906 are from his *Sussex* (Adam & Charles Black, 1906) – in which he is not credited as the author – quoting from the 1925 2nd edn, pp.148–9, 151. Belloc's prophetic warnings about the threats to Sussex – he was the first major writer to raise such issues – has been reflected most recently by Peter Brandon in the last chapter and epilogue to his *Sussex* (Robert Hale, 2006). He gives his own answer to Belloc's question put seventy years before.

Brandon's *cri de cœur* is again argued in *The Future of the South Downs*, edited by Gerald Smart and Peter Brandon (Packard Publishing, 2007). His essay 'The South Downs before and after 1939' traces the development of the public adulation of the Downs in the 20th century by writers such as Belloc and Virginia Woolf, its changing land use and conflicts between planners, developers and conservationists.

Belloc also expressed his identification with Sussex in *The Four Men: A Farrago* (Thomas Nelson, 1912) that takes the form of a walk from east to west, rooted in his philosophy and love for the county. The quotation that concludes this article – '... if a man ...' is from p.309 of this edition and the quotation in the Preamble is from pp.18–19; the line linking Sussex with Paradise used as a preliminary quotation at the beginning of the book is from p.84. See also Bob Copper, *Across Sussex with Belloc: In the Footsteps of 'The Four Men'* (Alan Sutton, 1994).

Belloc's life and work in Sussex is well covered in two biographies: A.N. Wilson, *Hilaire Belloc* (Hamish Hamilton, 1984) and Joseph Pearce, *Old Thunder: A Life* (HarperCollins, 2002).

Belloc's essay 'The Mowing of a Field' – used in J.B. Priestley's anthology quoted here – was first published in Belloc's book *Hills and The Sea* (Methuen, 1906).

Belloc closes his 1936 book with the Latin tag 'Ubi Troja fuit' in allusion to lines in Virgil's *Aeneid* and the destruction of Troy with nothing but emptiness left behind. As Troy, so Sussex...?

The advertisements for houses and land at High Salvington and Craigweil-on-Sea are from a little pocket magazine called *Sussex Homes* for 'homeseekers' wanting to live 'in England's fairest county' (vol.1 issue 3, (1937).

In the grounds of **CRAIGWEIL HOUSE**

Backed by SUSSEX DOWNS

Fronted by the SEA

Freehold prices from £1,000 to £2,775. Sites from £300 for houses built to accepted plans and houses available for renting. Bathing huts available on private beach.

**CRAIGWEIL-ON-SEA BOGNOR REGIS**

*Inspect also the Company's Inland Estate at Newberries, Radlett.*

# Copyright Acknowledgements

## Note on Photographs

The following copyright photographs by Kim Leslie were taken in 2008, except where dates indicated:

Bow Bells milestone, East Grinstead (16); Knepp Castle, Shipley (17); A272 and West Grinstead Paved Way (19); Mock Bridge, Henfield (20); Hunger Lane and Rotherbridge, near Petworth (21,23); Manor House, Lodsworth (25); Pophole and Hammer, Lynchmere (28); county boundary stone – 2003 – and Downley Bottom, Harting/Buriton (29); Ladyholt, Harting (32); Cutmill Creek, Bosham (34-5); Hayling Island Wadeway, Bremere Rife and Pagham Harbour (37); Lower Wadeway sign, Selsey (41); Sparkes' grave, Middleton-on-Sea (43); Becket banner, Pagham (45); Slindon tower, Langton memorial and Aldwick plaque (46); High Street, Worthing (52); Portsmouth plaque and monument (61); White memorials, Broadwater (62); Royal Pavilion gas lamp, Brighton (83); Brazier grave, Worth – 2003 (87); Chalk Pit Lane, East Lavant (96); Horsham Workhouse – 1970 (104); sculpture of Lord Egremont, Petworth (109); former Compton and Up Marden National School (115); Dangstein aviary and stained glass, Terwick – 2007 (125, 127); Petworth Prison office and bricks (133); Pullinger plaque, Selsey (136); Gordon grave and window, Harting (139); Hare grave, Herstmonceux (147); 'Foxes-brewings' – taken between Harting and Elsted (151); Gill inscriptions, Chichester Cathedral (155); Chichester Cemetery graves and war cross – 2007 – and Pidgeon grave (163); Eastergate war memorial – 2007 (164); Amberley Mount and Arun valley (168, 171); Humphrey's Homestead and Shed Hall, Greatham (173); Trent House and village sign, Balcombe (175,176); M23 motorway sign (182); Sand-martins and plaque, Bognor Regis (184); Slindon Cottage (the Dower House) – 1993 – and Gumber plaque, Slindon (193, 194).

# Index

REFERENCE to the RAPES

| | | | |
|---|---|---|---|
| Chichester | 1. | Lewes | 4. |
| Arundel | 2. | Pevensey | 5. |
| Bramber | 3. | Hastings | 6. |

S  U  R

H  A  N  T  S

HASLEMERE

Rusper
Kingsfold
Rudgwick
Worth
St.
Leonards
Forest
Balcomb
Hand Gr.
HORSHAM
Warnham

Linchmere
Shillinglee Park
Plaistow
North Chap.
Loxwood
Slinfold

Milland Chap.
Linch
Lurgasall Kirdford
Wisborough Gr.
Petworth Park

Rogate
Fittleworth
Woolbeding
Lodsworth
Wphurst

Springfield
Deane Park
Ashfold Lo.
Slaugham

W. Harting
Trotton
Stedham
MIDHURST
Tillington
PETWORTH
Endean
Coates

Billingshurst
Nuthurst
Woodgetters
Thorndean
Park
Cuc

S.th Harting
Elsted
Bepton
Heishot
Bury
Coldwaltham
Sutton

Hadfoldshern
Cowfold
Broadford Br.
Shipley
Knepp Cas.
W. Grinstead
Bolney

Ladyholt Park
Trayford
Didling
th Marden
Ducking
Grarfham

Compton
E. Marden
Up.r Marden
Singleton
Upwaltham

Horsham
Burton
Warminghurst
Thakeham
W. Chiltington
Ashurst
Shermanbury
Henfield
W. Grinstead P.r
W. Grinstead
Twinehanor
Twineham
Highfield
Hurst
Pierpont

Marden
Stoughton
W. Dean
E. Dean
Bignor
Barham

Greatham
Storrington
Ashington
Buncton Chap.
Washington
Woodmancote
Newtimber
Albourn
Kemp

West Bourn
Binderton
Midlavan
Earstham
Houghton
Dole Pa.
Stoke
N. Stoke
Timberley
Amberley
Sullington
Weston

STEYNING
Botolphs
Edburton
Poynings
Beeding
Potcham

Funtinton
Goodwood
W. Hampnet
Slindon
Boxgrove
Walberton
ARUNDEL
Burpham
S. Stoke
Muntham

Clapham
Findon
Sompting
Combs
Old Shoreham
Hangleton
Blatchington

Oakwood Hal
Tangmere
Aldingbourn
Binsted
Leominster
Ford

Pagham
Angmering
Patching
Darlington
Broadw.

CHICHESTER
Oving
Yapton
Clintping

Ichenor
Bosham
Appledram
Arundel
Portsmouth Ca.
S.th Bersted

W. Thorney
Donnington
W.m Mundham

Thorney I.

W. Itchenor
Hunston
Birdham
Sidlesham
Bognor

W. Wittering
Earnley
Selsey
Pagham
Middleton
Felpham

Arun
Kingston by Sea
Lancing
Worthing
Shoreham by Sea

Selsey Str.
Selsey Bill

E  N  G  L  I  S  H

Scale of Miles

1          5          10

S  U

CHICHESTER CATHEDRAL

Engraved for MOULES